1704408

Printed in the United States of America
Library of Congress Catalog Card Number: 64-66198

REGISTRATION AND
OF BROKERS AND

EZRA WEIS

COUNSEL TO THE NEW YORK RE
THE SECURITIES AND EXCHAN

FOREWORD F
HON. MANUEL F.
CHAIRMAN OF THE SECURITIES AND

BNA
BOO

BNA INCORPORATED •
1965

FOREWORD

The firms and individuals who assist the public in its selection, purchase, and sale of securities are engaged in a business, and a large and important one. It is also an unusual business in that, complex as it is and involving as it does intricate merchandise and the handling of other people's funds and securities, and the existence of relationships often based on trust and confidence, it has come to be surrounded by more legal restraints, and has imposed on itself more ethical standards than most other businesses. Yet it remains, for most of its segments, essentially a business of merchandising securities.

—Report of Special Study of
Securities Markets, Chapter III (1963).

It is hardly surprising that after thirty years of regulation by the Securities and Exchange Commission there has developed a need for a manual to guide broker-dealers; a body of law, like the community it governs, tends to grow more complex as it matures. In the case of the Commission this development seems to have been inevitable, for at least two reasons: first, the rapid growth of the securities markets, and second, the increased sophistication of techniques in the regulated industry, calling for more detailed and sophisticated responses on the part of the regulatory agency. The result has been some 40 volumes of decisions and reports by the Commission, and a set of rules which to the uninitiated must be as frightening as those under the revenue laws.

The growth in the industry has been truly remarkable. Out of the demoralized markets of the depression there has developed an active and thriving financial community, whose renascence can be dramatized statistically: compare, for example, the average of 514 registration statements, covering less than $2.5 billion of public offerings, which became effective during the first five years of the Commission's life, with the 1,121 registration statements, involving $17 billion, which became effective during the last fiscal year. And growth continues at an accelerated pace: in the last ten years alone, trading on the stock exchanges increased from an annual volume of $28 billion to a volume of $75 billion, and registration statements and dollar amounts of new offerings have almost doubled.

Inseparable from the increase in the volume of the trading markets has been the increase in public participation. More than seventeen million persons, a figure which has more than doubled since 1954, now own shares in publicly-held corporations. Countless others participate in the markets indirectly through the mutual funds, pension trusts, insurance companies, banks and similar aggregations of capital which the trade lumps together under the caption "institutions."

Much of this growth reflects, of course, expansion of the economy and of resources available for investment. But an essential ingredient has also been the activity of the registered broker-dealer. Technological advances in the modern securities industry have been of enormous value, not only in making the markets themselves more efficient, but in inducing greater public interest and activity. The new tools have been many and varied, tangible and intangible. Modern advertising techniques and advanced psychologically-oriented selling methods are as much a part of the developing securities industry as are almost-instantaneous communications and the high-speed tickers. That the use of some of these devices may be overdone—as evidenced by the 1962 market collapse and the frenetic market conditions which led up to that event—is proof only of their effectiveness. The most esoteric technological advance, electronic data-processing equipment, is yet to be absorbed in its fullest impact: realization of the computer's full potential is still in the future, although drawing steadily nearer.

Entirely apart from the technology of the industry is the character of those who comprise it. It has become a truism that the viability of the securities markets is dependent on public confidence, and that an essential in that confidence is the belief in the integrity of the broker-dealer. Fortunately, the vast majority of broker-dealers justify that belief. Perhaps the best evidence of this is the success of our system of "cooperative regulation," in which the self-regulatory agencies—such as the exchanges and the National Association of Securities Dealers—themselves enforce compliance with legal and ethical standards of conduct. This reliance on the industry to discipline its own members, combined with Federal regulation and the expanding efforts of state authorities, has created a three-tiered regulatory structure, each level of which has made its own contribution and left its particular stamp on the system.

Regulation by the Securities and Exchange Commission has nevertheless been the dominant force in legal controls over the securities industry. Armed with broad powers under the Acts it administers, the Commission has used all the devices available to an independent regulatory agency in developing a body of law adequate both to the protection of the public and, at the same time, to the business needs of the community. The complexity of the regulatory framework mirrors not only the complexity of the securities markets themselves. It reflects also the desire of the Commission to avoid procrustean rules which might inhibit the freedom of the industry to find its own solutions to constantly changing economic patterns.

The statutes administered by the Commission, and the rules and interpretive releases it has received from time to time, are only part of the body of federal securities law. The boundaries of permissible broker-dealer conduct have also been marked in significant part through decisions of the Commission as an adjudicatory body. Some critics of the administrative process have advocated removal of the judicial function from the independent agencies, and this may even be appropriate in particular situations. The Commission, however, has found adjudication a particularly useful device, enabling the development of policy against the background of actual facts and concrete cases, and allowing broad principles to be laid down not in the abstract but from proven factual bases.

For example, the rule has developed that a broker-dealer has obligations to his customers which are very much like those of a fiduciary to his cestui que trust. As Mr. Justice Frankfurter has pointed out, in a different but not wholly unrelated context:

> "But to say that a man is a fiduciary only begins analysis; it gives direction to further inquiry. To whom is he a fiduciary? What obligations does he owe as a fiduciary? In what respect has he failed to discharge these obligations? And what are the consequences of his deviation from duty?"*

Case-by-case adjudication has proven to be peculiarly well adapted to careful delineation of the nature of the duty to customers and the fashioning of remedies, allowing the Commission to move

---

* SEC v. Chenery Corp., 318 U.S. 80, 85-86.

positively but in a way responsive to the changing methods and requirements of the securities business.

There are few who could have brought this varied and complex material together as Ezra Weiss has done. He has been with the Commission, and a valued and respected colleague, for more than two decades. As Regional Counsel in the Commission's New York Regional Office, his domain includes Wall Street, that symbol of American capitalism and the largest concentration of broker-dealers in the United States. He knows the securities industry, its problems, and the impact of the securities laws on them, and has combined this invaluable practical experience with legal judgment in the writing of this truly useful handbook.

Manuel F. Cohen

Washington, D. C.
March, 1965.

PREFACE

Recent annual reports of the Securities and Exchange Commission ("Commission") reveal that the number of broker-dealers registered with the Commission increased from 4771 on June 30, 1957,[1] to 5868 on June 30, 1962.[2] With the constant rise of public activity in the securities markets,[3] moreover, the number of persons entering the securities business continues to grow.[4] Broker-dealers, their advisers, and attorneys representing such persons are confronted not only with the relatively simple problems of broker-dealer registration, but with acquainting themselves for the guidance of their clients with the principles governing the standards of conduct of brokers and dealers for the protection of the public. Securities have been characterized as "intricate merchandise";[5] and the regulatory provisions required to meet the complexities of the securities business are correspondingly varied and numerous.[6]

There does not appear to be any published work designed principally as a guide for both broker-dealers and practitioners in advising new as well as established broker-dealer clients with respect to their day-to-day problems. This manual will attempt to fill that basic need.

A brief amount of space will be devoted at the outset to an outline of the organization of the Securities and Exchange Com-

---

[1] 24 SEC Ann. Rep. 81 (1958).

[2] 28 SEC Ann. Rep. 61 (1963).

[3] See SEC *Report Of The Special Study of Securities Markets* [hereinafter called "Special Study Report"] H.R. Doc. No. 95, 88th Cong. 1st Sess. (1963), Parts 1-5, Pt. 1, Ch. 1, pp. 21-2.

[4] *Special Study Report*, Pt. 1, Ch. 1, pp. 22-3.

[5] H.R. Rep. No. 85, 73rd Cong. 1st Sess. (1933), p. 8.

[6] See *United States* v. *Guterma*, 189 F. Supp. 265, 275 (S.D.N.Y. 1960), where the court observed with respect to the federal securities laws. ". . . It is entirely reasonable and proper to employ a relatively sophisticated scheme for the regulation of relatively sophisticated transactions. Clarity is relative to context and in the context of a complex field of human activity, clarity is not precluded by a commensurate complexity of regulation. xx." And, in another securities case, *United States* v. *Crosby* 294 F.2d 928, 944 (2d Cir. 1961), the court pointed out that ". . . the ingenuity of the white collar criminal and quasi-criminal is mirrored in the complicated regulation of the securities industry. . . ."

mission and to the system of citations of authorities which are unique to the field administered by the Commission. Then, following a necessary threshold examination into the kinds of activities which bring persons within the terms "broker" and "dealer" as defined in the Securities Exchange Act of 1934, this book will review the registration requirements applicable to brokers and dealers, and devote part of that discussion to the problems of filling out the application for registration. The remainder of this work will concern itself with the principles governing the conduct of broker-dealers as enunciated in pertinent statutory provisions, rules, Commission and court opinions, and other authoritative pronouncements. Reference will be made to such matters as the bookkeeping rules, the financial reporting requirements, the restrictions as to the extension and maintenance of credit, the hypothecation rules, confirmation requirements, and the types of activities prohibited in connection with distributions of securities, as well as such exceptions from these prohibitions as the stabilization rules and rules having special application to rights offerings.

Additionally, there will be a rather detailed treatment of the body of principles covered by the anti-fraud and anti-manipulative provisions of the federal securities laws, first, in relation to their application to special types of broker-dealer activity, involving the "shingle" theory, and, secondly, in their general aspects. These will be followed by discussions of the criteria employed for the sanctions which may be imposed in the public interest against brokers and dealers as respects registration with the Commission and against other persons with regard to their remaining or becoming associated with a broker or dealer. Finally, brief reference will be made to the self-regulatory aspects of the securities business so far as concerns the federal securities laws. It will be seen how enforcement of the federal securities laws and its policies are carried out through national securities exchanges and registered securities associations. However, there will be no discussion of the rules of those organizations which have no direct bearing on the matter of such enforcement.

A number of the topics covered here have recently been the subject of scrutiny by the Securities and Exchange Commission through its Special Study of Securities Markets.[7] As the result of the study, the Commission has already adopted and proposed, and will undoubtedly continue to propose and adopt, new rules and make new pronouncements of interpretation and policy.[8] One series of amendments to the federal securities laws proposed by the Commission has already been enacted into law.[9] Whatever may continue to eventuate from the study, it is nevertheless felt that the bulk of the material in this book should still remain a reliable guide for most of the subjects covered. References to prospective changes in rules will be made at appropriate places in the text. In addition, a number of pertinent recommendations of the Special Study Report will be set out in full as Appendix A.[10]

Since this is primarily a handbook, discussion of the background behind various provisions and rules will be confined to what is deemed absolutely essential for an understanding of the topic under discussion. For the same basic reason, references to authorities will in most cases be limited only to those deemed necessary to authenticate the statements made. Yet, whenever it is thought that it will serve the reader, citations of authority will be repeated in full. Similar considerations dictate the restatement upon appropriate occasion of material covered elsewhere in the book.

Although this book is designed for the guidance of broker-dealers and their attorneys, it does not purport to serve as a primer on the general subject of the federal securities laws. Hence, such topics as what constitutes a security are not covered here other than by references to sources which should prove helpful to readers concerned with subjects mentioned but not developed. Moreover, this book does not deal with procedure and practice relative to investigations or administrative proceedings instituted by or conducted before the Securities and Exchange Commission. And it does not make references to any requirements of state laws applicable to brokers and dealers.[11]

---

[7] The results of the study are embodied in the *Special Study Report, supra,* n. 3.

[8] See Special Market Study Release No. 25, April 30, 1963, and Special Market Study Release No. 33, July 23, 1963.

[9] Securities Acts Amendments of 1964, 78 Stat. 565, Public Law 88-467.

[10] See, *infra,* Sec. 25-1.

[11] Section 28(a) of the Securities Exchange Act of 1934, 15 U.S.C. 78 bb (a) (1958), provides that nothing in the Act shall affect the jurisdiction of any state agency insofar as it does not conflict with the provisions of the Act.

Finally, it should be stated that the Securities and Exchange Commission, as a matter of policy, disclaims responsibility for any private publication by any of its employees. The views expressed herein are those of the author and do not necessarily reflect the views of the Commission or of the author's colleagues upon the staff of the Commission.

INTRODUCTION

Those who have had little or no contact with the Securities and Exchange Commission ("Commission") may find helpful a brief discussion of its organization and principal functions. They may also find useful some reference to the sources of research which have special application to the federal securities laws administered by the Commission.

A. *The Securities and Exchange Commission*

The Securities and Exchange Commission is an agency of the United States composed of five commissioners charged with the administration of several statutes collectively known as the federal securities laws.[1] Although the common thread found in these laws is the protection of investors in the public interest,[2] some of these statutes have rather narrow, specialized scope. The two pieces of legislation which are of general application on the subject are the Securities Act of 1933[3] and the Securities Exchange Act 1934.[4] The basic purpose underlying both Acts is that of providing public investors with full, adequate, and accurate disclosure of information relative to securities which they own or which they may be induced to purchase or sell.[5] A major concern of the Securities Act is that of providing full and fair disclosure to investors in connection with the distribution of securities by issuers, persons in control relationships with issuers, and the underwriters for either.[6]

---

[1] For descriptions of the statutes administered by the Commission, see SEC— *Statement of Organization, Conduct And Ethics, And Information Practices* (1962), 17 CFR 200.1-200.29, particularly the section on "Commission—Origin and Authority," 17 CFR 200.1-200.2.

[2] See SEC v. *United States Realty and Improvement Company*, 310 U. S. 434, 448 at n. 6 (1940).

[3] 15 U.S.C. §§77a-77aa (1958 and Supp IV 1963) [hereinafter called the "Securities Act"].

[4] 15 U.S.C. §§78a-78gg (1958 & Supp IV 1963) [hereinafter called, variously, the "Securities Exchange Act," the "Exchange Act," or simply, the "Act"]. All references to the provisions of the Act will be by section numbers of the Act.

[5] See *Morris Mac Schwebel*, SEC Securities Exchange Act Release No. 6424, Nov. 17, 1960, p. 12 (same as SEC Securities Act Release No. 4304).

[6] H. R. Rep. No. 85, 73rd Cong., 1st Sess. (1933), pp. 5, 15-16. The Securities Act also has anti-fraud provisions which are applicable to transactions of offer and sale of securities even in the absence of a distribution. See Section 17 of the

The Securities Exchange Act is directed at protecting the public principally with respect to trading in securities, through, among other things, the regulation of brokers and dealers and the securities markets.[7] The enforcement on behalf of the Commission of these provisions of the Exchange Act is, among other duties, the responsibility of the Division of Trading and Markets (successor to the Division of Trading and Exchanges)[8] at the headquarters office, Washington, D. C.[9] As part of the Division's functions, it provides brokers, dealers, and others affected by matters within the Division's province with guidance as to the applicability of the statute and pertinent Commission regulations.[10] The Commission has nine regional offices serving specified geographical regions.[11] Within its region, a regional office has the responsibility in conjunction with the Division of Trading and Markets (as well as other headquarters units in appropriate cases) to enforce the provisions regulating brokers, dealers, and the securities markets.[12] The regional office also provides interpretative guidance, as to matters within its province, relative to the application in given situations of the provisions of pertinent statutes, rules, and regulations.[13]

B. *Sources of Authorities*

It is not the purpose here to discuss systems of citations of general application, such as judicial opinions, statutes, rules, or the

---

Securities Act, 15 U.S.C. §77q (1958). For a discussion of the subject of what constitutes a "distribution" as distinguished from trading transactions, see, *infra,* Sections 13-1 and 13-12.

[7] H. R. Rep. No. 85, 73rd Cong., 1st Sess. (1933), pp. 15-16. See also, Section 2 of the Exchange Act; and see *Securities Acts Amendments,* 86th Cong., 1st Sess. (1959), p. 156.

[8] The name was changed to the Division of Trading and Markets on October 3, 1963, *SEC News Digest,* October 3, 1963, p. 1.

[9] SEC-*Statement of Organization, Conduct and Ethics, and Information Practices* (1962) (hereinafter called "Statement of Organization"), 17 CFR 200.19.

[10] See SEC Securities Exchange Act Release No. 351, Aug. 16, 1935; 8 SEC Ann. Rep. 44 (1942); 1 SEC Ann. Rep. 9-10 (1935); 2 SEC Ann. Rep. 11 (1936); See also SEC *Statement On Informal And Other Procedures,* 17 CFR 202.1 (1960).

[11] A list of the locations and addresses of these and of the branch offices appears as Appendix B. See, *infra,* Sec. 25-2.

[12] SEC Statement of Organization, Article 24, p. 7, 17 CFR 200.27 (1962).

[13] See SEC *Statement On Informal And Other Procedures,* 17 CFR 202.1 (1960); and see, *"The Approach Of The Practitioner To The SEC,"* Address by Chairman Edward N. Gadsby before the Annual Convention of the Federal Bar Association, Chicago, Illinois, September 17, 1960, pp. 1-3, on file at SEC, Washington, D. C., and New York, N. Y.

legislative history of federal statutes.[14] The discussion here will be confined, rather, to other sources furnishing authoritative guidance with respect to the federal securities laws.

The Commission expresses itself in a number of ways. Most frequently, this is done by printed public announcements available for public distribution. Such announcements are designated "Releases"; to the extent a release has special reference to any of the statutes administered by the Commission, that fact will be designated at the head of the release which will also bear the date together with the release number. If the Commission's latest release at a given time under the Securities Exchange Act be, for example, Securities Exchange Act Release No. 6900, the next release issued under that Act will be Securities Exchange Act Release No. 6901. Releases under the Securities Exchange Act are cited as, "SEC Securities Exchange Act Release No.," together with the number of release and date.[15] Similarly, releases under the Securities Act are cited as "SEC Securities Act Release No.," together with the number and date.[16] Releases under the other federal securities statutes are similarly designated.

Copies of all Commission releases are available for inspection at the main office of the Commission, Washington, D. C., and at most regional offices. As explained below,[17] arrangements can be made to receive releases on a current basis. To the extent the main office has a supply, back numbers of releases will be distributed by that office upon request.

If a release consists of the findings and opinion of the Commission in the context of adversary proceedings following notice and opportunity for hearing, it will in addition bear the name of the case.[18] Other releases, which may consist, for example, of interpretative pronouncements,[19] announcements of the institu-

---

[14] For a compilation of the legislative history of the federal securities laws, see Dunton, *Selected Bibliography Including Legislative History of Securities and Exchange Commission And The Statutes It Administers,* 28 Geo. Wash. L. Rev. App. 1, p. 1, Oct. 1959.

[15] E.g., SEC Securities Exchange Act Release No. 6424, Nov. 17, 1960.

[16] E.g., SEC Securities Act Release No. 3825, Aug. 12, 1957.

[17] See, *infra*, n. 31 and accompanying text.

[18] E.g., *Investment Service Co.,* SEC Securities Exchange Act Release No. 6884, Aug. 15, 1962.

[19] See e.g., SEC Securities Exchange Act Release No. 6778, April 16, 1962 (on the obligation of brokers and dealers to effect transactions with customers in timely fashion). See also SEC Securities Act Release No. 3825, Aug. 12, 1957 (report of Commission following investigation), and SEC Securities Exchange Act Release No. 4150,

tion of administrative proceedings,[20] intermediate administrative action,[21] or the proposal or adoption of a Commission rule,[22] are identified merely by the statutes to which they relate, the number of the release, and the date.

Announcements of the institution or results of litigation in the courts involving the Commission are made in the form of "Litigation Releases" bearing appropriate numbers and dates of issuance.[23] Additionally, the Commission makes pronouncements of policy in certain areas within its competence which are not given identification as releases.[24]

The Commission has other important avenues of expression through its annual reports to Congress,[25] as well as through published reports of the Commission and its staff on special subjects.[26] Additionally, valuable insights can be gained as to the Commission's views from the statements of its spokesmen before Congressional Committees,[27] as well as from the statements in the Commission's publication, the SEC News Digest, which reports, daily, a summary of important Commission developments.[28] That sums up the material available directly from Commission sources.[29]

October 23, 1959 (statement of Director of Division of Trading and Exchanges on subject of "Hot Issues").

[20] See e.g., SEC Securities Exchange Act Release No. 6838, July 3, 1962 (instituting broker-dealer revocation proceedings).

[21] See e.g., SEC Securities Exchange Act Release No. 6840, July 5, 1962 (setting broker-dealer revocation proceeding for a hearing), and SEC Securities Exchange Act Release No. 6904, Oct. 1962 (dismissing broker-dealer revocation proceeding without prejudice to renewal).

[22] See e.g., SEC Securities Exchange Act Release No. 6809, May 22, 1962 (proposing adoption of Rule 15C2-5 under the Exchange Act); and SEC Securities Exchange Act Release No. 6851, July 17, 1962 (announcing adoption of Rule 15C2-5).

[23] See e.g., SEC Litigation Release No. 1876, January 9, 1961 (announcing permanent injunction granted in suit for such relief instituted by the Commission).

[24] See e.g., SEC Statement Of Policy as amended (November 5, 1957), as to certain types of representations in the offer and sale of investment company securities regarded by the Commission as violating statutory standards.

[25] Cited e.g., 1 SEC Ann. Rep. 1 (1935).

[26] E.g., SEC Report On Investigation, In The Matter Of Richard Whitney (1938).

[27] See e.g., Statement of Ganson Purcell, Commissioner, Securities and Exchange Commission—Hearings on Proposed Amendments to the Securities Act of 1933 and to the Securities Exchange Act of 1934, 77th Cong., 1st Sess. (1941), Part III, pp. 893, 895, 897-9. See also, e.g., Testimony of Chairman Edward N. Gadsby of Securities and Exchange Commission—Securities Acts Amendments, 1959, 86th Cong., 1st Sess. (1959), pp. 156-185.

[28] The "News Digest" is cited as SEC News Digest with date of publication. These may be ordered from the Superintendent of Documents, Government Printing Office, Washington 25, D. C., at the price of $15 a year.

[29] Articles, speeches, and treatises by Commissioners and staff members are published from time to time relative to the Commission or the laws it administers. However, the Commission assumes no responsibility for the statements made by

Copies of the statutes administered by the Commission and the rules adopted thereunder, as well as the SEC News Digest, in addition to specified bound printed volumes, including the bound volumes containing the SEC Decisions And Reports (composed of Commission Findings and Opinions in adversary proceedings following notice and opportunity for hearing) and the SEC Annual Reports to Congress, among other publications, may be obtained at specified prices from the Superintendent of Documents, Government Printing Office, Washington, D. C.[30] Additionally, any one may arrange to have his name placed on the list to receive any one or more of 18 classifications of releases distributed to the public by the Commission by writing to the main office of the Securities and Exchange Commission, Washington, D. C., 20549, and designating which classes of releases he desires to receive.[31]

Loose-leaf reporting services published by Commerce Clearing House and Prentice Hall,[32] in the securities field, report, summarize, and make currently available, Commission releases, Court opinions, and other material relative to the federal securities laws.

Additionally, there is one authoritative treatise on the subject of federal securities regulation. That is, Loss on *Securities Regulation*,[33] an invaluable three volume reference work which touches on virtually every aspect of the federal securities laws.

In addition to the statutes administered by the Commission and the rules and regulations adopted thereunder, it may be of value to ascertain whether a rule of a national securities exchange or a registered securities association bears on a problem at hand.[34]

---

any staff member. See SEC, *Regulation Concerning Conduct of Members and Employees and Former Members and Employees of the Commission,* 17 CFR 200.32(f) (1960).

[30] These are detailed in SEC *List Of Publications* Rev., October 25, 1963, copies of which may be obtained at the Commission's main office, Washington, D. C., or at any of the regional or branch offices of the Commission. A copy of the current list is reproduced as Appendix C. See Sec. 25-3, *infra.* The list is revised from time to time reflecting changes in prices or in publications available.

[31] A copy of the most recent *Classification Of Releases* is reproduced as Appendix D. See Sec. 25-4, *infra.*

[32] See e.g., Prentice Hall, *Securities Regulation Report* (3rd ed) (cited P. H. Sec. Reg. Rep.); and Commerce Clearing House, *Federal Securities Law Reporter* (Cited, CCH Fed. Sec. L. Rep.).

[33] 2d ed. 1961.

[34] The subject of rules of national securities exchanges and registered securities associations are discussed later in this work. See, *infra* at Chapters 23 and 24.

Copies of these rules are available at the Commission's main office and most regional offices.[35]

Finally, resort may be had for such assistance as they may afford to various law review articles on specific aspects of the work of the Securities and Exchange Commission.[36]

---

[35] The rules of the New York Stock Exchange may also be found in CCH, *New York Stock Exchange Directory and Guide.*

[36] For a compilation of some of the more significant articles, see, Dunton, *Bibliography Including Legislative History Of Securities and Exchange Commission And The Statutes It Administers,* 28 Geo. Wash. L. Rev. App. 1, p. 1, October, 1959.

TABLE OF CONTENTS

PART VII. SELF-REGULATION UNDER COMMISSION SUPERVISION

PART I

REGISTRATION

Chapter 1

DEFINITIONS

Sec. 1-1. Broker, dealer. As will be detailed below, many important consequences flow from being a broker or dealer as those terms are defined in the Securities Exchange Act. In a large number of cases, registration would be required with the Commission, and registration brings in its train a host of regulations. A number of obligations are imposed on a broker or dealer who need not be registered.[1] Therefore, it is important to analyze whether a person's activities in connection with securities bring him within the statutory definition of broker or dealer.

With the exceptions noted below, a "broker" is a "person" engaged in the business of effecting transactions in securities for the account of others,[2] whereas a dealer is a person engaged in the business of buying and selling securities for his own account.[3] Contrasted with the activity which might render a person a broker acting on behalf of others, a dealer's activity must include both the buying and selling of securities.[4]

In appraising whether or not the definitions of "broker" or "dealer" apply to a given person, the subject of his transactions must be examined. If it is a "security" as defined in Section 3(a)

---

[1] Non-registered brokers and dealers are subject to the anti-fraud provisions applicable to all brokers and dealers, as well as to the net capital rule (discussed *infra* at Sec. 8-2). See SEC *Statement of The Securities and Exchange Commission With Respect to Proposed Amendments of Section 15(a) and (b) and Section 15A of the Securities Exchange Act of 1934,* June 18, 1963, p. 12. See also, e.g., *Arthur J. Decker, Trustee,* SEC Securities Exchange Act Release No. 7068, April 26, 1963.

[2] Sec. 3(a)(4) of the Act. The term "person" includes an individual, corporation, partnership, association, joint stock company, business trust, or unincorporated organization. Sec. 3(a)(9) of the Act.

[3] Section 3(a)(5) of the Act. By definition a "bank" performing any or all of these activities is not a broker or dealer. *Ibid,* and see Section 3(a)(4) of the Act. A "bank" is an institution engaged in specified activities under the supervision of State or Federal authority having supervision over banks. Section 3(a)(6) of the Act. Thus, a foreign bank not thus supervised which otherwise meets the test for a broker or dealer is a "broker" or "dealer," as the case may be, for all purposes of the Act.

[4] A person may be a "broker" if engaged solely in buying or solely in selling securities for others. See SEC Securities Exchange Act Release No. 721, June 6, 1936.

(10) of the Act, further exploration becomes necessary.[5] If not, that ends the matter.

Sec. 1-2. Engaged in the business. As seen, a broker is a person "engaged in the business" of effecting securities transactions for others, and a dealer is one "engaged in the business" of buying and selling for his own account. Moreover, Section 3(a)(5) of the Act excepts from the definition of dealer "any person insofar as he buys or sells securities for his own account, either individually or in some fiduciary capacity, but not as a part of a regular business."

To determine whether a person is a broker or dealer, therefore, it becomes necessary to explore whether or not he is "engaged in the business" within the meaning of that term as used in the definitions. This is a question of fact to be resolved by taking into account all relevant circumstances. In the vast majority of cases no problem would exist in determining whether the activities of a person amount to his being "engaged in the business" of buying and selling for his own account or of effecting transactions for the account of others. As in every area subject to regulation, however, there is an almost infinite variety of borderline type situations. Here are some of the more common examples, together with the author's views in each case.

A question frequently arises in connection with the utilization by an issuer[6] of the services of its directors, officers, and employees relative to a public offering of the issuer's securities. If the issuer engages in no other activity in securities, it is not engaged in the securities business. The more troublesome problems

---

[5] With exceptions which will be noted where appropriate, the definition of a "security" in Section 3(a)(10) of the Act is substantially the same as that term is defined in the Securities Act. See Section 2(1) of the Securities Act, 15 U.S.C. 77(b)(1). A discussion of the more unusual types of securities is found in SEC Securities Act Release No. 3892, January 31, 1958, and SEC Litigation Release No. 1876, January 9, 1961. These deal with the basic question of what constitutes an "investment contract," a subject examined by the Supreme Court in *SEC v. W. J. Howey Co.*, 328 U. S. 293 (1946) and *SEC v. C. M. Joiner Leasing Corp.*, 320 U. S. 344 (1943). See, also, 1 Loss, *Securities Regulation*, 455, 483—517 (2d ed. 1961). The arranging for passbooks with savings and loan associations involves the offer of a security. See *American Finance Company Inc.*, SEC Securities Act Release No. 4465, March 19, 1962, p. 6. Accordingly a person who is in the business of arranging for the opening of such accounts is a broker.

[6] The term issuer, as defined in Section 3(a)(8) of the Act, encompasses, in general, any "person" who creates or proposes to create a security. We have seen, *supra*, n. 2, that the term "person" includes an individual, corporation, partnership, association, joint stock company, business interest, or unincorporated association.

are posed, however, by the issuer's directors, officers, and employees who receive special compensation for soliciting subscriptions for the securities. It may be that any such person is an underwriter as defined in Section 2(11) of the Securities Act.[7] Nevertheless, he would not be a "broker" if he is under the issuer's supervision and control, he devotes his full time in rendering services for the issuer and he neither was previously engaged in the sale of securities, nor proposes to do so following completion of the offering. A so-called employee who has an application pending before the Commission for registration as a broker-dealer and who intends to go "independent" upon effectiveness of his registration would actually be "engaged in the business" of selling securities for the issuer prior to effectiveness of registration. If a director or officer of an issuer has an arrangement that he is to assume the responsibility for sale of the entire issue in return for a commission on sales, and if the selling expenses, including the compensation of salesmen, are to be borne by him, he is manifestly in business as "broker." Purchase by an officer or director of the securities from the issuer as principal, for resale to the public, would result in his being "engaged in the business" and thus being a "dealer."

What has been stated with reference to a director or officer of a corporation applies equally to general partners of a limited partnership who effect or participate in the public offering of interests by the limited partnership.

Any other person specially hired by an issuer on a commission basis to manage the public offering with the obligation to pay selling expenses and the right to hire salesmen would be in business as a "broker," irrespective of whether or not the issuer reserves the right to accept or reject subscriptions.

The problem may arise as to whether a person is "engaged in the business" of buying and selling securities in the context of merchandise sales promotions and sales contests. If a merchant offers a specified amount of securities purchased by him on the market to each customer who purchases a stated amount of merchandise, the merchant would be a "dealer" unless the offer is part of a promotion of very limited duration. Similarly, unless it is of definite and brief duration, a plan for the achievement of

---

[7] 15 U.S.C. 77(b)(11). See e.g., *Beta Frozen Food Storage, Inc.*, 37 SEC 387, 392 (1956); Cf., *Free Traders, Inc.*, 7 SEC 913, 921-2 (1940); *Shawnee Chiles Syndicate*, 10 SEC 109, 116-117 (1941).

higher goals for salesmen would result in the employer's acting as a dealer if the plan involves the disposition of securities among the salesmen which the employer purchases on the market. Also, the acceptance from customers by a merchant, on more than a very limited basis, of securities in part payment for merchandise and the resale of such securities would cause the merchant to be a "dealer."

Questions may be raised as to the activities of corporate treasurers who purchase stock in the market for company employees pursuant to stock purchase plans. If the treasurer enters into no other securities transactions which would indicate that he is "engaged in the business," he would not be a broker or dealer. The approach would probably be the same with reference to a corporation formed as a family vehicle with functions limited strictly to such non-discretionary matters as the transmission of orders to brokers and dealers and the maintenance of records of transactions engaged in by various members of the family. However, whether or not it be a family organization utilized for the purpose, if the organization should act on behalf of its members in giving orders to broker-dealers to buy or sell securities, and, in the process, make or influence investment decisions for the members, the broker-dealers having no direct relationship with the members, the organization would be a broker even though its charges are not based on commissions. The nominee of a bank, utilized purely as a conduit for the convenience of the bank in handling its securities transactions, does not, however, come within the definition of broker or dealer.

Trustees who have the basic responsibility for managing the portfolios of the trust estates to which they have title as trustees are not engaged in business as either a broker or dealer, particularly if they utilize the services of *professional* broker-dealers in engaging in securities transactions. Similarly, if investment advisers merely act as intermediaries for their customers in placing orders with the customers' brokers and dealers in respect of accounts carried by the latter in the names of such customers, such investment advisers would not be engaged in the business of buying or selling as a broker. Moreover, service type organizations providing mechanical facilities, such as routine billing, collection of receivables, and transmissions of collections to underwriters, are not brokers or dealers if their activities are confined to these mechanical tasks; in short if they engage in no activity which would be viewed as influencing the purchase of securities, and if their charges do not consist of commissions related to the size of transactions handled.

A person who has been a broker-dealer and who is in the process of terminating his business following withdrawal or revocation of his registration would not be continuing to engage in such business if he confines his securities activities to the liquidation of the securities positions of himself or his firm. However, a dealer who was once engaged in the sale of periodic plans for the accumulation of investment company shares would still remain a dealer, even though he is not selling new plans, if he continues to collect commissions on plans already sold.[8] A close issue can arise, however, in connection with a promotional organization which trains employees of issuers in the techniques of selling, which does not itself engage in the solicitation of subscriptions, but which maintains records of the performance of employees for follow-up purposes.

Problems would also arise in connection with certain practices of some broker-dealers (engaged principally in the sale of savings and loan association deposits, or of limited partnership, syndicate, or other interests in real estate issuers, or of securities of open end investment companies popularly known as "mutual funds") if these broker-dealers should circulate invitations to attorneys and accountants, upon the inducement of a commission, to sell to their clients the securities being offered by such broker-dealers. Apart from questions as to violation of anti-fraud provisions of the federal securities laws,[9] acceptance of these proposals would result in the accountants and attorneys becoming engaged in the business of effecting transactions in securities for the account of others, and thereby becoming brokers.

Sec. 1-3. Engaged in part-time business. It may be observed that there is nothing in the definitions of broker and dealer which would warrant a conclusion that a person cannot be engaged in the business in respect of securities merely because such business

---

[8] See *H. Law Weatherwax*, SEC Securities Exchange Act Release No. 7236, February 12, 1964. See also *Boruski, Jr.* v. *National Securities & Research Corporation*, 237 N.Y.S.2d 772 (1962).

[9] See *infra*, Sec. 10-1.

is only a minor part of the person's activities[10] or merely because the income from it represents only a small fraction of his total income. On the contrary, if the activity is engaged in for commissions or other compensation with sufficient recurrence to justify the inference that the activity is part of the person's business, he will be deemed to be "engaged in the business" within the meaning of that term as used in the definitions of broker and dealer.

On the other hand, a person is not a broker or dealer if his securities activities are performed on behalf of and are in fact under the complete and effective control and supervision of a broker or dealer. This follows whether or not the individual serves on a part-time basis or is characterized by the parties as independent contractor to avoid certain state and federal taxes, if his activities are actually under the supervision and control of the broker or dealer.[11] However, if an independent organization, or even an individual who is in fact an independent contractor, should sell securities on behalf of a broker-dealer for a commission, or should receive forwarding fees for channelling business to the broker-dealer, such organization or individual would be viewed as engaged in the securities business as a broker.

Sec. 1-4. Broker, dealer—miscellaneous considerations. It will be recalled that one part of the definition of a dealer is that it does not include "any person insofar as he buys or sells securities for his own account, either individually or in some fiduciary capacity, but not as a part of a regular business."[12] The purpose of this is to exclude from the definition of "dealer" members of the public who buy and sell securities for their own account as ordinary traders. Sometimes it is difficult to draw the line. But, when a person's interest in securities measured against his other interests is quite minor, and if he does not have memberships in exchanges or associations of dealers and does not provide the services to others that dealers customarily supply to customers, it may

---

[10] Such a broker-dealer is subject to the same obligations and standards of conduct as one engaged in the business full time. See e.g., *Boruski* v. *SEC,* 289 F.2d 738 (2d Cir. 1961), aff'g *Ernest F. Boruski, Jr.,* SEC Securities Exchange Act Release No. 6376, Oct. 7, 1960, p. 3.

[11] See SEC Securities Exchange Act Release No. 3674, April 9, 1945. As will be seen *infra,* Sections 17-12 and 19-9, absence of such supervision and control would violate fundamental standards of conduct applicable to brokers and dealers; and it constitutes an independent ground for disciplinary action.

[12] *Supra,* Sec. 1-2, Section 3(a)(5) of the Act.

be reasonable to infer that the individual is a mere trader and not a dealer.

One who writes, puts, and calls[13] with any degree of frequency would probably be considered as "engaged in the business" of buying and selling the underlying securities.[14] And an intermediary performing the functions of a broker in connection with the sale of puts and calls would appear to be within the definition of a broker.[15]

Before leaving the subject of who is a broker or dealer, it should be observed that the solicitation of prospective customers by a person intending to engage in business as a broker or dealer would be regarded as an activity which is tantamount to engaging in the business of a broker or dealer.[16] It would follow that a person, including any foreign individual or entity, is a dealer or broker, as the case may be, who advertises his willingness to buy and sell securities or to effect transactions in securities for the account of others.[17]

---

[13] A "put" is an option given to a person to sell to the writer of the put a specified amount of securities at a stated price within a certain time. "A call" is an option given to a person to buy from the writer a specified amount of securities at a stated price within a certain time. A "straddle" is a combination of both a put and a call. See SEC *Report on Put And Call Options* (1961), p. 9.

[14] In this connection, see the definitions in Sections 3(a)(13) and (14) of the Act as follows: "The terms 'buy' and 'purchase' each include any contract to buy, purchase or otherwise acquire" [Sec. 3(a)(13)]. "The terms 'sale' and 'sell' each include any contract to sell or otherwise dispose of" [Sec. 3(a)(14)].

[15] See *SEC* v. *Todd* (S.D.N.Y. Civil No. 55384, Judgment dated February 10, 1950), SEC Litigation Release No. 576, Feb. 10, 1950. *Cf.* also SEC Securities Exchange Act Release No. 4463, June 30, 1950.

[16] See *Ralph Siepel*, 38 SEC 256, 257-8 (1958), a case under the Investment Advisers Act of 1940, as amended, 15 U.S.C. §§80b-1—80b-21 (1958 & Supp. IV, 1963) [hereinafter cited as Investment Advisers Act by Section number of that Act.], where the Commission held that the solicitation of clients by one who offers investment advisory services is part of the business of an investment adviser.

[17] See *F. W. Horne & Company Inc.* 37 SEC 104, 108 (1957). And see *The Whitehall Corporation*, 38 SEC 259, 271 at n. 27 (1958).

Chapter 2

REQUIREMENTS

Sec. 2-1. Registration requirements. Unless he comes within stated exceptions, a broker or dealer may not "make use of the mails or of any means or instrumentality of interstate commerce to effect any transaction in, or to induce the purchase or sale of any security" if he is not registered with the Commission.[1] This includes a foreign broker or dealer.[2]

In appraising the possible need of a person to register, the first point of inquiry is whether the activities of the person are those of a broker or dealer. This is a subject which we have already explored.[3] It now becomes pertinent to inquire as to whether any one of the specified exceptions to the registration requirements is applicable.

Sec. 2-2. Exceptions—transactions confined to national securities exchanges. A broker or dealer who confines all of his securities activities to effecting transactions or inducing purchases and sales on national securities exchanges[4] need not be registered. If his activities be so limited, it is not essential to the exception that he be a member of any such exchange, provided all of his orders are executed by such a member on the exchange. A broker or dealer who is a member of an exchange would nevertheless have to register if he engages in any transaction in non-exempted securities in the over-the-counter market,[5] regardless of

---

[1] Securities Acts Amendments of 1964, Sec. 6(a). Section 15(a)(1) of the Act. "Use of the mails or of any means or instrumentality of interstate commerce" will sometimes be referred to herein as "jurisdictional means."

[2] See e.g., *Gregory & Company, Inc.*, 38 SEC 304 (1958).

[3] See *supra*, Sec. 1-1.

[4] A national securities exchange is one which is registered with the Commission pursuant to Section 6 of the Act. "Exchange" is defined in Section 3(a)(1) of the Act. See *infra*, Sec. 23-1 for a more detailed discussion.

[5] See SEC Securities Exchange Act Release No. 5790, Oct. 10, 1958. The categories of securities which are "exempted" will be touched upon below. See *infra*, Sec. 2-3. Any transaction not executed on a national securities exchange is deemed effected in the "over-the-counter market," Section 2 of the Act; Sen Rep. No. 1455, 75th Cong., 3rd Sess. (1938), p. 2; H. R. Rep. No. 2307, 75th Cong., 3rd Sess. (1938), p. 2. A transaction is "executed" by a broker or dealer when he (or someone he authorizes to act on his behalf) enters into a contract of purchase or

10

any claim on his part that such transactions are "personal" or have been made for his own investment purposes. The argument by a broker or dealer will not be accepted to the effect that his or its over-the-counter transactions constituted "personal" or "investment" activities as distinguished from business transactions. The business of a broker or dealer encompasses engaging in transactions in securities, and no distinction will be recognized between a transaction claimed to be "for investment" or "personal," on the one hand, and one claimed to be of a business character, on the other.[6]

Sec. 2-3. Exceptions—transactions in exempted securities. If a broker or dealer confines his over-the-counter transactions to "exempted" securities, however, he would not be required to register so long as his other transactions in securities are confined to transactions executed on a national securities exchange.[7] This follows because of provisions in Section 15(a)(1) of the Act that the registration requirements do not apply to a broker or dealer whose over-the-counter transactions are confined to exempted securities.[8] By the terms of Section 3(a)(12) of the Act, "exempted" securities include direct obligations of, and those guaranteed as to principal or interest by the United States, or a state or municipal government, or an agency or corporate instrumentality of such government. They also encompass those securities issued by corporations in which the United States has a direct or indirect interest as the Secretary of Treasury shall designate for exemption. Finally, they include:

> . . . such other securities . . . as the Commission may by such rules and regulations as it deems necessary or appropriate in the public interest or for the protection of investors, either unconditionally or upon specified terms or for stated periods, exempt from the operation of any one or more provisions of . . . [the

---

sale, as the case may be, in order to carry out the order of his customer. See SEC Securities Exchange Act Release No. 3040, Oct. 13, 1941, which discusses this term in another but comparable context.

[6] *F. R. Gentry & Co., Inc.,* SEC Securities Exchange Act Release No. 6986, January 2, 1963, p. 3; *Chester Richard Koza,* 39 SEC 950, 952 (1960). *Peoples Securities Company,* 39 SEC 641, 650-652 (1960); *affd.* 289 F.2d 268 (5th Cir. 1961); *Lawrence R. Leeby,* 32 SEC 307, 312-313 (1951). *R. D. French & Co.,* 36 SEC 603, 606-7 (1955). *Burley & Co.,* 28 SEC 126, 128 (1948).

[7] Section 15(a)(1) of the Act.

[8] Section 15(a)(1) of the Act also exempts from its registration requirements brokers and dealers whose over-the-counter transactions are confined to commercial paper, bankers' acceptances, and commercial bills.

Act] which by their terms do not apply to an 'exempted security' or to 'exempted securities.'[9]

It may be observed that the governmental obligations specified in Section 3(a)(12) are exempted securities for all purposes, and hence a broker or dealer who confines his activities to them need not register.

The Commission has adopted rules[10] designating certain types of securities as exempted securities for the purpose of Section 15 (a)(1) of the Act. The effect of these rules is to obviate the necessity for registration by a broker or dealer whose over-the-counter transactions are limited to the securities thus designated as "exempted."

Rule 15a-3 under the Act provides that securities registered or exempt from registration on a national securities exchange are exempted from the operation of Section 15(a)(1) of the Act under the special circumstances specified in the rule relative to the maintenance of orderly markets on an exchange. The purpose of this rule is to obviate the necessity for registration as a dealer by a specialist who, as a broker and dealer, confines his activities to transactions on an exchange with the exception of making purchases and sales over-the-counter of securities as to which he is designated by the exchange as a specialist, provided that such over-the-counter transactions are approved by the exchange in accordance with exchange rules designed to assist the specialist to maintain a fair and orderly market in the security on the exchange.[11]

Another security exempted by rule under Section 15(a)(1) of the Act is the stock of a corporation which entitles the holders to possession and occupancy of specific apartment units in property owned by such corporation organized and operated on a cooperative basis, provided the shares of stock are sold by or through a real estate broker licensed under the laws of the political subdivision in which the property is situated.[12]

---

[9] Section 3(a)(12) of the Act. Examples of these specially exempted securities will be given in contexts where they are relevant. SEC Securities Exchange Act Release No. 7448, Oct. 16, 1964.

[10] The Rules adopted by the Commission under the Act are the General Rules And Regulations under the Securities Exchange Act of 1934. All references to rules under the Act will be by rule number of such General Rules And Regulations. The rules under the Act are published in the Code of Federal Regulations as Title 17, Part 240. Thus, Rule 15a-3 corresponds to 17 CFR 240.15a-3.

[11] Rule 15a-3. Some reference to the term "specialist" and to the requirement for maintaining an orderly market will be made *infra* at Sec. 23-3.

[12] Rule 15a-2.

Finally, under Rule 15a-1, an evidence of indebtedness is exempted if it is secured by mortgage, deed of trust, or other lien upon real estate or upon leasehold interests therein and if the entire mortgage, deed of trust, or other lien is transferred with the entire indebtedness. This operates to exempt from registration brokers or dealers whose activities are thus confined.[13] Unlike the Securities Act, a guarantee of a security is not included in the definition of a security under the Act.[14] It may be that a broker or dealer need not register if he confines his transactions to guaranteed whole mortgages or other real estate liens and their corresponding evidence of indebtedness. Nevertheless, if the broker or dealer is himself the guarantor, or if the effect of the guarantee or the identity of the guarantor or other characteristics of the security dealt in by the broker or dealer bring it within the meaning of the term "investment contract," Rule 15a-1 will not serve to relieve the broker or dealer from the necessity to register.[15]

A broker or dealer who limits his activities to exempted securities is nonetheless a broker or dealer. Consequently, if he engages for any reason in any over-the-counter transaction in non-exempted securities by use of the mails or interstate instrumentalities, he must register.[16] It has been seen that he cannot claim dispensation from registration on the argument that such transactions are "personal" or for "investment."[17] Furthermore, he cannot escape registration even if his over-the-counter activities in non-exempted securities be engaged in without compensation merely for the accommodation of his customers. By the terms of the Act the test for registration is met if a broker or dealer effects or induces a transaction in a security over-the-counter,[18] and it need not be shown that he was specially compensated for that particular activity.[19]

Sec. 2-4. Exceptions—business exclusively intrastate. An

---

[13] See SEC Securities Exchange Act Release No. 784, July 25, 1936.

[14] See Section 3(a)(10) of the Act and Section 2(1) of the Securities Act.

[15] See the rather full discussion on this entire subject in *Public Offerings Of Investment Contracts Providing For the Acquisition, Sale or Servicing Of Mortgages or Deed of Trust*, SEC Securities Exchange Act Release No. 5633, January 31, 1958. This is the same as SEC Securities Act Release No. 3892.

[16] See SEC Securities Exchange Act Release No. 5790, Oct. 10, 1958.

[17] *Supra*, Sec. 2-2.

[18] Section 15(a)(1) of the Act.

[19] As already seen, a broker or dealer must by definition be "engaged in the business" of effecting transactions for the account of others or buying and selling for his own account, *supra* Sec. 1-1; Sections 3(a)(4) and 3(a)(5) of the Act.

other exemption from broker-dealer registration requirements applies to a broker or dealer "whose business is exclusively intrastate."[20]

The business of a broker or dealer is not exclusively intrastate if he is a participant in the distribution of securities of an out-of-state issuer, or even if he acts only as broker in the sale of an out-of-state block of securities from an out-of-state issuer to a local customer.[21] Similarly, a broker or dealer who advertises for business in a publication which crosses state lines without limiting his invitation to residents of the state in which he is situated is one who is not regarded as operating exclusively intrastate.[22] If any orders of a customer are executed on an exchange, his broker or dealer cannot successfully maintain that its business is exclusively intrastate.[23] The same conclusions would follow in the case where a broker or dealer places or responds to a quotation or other invitation for the transaction of business in a specified security in the daily quotation sheets of the National Daily Quotation Bureau, Inc. These cross state lines and therefore include inducements for the purchase or sale of the particular security in a manner that is not exclusively intrastate.[24]

However, if securities of an out-of-state issuer have genuinely

---

[20] Section 15(a)(1). Such brokers and dealers are nevertheless subject to the anti-fraud rules of Sections 15(c)(1) and 15(c)(2) and the financial responsibility requirements of section 15(c)(3). SEC *Statement of the Securities and Exchange Commission With Respect To Proposed Amendments of Section 15(a) and (b) and Section 15A of the Securities Exchange Act of 1934,* June 18, 1963, p. 12.

[21] *Professional Investors, Inc.,* 37 SEC 173, 175-6 (1956). *The Whitehall Corporation,* 38 SEC 259-271 (1958); *Peoples Securities Company,* 39 SEC 641, 650-652 (1960), *aff'd* 289 F.2d 268 (5th Cir. 1961).

[22] *Mutual Real Estate Investors, Inc.,* SEC Securities Exchange Act Release No. 7105, July 30, 1963, p. 1. And his use of the telephone across state lines in his business is similarly regarded. *Ibid.*

[23] *Professional Investors, Inc. supra,* n. 38, and *Brooklyn Manhattan Transit Corporation,* 1 SEC 147 173-4 (1935), where the Commission took official notice that ". . . a person selling a security over the [New York] stock exchange cannot in any way control the sale in order to prevent a purchaser from a state outside of New York bidding for and purchasing the securities offered and thereafter requiring their delivery in interstate commerce after the sale. . . . " See also SEC *Statement of the Securities and Exchange Commission with respect to Proposed Amendments of Section 15(a) and (b) and Section 15A of the Securities Exchange Act of 1934,* June 18, 1963, p. 13.

[24] See *Halsey Stuart & Co., Inc.,* 30 SEC 106, 127 (1949). "Thus the listings [in the over-the-counter daily quotation sheets] are commonly understood to have a serious meaning and business purpose. They are steps in sales negotiations and, at the very least, invitations to negotiate the sales. . . . And see *Idem.* at p. 113, n. 10, and see *The New York Times,* October 23, 1960. Section 3, p. F3. A discussion of these daily quotation sheets appears *infra* at Sec. 16-4.

come to rest in the hands of local customers,[25] a broker or dealer can engage in transactions in such securities so long as he otherwise confines his business intrastate.

Manifestly, the "exclusively intrastate" business exemption is based on the local and limited character of the broker's or dealer's business. The term "exclusively" is therefore given its literal meaning. Consequently, the exemption is destroyed, no matter how few the interstate transactions are; the claim that they were *de minimis* will not save the exemption.[26] Moreover, one who engages in interstate activities as regards exempted securities, cannot avoid registration on the claim that his activities in non-exempted securities over-the-counter are kept within the bounds of a single state. As we have seen, no credit would be given to the claim of exemption on the plea that such interstate transactions as have occurred were "personal" or for "investment."[27]

It may finally be noted that a person would be violating the broker-dealer registration requirements if he has filed an application for registration and begins to engage in business wholly within a single state pending effectiveness of the registration. The exception in Section 15(a)(1) of the Act relates to "one whose business is exclusively intrastate." If it is the intention of such person to expand his business across state lines upon effectiveness of the registration, it is plain that the business engaged in pending effectiveness is but part of an interstate business.[28]

Sec. 2-5. Exceptions—exemption by commission rules or orders. By recent amendment to the Act, the Commission is empowered to exempt from the registration requirements of Section 15(a)(1) of the Act any broker or dealer or any class of brokers or dealers specified by the Commission by its order or rules and regulations made or adopted in the public interest or for protec-

---

[25] A discussion of the concept of "distribution" and as to when securities come to rest in the hands of members of the investing public may be found *infra* at Sections 13-1 and 13-12.

[26] *Associated Investors Securities, Inc.*, SEC Securities Exchange Act Release No. 6859, July 24, 1962, p. 12, and see *The Whitehall Corporation*, 38 SEC 259, 271 (1958).

[27] See *supra* Sec. 2-2.

[28] *The Whitehall Corporation*, 38 SEC 259, 271 at n. 27 (1958). However, if a broker-dealer genuinely engaged in an exclusively intrastate business for a substantial period of time decides to file an application for registration as a broker-dealer with the Commission, he would not lose his intrastate exemption but may carry on as before until his broker-dealer registration becomes effective.

tion of investors. Such exemptions may be unconditional, or upon conditions, or for specified periods.[29]

Sec. 2-6. Recapitulation of broker-dealer registration requirements. Unless his business is exclusively intrastate, a broker or dealer must be registered if he uses the mails or any means or instrumentality of interstate commerce to effect any transaction in or induce the purchase or sale over-the-counter of any security other than commercial paper, bankers' acceptances, commercial bills, or exempted securities. If a broker-dealer effects transactions in or induces the purchase or sale of securities only on a national securities exchange, he need not register. Nor does he have to register if his over-the-counter transactions are limited to commercial paper, bankers' acceptances, commercial bills, and exempted securities. A broker or dealer does not conduct an exclusively intrastate business if he engages in any interstate transactions in exempted securities or in any transactions executed on an exchange, or if he places quotations in or otherwise invites interest in transacting business in a given security through the medium of the daily quotations sheets or other publications which cross state lines. Similarly the so-called intrastate character of his business is destroyed if he participates in the distribution of securities of an out-of-state issuer or deals in securities procured directly from out-of-state sources. Securities of out-of-state issuers which have genuinely come to rest in the hands of local customers can, however, be dealt in without loss of the "intrastate" character of the business.

No broker or dealer other than one whose business is "exclusively intrastate" can avoid registration, irrespective of the predominant character of his business, if he engages in any transaction over-the-counter in a non-exempted security. A broker or dealer cannot separate such transactions from his business on the ground that they are "personal" or for "investment." And no transaction crossing state lines will be viewed as *de minimis* in testing whether the intrastate exemption is available.

Sec. 2-7. Other threshold requirements. In addition to registration, if a broker or dealer is not a member of a registered securities association,[30] the broker or dealer and all natural persons

---

[29] Section 15(a)(2) of the Act; Securities Acts Amendments of 1964, Sec. 6(a).

[30] For a discussion of registered securities associations, see, *infra*, Chapter 24.

associated with such broker or dealer[31] must meet such specified and appropriate standards with respect to training, experience, and such other qualifications as the Commission finds necessary and desirable.[32] For this purpose, the Commission is authorized to adopt rules and regulations which may appropriately classify brokers and dealers and associated persons, taking into account such matters as types of business conducted and nature of securities sold,[33] which may specify which portion of such standards shall be applicable to any such class;[51] and which may require persons in any such class to pass prescribed examinations.[35] Additionally, the rules and regulations may provide that persons in any such class (other than a broker or dealer, partners, officers, or supervisory employees including branch managers) may be qualified solely on the basis of compliance with such specified standards of training and other prescribed qualifications.[36] The Commission may provide for examinations to be administered by a registered securities association or a national securities exchange, and may make provision for the payment to such association or exchange of reasonable fees and charges to defray their costs of administration. If an examination is administered directly by the Commission, it may similarly provide for reasonable fees and charges for such purposes.[37] Additionally, such a non-member registered broker or dealer will be required to pay reasonable fees and charges to defray the costs of additional regulatory duties imposed upon the Commission because the broker or dealer is not a member of such an association.[38] The added regulatory duties will include the enforcement of regulations "designed to promote just and equitable principles of trade, to provide safeguards against unreasonable rates of commissions or other charges, and in general, to protect investors and the public interest and to remove impediments to and perfect the mechanism of a free and open market."[39]

It will be seen that membership by a broker or dealer in a

---

[31] The categories of persons who come within the meaning of the term of a "person associated with a broker or dealer" are specified in Section 3(a)(18) of the Act. They will be discussed further in detail *infra,* at Sec. 19-1.

[32] Section 15(b)(8).

[33] Section 15(b)(8)(A).

[34] Section 15(b)(8)(B).

[35] Section 15(b)(8)(C).

[36] Section 15(b)(8)(D).

[37] *Ibid.*

[38] Section 15(b)(9).

[39] Section 15(b)(10).

registered securities association would tend to ease the Commission's regulatory burden in these areas with respect to a member broker or dealer.[40] Such associations are required to adopt and enforce rules providing for minimum standards of training, experience, and other qualifications for member brokers and dealers and persons associated with them.[41] And the association must adopt rules (and enforce them) which promote just and equitable principles of trade, provide safeguards against unreasonable rates of commissions or other charges, and, in general, protect investors and the public interest, and remove impediments to and perfect the mechanism of a free and open market.[42]

---

[40] Discussion on this topic will be deferred and dealt with at some length in Chapter 24 beginning at Sec. 24-2, *infra*.

[41] Section 15A(b)(5). Persons associated with a member of a registered securities association are defined in Section 3(a)(21). Reference to this matter in further detail will be made at Sec. 24-3, *infra*.

[42] Section 15A(b)(8).

CHAPTER 3

PROCEDURE

Sec. 3-1. Application—form, filing, execution. The procedure with respect to the execution and filing of an application for registration as a broker or dealer is found in Section 15(b) of the Act and in a number of rules adopted under that Section.

The first step is to file an application on a prescribed form[1] in accordance with the instructions in the form.[2]

The items of information set forth in the prescribed Form must be supplied, and, of course, they must be "true, correct and complete."[3] The application must be executed and filed in duplicate original with the Commission at its headquarters in Washington, D. C., and an exact copy should be retained for the applicant's files.[4] The application must be dated and signed. In the case of a partnership, a general partner must sign. In the case of a corporation, the signature must be by a duly authorized principal officer. If the applicant is an unincorporated organization or association which is not a partnership, it must be signed by a duly authorized person who directs or manages or participates in the direction or management of the applicant's affairs.[5] As a convenient check list, the Commission makes available to the public its *Guide For Broker-Dealer Form BD* to answer most of the questions which arise with respect to the filling out and execution of form BD.[6]

Sec. 3-2. Application—form of organization-registration as entity. It has been seen that a broker or dealer is defined in part

---

[1] SEC Form BD, March 2, 1959 [hereinafter called "Form BD"]. A copy of the form currently in use is set forth at Appendix E, Sec. 25-5, *infra.*

[2] Rule 15b-1. See Rule O-1(a)(4) which provides that the instructions accompanying forms are included in the term, "rules and regulations."

[3] The representations in Form BD under the caption, "Execution" are as follows: "The Applicant or Registrant Submitting This Form and The Person By Whom It Is Executed Hereby Represent That It Contains A True, Correct And Complete Statement Of All Information Required To Be Furnished."

[4] Form BD, General Instructions, No. 1.

[5] Form BD, "Execution."

[6] *SEC Guide For Broker-Dealer Form BD* [hereinafter called Guide to Form BD]. As seen from this Guide, unacceptable applications numbered as high as forty percent prior to its adoption. A copy of the Guide is set forth as Appendix F at Sec. 25-6, *infra.*

19

as a "person," which in turn is defined to include an individual, corporation, partnership, association, joint stock company, business trust, or unincorporated organization.[7] This reflects the Congressional purpose to treat the enterprise, regardless of form, as the business entity subject to the regulatory provisions of the statute. Accordingly, if a business enterprise is to be conducted in a manner requiring registration as a broker or dealer, it must register as an entity, whether it be composed of a joint account or any other conceivable form of unincorporated association or organization.

Sec. 3-3. Accuracy of information in application. The items of information called for by Form BD are designed to carry out the Congressional mandate of Section 15(b)(1) of the Act that the application for registration "shall contain such information in such detail as to such broker or dealer and any persons associated with such broker or dealer, as the Commission may by rules and regulations require as necessary or appropriate in the public interest or for the protection of investors."

Accordingly, it is fundamental to the regulatory plan as regards brokers and dealers that the items of information in the Form BD application be true, correct, and complete[8] irrespective of a claim that the information is available to the Commission elsewhere.[9] Although the form of application has been changed from time to time and corresponding changes have been made in the nature of the information required, it may be of some value to refer to the items in the present Form BD[10] which have

---

[7] *Supra*, Sec. 1-1, n. 2. See sections 3(a)(4), (5), and (9) of the Act.

[8] Form BD, General Instructions, No. 1, and Form BD, "Execution." See *S.A.E. Corporation*, SEC Securities Exchange Act Release No. 6956, Nov. 28, 1960, p. 2; *Mayflower Associates, Inc.*, 38 SEC 110, 112 (1957). As part of the "Guide For Broker Dealer Form BD" there is an "Important Notice," warning against failure to include or file required information or making false statements. A copy of this notice is set forth as Appendix G. See Sec. 25-7, *infra.*

[9] *Albert Wasserman*, 38 SEC 579, 580-1 (1958); *Gregory & Co., Inc.*, 38 SEC 304 (1958); *Sterling Securities Company*, 39 SEC 487, 495-6 (1959); *Morris J. Reiter*, SEC Securities Exchange Act Release No. 6849, July 13, 1962, p. 6. *Nicholas Jamieson*, SEC Securities Exchange Act Release No. 6440, Dec. 28, 1960, p. 3, and see *F C C v. W O K O, Inc.*, 329 U. S. 223 (1946).

[10] Adopted March 2, 1959, SEC Securities Exchange Act Release No. 5894. This states *inter alia* ". . . The form as revised makes it clear that it must contain not only true and correct information, but also all the information required to be furnished." As a result of *Special Study Report* recommendations (Pt. 1, Ch. II, p. 159, item 3) the Commission has indicated that it intends to adopt rules revising Form BD to contain information such as, major business activities, exchange and association memberships, branch office information, details as to wire connections, size of

resulted in Commission action. The failure to set forth accurately the address of the applicant's principal place of business, the name under which applicant would transact its business, or the address at which official Commission notices may be received, have each been the subject of adverse Commission comment.[11] One of the most common occasions for censure by the Commission on the subject of broker-dealer applications relates to the failure to disclose the identity of the persons actually in control, directly or indirectly, of the applicant or registrant.[12] Concealment, as regards principals of the applicants or registrant, of their previous connections with any other broker or dealer has also been the subject of Commission action.[13] Additionally, the Commission has had occasion to take action for failure to disclose with respect to principals or employees, previous Commission findings, court injunctions as regards violation of the federal securities laws or acts and practices respecting transactions in securities.[14]

The truth and accuracy of the application of a broker or dealer are the responsibility of the applicant and its principals.

---

sales staff, nature of research department, and names of supervisors of various activities and their prior experience. Special Market Study Release No. 25, April 30, 1963, p. 4.

[11] See e.g., *George Frederick Wheeler*, 38 SEC 403, 404 (1958); *Valley State Brokerage, Inc.*, 39 SEC 596, 598 (1959); *John B. Sullivan*, 38 SEC 643 (1958); *Intermountain Securities, Inc.*, 39 SEC 638, 640 (1960); *First Lewis Corp.*, 39 SEC 871, 872 (1960); *Ross Natale Barengo*, 38 SEC 824 (1959); *Ralph Mineo*, SEC Securities Exchange Act Release No. 6955, Nov. 28, 1962. See also facing page of Form BD and Item 9 of Form BD, Sec. 25-5, *infra*.

[12] See *W. K. Archer Company*, 11 SEC 635, 641 (1942), aff'd *Archer v. SEC*, 133 F.2d 795 (8th Cir. 1943), *Ross Natale Barengo*, 38 SEC 824 (1959); *Peoples Securities Co.*, 39 SEC 641, 643 (1960); *Herman Bud Rothbard*, 39 SEC 253, 258 (1959); *Maxwell M. Sacks*, 38 SEC 465 (1959); *First Lewis Corp.*; and *Intermountain Securities, Inc., supra; Southern States Securities Corporation*, 39 SEC 728, 732 (1960); *Edna Campbell Markey*, 39 SEC 274 (1959); *J. A. Latimer & Co., Inc.*, 38 SEC 790, 792 (1958); *Sol T. Pfeffer*, SEC Securities Exchange Act Release No. 6506, March 23, 1961, p. 3. See *Batten & Co., Inc.*, SEC Securities Exchange Act Release No. 6734, Feb. 14, 1962; *Lewis Wolf, Inc.*, SEC Securities Exchange Act Release No. 6949, Nov. 21, 1962, p. 1; *Security Service Inc.*, SEC Securities Exchange Act Release No. 7127, Aug. 27, 1963, p. 1. As reflected in all of these authorities, actual control must be disclosed in the application. Thus an individual controlling a parent of the applicant must be shown as controlling the applicant.

Items 3(c) and 6 of Form BD are designed to elicit whether someone not an officer or principal stockholder of applicant or registrant is actually in control.

[13] See item 7 of form BD, Sec. 25-5, *infra*, *Kelly Rubenstein, Inc.*, 38 SEC 583 (1958); *East Coast Investors Co., Inc.*, SEC Securities Exchange Act Release No. 7122, Aug. 21, 1963; p. 1; *Associated Underwriters Inc.*, SEC Securities Exchange Act Release No. 7075, May 10, 1963, p. 1.

[14] See e.g. *Alexander Dvoretsky*, 39 SEC 605-607 (1959). Items 8(a)(b) and (c) of Form BD call for this information. See also, *Nicholas Jamieson*, SEC Securities Exchange Act Release No. 6440, Dec. 28, 1960, p. 3.

No excuse will be entertained that subordinates, relied upon for details, had failed to fill in the items properly.[15]

Sec. 3-4. Documents accompanying application—statement of financial condition. There is a requirement under Rule 15b-8 that every broker or dealer who files an application for registration on Form BD shall file with such application a statement in duplicate original as at a date within 30 days prior to filing, disclosing the nature and amount of assets and liabilities and the net worth of such broker or dealer.[16]

The Commission has published a guide to assist applicants in following the requirements of the Rule.[17] This Rule 15b-8 Guide contains these instructions in part:

> "The statement of financial condition required by Rule 15b-8 must be that of the person or *entity* applying for registration and in sufficient detail to disclose the *nature* and *amount* of all assets and liabilities (of each category) and the resultant net worth. A *pro forma* statement as of a date in the future is not acceptable, although *pro forma* information may be included as a footnote or exhibit.

> "A sole proprietor must show *all* of his assets and liabilities and net worth, not just those assets dedicated to the broker-dealer business. If any assets are jointly owned, such should be indicated to the broker-dealer business.

> "If any liabilities are secured, the nature and amount of collateral should be indicated.

> A schedule of any securities in which the applicant has an interest must be included, showing the *number of units of each security and market value as of the date of the statement.*

> "A Corporation Should Reflect its Capitalization."

> "The statement required by Rule 15b-8 need not be prepared by an independent accountant.[18] "

Attached to the statement must be an oath or affirmation taken before an authorized official by the sole proprietor, duly

---

[15] *Kelly Rubenstein, Inc.,* 38 SEC 582, 583-4 (1958). *Peoples Securities Company,* 39 SEC 641, 643-4 (1960); cf. *Sterling Securities Company,* 39 SEC 487, 494-5 (1959); and *Freeman Securities, Inc.,* 39 SEC 355, 356 (1959).

[16] Of course, this statement must be true and correct, see *Sierra Securities Inc.,* SEC Securities Exchange Act Release No. 7257, Feb. 28, 1964.

[17] SEC *Guide For Preparation of Oath Or Affirmation And Financial Statement* [hereinafter called the "Rule 15b-8 Guide"]. A copy of the Rule 15b-8 guide is set forth as Appendix H, at Sec. 25-8, *infra.*

[18] [Author's note] Emphasis in original. Instructions as to manner of execution and on filling out the facing page of the Rule 15b-8 statement are contained in the Rule 15b-8 Guide, Sec. 25-8, *infra.*

authorized corporate officer, general partner or managing agent, as the case may be, of the applicant, depending on the form of its organization. If bound separately from the balance of the statement, the schedule containing the list of securities will not be available for public inspection except upon authorization of the Commission.[19]

Sec. 3-5. Documents accompanying application—consent to service of process—Non-Residents. In the case of a non-resident broker or dealer, a non-resident general partner of a broker-dealer partnership, or a non-resident managing agent of any other unincorporated association, the application must be accompanied by appropriate forms, properly executed and acknowledged, designating the Commission as agent for the service of process respecting causes of action instituted in any appropriate court in the United States and arising during the time the registration is in effect out of activities of such non-resident occurring within the jurisdiction of the United States in connection with the conduct of business of a broker or dealer, if such cause of action is founded directly or indirectly on any of all but one of the statutes administered by the Commission.[20]

Sec. 3-6. Documents accompanying application—records and undertaking as to records—non-residents. At the time a non-resident files an application on Form BD, the applicant must also file a notice specifying the address of the place within the United States where he will keep and preserve the true, correct, complete, and current copies of all books and records which a broker or dealer is required by Commission rule to make, keep current, maintain, and preserve.[21]

In the alternative, the non-resident applicant may file with the

---

[19] These schedules are available for official use to federal and state employees and officials; and those of a national securities exchange or association of which the applicant is a member. Rule 15b-8(b).

[20] The exception is the Public Utility Holding Company Act of 1935, 15 U.S.C. 79a-79z-6 (1958). For full details as to the extent of the power of attorney required, see Rule 15b-7 and SEC Forms 7-M, 8-M, 9-M and 10-M, December 9, 1958, the forms prescribed for use in the circumstances stated therein. Copies of these forms are set forth as Appendices I, J, K, and L, respectively, Sections 25-9, 25-10, 25-11, 25-12, *infra.* The requirements of Rule 15b-7 also arise should the broker or dealer, or a general partner or managing agent, become a non-resident after registration has become effective.

[21] Rule 17a-7(a). For a discussion of the records maintenance and preservation requirements see *infra,* Chapter 6.

application, and execute, a written undertaking, in substantially the form set forth in Rule 17a-7(b)(1), to furnish the Commission upon demand at its headquarters or at any designated Regional Office all or any part of the registrant's books and records required by the rules on its part to be made, kept current, maintained, and preserved.[22]

Sec. 3-7. Applications by predecessors and successors of applicants, successor partnerships, successor fiduciaries. An application for registration of a broker or dealer to be formed or organized may be made by a broker or dealer to which the broker or dealer to be formed or organized is to be the successor. The application must be made on Form BD, and it becomes effective on the 30th day after filing, but the registration will terminate on the 45th day after the effective date, unless, before then, the successor, in accordance with Commission rules and regulations, files a statement adopting the application filed by the predecessor.[23] Any such statement constitutes a representation that the information contained in the predecessor application and all supplements and amendments thereto are true and correct.[24]

Additionally, a broker or dealer succeeding to and continuing the business of a registered broker-dealer will be effectively registered upon succession, and for this purpose the predecessor's registration will be deemed to remain in effect 60 days after succession, if the *successor* files an application on Form BD within 30 days after succession.[25] It should be observed that this privilege exists

---

[22] A copy of the form of undertaking is set forth as Appendix M, at Sec. 25-13, *infra*. By paragraph (b)(2) of Rule 17a-7 the broker or dealer who maintains or preserves its books and records outside the United States and who files the requisite undertaking is also required to honor written demand by the Commission for all or part of its records by furnishing true copies of the requested material within 14 days after Commission demand to either the principal office or any Regional Office of the Commission as specified in the demand. It may be noted that the provisions of Rule 17a-7 become applicable even after effectiveness of registration if a broker or dealer becomes a non-resident.

[23] Section 15(b)(2) of the Act, Rule 15b-3. The Rule 15b-8 statement of financial condition should be filed by the successor at the time the application is adopted by the successor.

[24] Rule 15b-3.

[25] See paragraph (a) of Rule 15b-4. This application is a new one in all respects which must be accompanied by the successor's Rule 15b-8 statement and such other documents as may be called for upon the filing of a new application. See *supra*, Sections 3-4, 3-5 and 3-6. The filing of a "successor" application must be made no later than 30 days after succession. A later filing will not serve to keep the old registration alive for the benefit of the successor, and immediate broker-dealer

only if the successor takes over substantially all of the assets and liabilities of, and continues the business of, the predecessor. The privilege was, of course, not designed to enable persons to succeed to registered broker-dealers which are empty shells and have ceased to be actively engaged in business.[26]

In the case of a broker-dealer partnership, the death, withdrawal, or admission of a partner, or some change in the terms of the partnership agreement, might under applicable local law result in the termination of the old partnership and creation of a new one. Paragraph (b) of Rule 15b-4 provides that if a partnership succeeds to and continues the business of a predecessor registered partnership, the successor may file Form BD to reflect the changes in the partnership and information called for as to any new partners, and that such filing shall be treated as an application even though designated as an amendment. If a new partnership is in fact created under local law, a statement of financial condition under Rule 15b-8 must be filed with the Form BD filing.[27]

The registration of a broker or dealer becomes the registration of a fiduciary successor such as an executor, administrator, guardian, conservator, assignee for benefit of creditors, receiver or trustee in bankruptcy, appointed or qualified by order, judgment or decree of court of competent jurisdiction to continue the business of such registered broker or dealer. However, within 30 days after embarking on his duties, such successor fiduciary must file a statement setting forth as to him in his fiduciary capacity substantially the information required by Form BD.[28] This Rule has ap-

---

operations by the successor will be deemed in violation of Section 15(a) of the Act. See *First Securities Company,* SEC Securities Exchange Act Release No. 6446, January 9, 1961, p. 4.

[26] *F. W. Horne & Co., Inc.,* 38 SEC 104, 109 (1957); and see Item 1 of Form BD. Situations which do not fit this test for "successor" may be appropriate for an application for acceleration of the effectiveness of registration. See, *infra,* Sec. 3-8. It may be noted that the concept of "successor" as envisioned by Rule 15b-4 and enunciated in the text would preclude the possibility of a broker-dealer having two or more successors as would be the case if partners of a registrant dissolve the partnership and desire to engage in separate, individual businesses.

[27] Prior to the change in Rule 15b-8 effective September 15, 1957, the requirement to file a Rule 15b-8 statement did not apply "to a partnership succeeding to and continuing the business of another partnership registered as a broker or dealer at the time of such succession." However, the Rule in its present amended state has eliminated that exception. SEC Securities Exchange Act Release No. 5560, August 8, 1957.

[28] Rule 15b-5. If the fiduciary fails to file this statement within the 30 days, he will be required to file an application for new registration together with the statement of financial condition required by Rule 15b-8.

plication only when the fiduciary proposes to continue engaging in the business of a broker and dealer as distinguished from having the intention of limiting his activities to those necessary to liquidate the enterprise.

Sec. 3-8. Effectiveness of registration—acceleration. Except in cases where registration is deferred, postponed, or denied by Commission order,[29] the registration becomes effective thirty days after filing, "or within such shorter period of time as the Commission may determine."[30]

This provision affords scope for acceleration of the effective date of the application. The Act and Rules provide no procedure for this purpose, and they do not set up standards or guides which might be used in the exercise by the Commission of its discretion whether or not to accelerate. If an applicant wants acceleration, it would appear desirable from his standpoint to make the request at the earliest possible occasion. It stands to reason that he would be well advised to set forth in ample detail the basis for his request. Since the discretion of the Commission is absolute in this area, there is no guide-post as to the thrust of such application nor as to how the Commission might decide the matter in any given case.

Taking into account, however, that the thirty-day waiting period affords the Commission the opportunity to institute proceedings to deny registration, circumstances should be shown tending to establish that there is no practical need for the opportunity afforded by the thirty-day waiting period. For example, two individuals owning the entire interest as general partners in a registered broker-dealer partnership may decide to split up, each to take half of the business. Neither of the individuals would qualify as a "successor" to the partnership which, as seen, would mean succession to substantially all of the assets, liabilities, and business of an existing registrant.[31] Yet, were it not for the split, each, as partner of a registrant, would be actively engaged in the securities business. Coupled with the circumstances that a hiatus in the continuity of doing business might be disastrous to the business of each of the former partners, such a state of facts would provide persuasive rea-

---

[29] For the discussion of the authority for and procedure with reference to deferments, postponements, and denials, see, *infra* Chapters 19 and 20. Applications for registration can be withdrawn under certain conditions, see *infra,* Sec. 20-5.

[30] Section 15(b)(1) of the Act.

[31] *Supra,* Sec. 3-7.

sons for acceleration. Similar considerations would be applicable, for example, if, through not being well advised, a fiduciary as encompassed by Rule 15b-5 is compelled to file a new application for registration because of failure to make timely filing of the successor statement prescribed by the Rule.[32]

Sec. 3-9. Scope of registration. Upon effectiveness, a registrant is authorized to engage in all activities which require registration. He may act as broker or dealer, and, within the limits of the anti-fraud provisions discussed below,[33] may engage in business as both a broker and dealer. Any other limitations as to the type of business a registrant will conduct would be self-imposed. Upon registration the registrant is, therefore, commonly referred to as a registered "broker-dealer."[34]

---

[32] See *supra,* Sec. 3-7, for a reference to Rule 15b-5 as regards such fiduciaries as an executor, administrator, guardian, conservator, assignee for the benefit of creditors, receivers, and other court officers duly appointed to continue the business of a registered broker-dealer.

[33] See *infra,* Chapters 10 to 18, inclusive.

[34] But see n. 10, *supra,* which mentions that a broker may possibly in the future have to set forth in his application on Form BD the major type of activity he proposes to engage in in the securities business.

PART II

GENERAL REGULATORY PRINCIPLES

CHAPTER 4

JURISDICTIONAL CONSIDERATIONS

Sec. 4-1. Federal regulations. Federal regulations as to the conduct of brokers and dealers are founded variously on: membership on a national securities exchange, or transaction of a business through the medium of a member of such exchange,[1] or the use of any facility of a national securities exchange, the use of the mails or of any means or instrumentality of interstate commerce,[2] or broker-dealer registration, or a combination of these.[3] Any of these jurisdictional supports is commonly referred to as "Jurisdictional Means," and this term will be employed in that sense throughout this book.

The regulations discussed below governing the conduct of brokers and dealers apply, with possible minor and unimportant exceptions, to all registered broker-dealers, members of national securities exchanges, and brokers and dealers who transact a business in securities through the medium of such a member. Although these jurisdictional supports are essential as a basis for federal jurisdiction, it would be an exceptional case which could not be reached by one or the other of the jurisdictional supports in the Congressional arsenal, since they are not central to the Congressional purpose of regulating the conduct of brokers and dealers. Their use, therefore, need be only incidental to a transaction for

---

[1] See e.g., Secs. 7(c), 8, 11(d), and 14(b) of the Act. See also *Kook* v. *Crang,* 182 F. Supp. 388, 390 (S.D.N.Y. 1960). And see *George H. Hildegrand,* SEC Securities Exchange Act Release No. 7039, March 21, 1963, p. 2. If transaction of a business in securities through the medium of a member of a national securities exchange is the claimed basis for jurisdiction, it is not essential for such jurisdiction that the broker-dealer in question handle business in securities listed on the exchange; the only requirement being that some part of the business in question is carried out by the member's acting on behalf of the broker-dealer in any securities transaction. See *Fed. Reserve Bull.,* Nov. 1938, p. 951. It does not matter, moreover, if such transaction is isolated or represents only a small part of the broker-dealer's business. All of his business becomes subjected to federal jurisdiction. *Ibid* and see *Fed. Reserve Bull.,* Nov. 1939, p. 961.

[2] See e.g. Section 12 of the Act.

[3] See e.g. Sections 9, 17(a) of the Act.

the regulation to become applicable to activity specified in the Act.[4]

By recent amendment to the Act, moreover, it is provided that, wherever in the Act, an act, practice, or course of business is prohibited if the mails or interstate instrumentalities be used, registered broker-dealers are, by the fact of registration, prohibited from engaging in any such act, practice, or course of business, irrespective of any use of the mails or interstate instrumentalities in connection therewith.[5]

A discussion of the subject of jurisdiction over brokers and dealers would not be complete without reference to Section 30(b) of the Act. In pertinent part, this provision exempts from the operation of the Act ". . . any person insofar as he transacts a business in securities without the jurisdiction of the United States. . . ."

In approaching a problem as to the applicability of Section 30(b) to a given situation, it may be assumed that the business under scrutiny was transacted by use of jurisdictional means. The manifest purpose of the Section is to deal with transactions which would otherwise come within the compass of the Act, and to exempt them from its scope because the basic Congressional concern is with domestic conditions.[6] Hence, Congress intended the Act not to apply to business transacted wholly outside of the territorial jurisdiction of the United States.[7]

Despite use of the mails and of interstate and foreign transportation by a customer of a broker-dealer between the United States and Toronto, Canada, where the broker-dealer had its main office with which the customer transacted the essential aspects of the business in question, it was held in one case on the basis of Section 30(b) that such business was not within the scope of the Act.[8]

---

[4] See e.g. *Carroll* v. *U. S.,* F.2d (9th Cir. Dec. 10, 1963); *U. S.* v. *Cashin,* 281 F.2d 669 (2d Cir. 1960); *Matheson* v. *Armbrust,* 284 F.2d 670 (9th Cir. 1960); *Errion* v. *Connell,* 236 F.2d 447, 455 (9th Cir. 1960).

[5] Section 15(b)(4) of the Act. And see rule ô-8.

[6] *Kook* v. *Crang,* 182 F. Supp. 388 (S.D.N.Y. 1960).

[7] *Kook* v. *Crang, supra,* n. 6.

[8] *Kook* v. *Crang, supra,* n. 6.

CHAPTER 5

BASIC RESPONSIBILITIES

Sec. 5-1. Knowledge of laws—nondelegation of responsibility.
A broker-dealer is charged with the responsibility of acquainting himself with the requirements of the federal securities laws governing the conduct of his business. A plea of ignorance by a broker-dealer of the ground rules of his calling will not suffice to ward off appropriate sanctions.[1]

Furthermore, a broker-dealer cannot hide his failings behind alleged personal difficulties,[2] such as, for example, that he has domestic involvements, or that he is engaged only part-time as a broker-dealer and the demands of his other work interfere with performance of certain of his broker-dealer responsibilities, or that expanding facilities and inexperienced personnel account for his failure to follow the rules.[3] No excuse will be taken that another person, instructed or relied upon to carry out the broker-dealer's obligations, failed to follow through. The responsibilities of a broker-dealer cannot be delegated to another.[4]

Sec. 5-2. Accountability for acts of employees—direction and supervision. An individual using jurisdictional means who engages on behalf of a registered broker-dealer in effecting transactions in or inducing the purchase or sale of a non-exempted secu-

---

[1] See *Carter Harrison Corbrey*, 29 SEC 283, 288 (1949); and *Investment Registry of America, Inc.*, 21 SEC 745, 760 (1946), and cf. *Bollt and Shapiro*, 38 SEC 815, 821 (1959); *Aldrich, Scott & Co. Inc.*, 40 SEC 775, 778-9 (1961).

[2] See *John B. Sullivan*, 38 SEC 643, 644 (1958) (domestic difficulties); *Richard A. Sebastian*, 38 SEC 865, 869 (1958) (illness of accountant); *Herbert Perry & Co., Inc.*, SEC Securities Exchange Act Release No. 6896, September 13, 1962 (ill health).

[3] *Ibid;* and see *Reynolds & Co.*, 39 SEC 902, 916-18 (1960).

[4] See *Kelly Rubenstein*, 38 SEC 582 (1958); *John Munroe*, 39 SEC 308, 311 (1959); *John T. Pollard & Co., Inc.*, 38 SEC 594, 597-8 (1958); cf. *Bollt & Shapiro*, 38 SEC 815, 821 (1959). And see *Empire Securities Corp.*, SEC Securities Exchange Act Release No. 6791, April 27, 1962, pp. 2-3; *Aldrich, Scott & Co., Inc.*, 40 SEC 775, 778-9 (1961); *Lucyle Hollander Feigin*, SEC Securities Excahnge Act Release No. 6505, March 21, 1961, p. 3; *Thompson & Sloan, Inc.*, SEC Securities Exchange Act Release No. 6443, Jan. 3, 1961, pp. 6-7; cf. *F. R. Gentry & Co., Inc.*, SEC Securities Exchange Act Release No. 6986, January 2, 1963, pp. 3-4. *Associated Underwriters Inc.*, SEC Securities Exchange Act Release No. 7075, May 10, 1963, p. 2; *Advanced Research Associates Inc.*, SEC Securities Exchange Act Release No. 7117, Aug. 16, 1963, p. 33; *Valley Forge Securities Company, Inc.*, SEC Securities Exchange Act Release No. 7055, April 12, 1963, p. 3.

rity in the over-the-counter market would be regarded as engaged in business as a broker or dealer and would be required to register, unless he functions under the control, direction, and supervision of the registered broker-dealer. Stated otherwise, unless such an individual is under the "control" of the registrant, the registrant would be a participant in the violation by that individual of the broker-dealer registration requirements of the Act.

It is a basic design of broker-dealer registration requirements that a registrant be accountable for all violations of the federal securities laws committed by any person employed by him in any capacity;[5] or by any other individual who effects or induces transactions in securities for the registrant,[6] irrespective of whether the relationship be characterized as that of "independent contractor" or otherwise as between the parties.[7] It is accordingly incumbent upon the registrant to have such direction and supervision over individuals engaged in such activities as would enable the registrant to avoid any such violations. This principle, which has been the subject of Commission pronouncements in its opinions and otherwise, has now been codified in the Act through provisions calling for appropriate administrative sanctions against a person's failure to supervise another person subject to this supervision.[8] It follows that it is a concomitant obligation of the registrant to devise a system of internal controls adequate and effective for the avoidance of violations of the federal securities laws by controlled persons;[9] and it also follows that the registrant and its supervisory

---

[5] See *National Association of Securities Dealers, Inc.*, 20 SEC 508, 516 (1945); and see SEC Securities Exchange Act Release No. 3674, April 9, 1945, pp. 1-2.

[6] *Ibid.* And see *SEC* v. *Rapp* 304 F.2d 786 (2nd Cir. 1962).

[7] *Ibid.* And see *Fred L. Carvalho*, SEC Securities Exchange Act Release No. 7129, Aug. 29, 1963, p. 3. The broker-dealer registrant should reflect in its Form BD application that, however the parties may view their relationship for other purposes, the persons acting on behalf of the broker-dealer are employees for the purposes of the Securities Exchange Act of 1934.

[8] See Section 15(b)(5)(E) of the Act. Securities Acts Amendments of 1964, Sec. 6(b). These provisions will be mentioned again, *infra* at Sec. 19-9.

[9] *R. H. Rollins & Sons, Inc.*, 18 SEC 347, 390, 395 (1945); *Bond & Goodwin, Inc.*, 15 SEC 584, 599, 601 (1944); *Kidder Peabody & Co.*, 18 SEC 559 (1945); *R. H. Johnson & Company* v. *SEC*, 198 F.2d 690, 696-7 (2d Cir. 1952); *Alan Russel Securities, Inc.*, 38 SEC 599 (1958); see also particularly as to branch offices of large broker-dealer firms; *Address by SEC Commissioner Manuel F. Cohen, Presented At The Seminar On The Management Function In The Investment Banking Industry Sponsored By Education Committee, New York Group, Investment Bankers Association of America*, October 25, 1962, pp. 6-8 on file at SEC, Washington D. C. and New York, N. Y. The necessity for establishing procedures and a system for applying such procedures as would be reasonably expected to prevent and detect as far as practicable the violations by a supervised person is a requirement now specifically adverted to

personnel must look into all matters reaching their attention even remotely indicating irregularity; and failure to do so places the responsibility on supervisory personnel for violations of the federal securities laws committed by employees.[10] The supervision must be thorough and complete.[11]

It follows that a broker-dealer has a very high obligation to exercise more than ordinary care in hiring employees.[12] Indeed, a specific rule requires a broker-dealer to have a detailed questionnaire filled out by salesmen, other specified types of employees, and others associated with the broker-dealer, containing background information such as previous business connections, criminal or other record, and the like.[13]

Sec. 5-3. Amendment of application by registered broker-dealer. One of the basic obligations of a registered broker-dealer is "promptly" to amend his application whenever the information in it becomes inaccurate or incomplete.[14] This is done on Form

---

in the Act itself. Section 15(b)(5)(F) of the Act. Securities Act Amendments of 1964 Sec. 6(b). Further reference to this subject will be made *infra*, at Sec. 19-10.

[10] *Ibid.* And see *Reynolds & Co.*, 39 SEC 902, 916-19 (1960); *SEC* v. *Rapp* 304 F.2d 786 (2d Cir. 1962); *Luther L. Bost*, SEC Securities Exchange Act Release No. 6703, January 8, 1962, p. 4, n. 8; *Reilly Hoffman & Co., Inc.*, SEC Securities Exchange Act Release No. 6924, October 9, 1962, p. 2; *Borent & Co.*, SEC Securities Exchange Act Release No. 6367, September 19, 1960, pp. 9-10; *Alexander Reid & Co. Inc.*, SEC Securities Exchange Act Release No. 7016, Feb 7, 1963, p. 5.

[11] Permitting an employee to open fictitious accounts under assumed names is not permissible because it serves to insulate activities from necessary supervision and impede detection of wrongdoing. See *Leonard H. Zigman*, SEC Securities Exchange Act Release No. 6701, January 5, 1962, p. 3; *National Association of Securities Dealers, Inc.*, SEC Securities Exchange Act Release No. 6817, June 8, 1962. So, too, permitting a practice of customers making checks to the order of salesmen or of accepting salesmen's checks in payment of customers' obligations, invites serious violations and constitutes inadequate supervision. Also, the practice of giving customers' confirmations and checks to salesmen for delivery to customers reflects grossly inadequate supervision. *Reynolds & Co.*, 39 SEC 902, 911, 917 (1960).

[12] *Midas Management Corp.*, SEC Securities Excange Act Release No. 6569, May 25, 1961, p. 3. And see *Vickers Christy & Co., Inc.*, SEC Securities Exchange Act Release No. 6872, August 8, 1962, pp. 4-6; *SEC* v. *Rapp,* 304 F.2d 786 (2d Cir. 1962).

[13] Rule 17a-3(a)(12).

[14] Rule 15b-2. See the appendix for Important Notice attached to the guide to broker dealer form BD, Sec. 25-7, *infra. Banner Securities, Inc.*, SEC Securities Exchange Act Release No. 6985, Dec. 28, 1962, p. 4; *S.A.E. Corporation*, SEC Securities Exchange Act Release No. 6956, Nov. 28, 1962, p. 2; *Edmund S. Reed,* SEC Securities Exchange Act Release No. 6877, Aug. 10, 1962; *Sol T. Pfeffer*, SEC Securities Exchange Act Release No. 6506, March 23, 1961, pp. 2-3; *Makris Investment Brokers*, SEC Securities Exchange Act Release No. 6509, p. 4; *Thompson & Sloan, Inc.*, SEC Securities Exchange Act Release No. 6443, January 3, 1961, p. 5, n. 13; *Invesco Inc.*, SEC Securities Exchange Act Release No. 6993, Jan. 21, 1963, p. 1. See also *Batten & Co., Inc.*, SEC Securities Exchange Act Release No. 6734, Feb. 14, 1962; *Lewis Wolf, Inc.*, SEC Securities Exchange Act Release No. 6949, Nov. 21, 1962, p. 1;

BD which is executed and filed in duplicate original. Only those items need be answered as may be necessary to provide correct information.[15] Every item of information in the application is deemed basic. Hence, laxity in this regard on the theory that the information is not material or that it is available elsewhere, or for any other reason, will not be tolerated.[16]

Investment Brokers of N.J. Inc., SEC Securities Exchange Act Release No. 7017, Feb. 7, 1963, p. 1; *Joe Bert Sissom,* SEC Securities Exchange Act Release No. 7021, Feb. 11, 1963, p. 2; *Associated Underwriters Inc.,* SEC Securities Exchange Act Release No. 7075, May 10, 1963, p. 2; *Market Securities Inc.,* SEC Securities Exchange Act Release No. 7107, Aug. 2, 1963, p. 1; *Mitchell & Company Inc.,* SEC Securities Exchange Act Release No. 7109, Aug. 2, 1963, p. 1; *State Securities Corporation,* SEC Securities Exchange Act Release No. 7120, Aug. 20, 1963, p. 1; *East Coast Investors Inc.,* SEC Securities Exchange Act Release No. 7122, Aug. 21, 1963, pp. 1-2; *Security Service Inc.,* SEC Securities Exchange Act Release No. 7127, Aug. 27, 1963, p. 2.

[15] Rule 15b-2. Form BD gives these instructions as to amendments: "If items 3(b) or 3(c) [calling for lists of directors, officers and controlling persons] are amended, they must be answered in full. With respect to any other items, furnish only the corrected information." Sec. 25-5, *infra.*

[16] *Louis B. Cherry,* SEC Securities Exchange Act Release No. 7234, Feb. 12, 1964, p. 2; *Albert Wasserman,* 38 SEC 579, 580-1 (1958); *Gregory & Co., Inc.,* 38 SEC 304, 306 (1958); *Sterling Securities Company,* 39 SEC 487, 495-6 (1959); *Morris J. Reiter,* SEC Securities Exchange Act Release No. 6849, July 13, 1962, p. 6; *Samuel Janov,* SEC Securities Exchange Act Release No. 7005, January 25, 1963, p. 1. And see *FCC* v. *WOKO, Inc.,* 329 U. S. 223 (1946).

BASIC RULES FOR REGULATION
OF BUSINESS

CHAPTER 6

BOOKKEEPING RULES—INSPECTION AND VISITATION

Sec. 6-1 Records to be maintained. The most fundamental regulation for enabling the commission to carry out its administrative and enforcement functions as regards broker-dealers is the body of provisions in Rules 17a-3 and 17a-4 under the Act concerned with the making, keeping, and preserving of specified books and records by a broker-dealer relating to the conduct of his business.[1] The companion power in the Commission of inspection and visitation as to such books and records[2] is a correspondingly key implement in its administration of the Act.

The reach of the bookkeeping maintenance rule, Rule 17a-3, goes far beyond the requirement for making and keeping the usual accounting books and records pertinent to the conduct of the business of broker-dealer, such as blotters, other journals, ledgers and certain types of ledger accounts specified in paragraphs (1), (2), (3), (4), and (5) of Rule 17a-3(a).[3] It encompasses copies of every confirmation of the purchase or sale of securities and of every notice of debits or credits for securities, cash, and other items, as well as memorandums of all brokerage orders whether or not executed, including every internal "instruction" with respect to such order, and, in addition, the appropriate designation for each order entered pursuant to the exercise of a discretionary power.[4] It em-

---

[1] These rules are based upon specific authority contained in Section 17(a) of the Act. See *Midas Management Corp.*, 40 SEC 707, 709 (1961), where the Commission said: ". . . As counsel for our Division of Trading and Exchanges pointed out, our bookkeeping rules go to the very heart of the enforcement of the provisions of the Act and our rules thereunder concerning the conduct of securities brokers and dealers. . . ." See also *SEC v. Mainland Securities Corp.*, 192 F. Supp. 862 (S.D.N.Y. 1961).

[2] This authority is also found in Section 17(a) of the Act.

[3] In addition to the specifications in Rule 17a-3 there are requirements set forth in Regulation T in respect of certain types of customers' ledger accounts which must or may be maintained by broker-dealers. See *infra*, Chapter 9, in connection with the discussion of Regulation T. 12 CFR 220. 1-220.8. Other records are specified in Rule 15c1-7 to be made relative to the operation of discretionary accounts. These will be discussed, *infra* at Sec. 12-4.

[4] Paragraphs (6) and (8) of Rule 17a-5(a).

braces the requirement to make a separate memorandum as to each purchase or sale for the broker-dealer's own account, showing the price and where feasible the time of execution, irrespective of the fact that the daily blotter contains some of that information.[5]

Special records must also be maintained to give effect to the necessity for keeping close surveillance as to the location and flow of securities. Thus "blotters" (daily journals) must reflect accurate identification of securities by designation and quantity as well as accurate descriptions of securities transactions. Details must be recorded, for example, of trade dates and clearance dates of transactions, the number and identity of securities delivered and received, and the cost and price involved in each transaction. Ledger accounts must include, for example, the securities record ("stock record") which is a complete record of obligations with respect to securities as well as a statement of securities positions and of identifications of their locations.[6]

Broker-dealers must additionally make and prepare at least once a month trial balances reflecting the money balances of all ledger accounts.[7] Moreover, a detailed questionnaire, approved by an authorized representative of the broker-dealer, must be procured from and executed by each partner, officer, director, salesman, trader, manager, or any employee handling funds or securities or soliciting transactions or accounts for the broker-dealer, such questionnaire containing information relating to the background of the individual concerned in such detail as is called for by the nine separate items of Rule 17a-3(a) (12).[8]

---

[5] Paragraphs (7) of Rule 17a-3(a). *Joseph Blumenthal,* SEC Securities Exchange Act Release No. 6847, July 12, 1962, p. 2.

[6] See e.g., *Babson, Kaye & Robb Co.,* SEC Securities Exchange Act Release No. 7142, Sept. 13, 1963, p. 3.

[7] Rule 17a-3(a)(11). See *John M. A. Lecluse,* SEC Securities Exchange Act Release No. 6907, October 4, 1962.

[8] These include data such as date of birth, name, address, social security number, and date of commencement of association with the broker-dealer, a complete history of the individual's education, employment, disciplinary experience with any federal or state agency or national securities association or exchange, the record of all injunctions against the individual and against any of his former employers or other broker-dealers with whom he was once associated if the injunction was handed down while he was so employed or associated, the record of any denial, suspension, expulsion or revocation of membership of such individual or such former employer or associate, the record of any arrests, indictments or convictions, and the record of any other names which he has used or by which he is known.

An exemption from the requirements of filing this questionnaire is afforded by the rule if the broker-dealer maintains copies of similar questionnaires required by registered securities associations or exchanges specified in the rule. See subparagraph

Other specialized types of information which may be required to be included in a broker-dealer's records as a result of the Special Study Report are set forth in the margin.[9]

Broker-dealers may not determine for themselves which of the required records they will maintain. Deviations from the requirements of the rule are not permitted either upon the claim that the records are not needed in the given situation,[10] or that the broker-dealer engages in only certain aspects of the securities business on a part-time basis,[11] or that the information is otherwise available.[12]

However, the rule does provide that a member of a national securities exchange whose transactions are cleared through another member need not make or keep a record of the transactions so cleared where the clearing member makes and keeps the required records as to such transactions.[13] On the other hand, there is no such exemption available to a broker-dealer who is not a member of such an exchange or who attempts to clear his transactions through a non-member.

If a broker-dealer sells mutual fund shares or sells plans for the accumulation of mutual fund shares in circumstances under

(9) of Rule 17a-3(a) (12) A. Note that paragraph B of Rule 17a-3(a) (12) applies to, among others, all persons who handle securities or funds. These would normally include cashiers, bookkeepers, and others in the "back office" or "cashier's cage," but do not normally include messengers and runners.

[9] Item No. 3 of Chapter III-B of the report, Pt. 1, p. 329, recommends that rules be adopted to require "that every retail transaction be designated 'solicited' or 'unsolicited' in the permanent records of a broker-dealer; that all customer complaints be kept in a single file and available for inspection and examination by the Commission, the NASD, and the exchanges; and that customer account cards or similar records include such information as investment goals, occupation, and type of service desired. See in this connection Special Market Study Release No. 25, April 30, 1963, pp. 4-5. See, *infra*, Chapter 24, for references to NASD.

[10] *Wanda O. Olds*, 37 SEC 23, 26 (1956); See *Bradford* v. *SEC*, 278 F.2d 566, 567 (9th Cir. 1960); And see *Midland Securities, Inc.*, SEC Securities Exchange Act Release No 6413, Nov. 16, 1960, pp. 6-7; *Boren & Co.*, 40 SEC 217, 225-6 (1960); *Associated Securities Corp.*, 40 SEC 10, 18 (1960).

By the use of electronic data-processing machines, a broker-dealer may identify the customer on the purchases and sales blotters by identifying number, if the customer's name can be ascertained readily from other records. Paragraph (1) of Rule 17a-3(a) permits the identification on the blotter by customer's name or "other designation."

[11] *Boruski* v. *SEC*, 289 F.2d 738 (2d Cir. 1961); And see *Joseph Blumenthal*, SEC Securities Exchange Act Release No. 6847, July 12, 1962, p. 2.

[12] *Babson, Kaye & Rabb Co.*, SEC Securities Exchange Act Release No. 7142, Sept. 13, 1963, p. 3.

[13] Paragraph (b) of Rule 17a-3. Such transactions are said to be on a "disclosed" basis in circumstances under which, in net effect, the customer is the customer of the clearing member as well as of the forwarding broker, the clearing member carrying on its books such accounts in the name of the customer as are appropriate to the transactions engaged in.

which the check for the payment of the shares or the initial payment under the plan is made payable to a custodian bank for the fund, and the broker-dealer does not handle any money or securities for customers and receives a monthly statement from the custodian bank advising him of all payments made and the amount of commission due him, he will be in compliance with the books and records maintenance requirements if the broker-dealer maintains a card for each customer on which he briefly records the details of the initial transaction and all subsequent payments and dividends, and if he maintains copies of the orders or subscription blanks signed by the customers, and makes blotter entries necessary to reflect his receipt of commissions and cash disbursements. In these cases, however, the confirmation sent to the customer by the issuer, underwriter, or custodian must have all information required for a customer's ledger account, and the broker-dealer must keep copies of all confirmations pertaining to a particular customer together and arrange them chronologically.[14] An underwriter of mutual funds, irrespective of whether it acts as broker or dealer, must maintain ledger accounts or comparable records for the individual retail brokers and dealers, reflecting amounts receivable from the sale of mutual fund shares, and amounts payable for any redemptions by it of mutual fund shares. Such an underwriter cannot, under claim of acting merely as agent for the fund, limit its records to receipt of commissions, but must include such receivables and payables[15] on its books and records.

Indeed each transaction of a broker or dealer engaged in as

---

[14] Subdivision (a)(1) of Rule 17a-3, prescribing the use of "blotters," permits alternatively the use of "other records of original entry." Similarly, subdivisions (a)(2), (a)(3), and (a)(4) of the rule specifying the use of certain ledgers allow the use of "other records" in their stead. Obviously the "other records" must contain the same information as would be found in the prescribed ledgers. Therefore, the mutual fund broker-dealer who maintains the records outlined in the text may do so properly because of the "other records" provisions of the rule.

[15] The retail broker or dealer is a "customer" for which subdivision (3) of Rule 17a-3(a) requires the underwriter to maintain separate ledger accounts in the name of each. These mutual fund transactions are quite different from other trading transactions between broker-dealers as principals, which, upon failure of settlement on the clearance date are recorded in the "securities failed to receive and failed to deliver" ledgers envisioned by subdivision 4(E) of Rule 17a-3(a). SEC Securities Exchange Act Release No. 7169, Nov. 13, 1963. The "Securities failed to deliver" account shows amounts receivable from sales to other broker-dealers for which the broker-dealer in question is unable to deliver the securities sold at the specified clearance date. "Securities failed to receive" is the ledger account showing amounts payable to other broker-dealers for purchases as to which the other broker-dealers failed to make delivery on the clearance date. *Audits of Brokers or Dealers in Securities*, American Institute of Accountants (1956), pp. 10, 14, 27-28.

agent for any other broker must be reflected in an account carried by such agent in the name of such other broker-dealer. However, transactions between two broker-dealers acting as principals with respect to each other are initially recorded as blotter items only. If the transaction is settled on the contract clearance date by actual delivery and payment, it is not recorded in a ledger account. On the other hand, if there be failure of settlement by the clearance date, the transaction is recorded in the "Securities failed to receive" or "Securities failed to deliver" ledger[16] as may be appropriate to the case.

Books and records required to be maintained by a broker-dealer may be prepared and maintained by another person on behalf of the broker-dealer, so long as such other person furnishes an agreement in writing to the effect that such records are the property of the broker-dealer and will be surrendered to him promptly upon his request and be made available at all times for inspection by the Commission.[17]

Sec. 6-2. Records must be current and accurate. By the specific terms of the rule, the books and records must be kept current.[18] And the requirement that records be made and kept

---

[16] See SEC Securities Exchange Act Release No. 7169, Nov. 13, 1963. These ledger accounts have been explained in the preceding footnote. For reference to and recognition of the practice of recording unsettled principal transactions as between broker-dealers in the "fail" accounts, see items "(E)" of paragraph (4) of Rule 17a-3(a), and paragraph (c)(1) as well as subdivision "(D)" of that paragraph of Rule 15C3-1. The terms "fail to deliver" and "fail to receive" are also defined and discussed in the Special Study Report, Chapter III, part E, pp. 416-428. That report notes the impact on net capital computations of both of those ledger account items, and emphasizes that the "fail to deliver" is an asset account which can be swollen to the point of jeopardizing a broker-dealer's financial position. *Idem.* at p. 427. Accordingly, the report makes certain recommendations for the reduction of these accounts by suggested rules of registered securities associations. *Idem.* at p. 428.

[17] See by way of analogy Rule 31a-3 under the Investment Company Act of 1940, 15 U.S.C. 80a-1 to 80a-49 (1958) [hereinafter called the Investment Company Act]. The Rules under the Investment Company Act are published in the Code of Federal Regulations as Title 17, Part 270. Rule 31a-3 under the Investment Company Act was announced as adopted in SEC Investment Company Act Release No. 3578, November 28, 1962.

[18] Paragraph (a) of Rule 17a-3. See *Carl J. Bliedung*, 38 SEC 518, 519 (1958); *Alexander Dvoretsky*, 39 SEC 611, 612 (1959); *John M. A. Lecluse*, SEC Securities Exchange Act Release No. 6907, Oct. 4, 1962; *Whitney & Company, Inc.*, SEC Securities Exchange Act Release No. 6787, April 24, 1962, p. 2; *Florida Underwriting And Securities Services Corp.*, SEC Securities Exchange Act Release No. 6789, April 24, 1962, p. 2; *Vincent Associates Ltd.*, SEC Securities Exchange Act Release No. 6806, May 16, 1962; *Sherwood and Co.*, SEC Securities Exchange Act Release No. 6876, Aug. 10, 1962; *Robert H. Davis*, SEC Securities Exchange Act Release No. 6730, February 12, 1962; *Fidelity Securities Corporation*, SEC Securities Exchange Act

embodies the requirement that they be true and correct.[19] The range of possibilities as to the falsification of books and records is infinite. However, one practice merits mention in the margin.[20]

Sec. 6-3. Records—miscellaneous considerations. The book-keeping rules were adopted in 1939 and have since remained in effect with only slight modifications. By this time, there are but a few open questions as to their application and meaning. The Commission has invited the attention of brokers and dealers to the publication, "Audits of Brokers or Dealers In Securities" (1956), published by the American Institute of Accountants.[22] This should be of assistance to persons who desire to keep and maintain the books and records required by Rule 17a-3. Also, the National Association of Securities Dealers, Inc., recommends a suggested set of bookkeeping forms for use by small securities firms.

Records of a broker-dealer partnership or other unincorporated association are those of the business entity and not of the constituent individuals. Records of sole proprietorships should, in

Release No. 6987, January 4, 1963, p. 1; *Aircraft Dynamics International Corp.*, SEC Securities Exchange Act Release No. 7113, Aug. 8, 1963, p. 7.

A broker-dealer using an outside data-processing service may not be in a position to comply with the requirements for keeping his books and records current if the data cards are not delivered to the service on a daily basis and if such data cards can not be run off on to permanent records on a daily basis.

[19] *Lowell Niehbur & Co., Inc.*, 18 SEC 471, 475 (1945); *Southeastern Securities Corp.*, 29 SEC 609 (1949); *R. L. Emacio Co., Inc.*, 35 SEC 191, 202 (1953); *C. Herbert Onderdonk*, 37 SEC 846 (1957); *P. J. Gruber & Co., Inc.*, 38 SEC 223, 225 (1958); *Gill-Harkness & Co.*, 38 SEC 646, 652-3 (1958); *Southern States Securities* 39 SEC 728, 732 (1960); *Reilly Hoffman & Co., Inc.*, SEC Securities Exchange Act Release No. 6924, Oct. 29, 1961; *Thomas Bennett Allen*, SEC Securities Exchange Act Release No. 6881, August 10, 1962; *Thompson & Sloan, Inc.*, SEC Securities Exchange Act Release No. 6443, January 3, 1961, p. 5; *First Securities Company*, SEC Securities Exchange Act Release No. 6446, January 9, 1961, p. 4; *George H. Hildebrand*, SEC Securities Exchange Act Release No. 7039, March 21, 1963, p. 3; *P. De Rensis & Co.*, SEC Securities Exchange Act Release No. 7114, Aug. 9, 1963, p. 2; *Continental Bond & Share Corporation*, SEC Securities Exchange Act Release No. 7135, Sept. 9, 1963, pp. 1-2.

[20] This relates to the practice of some of the less reputable broker-dealers of confirming sales of securities to customers who did not order them. The copies of the confirmations and the entry of the purported sales on the books and records and their subsequent cancellation on the records constitute false records. See e.g., *Shelley Roberts & Co. of California*, 39 SEC 744, 751 (1958); *Alfred D. Laurence & Co.*, 38 SEC 220, 225 (1958); *Midland Securities, Inc.*, SEC Securities Exchange Act Release No. 6413, Nov. 16, 1960, pp. 6-7. This practice is also a violation of the anti-fraud provisions of the federal securities laws. See *infra*, Sec. 17-4.

[21] SEC Securities Exchange Act Release No. 2304, Nov 13, 1939.

[22] SEC Securities Exchange Act Release No. 5560, Aug. 8, 1957, p. 2. See also, National Association of Securities Dealers, Inc. *Memorandum Re: Rule 17a-3*, NASD Manual, pp. 1-15 to 1-23 (NASD 4-1-59).

the main, include all assets devoted to the securities business as well as liabilities arising out of the business, and should present all information relative to the securities business. For certain purposes, such as the question of compliance with the "net capital rule"[23] or of the financial reporting requirements,[24] it may be pertinent to inquire into the other assets, liabilities, and business, if any, of the sole proprietor.[25]

We have seen that no securities transaction by a broker-dealer will be viewed as "personal" as distinguished from "business" transactions.[26] Hence every transaction in a security engaged in by a sole proprietor for any purpose whatever must be reflected on his books and records.[27]

Sec. 6-4. Preservation requirements. The rules of the Commission also encompass a program for the preservation of specified records for stated periods of time.[28] In the main, all records must be preserved in an easily accessible place for two years. Some must be preserved for six years (paragraphs (a) and (c) of Rule 17a-4), others for three years (paragraph (b) of Rule 17a-4). Fundamental documents, such as charters, by-laws, partnership articles, and the like, must be kept for the life of the enterprise.[29] With respect to the preservation requirements, one observation may warrant mention. This is that the preservation rule calls for the preservation of records which the maintenance rule does not require to be made. For example, subdivision (4) of paragraph (a) of Rule 17a-4 calls for the preservation for a prescribed period of time of "originals of all communications received and copies of all communications sent by such member, broker, or dealer (including interoffice memoranda and communications) relating to his business as such." Of course, the number, variety, and kinds of such communications and memoranda are not prescribed. But once any such written communications or memoranda are made or received, they must

---

[23] Rule 15c3-1. See *infra,* Sections 8-3 and 8-4.

[24] Rule 17a-5. See *infra,* Chapter 7.

[25] Broker-dealer partnerships, corporations or unincorporated associations which carry on other businesses must comply in all respects with the bookkeeping and records requirements, and must reflect in the books and records all matters pertaining to such other business.

[26] *Supra,* Sec. 2-2 n. 23.

[27] *F. R. Gentry & Co., Inc.,* SEC Securities Exchange Act Release No. 6986, January 2, 1963, p. 3; and see the other authorities cited at Sec. 2-2 n. 23, *supra.*

[28] Rule 17a-4.

[29] Paragraph (d) of Rule 17a-4.

be preserved. These include, for example, copies of all correspondence between salesmen and customers, and of form letters with a record of the names and addresses of the persons to whom sent.[30] And they include all written communications made between brokers and dealers relative to the insertion of quotations in the daily quotation sheets of the National Daily Quotation Service, Inc.

Sec. 6-5. Inspection provisions. Section 17(a) provides in part that the books and records of a broker-dealer ". . . shall be subject at any time or from time to time to such reasonable periodic, special, or other examinations by examiners or other representatives of the Commission as the Commission may deem necessary or appropriate in the public interest or for the protection of investors." This means simply that the books and records of a broker-dealer must be made available for Commission inspection without notice at any reasonable time.[31] Absent the inspection powers, much of the benefits of the bookkeeping requirements would be dissipated, since, as already noted, inspections are designed to ascertain from the books and records whether or not a broker-dealer is complying with the federal securities laws, including Commission regulations governing conduct of the business.[32]

---

[30] *Boren & Co.*, 40 SEC 217, 225 (1960); *Fred T. Garner,* 39 SEC 626, 628 (1960). See *Joseph Blumenthal,* SEC Securities Exchange Act Release No. 6847, July 12, 1962, p. 3.

[31] See *Whitney Phoenix Company, Inc.,* 39 SEC 245, 250 (1959); *Fred T. Garner,* 39 SEC 626, 628 (1960); SEC Litigation Release No. 1596, Feb. 23, 1960; SEC Securities Exchange Act Release No. 5963, May 14, 1959; *Albert Harris,* SEC Securities Exchange Act Release No. 7782, April 1, 1964, p. 2. The maintenance and production of records required by Section 17(a) and the corresponding rules cannot be used as a foundation for a plea of immunity from criminal prosecution. See *Shapiro* v. *U. S.,* 335 U. S. 1, 7-8, 8-19, 22-24 (1948); and *M. Marshall Landy* v. U. S. 283 F.2d 303 (5th Cir. 1960).

For application of the preservation requirements see *Sherwood and Co.,* SEC Securities Exchange Act Release No. 6876, Aug. 10, 1962.

[32] SEC News Digest, August 8, 1957, p. 3.

CHAPTER 7

ANNUAL REPORTS OF FINANCIAL CONDITION

Sec. 7-1. General requirements. Another key instrument available to the Commission to discharge its supervisory role is the financial reporting requirement applicable to brokers and dealers.[1]

With some minor exceptions, each broker, dealer, and member of a national securities exchange is required each year to file a report of his financial condition in the prescribed manner as called for by Rule 17a-5(a).[2]

The report must be filed as of a date within each calendar year and within 45 days after the date as of which it speaks.[3] It need not be filed on the anniversary of the previous filing; the requirement being merely that a report must be filed once each calendar year. However, reports for any two consecutive years may not be as of dates within four months of each other.[4]

The first report of a member or broker-dealer must be filed not less than one month nor more than five months after the date on which he becomes subject to the rule, which, in the case of a registered broker-dealer, is the date the registration becomes effective.[5] If, however, a member, broker, or dealer becomes

---

[1] See *W. E. Leonard & Company, Inc.,* 39 SEC 726, 727 (1960); *Seymour J. Schlesinger,* SEC Securities Exchange Act Release No. 6957, November 28, 1962, p. 2. "Reports are important not only to inform investors, but because they may open avenues of inquiry which may well lead to collateral information having a direct bearing upon the broker-dealer's compliance with other rules of the Commission." *Scientific Investors Corporation,* SEC Securities Exchange Act Release No. 7126, Aug. 27, 1963, p. 1.

[2] This rule is based on Section 17(a) of the Act requiring broker-dealers to make such reports as the Commission may by rule prescribe as necessary or appropriate in the public interest or for the protection of investors.

[3] Paragraph (a) of Rule 17a-5. Paragraph (d) of Rule 17a-5 provides for extensions of time to a specified date not more than 90 days after the date as of which the financial condition is reported. Requests for extension must be by written application stating reasons why the broker-dealer or member cannot file the report within the year as required without undue hardship. The application must specify a date before which the report will be filed and contain an agreement that it will be filed on or before that date.

[4] Paragraph (a) of Rule 17a-5.

[5] *Ibid.*

subject to the rule because of his succession to the business of another, the successor need not file a report within the calendar year during which the predecessor already filed a report. This proviso, it may be noted, applies only if the successor succeeds to substantially all of the assets and liabilities and continues the business of the predecessor. In brief, although there might be a change of entity, the financial position of the one would in effect have to be the same as that of the other.[6]

Sec. 7-2. Form of report—certification requirements. The report must be as prescribed by Form X-17A-5[7] which is to be used as a guide and not a medium for the filing of the report; the filing must be made in duplicate original with the Regional Office of the Commission for the region in which the member, broker, or dealer has his principal place of business.[8] Form X-17A-5 contains the instructions which must be followed, and, apart from the exemptions mentioned below, the report must be certified. The certifying accountant must be either a certified public accountant duly registered and in good standing under the laws of the place of his residence or principal office, or a public accountant entitled under the laws of the place of his residence or principal office to practice as such.[9] The technical requirements as to date and signature, the representations as to the scope of the audit and the form of certificate are matters also covered by the rule.[10]

---

[6] Cf. *F. W. Horne & Co., Inc.*, 38 SEC 104, 109 (1957). See also the discussion above on the subject of successor applications for registration, *supra*, Sec. 3-7. However, the successor to a registered broker-dealer would have to file the financial statement required by Rule 15b-8. See SEC Securities Exchange Act Release No. 5560, Aug. 8, 1957, p. 2.

[7] SEC Form X-17A-5 [hereinafter called Form X-17A-5]. Paragraph (c)(1) of Rule 17a-5 permits an alternative to a member broker or dealer required to file a financial statement with a national securities exchange, or with an agency of a State as a condition of doing business in securities in that State. A copy of such a statement may be filed in lieu of a Form X-17A-5 report, if the copy reflects the financial condition as of a date not more than 45 days prior to the filing with the Commission and if the report meets the requirements of Rule 17a-5 and Form X-17A-5, including certification and contains the information called for by that form.

[8] An exception to this provision is found in Paragraph (c)(2) of Rule 17a-5 relative to a member, broker, or dealer which is registered as an investment company under the Investment Company Act of 1940, or is a sponsor or depositor of such registered investment company, effecting transactions in securities only with or on behalf of the investment company, if such member, broker, or dealer has filed in the calendar year a statement of financial condition under Section 30 of the Investment Company Act of 1940 or under Section 13 or 15(d) of the Securities Exchange Act of 1934. If such a filing meets the requirements of other rules governing it as to time of filing and content, it will be deemed to satisfy Rule 17a-5.

[9] Rule 17a-5(f).

[10] Paragraphs (g)(1)(2) and (3) and (h) and (i) of Rule 17a-5. These provide that the accountant's certificate be dated, signed manually, and that it identify with-

Form X-17A-5, sets forth, in addition, the "Minimum Audit Requirements" to be followed.[11] It is clear from the rule that the certifying accountant must be independent.[12] Irrespective of the need for, or exemption from, certification, the sole proprietor, general partner of a partnership, or duly authorized corporate officer, as the case may be, of a broker-dealer or member must make an oath or affirmation, annexed to the report to the effect that the financial statement and supporting schedules are true and correct[13] and that the member broker or dealer or any partner,

---

out detailed enumeration the items covered by the certificate. It must also contain reasonably comprehensive statement as to the scope of the audit made, including whether there was a review of procedures for safe-guarding securities of customers, whether any auditing procedures generally recognized as normal have been omitted with respect to significant items of the report covered by the certificate, and, if so, a designation of such procedures and a statement as to the reasons for their omission. The certificate must also state whether the audit was made in accordance with generally accepted auditing procedures applicable in the circumstances and whether the audit omitted any procedure deemed necessary by the accountant in the circumstances of the particular case. Finally, the certificate must state clearly the opinion of the accountant with respect to the financial statement covered by the certificate and the accounting principles and practices reflected therein. Any exceptions in the certificate must be clearly stated and identified, and the effect thereof on the related item in the report should be given where feasible. Subdivision (3) of Rule 17a-5(g) provides that nothing in the rule should be construed as permitting the omission of any standard auditing procedure.

[11] In some instances these prescribed procedures go beyond what might otherwise be deemed generally accepted auditing standards. See e.g., the "Note to Item (5)" in the form currently in use at the time of this writing, respecting confirmation of accounts which requires the auditor to mail second requests for confirmation to those not replying to the first requests. This note also contains a special provision relaxing the confirmation requirements without sacrifice to public safety relative to confirmation of accounts in connection with periodic investment plans sponsored by specified types of member firms of a national securities exchange. SEC Securities Exchange Act Release No. 6102, Oct. 28, 1959 (same as SEC Accounting Series Release No. 83).

[12] Rule 17a-5(b)(1). A compilation of administrative rulings on the question of independence may be found in SEC Accounting Series Release No. 81, Dec. 11, 1958, and the bibliography found in the Appendix to that release. See also *Fred T. Garner*, 39 SEC 626, 628 (1960); *Harmon R. Stone*, SEC Accounting Series Release No. 97, May 21, 1963, pp. 4-5. Generally stated, an accountant is not independent if he or a member of his firm is a member of the management of the broker-dealer or an employee, close relative, or lawyer of a person in management of the broker-dealer, or if the accountant or a member of his firm has made entries in the broker-dealer's books, or if he has a pecuniary interest in the broker-dealer which is substantial either in terms of his own resources or the broker-dealer's capital. All questions concerning independence of accountants should be directed to the Chief Accountant of the Commission. See SEC *Statement of Organization, Conduct and Ethics and Information Practices*, 17 CFR 200-22 (1962).

[13] Paragraph (b)(2) of Rule 17a-5. Just as the requirement to make and keep current prescribed books and records embraces the obligation that they be true and correct, so the financial reporting obligation includes the imperative that the report be "true and correct." See *C. Herbert Onderdonk*, 37 SEC 847, 848-9 (1957); *Valley State Brokerage, Inc.*, 39 SEC 596, 598 (1959). The fact that the information is otherwise available to the Commission does not obviate the necessity for including it in the financial statement. *Wendell Maro Weston*, 30 SEC 296, 311-312 (1949). And,

officer, or director, as the case may be, has no proprietary interest in any account classified solely as that of a customer.[14] Certain schedules required by Form X-17A-5 will, if bound separately, not be available for public inspection except upon Commission authorization.[15]

Two areas governed by the rule and Form X-17A-5[16] are still somewhat unsettled. The first of these encompasses problems arising from the circumstance that a sole proprietor may be carrying on a business separate and apart from his securities business and the second arises from the broadening of the certification requirements by amendments to the rule adopted in 1957.[17] These will be discussed in turn.

Sec. 7-3. Form of report—"other" liabilities of sole proprietor.

It has already been seen that a broker-dealer registrant is accorded an entity resulting from the functional approach of the Act, as distinguished from concepts of entity prevailing in other fields of jurisprudence.[18] It may also be recalled that the books and records required to be made and kept current are those specified as relating to a broker-dealer's securities business.[19] The result is that none of the assets, liabilities, and transactions of any other separate enterprise of a sole proprietor are reflected in the books and records prescribed by rule.[20] However, since all gen-

---

if a material event occurs between the date as of which the report speaks and the date of filing relative to an item covered in the financial statement, the report must contain such change. *Idem.* at pp. 310-311.

[14] Paragraph (b)(2) of Rule 17a-5.

[15] Schedules called for by items (a), (b), and (c) of Part II of the form. See paragraph (b)(3) of Rule 17a-5. This part of the rule provides, however, that such schedules are available for official use by federal or state employees or officials, or those of a national securities exchange or association of which the member or broker-dealer is a member.

[16] Form X-17A-5 in force at this writing was adopted by the Commission upon the request of the industry for a form of a report likely to be adopted by other regulatory bodies such as state authorities, national securities exchanges, and national securities associations. The form as promulgated evolved from close cooperation between representatives of the Commission, on the one hand, and those of the industry on the other. See 9 SEC Ann. Rep. 21 (1943). The booklet *Audits of Brokers and Dealers in Securities* published by the American Institute of Accountants (1956) had additionally greatly contributed to clear understanding of the reporting requirements.

[17] See SEC Securities Exchange Act Release No. 5560, Aug. 8, 1957.

[18] *Supra,* Sec. 3-2.

[19] *Supra,* Sec. 6-1, see paragraph (a) of Rule 17a-3.

[20] Of course any transaction by a sole proprietor in securities is conclusively presumed to be part of his business as a broker-dealer, see *supra,* Sec. 2-2; they therefore must be reflected on the books and records of the broker-dealer entity. *F. R. Gentry & Co., Inc.,* SEC Securities Exchange Act Release No. 6986, January 2,

eral unsecured creditors of an individual have an equal claim on all of his assets, the liabilities of the individual arising from non-broker-dealer activity may affect his net worth as reflected in the financial statements of the broker-dealer business. Accordingly, note (e) of Part II of Form X-17A-5 requires from a sole proprietor the details of any liabilities not reflected in the Part I financial statement "if such liabilities would materially affect net worth as reported." The chief concern here is whether, apart from the securities business, the individual's other liabilities exceed his other assets. Information as to such other liabilities and assets must be obtained by the certifying accountant in the form of a written statement as to the "assets, liabilities and accountabilities, contingent or otherwise" not recorded on the broker-dealer books and records.[21] Of course, the auditor must make such investigations as to the contents of the written statement as may be necessary to enable him to certify as to the reliability of the statement in Item (e) of Part II to the effect that details of liabilities have been given to the extent that such liabilities would affect net worth as reported in the financial statement in Part I.[22]

Sec. 7-4. Exemptions from certification requirements—general discussion. Fully paid customers' securities placed in the custody of broker-dealers for safekeeping are not reflected in the books of account. Apart from Commission inspection powers, the technique for safeguarding the public in this area is the requirement that, with minor exceptions, the Rule 17a-5 report of a member broker or dealer must be certified by an independent public accountant.[23] The certification requirement is accordingly

1963, p. 3; *Chester Richard Koza,* 39 SEC 950, (1960); *Lawrence R. Leeby,* 32 SEC 307, 312-313 (1951); *R. D. French & Co.,* 36 SEC 603, 606-7 (1955). If the registrant is a corporation or partnership which is engaged in a business other than the securities business, it must nevertheless reflect all of its business transactions, including those not relating to securities, on its books and records, and its reports must include all of the assets and liabilities arising out of such other business.

21 Item "(6)" of Minimum Audit Requirements, Form X-17A-5.

22 For similar reasons, a similar approach is taken as regards separate partnerships operating separately a securities and other business composed of the same partners having the same respective interests. Cf. *Burley & Co.,* 28 SEC 126, 128 (1948).

23 "Such inspections are not a substitute for an audit by an independent accountant, but are primarily designed to make certain that the broker-dealer is complying with the Federal Securities laws and regulations of the Commission. . . ." *SEC News Digest,* August 8, 1957, p. 3. See also *National Association of Securities Dealers, Inc.,* 12 SEC 322 (1942), p. 329, n. 9. And see SEC Securities Exchange Act Release No. 5264, Dec. 12, 1955, in which the Commission announced proposed amendments to Rule 17a-5 which would have required all reports under that rule

central to the protection to be afforded the public by the financial reporting rule.[24]   The certification requirement is therefore absolute except for ". . . three very limited exemptions . . ."[25]

Sec. 7-5. Exemptions from certification requirements—specialists and floor traders. The first of these exemptions[26] applies to a member of a national securities exchange[27] who, from the date of the previous report, did not transact a business in securities directly with or for other than exchange members, did not carry any margin account, credit balance, or security for any person other than a general partner, and has not been required to file a certified financial statement with any exchange. This exception, hedged about with definite restrictions, applies in fact only to, and was intended to apply only to, floor traders and specialists of an exchange whose transactions take place on the floor only with members, and whose activities do not require them to file certified reports with the exchange.

Sec. 7-6. Exemptions from certification requirements—limited real estate mortgage transactions. Another exemption is the one available to a broker or dealer who, from the date of his last report, limited his securities business to buying and selling evidences of indebtedness secured by liens on real estate and did not carry any margin accounts, credit balances, or securities for securities customers.[28] Couched in very narrow terms, this exemption is designed to reach only a small number of registered broker-dealers whose business is primarily real estate but whose dealings in securities are confined to a form of split mortgages.[29]

---

to be certified, because the then existing exemptions from certification, which were broader than now, did not afford adequate investor protection. The Commission said: "It has been suggested that brokers and dealers now exempt from the certification requirements may owe money or securities to customers in substantial amounts in connection with their transactions and that such customers should have the protection afforded through examination of the books and records and the certification of the financial statements . . . by independent accountants."

[24] *Ibid.*

[25] *SEC News Digest,* August 8, 1957, p. 3. The burden of proving an exemption is on the one who claims it. See *SEC* v. *Ralston Purina Co.,* 346 U. S. 119, 126 (1953).

[26] Subdivision A of paragraph (b)(1) of Rule 17a-5.

[27] By its terms, this exemption applies only to a "member" of a national securities exchange.

[28] Subdivision C of paragraph (b)(1) of Rule 17a-5.

[29] We have seen, *supra,* Sec. 2-5, that real estate brokers duly licensed by state law who deal in whole mortgages transferred with the entire indebtednesses to which they relate are not required to register as broker-dealers so long as they do not perform services or engage in activities which may be deemed to constitute investment contracts.

Sec. 7-7. Exemptions from certification requirements—agent of issuer in soliciting subscriptions—conditions and limitations. Finally, there is an exemption available to a person whose securities business from the date of his previous report was limited to that of a "broker" engaged only as "agent" for an issuer in soliciting subscriptions for securities of the issuer and who has promptly transmitted to such issuer all funds and promptly delivered to the subscriber all securities in connection therewith, and who has not otherwise held funds or securities for or owed money or securities to customers.[30] The scope of this exemption has frequently been misunderstood and it therefore merits some analysis.

In pondering the availability of the exemption, a threshold consideration might be whether or not the broker-dealer "held funds or securities for or owed money or securities to customers." Here, the question sometimes arises as to who is a customer. Since this exemption is designed to relieve from certification the report of a person exempt from the net capital requirements of Rule 15c3-1 by reason of paragraph (b)(1) of that rule,[31] the definition of "customer" in Rule 15c3-1 would apply. Under that rule, except for a partner who has agreed to contribute to the partnership capital the equity in his account, the term customer means "every person except the broker or dealer."[32] This definition would nevertheless not encompass a person if the obligation to him is not connected directly with the carrying on of a business in securities. Otherwise, as a practical matter, the exemption would never be available, since in the ordinary course of business the broker would be apt to owe money for rent, supplies, and the like. However that may be, obligations of a broker-dealer to sales representatives engaged in selling securities for the broker-dealer, or the obligations of a principal underwriter of securities of an open end investment company ("mutual fund") to selling dealers, would constitute money owed to customers. And a principal underwriter for the stock of a mutual fund which keeps in its own name whole or fractional shares belonging to investors is holding securities for and owing securities to customers.

To qualify for this exemption from certification, moreover,

---

[30] Subdivision B of paragraph (b)(1) of Rule 17a-5.
[31] SEC Securities Exchange Act Release No. 5560, August 8, 1957, p. 2.
[32] Paragraph (c)(8) of Rule 15c3-1.

all of the reporting person's activities must be as "broker" only, and in the capacity of "agent" for an issuer in soliciting subscriptions for the issuer's securities. It follows that one who is a dealer confirming sales to customers as a principal does not fall within the exemption. Additionally, it is essential for the claimant of the exemption to be in privity of contract with the "issuer" to sustain his claim that he is agent for the issuer.[33] Moreover, the claimant can engage in no other securities transactions, personal or otherwise,[34] than those involving his acting as agent for the issuer. This precludes, of course, his acting as agent for the customer.[35] Additionally, to gain the exemption, the claimant's activities as agent for the issuer must be limited to soliciting subscriptions for securities of the issuer.

Assuming that the transactions of a broker are "limited" to those specified in the rule, he does not obtain the exemption unless he "promptly" transmits to the issuer all funds and "promptly" delivers to the subscriber all securities received in connection therewith. Although the term "promptly" is not defined, it has a relationship to a basic obligation of a broker-dealer to transmit funds of customers for securities and deliver securities to customers promptly in accordance with trade custom.[36]

Before we leave the subject of exemptions from certification, it should be emphasized that the failure to transact any business or the transaction of a "limited business" in securities since the date of the previous report does not constitute a ground for an exemption. No credit is given to the argument of a registered broker-dealer that if an exemption applies to a person who engages

---

[33] Broker-dealers under contract with a principal underwriter to sell stock of open end investment companies as well as plans for the accumulation of such securities fail on two counts to come within the exemption. First, they are not agents for the issuer. Invariably as a matter of trade custom, moreover, the contracts provide that the broker-dealer is to buy and resell the securities as principal for his own account. It is doubtful whether a principal underwriter would qualify for the exemption, even if as a matter of fact it could establish that it acts as agent for the issuer. It is the rare case in which such an underwriter does not owe money to selling dealers or hold securities for customers.

[34] See *supra*, Sec. 2-2.

[35] See *Thomas Lee Jarvis*, 40 SEC 692, 693-4 (1961).

[36] This and other aspects of a broker-dealer's high standards of obligation owed to customers will be discussed below in connection with Rule 15c2-4 and with the "Shingle Theory." *Infra*, Sections 13-7, 13-8, and 16-9. When this exemption was originally adopted in connection with Rule 15c3-1, the Commission pointed out that "securities issued in these situations would usually be issued in the name of the purchaser or his nominee, not in the name of the broker." SEC Securities Exchange Act Release No. 5244, Oct. 25, 1955.

in specified activities it must necessarily apply to one who has engaged in no activities.[37] The possibility that a registered broker-dealer might transact no business as a broker-dealer is wholly outside the scope of the contemplation of the exemptive provisions of paragraph (b)(1) of Rule 17a-5 which relates to specified, even though limited, activities in securities. For one thing, the last sentence of Section 15(b)(6) of the Act provides for cancellation of the registration of a broker-dealer who has "ceased to do business as a broker or dealer . . ." Indeed, a person who does not intend to engage in business as a broker-dealer should not register.[38] Once registered, however, he brings into play the functions of the Commission for the surveillance of his activities. And the requirement that financial reports be filed on time and in proper form is a "keystone" of such surveillance functions.[39] Rule 17a-5 certification requirements apply to every registered broker and dealer with the exception of those specifically exempted. Certification is designed to provide some reasonable assurance of the accuracy of a report filed under Rule 17a-5.[40] By the fact of registration, a broker-dealer holds himself out as engaging in the securities business generally and without limit. A requirement of certification is a rational means for providing assurance of the truth of the claim that no business in securities has been engaged in, and it does not matter that other rational means might have been employed to ascertain this fact.

It may also be noted that no exemption or excuse from the certification requirements is obtained on the basis that the broker-dealer's records are in such a state that an accountant is unable to certify a report.[41]

Since each exemption relates to persons whose activities are "limited" to the transactions specified in the given exemption, a person who engages in a combination of such activities does not have any exemption.

---

[37] See *Thomas Lee Jarvis* 40 SEC 692, 694-5 (1961). It will be seen, moreover, *infra*, Sec. 7-9, that failure to do business in the reporting period prvides no exemption from filing a Rule 17a-5 report.

[38] *John J. Murphy*, 38 SEC 430 (1958). See also Sec. 20-6, *infra*, where the matter of cancellation is discussed.

[39] *W. E. Leonard & Company, Inc.*, 39 SEC 726, 727 (1960).

[40] *CF Bollt & Shapiro*, 38 SEC 815, 817 (1959); and see supra, n. 23.

[41] *Wakefield, Carder & Holt, Inc.*, 40 SEC 675, 678 (1961); *Ernest F. Boruski Jr.*, SEC Securities Exchange Act Release No. 7418, Sept. 11, 1964, pp. 4-5.

Sec. 7-8. Procedure for obtaining exemption. The remaining point for discussion as regards exemption from certification requirements is the form in which the claim must be made. The last sentence of paragraph (b)(1) of Rule 17A-5 provides that: "A member, broker or dealer who files a report which is not certified shall include in the oath or affirmation required by paragraph (b)(2) of this rule a statement of the facts and circumstances relied upon as a basis for the exemption from the certification requirements."[42] Such statement in the affidavit must, of course, be true.[43]

Sec. 7-9. Doing no business does not exempt from filing requirements. It should be noted that, whether or not there may be an exemption from the certification requirements, there is absolutely no exemption from filing the report. As is the case with the certification requirement discussed immediately above in the text, the fact that the member, broker, or dealer has transacted no business in securities from the date of the previous report affords no basis for failure to file the report.[44]

---

[42] This is a prerequisite for a consideration of the claim for such an exemption. See *Thomas Lee Jarvis,* 40 SEC 692, 693 (1961). Paragraph (b)(2) of Rule 17a-5 requires as an attachment to the report an oath or affirmation by the sole proprietor, partner, or corporate officer of the registrant, as the case may be, to the effect that the financial statement and supporting schedules are true and correct and that neither the broker-dealer nor any partner, officer, or director has any proprietary interest in an account classified solely as that of a customer.

[43] *Fidelity Securities Corporation,* SEC Securities Exchange Act Release No. 6987, January 4, 1963, p. 2.

[44] *John J. Murphy,* 38 SEC 430 (1958); *W. E. Leonard & Co., Inc.,* 39 SEC 726, 727 (1960); *Lewis A. Adams,* 35 SEC 311 (1953); *Harriet Blitz,* 40 SEC 375, 376 (1960). See also *Certified Planning Corp.,* SEC Securities Exchange Act Release No. 6910, Oct. 8, 1962; *John M. A. Lecluse,* SEC Securities Exchange Act Release No. 6907, Oct. 4, 1962; *Seymour J. Schlesinger,* SEC Securities Exchange Act Release No. 6908, Oct. 4, 1962; *Harry George Ames,* SEC Securities Exchange Act Release No. 7004, Jan. 24, 1963.

The only exception to the requirement of filing a report relates to a member of a national securities exchange who is not a registered broker-dealer who transacts a business exclusively with members of the exchange. Rule 17a-5(a).

CHAPTER 8

FINANCIAL RESPONSIBILITY REQUIREMENTS

A. *Net Capital Requirements*

Sec. 8-1. Background. Viewed in proper focus, the business of broker-dealers includes important banking activities. Brokers and dealers lend money to margin purchasers, retaining the purchased securities as collateral. They receive and retain cash or "free credit balances" in the accounts of customers, and they hold for safekeeping fully paid securities of customers as well as securities constituting excess collateral not needed to secure customers' margin accounts. The danger to the public investor from these broker-dealer functions is heightened whenever brokers also act as dealers who purchase and sell securities for their own account and engage in underwriting activities.

It was in recognition of the need to protect investors from the hazards to which they are exposed in dealing with broker-dealers having banking functions that Congress enacted Section 15(c)(3) of the Act, and that Rule 15c3-1, the "net capital" rule, was adopted by the Commission under authority of that section.[1] The rule has been characterized as "one of the most important weapons in the Commission's arsenal to protect investors."[2]

Sec. 8-2. Rule 15c 3-1—broad outlines. Definitions and exemptions apart, the rule is starkly simple. Its general, broad pro-

---

[1] Section 15(c)(3) was enacted in 1938 as part of the Maloney Act, Public No. 719, 75th Congress (approved June 25, 1938). It was based partly on conditions mentioned in SEC, *Report on the Feasibility and Advisability of the Complete Segregation of the Functions of Dealer and Broker* (1936), pp. 58, 68-69. Following enactment of the statute, the Commission's attention was directed to the necessity for adopting an appropriate rule. See SEC, *Report on Investigation of Richard Whitney* (1938), pp. 167-170, and the rule was adopted in 1942. *National Association of Securities Dealers, Inc.*, 12 SEC 322 (1942). The effective date of the rule, however, was held up until 1944 when the Commission adopted elaborate definitions of the terms, "net capital" and "aggregate indebtedness." SEC Securities Exchange Act Release No. 3602, Aug. 11, 1944, and SEC Securities Exchange Act Release No. 3617, Nov. 8, 1944. It has been amended only in minor particulars since then.

[2] *Blaise D'Antoni & Associates* v. *SEC*, 289 F.2d 276, 277 (5th Cir. 1961). See also *SEC* v. *Mainland Securities Corp.*, 192 F. Supp. 862 (S.D.N.Y., 1961). *SEC* v. *General Securities Co.*, 216 F. Supp. 350, 351 (S.D.N.Y., 1963).

vision is that: "No broker or dealer shall permit his aggregate indebtedness to all other persons to exceed 2000 per centum of his net capital."[3] The full impact of the rule is felt mainly from the definitions of the terms "aggregate indebtedness" and "net capital." It will be seen from these definitions that the primary objective of the rule is not mere solvency in a balance sheet or other conventional sense;[4] it is liquidity, and therefore only liquid assets are taken into account.

Customers' cash ("free credit") balances are payable, and fully paid customers' securities held by broker-dealers are deliverable, on demand. Public confidence in the securities markets[5] depends in no small measure on the ability of broker-dealers promptly to meet such demands. Additionally, as already seen, fully paid securities of customers held for safekeeping are not reflected in the books of account of a broker-dealer;[6] and in adopting the rule, the Commission had in mind that the non-liquid assets of the broker-dealer should provide a partial cushion for the non-recorded obligations.[7]

Sec. 8-3. Rule 15c 3-1—net capital. Paragraph (c)(2) of the rule provides that the term "net capital" shall be deemed to mean the net worth of a broker or dealer, that is, the excess of total assets over total liabilities adjusted by, among other things, the deduction of fixed assets and assets which cannot be readily converted into cash.[8] Thus, to start with, the rule calls for the deduc-

---

[3] Paragraph (a) of Rule 15c3-1. This basic requirement was foreshadowed by the ratio specified in Section 8(b) of the Act as applied to members of national securities exchanges and others.

[4] It has been held that, in adopting the rule, the Commission was not limited to dealing with the matter of broker-dealer financial responsibility from the standpoint merely of commonly understood accounting concepts. *SEC* v. *Graye*, 154 F. Supp. 544, 546-7 (S.D.N.Y., 1957). Nevertheless, accounting terms which are used in the rule are to be given their commonly accepted accounting meanings. *Cornelis DeVroedt*, 38 SEC 176, 180 (1958).

[5] This is one of the cardinal objectives of the Act, section 2 of the Act, Sen. Report No. 792, 73rd Congress, 2d Sess. (1934), p. 3.

[6] *Supra*, Sec. 7-4.

[7] *National Association of Securities Dealers, Inc.*, 12 SEC 322, 328-9 (1942). See also *Metropolitan Securities Inc.*, SEC Securities Exchange Act Release No. 7010, Jan. 31, 1963, p. 3.

[8] Paragraph (c)(2) specifically mentions some of the types of assets which are to be deducted from the assets which may serve as a basis for computation of net capital. Subdivision (b) of the paragraph calls for deduction from assets of ". . . fixed assets which cannot be readily converted into cash (less any indebtedness secured thereby) including, among other things, real estate; furniture and fixtures; exchange memberships; prepaid rent; insurance and expenses; good will; organization expenses; all unsecured advances and loans; customers' unsecured notes and

tion of all liabilities from only the liquid assets to arrive at "net capital." It furthermore calls for additional adjustments as to assets and liabilities in computing net capital. Some of these merit special mention.

In the case where an asset otherwise not readily convertible into cash has actually been accepted as collateral in a genuine transaction for a cash indebtedness, the asset is regarded as liquid to the extent of that indebtedness. In effect the asset has thus actually been partly converted into cash. In any event, it is regarded as having a readily realizable cash value to the extent of the indebtedness it secures. In such circumstances, therefore, only the balance of the asset above the indebtedness it secures is deducted from assets in computing net capital.[9]

One of the measures used by the rule for further reducing the assets for net capital computation purposes is the so-called "haircut." Subject to minor, insignificant exceptions, this calls for deductions from net capital of specified percentages of the market value of securities (other than exempted securities) in proprietary and other accounts reflecting capital contributions.[10] The haircut provision is consistent with the concept of liquidity, taking into account the fluctuating values of securities.[11] It must be kept in view at all times that, in order to be given any value at all, par-

---

accounts; and deficits in customers' accounts, except in bona fide accounts within the meaning of Section 4 (c) of Regulation T of the Board of Governors of the Federal Reserve System." By its terms, this list is not all inclusive. See *Joseph Blumenthal,* SEC Securities Exchange Act Release No. 6847, July 12, 1962, p. 3.

[9] See *Babson, Kaye & Robb Co.,* SEC Securities Exchange Act Release No. 7142, Sept. 13, 1963, pp. 2-3. And see subdivision (B) of paragraph (c)(2) of the rule. This will not be the case, however, if other additional collateral is placed to secure the loan. In such case, the broker-dealer cannot meet the burden that the asset in question is readily convertible into cash. Advances to securities salesmen which are repayable to a broker-dealer are not viewed as readily convertible to cash, even if the broker-dealer takes a lien on future commission. The asset must be actually used as collateral.

[10] In general, the value of common stocks is reduced by 30 percent; that of preferred stocks meeting certain standards, by 20 percent; and that of non-convertible debt securities having specified characteristics, by 5 percent. Subdivision (C) of paragraph (c)(2) of the Rule. In order to be taken into account as assets at all, the securities must be, long or short, in the capital, proprietary and other accounts of the broker or dealer, or must be a subordinated obligation pursuant to a "satisfactory subordination agreement," or they must be securities in the "accounts of partners" as those terms are defined in the rule. These definitions will be discussed below in this section. The 30 percent haircut is also given to the market value of all long and short future commodity contracts in the accounts above mentioned. Subdivision (D) of Paragraph (c)(2) of the rule. No "haircut" is applied to "exempted" securities. Subdivision (C) of Paragraph (c)(2).

[11] *SEC* v. *Peerless—New York, Inc.,* 157 F. Supp. 328, 330 (S.D.N.Y. 1958).

ticular securities, like any other assets of a broker-dealer, must qualify as assets which can be readily converted into cash.[12] Consequently, securities are given no value which cannot be publicly offered by jurisdictional means without prior compliance with the registration requirements of the Securities Act of 1933 or which are the subject of restrictions as to sale imposed by agreement.[13] Of course, a security having no ready market or market value cannot be viewed as an asset which can be readily converted into cash.[14]

The haircut is also applied with minor exceptions and adjustments to each net long and short position contemplated by existing open contractual commitments in the capital and other accounts reflecting capital contributions, and the net capital is reduced by the amount of such haircut.[15] Such contractual commitments include, among others, firm commitment underwriting contracts and when issued, when distributed and delayed delivery contracts as to securities which are not exempted securities.[16]

The rule calls for adjustments to assets and liabilities in other areas in the computation of net capital. For example, in the case of a broker-dealer who is a sole proprietor, there is deducted the excess of liabilities not incurred as broker-dealer over the assets not used in his business.[17] The two most significant remaining items of adjustment relate to "accounts of partners" and to "sub-

---

[12] *SEC v. C. H. Abraham & Co., Inc.*, 186 F. Supp. 19 (S.D.N.Y. 1960).

[13] *Whitney Phoenix Company, Inc.*, 39 SEC 245, p. 249, n. 14 (1959). Securities which are registered but which may not be offered until the Commission permits a post effective amendment cannot be treated as assets readily convertible into cash until the Commission approves the amendment.

[14] *SEC v. Abraham & Co., Inc., supra*, n. 12; *Pioneer Enterprises Inc.*, 36 SEC 199, 207 (1955).

[15] Subdivision (E) of paragraph (c)(2).

[16] Such commitments also include the endorsement of puts and calls and commitments in foreign currencies and spot commodities contracts, but do not include uncleared regular way purchases and sales of securities or contracts in commodities futures. Paragraph (c)(5) of the Rule.

Any fixed money liability involved in the open contractual commitment must, like all other such liabilities, be reflected on the broker-dealer's books of account and be deducted from assets in computing net capital. Such a liability may not be obviated in the case of a firm commitment contract where there is a binding agreement in letter form rather than formal contract containing the usual terms of a firm commitment underwriting. In cases where the commitment of a co-underwriter is limited to the securities actually sold after effective registration, he will have no net long or short position, hence the haircut provisions do not apply.

[17] Subdivision (G) of paragraph (c)(2) *cf. supra*, Sec. 7-3, as to treatment of this matter in financial reports. A corporation or partnership which conducts another business, however, must include all of its liabilities, including those arising out of its other business, in computing its net capital.

ordination agreements." "Accounts of Partners" of a broker-dealer partnership are defined as ". . . accounts of partners who have agreed in writing that the equity in such accounts maintained with such partnership shall be included as partnership property." The unrealized profits of such accounts are added to assets, whereas unrealized losses and deficits in such accounts are deducted.[18]

Subdivision (F) of paragraph (c)(2) of the Rule provides for the exclusion from the liabilities of a broker-dealer of those which are subordinated to the claims of general creditors pursuant to a "satisfactory subordination agreement" as defined in the rule. What constitutes a satisfactory subordinate agreement will be discussed at length below.[19] The liability covered by such an agreement is mentioned here to note it as an adjustment item in the computation of "net capital." Before leaving this discussion of net capital for some appropriate references to the other part of the ratio, "aggregate indebtedness," it may be observed that the term liabilities, like any other accounting term employed in the rule, is to be given its commonly accepted accounting meaning.[20]

It includes, for example, appropriate provision for estimated taxes.[21]

---

[18] Subdivision A of paragraph (c)(2) of the rule provides for the addition to assets of unrealized profits in the accounts of the broker or dealer, and if the broker-dealer is a partnership, the addition of equities in "accounts of partners." The same subdivision provides for deduction from assets of unrealized losses or deficits in the enumerated accounts. The definition of "accounts of partners" is found at Paragraph (c)(4) of the rule.

If the partner's account includes securities in which a third person has some beneficial interest, the value of those securities are deducted from "accounts of partners" and are therefore deducted from net capital. However, should the third person subordinate his interest in such securities pursuant to a "satisfactory subordination agreement," discussed *infra* at Sec. 8-6, the securities may then be included in computing net capital.

[19] *Infra*, Sec. 8-6.

[20] A broker-dealer as underwriter who agrees with the issuer to act as the issuer's agent in a public offering of the issuer's securities and to use its best efforts in that connection has no liability to the issuer for failure of payment for securities on the part of selected dealers chosen by him to assist in the distribution where the selected dealers are not the underwriter's agents. Accordingly, the amounts which such dealers have failed to pay need not be reflected on the underwriter's books as liabilities to the issuer. Hence, such amounts need not be deducted from assets in computing the underwriter's net capital. *Investment Bankers of America, Inc.*, SEC Securities Exchange Act Release No. 6886, Aug. 16, 1962, p. 1, and *Investment Bankers of America, Inc.*, SEC Securities Exchange Act Release No. 6994, Jan. 21, 1963. The precise question decided by the Commission in these cases was held open in *SEC* v. *Investment Bankers of America, Inc.*, 181 F. Supp. 346, 348 (D.D.C. 1960).

[21] *Cornelis DeVroedt*, 38 SEC 176, 180 (1958). "The language of the rule is to be read in the light of generally accepted accounting principles regarding the meaning of 'liabilities' and 'net worth' and there is nothing in the rule, nor have registrants cited any authority in the contrary." However, where a broker-dealer is

Sec. 8-4. Rule 15c 3-1—aggregate indebtedness. Having arrived at the computation of "net capital"[22] as one element of the ratio, it is necessary to determine "aggregate indebtedness" as the other component. Here again, the basic definition is plainly stated. In general terms "aggregate indebtedness" means the "total money liabilities" of a broker-dealer arising in connection with any transaction whatsoever[23] less certain types of liabilities specifically designated to be excluded. The main thrust of the inquiry as to what constitutes aggregate indebtedness lies in the area of which liabilities are specifically excluded.[24] It should be noted, however, that the exclusion of a liability from aggregate indebtedness does not mean its exclusion from the computation of net capital, unless there is express provisions for such treatment. A number of liabilities which are excluded from aggregate indebtedness encompass specified items of indebtedness which are adequately collateralized.[25] Another type of obligation which may be

---

entitled to commissions as selling agent, and they are not payable until some specified later date, the related deferred tax liability may be offset against such commissions receivable, so that such liability need not be included as a liability if the commissions are deducted from net capital as an asset not readily convertible into cash. As to the necessity for accruing liabilities for income taxes, in general, see *H. P. Black & Company*, SEC Securities Exchange Act Release No. 7174, November 22, 1963.

[22] The final figure arrived at for "net capital" after all adjustments have been made for assets and liabilities as specified in the rule is termed "adjusted net capital."

[23] The rule enumerates items to be included, but these are more in the nature of reminders than limitations. They are ". . . money borrowed; money payable against securities loaned and securities 'failed to receive'; the market value of securities borrowed (except for delivery against customers' sales) to the extent to which no equivalent value is paid or credited; customers' free credit balances; credit balances in customers' accounts having short positions in securities; and equities in customers' commodities futures accounts. . . ." All of these liabilities are reflected on the books and records of the broker-dealer as liabilities for a sum certain, with the exception of the obligation to return borrowed securities, or their market value at the time of return.

In the case of a best efforts "all or none" type of underwriting (see *infra*, Sec. 13-8, for the discussion on Rule 15c2-4) a broker-dealer underwriter is placed in the position that his liabilities continue to mount with the receipt of payment for the securities being distributed, because the funds cannot be turned over to the issuer until the requisite minimum amount of securities have been sold. The only acceptable method of elimination of such liabilities from computation of aggregate indebtedness prior to sale of the requisite minimum number of units of securities is to place the proceeds in escrow with a bank as envisioned by paragraph (B) of Rule 15c2-4(a)(2). See *infra*, Sec. 13-8, and Appendix P, Sec. 25-16.

[24] These are listed in subdivisions (A) to (I) inclusive of paragraph (c)(1) of the rule.

[25] These embrace indebtedness to others, including other broker-dealers, adequately collateralized by securities owned by the broker-dealer or by exempted securities. *Idem.* at subdivisions (A), (B), and (E). Paragraph (c)(6) of the rule provides that "indebtedness shall be deemed 'adequately collateralized' within the meaning of the rule, when the difference between the amount of the indebtedness

eliminated from aggregate indebtedness is a fixed liability adequately secured by a non-liquid asset which is not included in the computation of net capital.[26] It may be observed that these are obligations which are offset by corresponding specific assets. On a similar vein, aggregate indebtedness is reduced by amounts payable against securities loaned, which securities are owned by the broker-dealer, and also by amounts payable against securities failed to receive, which securities were purchased for the account of, and have not been sold by, the broker-dealer.[27] Amounts segregated in accordance with the Commodity Exchange Act and corresponding rules are also not included,[28] and liabilities on open contractual commitments are similarly deducted.[29] There is additionally deducted indebtedness subordinated to the claims of general creditors pursuant to a satisfactory subordination agreement.[30]

When the money liabilities are adjusted by the prescribed items of exclusion, the net result is "aggregate indebtedness," the second component of the net capital ratio.

Sec. 8-5. Rule 15c 3-1—origin of terms used in rule. The net capital rule is not really as complex as its numerous provisions would indicate. In the first place, many of the terms in the rule are terms of art in every day use in the securities business. Such

---

and the market value of the collateral is sufficient to make the loan acceptable as a fully secured loan to banks regularly making comparable loans to brokers or dealers in the community; . . ."

[26] Subdivision G of paragraph (c)(1).

[27] Paragraph (c)(1) of the rule, subdivisions (C) and (D). For a discussion of "securities failed to receive" see *supra*, Sec. 6-1, notes 15 and 16. The net purport of this exclusion of the indebtedness reflected in the fail-to-receive account is that such exclusion is permitted only if the securities in question have not been sold by the broker-dealer. If they have been sold, the indebtedness in the fail-to-receive account relating to such securities must be included in aggregate indebtedness even though the securities be exempted securities. In such circumstances, this is not regarded as the equivalent of adequately collateralized exempted securities in subdivision (E) of paragraph (c)(1) of the Rule.

[28] *Idem.* at subdivision (F). These are amounts segregated for regulated commodity accounts.

[29] *Idem.* at subdivision (H). It should be noted, however, that obligations incidental to an underwriting such as liabilities as to unexpended portions of advances for expenses in connection with a best efforts offering are liabilities which are not part of an open contractual commitment and are part of aggregate indebtedness. *Keith Richard Securities Corporation*, 39 SEC 231, p. 237, n. 17 (1959).

[30] Subdivision (I) of paragraph (c)(1) of the rule. A discussion of the subject of subordination agreements follows shortly in the text. Equities in the accounts of partners of a broker-dealer partnership are not treated as liabilities if the partners have agreed in writing that such equities shall be included in partnership property. Paragraphs (c)(8) and (c)(4) of the Rule. See discussion of accounts of partners *supra*, Sec. 8-3.

terms as "fail to receive," "spot commodities contracts," "contractual commitments" and the like are well-known elements of the everyday parlance in the securities field. Secondly, the very terms "net capital" and "aggregate indebtedness," as concepts which are given definitional body in the rule, have their roots in regulatory practices in the financial community which antedated the adoption of the rule.[31]

Sec. 8-6. Rule 15c 3-1—satisfactory subordination agreement. Indebtedness subordinated to the claims of general creditors pursuant to a satisfactory subordination agreement as defined in the rule is deducted both from aggregate indebtedness and from the liabilities embraced in the computation of net capital.[32] A "satisfactory subordination agreement" between a broker-dealer and a lender[33] is one which is written, is binding and enforceable in accordance with its terms on the lender, his creditors, heirs, executors, administrators, and assigns, and which effectively subordinates any right of the lender to demand or receive payment or return of the cash or securities loaned to the claims of all present and future general creditors of the broker-dealer.[34] In addition, the agreement may not be subject to cancellation at the will of either party and must be for a specified term of not less than one year.[35] It must specifically provide, moreover, (a) that it shall not be terminated, rescinded, or modified by mutual consent or otherwise, if the effect thereof would be to make the agreement

---

[31] See SEC Securities Exchange Act Release No. 3617, Nov. 8, 1944, in which the Commission points out that at that time a number of securities exchanges had "settled practices" imposing financial responsibility requirements on their members which included rules defining the terms "net capital" and "aggregate indebtedness" as well as "their component parts" and which provided for specified ratios of aggregate indebtedness to net capital.

[32] Subdivision (I) of paragraph (c)(1) of the rule, and subdivision (F) of paragraph (c)(2) of the rule.

[33] The creditor who subordinates his obligation is called the "lender." Paragraph (c)(7) of the rule.

[34] See subdivision (A) of paragraph (c)(7). The wording of this provision is viewed as not providing scope for treating as subordinated under the rule debts arising from defaults on the part of a broker-dealer in respect of an obligation to a customer.

[35] *Idem.* at subdivision (B). The rule contemplates that the creditor should subordinate his right to demand or receive payment of the indebtedness so long as it is outstanding, even though that be for a period beyond the stated term of the agreement. A subordination agreement would therefore not be "satisfactory" if it provides that the indebtedness be subordinated only for the term of the agreement. The basic objective of the one year provision is that the obligation may not mature in less than one year. For this reason, moreover, installments of principal may not be payable in less than one year.

inconsistent with the conditions of the rule or to reduce the net capital of the broker-dealer below the amount required by the rule;[36] (b) that no default in the payment of interest or in the performance of any other covenant or condition by the broker-dealer shall have the effect of accelerating the maturity of the indebtedness;[37] (c) that any notes or other written instruments evidencing the indebtedness shall bear on their face an appropriate legend stating that such notes or instruments are issued subject to the provisions of a subordination agreement adequately referred to and incorporated by reference;[38] and (d) that the subject of the agreement, whether it be securities or other property including the proceeds of cash loans or advances, may be used and dealt with by the broker-dealer as part of his capital and shall be subject to the risks of the business.[39] If the agreement has these characteristics, it is "satisfactory" as defined. The effect of such an agreement is to eliminate the indebtedness from liabilities for purposes of the net capital rule, at least during the life of the agreement, and thus, to effect on behalf of the lender a capital contribution for purpose of the rule to the broker-dealer for not less than the stipulated period.

Since all non-contingent indebtedness of a broker-dealer is encompassed by the term "liabilities," a broker-dealer claiming the right to exclude a liability from net capital and aggregate indebtedness as "subordinated," has the burden of proving the existence of a "satisfactory subordination agreement."[40] In practice, this proof takes the form of the opinion of an attorney that, under applicable laws, the agreement effectively subordinates the claim of the lender to the claims of all present and future general

---

[36] *Idem.* at subdivision (C).

[37] *Idem.* at subdivision (D). Accrued interest on the loan is not itself subordinated unless the agreement so provides. However, it is a liability which must be included in aggregate indebtedness and in computing net capital.

[38] *Idem.* at subdivision (E).

[39] *Idem.* at subdivision (F). Accordingly, any provision in the agreement which limits or restricts the broker-dealer from exercising full dominion over the proceeds of the loan, or which has the effect of retaining in the creditor any rights to deal with the subject of the loan will render the agreement not satisfactory.

[40] Those who claim an exception or exemption from a general requirement have the burden of proving it. See *SEC* v. *Sunbeam Gold Mines, Inc.,* 95 F.2d 699, 701 (9th Cir., 1938); cf. *SEC* v. *Ralston Purina Co.,* 346 U. S. 119, 126 (1953); *Ira Haupt & Co.,* 23 SEC 589, 595 (1946).

creditors of the broker-dealer.[41] In the case of a corporate lender, an attorney's opinion is supplied that the making of the agreement is within the powers of the lender and that the agreement is binding on the lender.[42] Of course, the agreement must contain the specific provisions called for by paragraph (c)(7) of the rule. Broker-dealers relying on subordination agreements are requested by the Commission's staff also to furnish two conformed copies of the agreement together with conformed copies of the note or other written instrument evidencing the indebtedness which is the subject of the agreement or a written representation that no such note or other instrument is in existence.[43] To establish that proper compliance is being had with the records requirements of Rule 17a-3, the broker-dealer is also called upon to provide satisfactory evidence that he has reflected the fact of subordination on the records by appropriately identifying it on the books in a special account appropriately titled and designated as "subordinated."[44] In the event the parties wish to effect prepayment where prepayment would not place the broker-dealer in violation of net capital requirements, no question is raised, provided that thirty days advance written notice is given to the regional office of the Commission of the region in which the broker-dealer has his principal place of business.[45] Moreover, if the subject of the agreement is securities, no question would be raised if there is provision for substitution which requires that the securities substituted be equally marketable with, and have a market value of not less than the market value of the securities for which they are being substituted, and which, in the case of substitution of securities for cash, requires that the securities must have a ready market and have a market value such that, after applicable deduction provided for by paragraph (c)(2)(C) of the rule (the haircut), the substitution will not result in diminution of the net capital of the broker-dealer below that prescribed by the rule in the circumstances.[46]

---

[41] See Appendix N for a copy of the *Guide To Preparation Of Subordination Agreements,* employed by the New York Regional Office of the Commission [hereinafter called Guide To Preparation of Subordination Agreements]. Sec. 25-14, *infra.*

[42] *Ibid.*

[43] *Ibid.*

[44] *Ibid.*

[45] *Ibid.*

[46] *Ibid.* It may be noted that a broker-dealer successor to one who is party to a subordination agreement cannot have the liabilities which are the subject of the agreement reduced either from net capital or aggregate indebtedness. The basic requirement of a satisfactory subordination agreement is that the lender's rights

Procedure as respects execution also includes the acknowledgment of the signatures of the parties by a notary public or other appropriate official[47] and the opinion of counsel, additional to other such opinions called for,[48] that the lender has good title to the moneys or securities which are the subject of the agreement.[49]

We have seen that the effect of subordinating a liability pursuant to a satisfactory subordination agreement is to permit such indebtedness to be treated as part of capital for the purposes of the rule.[50] However, for other purposes, such as to ascertain whether a broker-dealer is solvent, the indebtedness is given full effect as a liability to be measured against assets.[51]

It may be noted that no other means than a satisfactory subordination agreement can be utilized to accord a liability the treatment of being added to capital for purposes of the net capital rule. For example, the guarantee of a liability, no matter how substantial or solvent the guarantor, will not eliminate a liability from computation of net capital and aggregate indebtedness.

Sec. 8-7. Rule 15c 3-1—(e) exemptions from operation.
Two basic types of exemption from its operations are set forth in Rule 15C3-1. One is granted to members of specified national securities exchanges which are deemed by the Commission to have rules and settled practices more comprehensive than the requirements of the rule.[52]

---

are subordinated to the claims of all present and future general creditors of *the particular broker-dealer* whose liabilities are being considered in relation to compliance or non-compliance with net capital requirements. This is not the same as an agreement to subordinate rights to those of creditors of another broker-dealer, albeit he be a successor.

[47] Guide to Preparation Of Subordination Agreements, *supra,* n. 41.

[48] *Ibid.*

[49] *Ibid.*

[50] See *supra,* Sec. 8-3; see SEC Securities Exchange Act Release No. 5156, April 11, 1955, p. 1.

[51] See *infra,* Sec. 16-10, for a discussion of the implied representation on the part of a broker-dealer that he is solvent.

[52] These are: American Stock Exchange, Boston Stock Exchange, Midwest Stock Exchange, New York Stock Exchange, Pacific Coast Stock Exchange, Philadelphia-Baltimore Stock Exchange, and Pittsburgh Stock Exchange. The rule has a proviso that the Commission may suspend or withdraw the exemption as to members of a particular exchange by sending at least ten days' notice in writing to the exchange, if such steps appear necessary or appropriate in the public interest or for the protection of investors. Paragraph (b)(2) of the Rule. For an application of the power of withdrawal of the exemption from the Salt Lake Stock Exchange, see SEC Securities Exchange Act Release No. 6691, Dec. 21, 1961, in which the Commission pointed out that this type of exemption is conditioned on the exchange's maintaining procedures to assure itself and the Commission that the capital require-

The second is the exemption that is available to one who is a broker only and whose securities business is limited to soliciting subscriptions as agent for issuers and who transmits funds and securities promptly and does not otherwise hold funds or securities for or owe money or securities to customers.[53] This test is identical with that employed for exemption from the certification requirements as to annual reports of broker-dealers in subdivision (b) of paragraph (b)(1) of Rule 17a-5. All of the observations made in the discussion on that topic are applicable to the paragraph (b)(1) exemption of the net capital rule.[54]

Sec. 8-8. Prohibitions of section 15(c)(3) of the act. Under Section 15(c)(3) of the Act a broker or dealer is prohibited from using the mails or any means or instrumentality of interstate commerce to effect any transaction in or attempt to induce the purchase or sale of any security (other than an exempted security or commercial paper, bankers' acceptances, or commercial bills) otherwise than on a national securities exchange if he is not in compliance with rules adopted by the Commission in the public interest or for the protection of investors to provide safeguards with respect to the financial responsibility of brokers and dealers. Rule 15c3-1 is the rule prescribed by the Commission for such purposes, and a person using jurisdictional means to effect or induce transactions in securities while he is not in compliance with the net capital requirements of Rule 15c3-1 would be engaged in a violation of Section 15(c)(3) of the Act.[55]

Non-compliance with the requirements of the net capital rule is viewed with the utmost seriousness. Broker-dealers who engage in transactions while not in compliance expose their customers to undue financial risks; the broker-dealer shifts the risk of finan-

---

ments of the exchange will be enforced, the exchange having represented in that case that it was too burdensome for it to conduct the necessary inspections and other procedures to enforce compliance.

During the period a member is suspended from membership in a specified exchange, he is regarded as not being a member and, therefore, must comply with the Commission's net capital rule. *Strand Investment Co.,* SEC Securities Exchange Act Release No. 6705, January 10, 1961.

[53] Paragraph (b)(1) of the rule.

[54] See *supra,* Sec. 7-4 to Sec. 7-7.

[55] See e.g., *Whitney & Company, Inc.,* SEC Securities Exchange Act Release No. 6787, April 24, 1962, p. 2.

To "effect" a transaction refers to any "participation in a transaction whether as principal, agent, or both." SEC Securities Exchange Act Release No. 605, April 17, 1936.

cial loss from the operation of his business from himself to his customers, and this neither the Commission nor the Courts will countenance.[56]

Sec. 8-9. Proposed changes in net capital rule.

As a further curb to speculative activity by broker-dealers at the risk of customers which the net capital rule is designed to discourage,[57] the Special Study Report as well as recently enacted legislation foreshadow stricter capital controls. The Special Study Report[58] recommends the imposition of minimum net capital requirements varying with the type of business conducted, with a suggested absolute minimum of at least $5000 plus about $2500 for each branch office and $500 for each salesman. Broker-dealers who would be engaged in the underwriting of securities, either on a "best efforts" or a "firm commitment" basis, would be required to have and maintain a minimum net capital of $50,000 plus about two percent of the underwriting commitments or undertakings in the most recent twelve-month period.[59] Still another recommendation would call for a reserve of about fifteen percent of the aggregate amount of free credit balances in the form of cash or United States Government securities.[60]

All of these suggestions are under active consideration by the Commission.[61] Additionally, recently enacted legislation empowers

---

[56] *Blaise D'Antoni & Associates, Inc.* v. *SEC*, 289 F.2d 276, 277 (5th Cir. 1961). And see *Owens & Co.*, 38 SEC 918, 920 (1959); *Kenneth E. Goodman & Co.*, 38 SEC 309, 313 (1958), and see *SEC* v. *Graye*, 156 F. Supp. 544 (S.D.N.Y. 1957); *SEC* v. *Peerless-New York, Inc.*, 157 F. Supp. 328 (S.D.N.Y. 1958); *SEC* v. *Mainland Securities Corp.*, 192 F. Supp. 862 (S.D.N.Y. 1961); *Bennett-Manning Company*, SEC Securities Exchange Act Release No. 6632, Sept. 26, 1961, p. 4.

[57] See *Metropolitan Securities Inc.*, SEC Securities Exchange Act Release No. 7010, Jan. 31, 1963, p. 3, where the Commission said: "While the net capital rule does not prohibit accumulation of inventory by broker-dealers, it does require that the margin of safety provided by the rule for the benefit of all customers not be imperiled by speculation by the . . . [broker-dealer]."

[58] Special Study Report, Pt. 1, Ch. II, Recommendation "11," pp. 161-2.

[59] Special Study Report, Pt. 1, Ch. II, Recommendation "12," p. 162.

[60] Special Study Report, Pt. 1, Ch. III, Part D, Recommendation "1," p. 415.

[61] See Special Market Study Release No. 25, April 30, 1963, pp. 4, 5. The Commission has in fact informally circulated a proposed rule calling for minimum net capital requirements conforming generally with, but varying in some important details from, the recommendations in the Special Study Report. Under the proposal, for example, the reserve of cash and United States securities would be required to be not less than twenty-five percent of customers' free credit balances. See *The Wall Street Journal*, May 25, 1964, p. 3, Col. 1; and see *Special Report To NASD Members* (National Association of Securities Dealers, Inc.), May 25, 1964, p. 3. As to the meaning of the term "free credit balance," see the discussion below under the next sub-heading "Other Financial Responsibility Requirements," Sec. 8-10.

registered securities associations to impose financial responsibility requirements on members.[62]

B. *Other Financial Responsibility Requirements*

Sec. 8-10. Free credit balances—requirements. The Commission has recently adopted a rule of financial responsibility known as the "free credit balances" rule.[63] "Free credit balances are those amounts of cash owed by broker-dealers to customers which the customers have an immediate right to withdraw."[64] The rule was adopted upon the recommendation of the Special Study[65] which pointed out that customers with free credit balances are generally not aware that funds which they have the unrestricted right to withdraw are customarily commingled by the broker-dealer with other assets used in the operation of the business, the relationship between the broker-dealer and customer being merely in this instance that of debtor and creditor.[66]

Under the rule, a broker-dealer may not use in his business any funds arising out of any free credit balance carried for the account of any customer unless he has established adequate procedures pursuant to which each customer for whom a free credit balance is carried will be given or sent, together with or as part of the customer's statement of account, whenever sent but not less frequently than once every three months, a written statement informing such customer of the amount due to the customer by the broker-dealer on the date of such statement, and containing a written notice that (1) such funds are not segregated and may be used in the operation of the broker-dealer's business, and (2) such funds are payable on the demand of the customer.[67] Of

---

[62] Section 15A(b)(5)(E). See Sec. 24-3, *infra*.

[63] Rule 15c3-2. See SEC Securities Exchange Act Release No. 7325, May 27, 1964. The rule was proposed by SEC Securities Exchange Act Release No. 7266, March 12, 1964.

[64] Special Study Report, Pt. 1, Ch. III, p. 393. In the release adopting the rule, the Commission noted: "Free credit balances generally arise when a customer gives cash to a broker-dealer to hold pending receipt of instructions to purchase securities; or when free securities are sold and the proceeds are held pending further investment or further instructions from the customer; or from interest or dividends on the customer's securities being held by the broker-dealer." SEC Securities Exchange Act Release No. 7325, May 27, 1954, p. 1, n. 1.

[65] Special Study Report Pt. 1, Ch. III, Recommendation "1," p. 415.

[66] *Idem*. at p. 402.

[67] Rule 15c3-2. By its terms, the rule does not apply to a broker-dealer which is also a banking institution supervised and examined by State or Federal authority having supervision over banks. The rule defines the term, "customer," as "every person other than a broker or dealer."

course, it follows that the required notice and statement must be sent in accordance with such established procedures.

These requirements do not apply to a broker-dealer who adequately segregates customers' free credit balances and does not use them in his business.[68]

---

[68] SEC Securities Exchange Act Release No. 7325, May 27, 1964, p. 2. The placing of all free credit balances in a separate bank account as an agency or trust account would, in the opinion of the author, constitute adequate segregation, provided, of course, that the broker-dealer does not have any of his own funds in such bank account. The bookkeeping requirements discussed *supra*, at Chapter 6, would call for the maintenance by the broker-dealer of precise records with respect to such bank account indicating the dates and amounts of deposits and withdrawals, the name of each customer having an interest in the account, and the exact amount of his interest in it.

CHAPTER 9

EXTENDING, MAINTAINING, AND ARRANGING FOR CREDIT

Sec. 9-1. Regulation T—in general. Excessive speculation in securities was a major factor in impelling Congress to pass the Exchange Act.[1] Accordingly, Section 7 of the Act grants important powers to the Board of Governors of the Federal Reserve System[2] with respect to the amount of credit which may be initially extended and subsequently maintained on securities, such powers having been furnished "for the purpose of preventing excessive use of credit for the purchase or carrying of securities. . ."[3] Among other things, Section 7(c) of the Act makes it unlawful for any member of a national securities exchange or any broker or dealer who transacts a business in securities through the medium of any such member[4] to extend or maintain credit or arrange for the extension of maintenance of credit to any customer (a) without collateral or on any collateral other than exempted securities or securities registered for listing on a national securities exchange except as permitted by Federal Reserve rules; and (b) on any security (other than an exempted security) registered on a national securities exchange[5] in contravention of such rules.[6] The Federal

---

[1] See Sen. Rep. No. 792, 73rd Cong., 2d Sess. (1934), p. 3.

[2] When the Act was passed, the name of the agency was the Federal Reserve Board. The name was changed by Section 203(a) of the Banking Act of 1935, 12 U.S.C. 221 (1958), to the Board of Governors of the Federal Reserve System [hereinafter sometimes called the "Board"].

[3] Section 7(a) of the Act. And see Sen. Rep. No. 792, 73rd Cong., 2nd Sess. (1934), p. 3; H.R. Rep. No. 1383, 73rd Cong., 2nd Sess. (1934), pp. 5-6.

[4] If, as part of his business, no matter how small, a broker or dealer effects or induces a transaction in a security executed on a national securities exchange then perforce he transacts a business in securities through the medium of an exchange member. See Fed. Res. Bull., Nov. 1938, p. 951 and Fed. Res. Bull., Nov. 1939, p. 961. As pointed out under the heading "Jurisdictional Considerations," *supra*, Sec. 4-1, it would be a rare case for a broker-dealer not to be within the purview of Section 7. See also *Palumbi Securities Co., Inc.*, SEC Securities Exchange Act Release No. 6961, Nov. 30, 1962, pp. 6-7. But see *Kook* v. *Crang*, 182 F. Supp. 388, 390 (S.D.N.Y. 1960), for implications to the contrary.

[5] The term "registered security," as defined in the governing Federal Reserve rules, includes securities registered for listing on a national securities exchange, or securities having unlisted trading privileges on such an exchange, or securities desig-

Reserve rules adopted under Section 7(c) of the Act are embodied in Regulation T.[7]

A detailed discussion of Regulation T will not be undertaken in this book. However, a few salient features of the regulation will be mentioned.

Apart from provisions relative to borrowings by members and broker-dealers subject to Section 8(a) of the Act,[8] Regulation T is concerned in the main with two subjects. The first is the maximum loan value of, and margin requirements as to, securities on which credit may be extended and maintained.[9] The second relates to the securities as to which credit may not be extended.

Regulation T accomplishes its results by prescribing that

nated by rule of the Securities and Exchange Commission under Section 7(c)(2) of the Act. See Section 2(d) of Regulation T, 12 CFR 220.2(d) (1959).

All sections of Regulation T are published in the Code of Federal Regulations as Title 12, part 220, cited as 12 CFR 220. References to provisions of Regulation T will be made in the text by section number of the regulation.

By adopting Rule 7c2-1 under the Act, the Securities and Exchange Commission in effect designated as included within the term "registered security," as defined in Regulation T, securities listed on an exchange exempted from registration as a national securities exchange.

[6] Sections 7(c)(1) and (2) of the Act. Another source of rule-making authority for the Board of Governors of the Federal Reserve System is found in Section 23(a) of the Act.

Questions may arise in given cases as to whether credit is actually being extended for the purchase of securities, such as in cases involving installment sales of securities or subscription agreements calling for a down payment and for periodic payments which may or may not involve delivery of securities upon the making of each payment. Each such case must be considered on the basis of its own special facts.

[7] Regulation T also contains the Federal Reserve rules envisioned by Section 8(a) of the Act respecting restrictions as to the sources from which members and broker-dealers subject to the regulation may borrow on registered non-exempted securities. Apart from permissible borrowings and extensions of credit as among members and broker-dealers subject to the regulation, the pertinent rules limit the sources of such borrowings to either (1) a member bank of the Federal Reserve System, or (2) a non-member bank which files an agreement with the Board in prescribed form. Section 5 of the regulation (12 CFR 220.5). See *J. A. Latimer & Co., Inc.*, 38 SEC 790, 793 (1958).

[8] See n. 7, *supra*.

[9] "Maximum loan value" represents the maximum amount which may be loaned on a given security and is stated as a percentage of the "current market value." See Section 8(a) of Regulation T; 12 CFR 220.8(a). The term "margin requirement" means the minimum amount which a purchaser must pay on account of a security. Expressed as a percentage of the current market value, "margin requirement" is the converse of "maximum loan value." Thus if the maximum loan value of a security is set at 70 percent of current market value, the margin requirement is 30 percent of current market value. *Ibid.* and see Section 8(b) of Regulation T; 12 CFR 220.8(b). Current market value throughout the day of purchase or sale is the total cost or the proceeds of sales, as the case may be, or the closing sale price on the preceding business day as shown by a regular quotation service or a reasonable estimate. Section 3(c)(4) of Regulation T; 12 CFR 220.3(c)(4).

designated kinds of transactions with customers be reflected, respectively, in specified types of ledger accounts[10] which creditors[11] maintain for customers.[12] These include the "general" or margin account, on the one hand, and, on the other, a series of "special" accounts required to be maintained with reference to transactions either presenting special situations for the elimination or modification of margin requirements or not involving the extension of credit.

Sec. 9-2. Regulation T—the general or margin account. All financial relations between a creditor and a customer, whether recorded in one record or more than one record, are deemed to be parts of the customer's general account with the creditor, with the exception of the particular relations specified in various designated special accounts.[13]

Section 3(b) of the Regulation (12 CFR 220.3(b)) makes it unlawful for a creditor to effect for or with any customer in the general, or margin, account any transaction which, in combination with the other transactions effected in the account on the same day creates an excess or increases an existing excess of the "ad-

---

[10] In explaining this approach, an official of the Board made these statements, among others: "The regulation should be as far as possible in the language of the brokers and margin clerks who must work under it, not in the language of the banker or the lawyer. It is in accord with this principle that the regulation is drawn in terms of transactions, accounts, debit balances, etc., notwithstanding the fact that the Securities Exchange Act is drawn chiefly in terms of the extension and maintenance of credit." Address by Carl E. Parry, Chief, Division of Security Loans, Board of Governors of the Federal Reserve System before the Senior Margin Clerks' Section, Association of Stock Exchange Firms, New York, N. Y., December 15, 1938.

[11] By definition in Section 2 of the regulation (12 CFR 220.2), the term "creditor" includes any member or broker-dealer subject to the regulation. A member firm and any partner of such firm is included in the definition of "member." Section 3(a)(3) of the Act.

[12] The term "customer" includes not only individuals, corporations, partnerships, and business associations such as joint accounts, as would in the ordinary usage of trade be considered a customer. It encompasses, also, any partner of the creditor firm who would be a customer were he not a partner, as well as any joint venture in which a creditor participates and which, absent such participation, would be a customer of the creditor. Section 2(c) and see Section 6(a) and (b) of Regulation T; 12 CFR 220.2(c), and 220.6(a) and (b).

[13] Section 3(a) of Regulation T. 12 CFR 220.3(a). For this reason, among others, a broker-dealer creditor cannot obviate the credit restrictions of Regulation T by engaging in so-called "personal" transactions as principal or dealer with a customer which do not conform with the requirements of Regulation T. We have seen that no securities transaction of a broker-dealer will be viewed in any light other than as a part of its business as a broker-dealer. See *supra*, Sec. 2-2.

justed debit balance"[14] of the account over the maximum loan value[15] of the securities in the account. In the event such excess is created or increased, the creditor must obtain as promptly as possible, and before the expiration of four business days following the transaction, the deposit of cash or securities in such amount as to equal the excess created or the increase created with reference to existing excess, of adjusted debit balance over maximum loan values.[16] Failing such deposit, the creditor must, prior to the expiration of the four-day period, sell registered non-exempted securities in the account to such extent as may be sufficient to eliminate such excess or increase.[17]

Credit initially extended without violation of the margin requirements may be maintained regardless of subsequent reductions in the customers' equity resulting from changes in the market price or the fact that a security in the account has ceased to be registered or exempt, or of any changes later made by the Board as to loan values or margin requirements.[18] The creditor, as well as the exchange of which a creditor is a member, is free, how-

---

[14] A debit balance in the account of a customer represents the balance owing from the customer to the creditor. The "adjusted debit balance" is arrived at by taking the net debit balance, if any, of the account and adding to it and subtracting from it the various items set forth in Sections 3(d) and (h) and Sections 6(a) and (b) of Regulation T. Among other things, there is added to the net debit balance the cost of securities bought for the account and not yet debited and the current market value of securities sold short in the account, plus, with minor exceptions, the amount of margin required for such short sales.

[15] The maximum loan value of a registered security is prescribed from time to time by the Board. Sections 3(c)(2) and 8 of Regulation T. 12 CFR 220.3(c)(2) and 8; as is the margin required for short sales. *Ibid.* and see Section 3(d)(3) of the regulation; 12 CFR 220.3(d)(3). The maximum loan values of "exempted" securities are those determined by the creditor in good faith. Section 3(c)(2) of the regulation; 12 CFR 220.3(c)(2). No collateral other than a registered or exempted security has any loan value in the general account. *Ibid.*

[16] Section 3(b)(1) of the regulation, 12 CFR 220.3(b)(1).

[17] Section 3(e) of the regulation, 12 CFR 220.3(e). There is a provision for extension of the four-day period as to a creditor who applies for such extension to regularly constituted committees of the exchange of which the creditor is a member or through which the creditor's transactions are effected, provided that the committee is satisfied that the creditor is acting in good faith and the circumstances are exceptional and warrant such extension. Section 3(f) of the regulation, 12 CFR 220.3(f).

Section 3(e) of the regulation specifies that, if there are insufficient registered non-exempted securities for elimination of the deficiency, other liquidating transactions must be effected in the account prior to the expiration of the four-day period (or any extension thereof as provided for by Section 3(f) of the regulation).

[18] Section 7(b) of the regulation, 12 CFR 220.7(b). Credit extended for part of a business day pending clearance of a transaction through the clearing agency of a national securities exchange is not governed by the margin requirements of Section 3 of the regulation. See Section 6(i); 12 CFR 220.6(i).

ever, to require from the creditor additional margin or other protection.[19]

Despite the propriety of thus maintaining credit where the adjusted debit balance exceeds the maximum loan value of the securities in the general account, the general account is regarded as restricted. Transactions in the account may occur if in combination with other transactions on the same day the excess is not increased. But as seen, if the "same day" transactions effect an increase in such excess, the creditor must take the appropriate steps within four business days thereafter to obtain the appropriate deposit of cash or securities or to sell enough registered non-exempted securities to eliminate the excess so created or increase so caused.[20] Moreover, apart from the exceptions noted below, no withdrawal may be made from such account of any cash or registered or exempted securities.[21] Among these exceptions are that cash may be withdrawn upon the deposit in the account of registered or exempted securities having a maximum loan value at least equal to the amount of cash withdrawn.[22] Another exception is that, upon the sale, other than a short sale, of registered or exempted securities in the account, cash may be withdrawn in an amount equal to the difference between the current market value of the securities sold and the "retention requirement" of those securities.[23] The "retention requirement" of a registered non-exempted security is prescribed by the Board from time to time.[24] Upon the assumption that the "retention requirement" of a registered security is 50 percent at the time a registered non-exempted security is sold from a restricted general account for $1000, only $500 of the cash can be withdrawn from the account by the customer. The remaining $500 must remain in the account.[25]

It is additionally provided that a customer may withdraw from the restricted account registered or exempted securities,

---

[19] *Ibid.* and see Sections 7(e) and 3(d)(5) of the regulation. 12 CFR 220.7(e) and 12 CFR 220.3(d)(5).

[20] *Supra,* n. 16 and accompanying text.

[21] Section 3(b)(2) of Regulation T. 12 CFR 220.3(b)(2).

[22] *Ibid.*

[23] *Ibid.*

[24] Section 3(b)(2) of Regulation T; 12 CFR 220.3(b)(2), and see Section 8(c) of Regulation T; 12 CFR 220.8(c). The retention requirement of an "exempted" security is the s᾽ me as its maximum loan value. *Ibid.*

[25] *Ibid.*

provided he deposits in the account cash (or registered or exempted securities counted at their maximum loan value) at least equal to the "retention requirement" of any registered or exempted securities withdrawn.[26]

With stated exceptions, every extension of credit on a nonexempted registered security is presumed to be for the purpose of purchasing or carrying or trading in securities;[27] and, although a creditor may arrange with others for the extension or maintenance of credit to or for any customer, such arrangements may with one narrow exception be for the extension and maintenance of credit only upon the same terms and conditions as the creditor may himself extend to or maintain for such customer.[28] The regulation does not prohibit a creditor from making bona fide cash deposits as collateral for securities (whether registered or unregistered) borrowed, either because of a failure to receive a security the creditor must deliver, or to cover a short sale; or for other similar cases. And a creditor may lend securities for such purposes against such deposit.[29] Margin accounts transferred from one creditor to another are regarded as though they have been maintained by the transferee from the date of origin if the transferee accepts from the transferor or (if this is not practicable) from the cus-

---

[26] Section 3(b)(2) of Regulation T. 12 CFR 220.3(b)(2).

[27] Section 7(c) of the regulation. 12 CFR 220.7(c). This presumption may be overcome by the filing of a written statement by the customer with the creditor as to the use to be made of the credit and containing a representation that such credit is not for the purpose of purchasing or carrying or trading in securities nor for evading Regulation T. This statement may be relied upon unless the creditor knows it to be false or has information which would lead a prudent man to discover its falsity. *Ibid.* If a loan to a customer is not for the purpose of purchasing, carrying, or trading in securities, the loan may be on such terms, even without collateral, as the creditor sees fit. Section 4(f)(8) of Regulation T, 12 CFR 220.4(f)(8).

[28] Section 7(a) of the regulation, 12 CFR 220.7(a). The exception to this restriction as to "arranging" for credit on terms other than the creditor can himself extend or maintain, exists if a creditor makes a direct arrangement (not through an intermediary) for a bank subject to Regulation U (12 CFR 221.1-221.4) to extend or maintain credit on registered or exempt securities. Under this exception, a creditor cannot arrange with a Regulation U bank to extend or maintain credit on non-registered non-exempt securities. Section 7(a) of the regulation. 12 CFR 220.7(a).

Apart from this limited exception, no other types of arrangements may be made even with professional non-bank money lenders. Moreover, arrangements for extension or maintenance of credit on other than Regulation T terms cannot be accomplished by indirection. The mere following of a customer's instructions who made his own non-Regulation T arrangements is not a violation of the regulation by a broker-dealer; yet, if the broker-dealer engages in any step as an intermediary for his customer, even limited to the conveying of messages, the broker-dealer will be guilty of arranging. *Sutro Bros. & Co.,* SEC Securities Exchange Act Release No. 7052, April 10, 1963, pp. 9-14.

[29] Section 6(h) of the regulation 12 CFR 220.6(h).

tomer a signed statement that no cash or securities need to be deposited in connection with any transaction that has been effected in the account.[30] An account transferred from one customer to another may be treated by the creditor as if it had been maintained for the transferee from the date of origin of the account if this is not effected to evade Regulation T, and if the creditor accepts in good faith and keeps with the transferee account a signed statement of the transferor describing the circumstances giving rise to the transfer.[31]

In broad outline, these are the regulations governing the margin or general account.[32]

Sec. 9-3. Regulation T—special accounts in general. Discussion on this topic will be confined to certain of the more significant "special" accounts prescribed by Regulation T.[33]

There is a general admonition applicable to each special account to the effect that each shall be recorded in full detail separately and be confined to transactions and relations specifically authorized or incidental to those specifically authorized for such account by the provisions applicable to such account. Moreover, a special account may not be used as a vehicle for evading or circumventing applicable margin requirements.[34]

A number of these accounts are designed to permit activity without the credit restrictions which would otherwise be applicable by Section 3. In brief, they are exceptions to the general rule, presumably because it was not the intent of the statute to embrace situations covered by the exceptions. Typical of such accounts are (1) the Special Arbitrage Account in which a member of a national securities exchange may effect and finance for any customer *bona fide* arbitrage transactions[35] in securities; (2) the

---

[30] Section 6(d) of the regulation, 12 CFR 220.6(d).

[31] *Ibid.*

[32] Whenever a change in maximum loan value or margin requirements is made, a customer's purchase order executed before the change is governed by the requirements before the change, even though delivery of the securities takes place thereafter. Federal Reserve Press Release, Nov. 8, 1963.

[33] The provisions of Section 7(a) of the regulation, 12 CFR 220.7(a), prohibiting a creditor from arranging for credit on terms different from those which apply to the creditor are restrictions which apply to transactions in the various special accounts discussed directly below in the text with the same force as to transactions in the general account.

[34] Section 4(a)(2) and (3) of the regulation, 12 CFR 220.4(a)(2) and (3).

[35] The term "Aribitrage" means (1) a purchase or sale of a security in one market together with an offsetting sale or purchase of the same security in a

Special Commodity Account confined to customers' commodities transactions; (3) the Special Miscellaneous Account;[36] and (4) the Special Omnibus Account. The latter is a type of account maintained by a member firm of a national securities exchange, usually for a non-member broker-dealer who places securities of his customers in an account carried by the member firm in the name of the non-member broker-dealer. This is done among other things to facilitate the execution on the exchange of the orders of the customers of the non-member broker-dealer.

In the Special Omnibus Account,[37] the member firm may effect and finance transactions for the broker-dealer without regard to margin restrictions, provided that the member accepts in good faith a signed statement to the effect that the broker-dealer is subject to Regulation T as regards adherence to margin requirements with reference to transactions with the broker-dealer's customers, or that the broker-dealer does not extend or maintain credit to or for customers except in accordance with the regulation

---

different market at as nearly the same time as practicable, for the purpose of taking advantage of a difference in prices in the two markets, or (2) a purchase of a security which is, without restriction other than the payment of money, exchangeable or convertible within 90 calendar days following the date of its purchase into a second security together with an offsetting sale at or about the same time of such second security, for the purpose of taking advantage of a disparity in the prices of the two securities. Section 4(d) of Regulation T. 12 CFR 220.4(d).

[36] Section 4(f) of the regulation. 12 CFR 220.4(f). This account is available for use as a sort of hodge podge for special types of transactions such as those engaged in by consent of a committee of a national securities exchange to meet the emergency needs of any creditor, or transactions involving loans made under specified conditions to members, or partners or stockholders of member firms or affiliated companies of member firms, if the proceeds of the loans are used to purchase stock of such companies or to make capital contributions. Additionally, in this account, a creditor may effect and finance transactions of an odd lot dealer member of a national securities exchange as well as transactions, in which the creditor participates, of certain special types of underwritings or distributions of all or part of an issue of securities. In this account, also, a creditor may effect cash transactions of sale with a broker-dealer customer, with payment to be made as promptly as practicable in accordance with the ordinary usage of trade. The account furthermore may reflect transactions effected for customers, such as the collections and exchange of securities, receipt of money or securities and payment or delivery of money or securities if such transactions do not involve sales or purchases of securities. It may reflect, moreover, transactions in foreign exchange; and finally, the extension and maintenance of credit to a customer with or without collateral for any purpose other than purchasing, carrying or trading in securities. In this latter connection, the sale by a broker-dealer would not be a violation of Regulation T if the sale of the securities be made to the issuer of such securities on credit terms not conforming to Regulation T margin requirements, where the issuer is purchasing the securities for the purpose of retiring such securities. In such case, the issuer does not retain ownership in such securities but is simply reducing the number of units outstanding.

[37] Section 4(b) of the regulation. 12 CFR 220.4(b).

as though he were subject to it. Thus, by the Special Omnibus Account, application of Section 7(c) of the Act and Regulation T may reach the rare broker-dealer who might otherwise not come within their purview. The broker-dealer must additionally provide the creditor with written notice that any short sales effected in the account will be made only on behalf of customers of the broker-dealer other than a partner of the broker-dealer.[38]

Other special accounts, such as the Specialists' Account[39] and the Special Subscriptions Account,[40] are designed to effect modifications of the margin requirements as to such accounts in certain particulars.

The special account of most general significance is the Special Cash Account provided for by Section 4(c) of the regulation. 12 CFR 220.4(c).

Sec. 9-4. Regulation T—the special cash account. The Special Cash Account is used to effect *bona fide* cash transactions with customers and is the one most often used to reflect purchases and sales of non-registered securities that are not exempted. Purchases for or sales of any security to any customer may be effected in this account if sufficient funds for the purpose are already in the account or if the transaction is effected upon an agreement accepted by the creditor in good faith that the customer will promptly make full cash payment for the security and that the customer does not contemplate selling the security prior to making payment.[41] Additionally, the creditor may sell any security for or

---

[38] An additional written notice must be given to the member firm by the broker-dealer to the effect that all securities carried in the account will be carried only for customers of the broker-dealer. This requirement is merely a restatement of the obligation imposed by the Commission on broker-dealers under the hypothecation rules. Rule 8c-1 and 15c2-1 under the Act. Discussion of the significance of this requirement will be found *infra* at Sec. 11-7.

[39] This is an account of a creditor maintained for a member of a national securities exchange who is registered and acts as specialist in specified securities registered on the exchange. Section 4(g) of the regulation. 12 CFR 220.4(g).

[40] Section 4(h) of the regulation. 12 CFR 220.4(h). In general, this account permits the relaxation of margin requirements with respect to the financing of the acquisition of a registered security for a customer through the exercise of rights evidenced by a warrant or certificate issued to stockholders and expiring within ninety days of issuance. It may be noted that the exercise of rights issued to other security holders such as debenture holders or bond holders may not be reflected in this account.

[41] Section 4(c)(1)(i) of the regulation. 12 CFR 220.4(c)(1)(i). During any period when the Board specifies in Section 8 of the regulation (12 CFR 220.8) that registered securities (other than exempted securities) shall have no loan value in a general account, any transaction consisting of a purchase of a security other than a pur-

purchase any security from any customer in a special cash account, provided the security is in the account, or the creditor is informed that the customer or his principal owns the security and the purchase or sale is in reliance upon an agreement accepted by the creditor in good faith that the security is to be promptly deposited in the account.[42] By virtue of this provision, a customer is effectively prevented from making a short sale of any unregistered security, except in the general account.

If a customer purchases a security in a Special Cash Account and fails to make full cash payment within 7 days after the date on which he purchases the securities, the creditor must promptly "cancel or otherwise liquidate the transaction or the unsettled portion thereof."[43] The customer doesn't violate Regulation T by such non-payment, but the creditor violates the regulation for failure promptly to cancel or liquidate within the prescribed period.[44]

---

chase of an exempted security, or a purchase of a security to reduce or close out a short position, must be effected in the Special Cash Account provided for by Section 4(c) of the regulation. 12 CFR 220.4(c); or in some other appropriate special account provided for by Section 4 of the regulation. See Section 3(a) of Regulation T. 12 CFR 220.3(a).

[42] Section 4(c)(1)(ii) of the regulation. 12 CFR 220.4(c)(1)(ii).

[43] Section 4(c)(2) of the regulation, 12 CFR 220.4(c)(2). The customer cannot extend the seven days by making late payment. Such payment should be rejected and the transaction cancelled or otherwise liquidated. But see *Investment Bankers of America, Inc.*, SEC Securities Exchange Act Release No. 6886, Aug. 16, 1962, p. 2. The seven-day period refers to seven full business days. Section 4(c)(7) of the regulation, 12 CFR 220.4(c)(7). In the case of the purchase by a customer of an unissued security, the seven days start to run from the "date on which the security is made available by the issuer for delivery to purchasers"; and, in the case of a "when distributed" security to be distributed in accordance with a published plan, the seven-day period commences with the date on which the security is to be so distributed. Section 4(c)(3) of the regulation. 12 CFR 220.4(c)(3). The provision as respects an unissued security that the seven-day period commences only when the security is made available by the issuer is designed to apply only when the entire issue has not been made so available, so that the entire issue is traded on a "when issued" basis. Consequently, such an extension of the seven-day period does not apply as to the sale of mutual fund securities merely because, as a matter of mechanics the issuer does not issue the security technically at the time of its sale by a dealer to a customer. This delay is viewed as merely allowing for the mechanics of transfer and delivery. 12 CFR 220.118. The time required for shipment incidental to consummation of the transaction, up to an additional seven days, may be added to the basic seven-day period. Section 4(c)(4) of the regulation. 12 CFR 220.4(c)(4). An appropriate committee of a national securities exchange or national securities association has the power to extend the time periods relative to payment in respect of *bona fide* cash transactions in a cash account if satisfied of the creditor's good faith and if the exceptional circumstances warrant such extension. Section 4(c)(6) of the regulation 12 CFR 220.4(c)(6). Such a committee may, on the same basis, permit transfer of the transaction to a general account or special omnibus account if the security is a registered or exempted security. *Ibid.*

[44] Section 4(c)(2) of the regulation. 12 CFR 220.4(c)(2).

One exception to this obligation on the part of a creditor relates to the purchase for or sale to a customer of a security where payment is to be made against delivery and the understanding is that the creditor acting in good faith is to deliver the security promptly to the customer. In such case, the creditor may at his option treat the transaction as one in which payment is to be made within 35 days after the date of the transaction.[45]

Section 4(c)(8) of the regulation, 12 CFR 222.4(c)(8), is the famous provision against "free riding." Unless sufficient funds for the purpose are already in the special cash account of a customer, no security other than an exempted security may be purchased for or sold to the customer in the account if any non-exempted security was purchased in that account by the customer during the preceding 90 days, and if for any reason whatever, without having been previously paid for in full, it was sold in the account by the customer or delivered out to any broker or dealer.[46] By the terms of the rule, the cancellation of a transaction by a customer is treated as a sale. However, the delivery to another broker-dealer may be disregarded if the delivery was into a special account carried by the other broker-dealer for the same customer, in which

---

[45] This is commonly known as the C.O.D. provision. Section 4(c)(5) of the regulation, 12 CFR 220.4(c)(5). The provision is not a *carte blanche* for evasion of the seven-day period. The delivery must be made promptly and the customer must be ready with the cash for payment on delivery. The *bona fides* of the creditor is bound up with whether or not it is realistic to expect the customer to pay, as whether or not the customer has the required resources for the purpose. The delay countenanced under this provision is only that which arises from the mechanics of the trade, such as the delay arising from a failure to receive the security purchased for the customer, or from the fact that the creditor sold the security without having it in inventory and has to go into the market for it. Consistent with not unduly upsetting a volatile market, the creditor must not delay in acquiring the security for delivery. 26 Fed. Reserve Bull. 1172-4 (1940). See e.g., *Coburn and Middlebrook, Inc.*, 37 SEC 581, 587 (1957). And see *Palombi Securities Co., Inc.*, SEC Securities Exchange Act Release No. 6961, Nov. 30, 1962, p. 7. In any event, the customer's request for delay in delivery and payment beyond the seven-day period cannot be honored. Moreover, unless the agreement between customer and creditor is specific that the transaction be one of payment against delivery, the transaction cannot be so treated to effect an extension of the seven-day period. In the ordinary case, when a customer's order is accepted the customer has the right to delivery. The mechanics of issue and transfer do not serve to extend time of payment. *Palombi Securities Co., Inc., supra.* The 35 days refer to 35 calendar days. Section 4(c)(7) of the regulation, 12 CFR 220.4(c)(7).

[46] Section 4(c)(8) of the regulation, 12 CFR 220.4(c)(8). Upon application, an appropriate committee of a national securities exchange or national securities association may authorize a creditor to disregard a given instance of sale before payment of the type described, if the committee is satisfied that both the creditor and the customer are acting in good faith and that the circumstances warrant such authorization. *Ibid.*

account there were already sufficient funds to pay for the security.[47] Similarly, the creditor may disregard a sale without prior payment if full cash payment was received into the account before the expiration of seven days from the date of purchase and the customer did not withdraw the proceeds of sale on or before the day on which such payment was received.[48] Absent these provisions, or authorization to a creditor by an appropriate committee to disregard a sale prior to payment of a security purchased within 90 days,[49] a creditor may not purchase for or sell to the customer any non-exempted security in the special cash account if the account does not have funds sufficient for the purpose. In brief, the creditor can no longer be regarded as relying upon an agreement accepted by the creditor in good faith that the customer will promptly make full cash payment for the security and that the customer does not contemplate selling the security prior to making such payment.[50]

Failure to comply with the conditions of Section 4(c)(1)(i) and (ii) of the regulation, as well as non-compliance with the provisions of Section 4(c)(2) and violations of Section 4(c)(8) of the regulation[51] relative to the anti-"free-riding" restrictions have been viewed with the utmost seriousness by the Commission, and they have resulted in appropriate sanctions.[52] Although Section 6(k)

---

[47] The creditor may accept in good faith the written statement of the other broker-dealer to this effect. *Ibid.*

[48] If such cash payment by the customer be by check, the proceeds of the check must have actually been collected before the expiration of the seven days. On the other hand, a customer is deemed to "withdraw" such proceeds immediately upon the issuance of the creditor's check to the customer. Hence, if the creditor's check is issued after receipt of the customer's check but before the customer's check has been collected, the customer will be deemed to have withdrawn the proceeds of sale before he made payment.

[49] See n. 43, *supra.*

[50] Section 4(c)(1)(i) of the regulation, 12 CFR 220.4(c)(1)(i).

[51] These are the sections relative to the Special Cash Account which have just been discussed.

[52] See e.g. *Coburn and Middlebrook, Incorporated,* 37 SEC 581 (1957); *Kramer & Company, Incorporated,* 39 SEC 265, 266-7 (1959); *Denton & Company, Incorporated,* 37 SEC 739 (1957); *Allen E. Beers Company,* 38 SEC 27 (1957); *Shelley, Roberts & Company of California,* 38 SEC 744, 751 (1958); *Allied Securities Corporation,* 38 SEC 870, 873 (1959); *James H. Drass, Inc.,* 39 SEC 368, 370-1 (1959); *Earl L. Robbins,* 39 SEC 847, 849 (1960); *Dennis Securities Corporation,* 39 SEC 364, 366-7 (1959); *T. J. Campbell Investment Company, Inc.,* 39 SEC 940, 943 (1960); *Thompson & Sloan, Inc.,* 40 SEC 451, 455 (1961); *Ross Securities, Inc.,* 40 SEC 1064, 1067 (1962); *Empire Securities Corporation,* 40 SEC 1104, 1105 (1962); *Michael J. Bogan, Jr.,* SEC Securities Exchange Act Release No. 6810, May 23, 1962, p. 2; *Palombi Securities Co., Inc.,* SEC Securities Exchange Act Release No. 6961, Nov. 30, 1962, p. 7. *George H. Hildebrand,* SEC Securities Exchange Act Release No. 7039, March 21, 1963, p. 2;

of the regulation, 12 CFR 220.6(k), holds that a non-compliance with the rule as the result of innocent mistake is not a violation, the creditor has the burden of establishing good faith, a heavy burden which is not met either by a plea of unusual volume of business and consequent inadequate and inexperienced help,[53] or by the claim of reliance on alleged informal, unwritten Commission staff opinion or indefinite opinion of counsel.[54]

The discussion of Regulation T in this chapter has been with the basic purpose of conveying its salient features in broad outline. For precise details the regulation itself should be consulted.[55]

Proposals for the amendment of Section 7 of the Act in various particulars and for action by rule by the Board of Governors of the Federal Reserve System are the subject of recommendations in the Special Study Report.[56]

Sec. 9-5. Special restrictions as to new issues. Apart from the restrictions of Section 7 of the Act and Regulation T as to the extending, maintaining, and arranging for the extension or maintenance of credit, there is an additional restriction imposed as to such activities by a broker-dealer in respect of a new issue of non-exempted securities as to which the broker-dealer is or has been a participant in a distribution. This is the limitation imposed by Section 11(d)(1) of the Act upon a participant in such distribution

---

A. T. Brod & Company, SEC Securities Exchange Act Release No. 7139, Sept. 11, 1963, p. 2.

[53] *Ross Securities, Inc., supra,* n. 52.

[54] *Palombi Securities Co., Inc. supra,* n. 52.

[55] For an illuminating exposition of Regulation T, see Bogen & Kroos, *Evolution of Security Credit Regulation* (1960), pp. 99-113, 125-6.

Although the Commission has the function of enforcing Regulation T (Section 21 of the Act), the Board of Governors of the Federal Reserve System provides an interpretative advisory service. It has a standing request that any inquiry relative to the regulation be addressed to the national securities exchange of which the person making the request is a member or the facilities of which are used for his transactions or, if this be not practicable, that the inquiry be directed to the Federal Reserve Bank of the district in which the inquiry arises.

Apart from the sanctions imposed by statute for willful violations of the provisions of the Act and the rules promulgated under its authority, it may be that a broker-dealer extending, maintaining, or arranging for credit to or for a customer in violation of Regulation T would have to respond in damages to the customer if the customer could establish that the violation was the proximate cause for his losses. See *Remar* v. *Clayton Securities Corporation,* 81 F. Supp. 1014 (D. Mass. 1949); *Appel* v. *Levine,* 85 F. Supp. 240 (S.D.N.Y. 1948); *Kook* v. *Crang,* 182 Fed. Supp. 388 (S.D.N.Y. 1960); *Reader* v. *Hirsch & Co.,* 197 F. Supp. 111 (S.D.N.Y. 1961); *Warshow* v. *Hentz & Co.,* 199 F. Supp. 581 (S.D.N.Y. 1961); cf. *Meisel* v. *North Jersey Trust Co.,* 218 F. Supp. 274 (S.D.N.Y. 1963).

[56] *Special Study Report,* Pt. 4, Ch. X, pp. 37-39.

who engages in business both as broker and a dealer.[57] This section provides in substance that it is unlawful for such a broker-dealer directly or indirectly to extend, maintain, or arrange to extend or maintain, credit to or for a customer "on any security" (other than an exempted security) which was part of a new issue, in the distribution "of which he participated as a member of a selling syndicate or group within thirty days prior to such transaction. . ."[58] Thus, apart from the specific exceptions noted below, an underwriter or selling group member may not extend, maintain, or arrange for credit in respect of a security distributed by him as part of a new issue until thirty days have elapsed from his last sale of part of the new issue.

Examination into some of the points covered by Section 11(d)(1) might be advanced if the basic purpose of the provision be explored. The provision appears as part of a section entitled, "Segregation and Limitation of Functions of Members, Brokers and Dealers." In brief, the section is concerned with safeguarding public investors against risks inherent from dealing with a person who acts as both broker and dealer. In particular, Section 11(d)(1) was directed ". . . at one of the greatest potential evils attributable to the combination of the broker and dealer functions in the same person by prohibiting him from aiding his customer to buy

---

[57] In actual terms, the limitation is imposed upon a member of a national securities exchange who is both a broker and dealer and upon any person who both as a broker and a dealer transacts a business in securities through the medium of a member or otherwise. It has already been seen that, for all practical purposes, this will reach all but a very few persons engaged in business as a broker and dealer. *Supra*, Sec. 4-1.

It is plain, however, that, if a person transacts business only as a dealer and never as a broker, the Section 11(d)(1) restrictions do not apply to any transactions by him. *Letter of Philip A. Loomis, Jr., Director, Division of Trading and Exchanges of Securities and Exchange Commission,* March 5, 1962 CCH Fed. Sec. L. Rep. No. 76, 840.

But if the dealer is a specially created wholly owned subsidiary of a broker-dealer which acts as broker, the form of the arrangement would give way to substance and the Section 11(d)(1) restrictions would be applied. SEC Securities Exchange Act Release No. 6726, Feb. 8, 1962, p. 2.

[58] Stated in the jurisdictional terms set forth in the statute, it is unlawful for such a broker-dealer to engage in the proscribed activities "through the use of any facility of a national securities exchange or of the mails or of any means or instrumentality of interstate commerce, or otherwise in the case of a member [of a national securities exchange] . . ." The section grants an exception in the case of a C.O.D. transaction if delivery and full payment are effected within 35 days, comparable to the C.O.D. exception provided by Section 4(c)(5) of Regulation T discussed *supra* at Sec. 9-4, n. 45 and accompanying text.

The question as to what is meant by a "new issue" will be discussed shortly below in the text.

on credit securities which he has undertaken to distribute to the public. . ."[59] Unlike the provisions of Section 7(c) of the Act and Regulation T, the Section 11(d)(1) restrictions have thus not been imposed to fit in with the nation's credit structure as a whole or to serve a broad economic purpose. Rather, it is with public investor protection with which Section 11(d)(1) is specially concerned. And the Board of Governors of the Federal Reserve System has no functions with reference to it.

What is a "new issue"? This term manifestly encompasses all primary distributions.[60] And it has been viewed as including all secondary distributions[61] which follow within a short time transactions which have the practical effect of facilitating the distribution of the security. Thus, stock splits or other reclassifications, recapitalizations or reorganizations which occur shortly before the distribution may be regarded as creating a "new issue" for the purposes of Section 11(d)(1).[62]

There are some exemptions from the application of Section 11(d)(1) which are provided by rule directed at situations viewed as not being within the purpose of the section.[63] The restriction does not apply if the customer in good faith and without subterfuge purchases the security elsewhere and then places it in the customer's general account with the broker-dealer;[64] nor does it

---

[59] SEC *Report On The Feasibility and Advisability Of the Complete Segregation Of the Functions of Dealer and Broker* (1936), p. 56. It is the Commission's view that Section 11(d)(1) was intended to "xx discourage any tendency on the part of members who bring out new issues to place such issues in the margin accounts of customers." *Idem.* at p. 57.

[60] A primary distribution is an original offering by an issuer to the public of an issue of securities, the consideration for which is received directly or indirectly (as by a firm commitment underwriting) by the issuer. *Idem.* at p. 185.

[61] A secondary distribution refers to the sale of all or part of an issue of securities which was previously the subject of a primary distribution. *Ibid.* In brief, it is a distribution in respect of which the issuer does not receive the proceeds directly or indirectly.

[62] See Loomis *The Securities Exchange Act of 1934 And The Investment Advisers Act of 1940*, 28 Geo. Wash. L. Rev. (1959) p. 234 n. 6. On somewhat the same approach, the distribution by a seller who would be an underwriter within the meaning of Section 2(11) of the Securities Act of 1933 would probably be regarded as involving a new issue within the meaning of that term as used in Section 11(d) (1). A "new issue" is also involved in situations which arise from securities issued upon the exercise of warrants or upon the exercise of conversion privileges. Shares of open end investment companies (mutual funds) are constantly the subject of primary distribution by the issuer. Loans arranged by a broker-dealer to a customer for life insurance premiums for life insurance sold in connection with the sale of mutual fund shares represent credit arranged for the customer in connection with a "new issue."

[63] Rule 11d1-1.

[64] *Idem.* at paragraph (a).

extend to a security acquired by the customer in exchange for an outstanding security of the same issuer on which credit was lawfully maintained at the time of the exchange,[65] and the credit restriction has no application if the customer is a broker or dealer or bank.[66] Moreover, if the security is acquired by a customer through the exercise of a right evidenced by a warrant or certificate expiring within 90 days after issuance, there are no Section 11(d)(1) credit restrictions if the right was originally issued to the customer as stockholder of the corporation issuing the security on which credit is to be extended.[67]

Finally, there is an exemption from Section 11(d)(1) prohibitions within narrow limits in cases where the "new issue" consists of additional units of the same class as units which are already outstanding and not subject to the restriction. The exemption refers to a security of such a "mixed class" if the class is not "predominantly new"; that is, if the "new issue" amounts to less than 50 percent of all of the securities of the same class which will be outstanding after the distribution is completed.[68] In the case of such a predominantly old issue, the Section 11(d)(1) restriction will not apply to a broker-dealer who sells the security to a customer or buys it for the customer's account "on a day when he is not participating in the distribution of any new issue of such security."[69] According to paragraph (e) of Rule 11d1-1 a "broker

---

[65] *Idem.* at paragraph (b). This applies, of course, only to an exchange of securities by the same issuer, and not to an offer by one issuer to the security holders of another issuer to exchange securities.

[66] *Idem.* at paragraph (c).

[67] *Idem.* at paragraph (d). In other words, this exemption would not apply to a person who purchased the right from someone else. However, a right is deemed to have been issued to the customer as stockholder of the company if he actually owned the stock giving rise to the right when the right accrued, even if the stock was not registered in the customer's name. On this point the broker-dealer acting in good faith may rely on a signed statement of the customer. *Ibid.* Securities acquired by a customer on the exercise of rights issued to him as stockholder of a company distributing the security to effectuate the reorganization provisions of the Public Utility Holding Company Act of 1935 are also not subject to the restriction. *Ibid.*

[68] SEC Securities Exchange Act Release No. 4404, Feb. 4, 1948; Paragraph (e) of Rule 11d1-1.

[69] Paragraph (e) of Rule 11d1-1. It may be noted that the Section 11(d)(1) prohibition as to a particular broker-dealer participant in a distribution extends to 30 days after he has completed his participation in the distribution. The effect of the paragraph (e) exemption is thus to eliminate this 30-day waiting period as to a broker-dealer who has sold his entire participation, provided, as will be seen in the text, he does not otherwise remain a participant in the distribution. One effect of the paragraph (e) exemption relates to a broker-dealer, not otherwise a participant in a rights offering of a predominantly old issue, who accepts recurrent

or dealer shall be deemed to be participating in the distribution of a new issue if (1) he owns, directly or indirectly, any undistributed security of such issue, or (2) he is engaged in any stabilizing activities to facilitate a distribution of such issue, or (3) he is a party to any syndicate agreement under which such stabilizing activities are being or may be undertaken,[70] or (4) he is a party to an executory agreement to purchase or distribute such issue."[71]

---

lay-offs of the new security from an underwriter and disposes of such new security. The restriction does not apply on such days as the broker-dealer has no unsold portion of the new issue and is not otherwise participating in the distribution in the manner specified in paragraph (e) as pointed out directly below in the text.

It may be observed that, if an underwriter of a predominantly old issue as defined in paragraph (e) is no longer participating in the distribution of the new issue within the intendment of that paragraph, the underwriter, also, is relieved of the thirty-day restriction of Section 11(d)(1).

[70] [Author's note] The subject of "stabilizing" will be discussed *infra* at Sec. 13-18.

[71] If the underwriting agreement has been terminated except for the covering of a short position remaining after all offered securities have been sold, it may be that the agreement is no longer viewed as executory.

PART IV

SPECIAL ANTI-FRAUD PROVISIONS TO PREVENT SPECIFIC FRAUDULENT PRACTICES

CHAPTER 10

PRELIMINARY OBSERVATIONS

Sec. 10-1. Provisions—in general. In one sense, it may be said that all rules governing the conduct of broker-dealers are designed to protect the investing public against fraud and over-reaching. Apart from net capital requirements and the credit restrictions, the regulations we have already met have in the main been concerned with providing for and giving access to basic information as to the activities of broker-dealers. Adherence to these basic requirements is essential to enable the Commission to resort to records to test broker-dealers' observance of standards fashioned to protect the public investor. But broker-dealer fraud can take many forms which may or may not be reflected in the filings or the books, records, or financial reports.[1] Consequently, apart from the filing requirements, the net capital, bookkeeping, and reporting rules, and Regulation T credit restrictions, the direct thrust of broker-dealer regulation is in the area of fraud prevention.[2]

The federal securities laws contain a number of provisions declaring it unlawful by jurisdictional means to engage in sales or purchases of securities by means of fraud or deception in any conceivable form. All of these are applicable to broker-dealers among others, and some, by their terms, apply only to brokers and dealers. In engaging in any fraudulent, deceptive, or manipulative conduct in carrying on its business, therefore, a broker-dealer would be violating a number of separate prohibitions applicable to the same activity.

Typical of the broad sweep of the general anti-fraud and

---

[1] It has been said that: "The business of trading in securities is one in which the opportunities for dishonesty are of constant recurrence and ever present. . . ."; and that the frauds to be dealt with in this field ". . . may take on more subtle and involved forms than those in which dishonesty manifests itself in cruder and less specialized activities . . .". *Archer* v. *SEC,* 133 F.2d 795, 803 (8th Cir. 1943).

[2] This, of course, is the ultimate objective of the credit restrictions provided for by Section 11(d)(1) of the Act mentioned *supra* at Sec. 9-5; and, also, of the net capital requirements, *supra,* Sections 8-1 to 8-8.

anti-manipulative provision is Section 15(c)(1) of the Act[3] as implemented by Rule 15cl-2 which provides:

(a) The term "manipulative, deceptive, or other fraudulent device or contrivance," as used in Section 15(c)(1) of the Act, is hereby defined to include any act, practice, or course of business which operates or would operate as a fraud or deceit upon any person.

(b) The term "manipulative, deceptive, or other fraudulent device or contrivance," as used in Section 15(c)(1) of the Act, is hereby defined to include any untrue statement of a material fact and any omission to state a material fact necessary in order to make the statements made, in the light of the circumstances under which they are made, not misleading, which statement or omission is made with knowledge or reasonable grounds to believe that it is untrue or misleading.

(c) The scope of this rule shall not be limited by any specific definitions of the term "manipulative, deceptive, or other fraudulent device or contrivance" contained in other rules adopted pursuant to Section 15(c)(1) of the Act.[4]

The full sweep of these and other general anti-fraud provisions will be discussed later.[5] What will be taken up at this point are special provisions directed at specific types of activity which may arise in the conduct of the business of a broker-dealer. These provisions relate to certain practices which experience has shown

---

[3] This section provides: "No broker or dealer shall make use of the mails or of any means or instrumentality of interstate commerce to effect any transaction in or to induce the purchase or sale of, any security (other than commercial paper, bankers' acceptances, or commercial bills) otherwise than on a national securities exchange, by means of any manipulative, deceptive, or other fraudulent device or contrivance. The Commission shall, for the purposes of this sub-section, by rules and regulations define such devices or contrivances as are manipulative, deceptive or otherwise fraudulent."

[4] Particular note should be made of this last proviso as set forth in paragraph (c) of the rule. It may be observed that, conversely, any specific activity defined in rules and regulations under Section 15(c)(1) of the Act as a manipulative, deceptive, or other fraudulent device or contrivance would come within the compass of Rule 15cl-2 absent such more precise definition. See *Norris & Hirshberg, Inc.*, 21 SEC 865 (1946) at p. 89, n. 31. It may also be noted that another anti-fraud regulation, Rule 10b-5 under Section 10(b), which is in terms and effect as sweeping as Rule 15cl-2, applies to all persons, including broker-dealers and to all transactions in non-exempted securities, whether or not registered for listing on a national securities exchange and whether or not effected on such an exchange. Finally, as regards offers to sell and sales of any security by jurisdictional means, Section 17(a) of the Securities Act of 1933 is as broad in its anti-fraud and anti-manipulative reach as Sections 10(b) and 15(c)(1) of the Securities Exchange Act of 1934 and Rules 10b-5 and 15cl-2 thereunder. *Norris & Hirshberg, supra,* and see *Charles Hughes & Co. v. SEC,* 139 F.2d 434 (2d Cir. 1943). All of these general anti-fraud provisions will be discussed in greater detail below. See *infra,* Sec. 18-3.

[5] *Infra,* Sec. 18-3.

have been used as devices for fleecing unsophisticated and trusting customers. Such practices, it will be seen, are dealt with by the Act and the rules through the root and branch type of approach which concentrates on the general adverse effect of these practices on the public, as distinguished from whether, in given cases, there is claimed absence of harm or of evil motivation.

One group of rules is directed to the protection of customers against dangers inherent in certain normal operations of the securities business. In this category are the standards laid down with reference to the hypothecation of securities of customers. Another collection of rules is concerned with the special trust and confidence which exists as between some customers and their broker-dealers. These are designed to guard against breaches of fiduciary obligations. Certain manipulative and deceptive techniques and practices have in the past been employed in the effectuation of distributions of securities. A number of rules are accordingly directed to those activities. Manipulative and deceptive devices and practices employed in the past by some broker-dealers in the sale of securities irrespective of their being the subject of a distribution are also the subject of rules designed to eliminate such evils. Finally, a number of representations implicit in the conduct of the business of a broker-dealer will be examined. Failure to measure up to these is regarded as a violation of anti-fraud rules.

Following a discussion of various specific rules and related standards as they refer uniquely to the conduct of a business as a broker-dealer, references will be made to the more general types of fraud frequently recurring in securities transactions by persons who may or may not be broker-dealers.[6]

---

[6] *Ibid.*

CHAPTER 11

HYPOTHECATION RULES

Sec. 11-1. Rules—in general. In the discussion as to margin requirements, it has been seen that one aspect of the business of a broker-dealer is the extension and maintenance of credit to and for customers for the purchasing and carrying of securities. These securities, it will be recalled, are placed in the general account maintained for the customer and are taken by the broker-dealer as collateral for the indebtedness of the customer.[1] In turn, it is the practice of the broker-dealer to rehypothecate such securities to procure cash needed in the operations of his business. Additionally, in order to facilitate his own trading and speculation in securities, or merely to raise cash for other business purposes, the broker-dealer will hypothecate securities which he owns and in which he maintains a position.

This practice of the business relative to the rehypothecation and hypothecation of securities is dealt with in a set of rules known as the hypothecation rules.[2] These rules contain three basic prohibitions. First, securities carried for the account of any customer may not be commingled under a lien with securities carried for the account of any other customer, unless the broker-dealer has previously obtained the written consent to such hypothecation from each such customer.[3] Secondly, there is a flat prohibition against the commingling of securities carried for the account of a customer with securities carried for the account of a

---

[1] See *supra,* Sec. 9-2.

[2] Rule 8c-1 and Rule 15c2-1 under the Act. Each rule is identical with the other except for introductory language bringing it within the framework of the jurisdictional design of the section of the Act under which it was adopted. The net effect of the combined jurisdictional sweep of both rules, however, is to bring virtually every broker and dealer within the compass of either the one or the other rule. Since both rules are paragraphed and subdivided identically, the paragraphs and subdivisions will be referred to for convenience as though only a single rule were involved.

[3] Paragraph (a)(1) of the rule. See *Joe Bert Sissom,* SEC Securities Exchange Act Release No. 7021, Feb. 11, 1963, p. 1. The term "customer" as stated in paragraph (b)(1) of the rule does not include any general or special partner or any director or officer of the broker-dealer, or any participant as such in any joint, group, or syndicate account with the broker-dealer or any of its partners, officers, or directors.

person not a customer under a lien for a loan made to the broker-dealer.[4] The normal impact of this restriction is the prohibition of hypothecation of securities of the broker-dealer with securities carried for the account of a customer under the same lien given by the broker-dealer to collateralize his own loan. The third activity proscribed is the hypothecation of securities carried for the account of customers to secure a loan which exceeds the aggregate indebtedness of all customers of the broker-dealer arising out of the securities carried for their accounts.[5]

Each of these prohibitions has exceptions to take out of its scope certain types of transactions that do not involve the dangers which the rule was cast to prevent. Before referring to these, however, it may be helpful to discuss the prohibitions in the light of the conditions they are designed to correct and to study the definitions of certain terms used in the rule.

In adopting the hypothecation rules, the Commission had as its broad purpose to "prohibit brokers and dealers from risking the securities of their customers as collateral to finance their own trading, speculating, or underwriting ventures."[6] Securities carried for the account of a customer in a "special cash account" as that term is defined by Section 4(c) of Regulation T[7] would not ordinarily be the subject of a written consent by the customer to the commingling of such securities with securities carried for the account of other customers. With minor exceptions noted below as to certain mechanics of a transaction in a customer's special cash account, no proper basis normally exists for subjecting to any

---

4 Paragraph (a)(2) of the rule. For an example of the application of this provision of the rule in the context of a proceeding for the revocation of the registration of a broker-dealer, see *First Securities Company*, 40 SEC 462, 464 (1961); and *Joe Bert Sissom*, SEC Securities Exchange Act Release No. 7021, Feb. 11, 1963, p. 1.

5 Paragraph (a)(3) of the rule. The Commission has under consideration the recommendation of the *Special Study Report* for rules requiring a "reasonable relationship" between the amount of each customer's securities that can be hypothecated or lent by a broker-dealer and the amount of the particular customer's indebtedness. See *Special Study Report*, Pt. 1, Ch. III-D, p. 415, and see Special Market Study, Release No. 25, April 30, 1963, p. 5. The present rule is a restriction on the over-all amount which can be borrowed on customers' securities in relation to aggregate indebtedness of all customers. However, improper use of customers' free or excess securities would violate general anti-fraud provisions. See *infra*, Sec. 16-9.

6 SEC Securities Exchange Act Release No. 2690, Nov. 15, 1940, p. 1. This is consonant with the Congressional intent of Section 8(c) of the Act, which is one of the sources of the Commission's rule-making power on the subject. See Sen. Rep. No. 792, 73rd Cong., 2d Sess. (1934), p. 11; H.R. Rep. No. 1303, 73rd Cong., 2d Sess. (1934), p. 20.

7 See *supra*, Sec. 9-4.

lien securing a loan to a broker-dealer any security carried for a customer in a special cash account. On the other hand, it has been seen that broker-dealers ordinarily have to rehypothecate securities carried on margin. Accordingly, the usual agreement between broker-dealer and customer will contain the consent of the customer to the commingling of securities carried for his account with securities carried for the account of other customers.[8]

It needs no demonstration that a broker-dealer who commingles his own securities with those of his customers under a single lien would be doing so to borrow an amount in excess of that needed to refinance the credit he has extended to and maintained for customers. The excess would represent borrowings by the broker-dealer to finance his own position and trading in securities. Thus, such a commingling would present the danger that should the broker-dealer experience financial difficulties, the securities of customers would be subject to the same risk of loss as those of the broker-dealer.[9] The basis for the prohibition against such commingling is therefore manifest.

When a broker-dealer borrows a sum of money on his customers' securities in excess of the amount of their aggregate indebtedness to him in respect of securities carried for their accounts, it is similarly quite plain that he is unduly jeapordizing the securities of his customers. In effect, he would be using securities of his customers to raise cash for an amount exceeding the sum required to refinance the credit he extends to and maintains for customers. Thus, with minor exceptions noted below, a broker-dealer may not permit securities carried for the account of customers to be hypothecated for a sum which exceeds the aggregate

---

[8] See National Association of Securities Dealers, Inc., *Explanatory Memorandum Re SEC Rules X-8C-1 and X-15C2-1 Which Govern The Pledging Of Securities As Collateral By Over-The Counter Brokers and Dealers,* February 6, 1941 (NASD 2-6-41), p. E21. The usual agreement also contains the written consent of the customer to the lending of securities carried for the account of the customer. Absent such written consent, the lending of such securities by a broker-dealer is prohibited. Section 8(d) of the Act. The Commission has under consideration the recommendation of the Special Study Report to adopt rules safeguarding the interests of customers with respect to the power of the broker-dealer to borrow or lend securities representing excess margin or fully paid securities. *Special Study Report,* Pt. 1, Ch. III-D, p. 415, and see SEC Special Market Study Release No. 25, April 30, 1963, p. 5. See Appendix O for a copy of the "Customer's Agreement" prepared by the Association of Stock Exchange Firms, a form currently recommended by that Association as conforming to industry needs and legal requirements. Sec. 25-15, *infra.*

[9] SEC Securities Exchange Act Release No. 2690, Nov. 15, 1940, p. 2.

indebtedness of all customers in respect of securities carried for their accounts.[10]

Following a reference to the meaning of the terms, "aggregate indebtedness" and "securities carried for the account of a customer" as used in the rule, the circumstances may then be examined as to the availability of specific exemptions from the enumerated prohibitions.

Sec. 11-2. Definitions—aggregate indebtedness. "Aggregate indebtedness" is, first, the aggregate of all of the debits in the accounts of customers carried by the broker-dealer "in respect of securities carried for their accounts." This amount is not reduced by any uncleared customer's checks despite the fact that a bookkeeping entry may reflect payment and consequent reduction of the customer's indebtedness upon receipt of the check as distinguished from actual collection.[11] In the case of two accounts, one of which guarantees the other, both accounts are to be considered as a single account and treated on a consolidated basis.[12] And, in the case of accounts in which both long and short positions are carried, "aggregate indebtedness" includes the amount equal to the market value of the securities short in such accounts.[13]

Sec. 11-3. Definitions—securities carried for account of customers. "Securities carried for the account of any customer" includes (1) securities received by or on behalf of the broker-dealer for the account of a customer; (2) securities sold to and "appropriated" by the broker-dealer to a customer; and (3) securities sold to, but not appropriated by the broker-dealer to, a customer who has made any payment therefore, to the extent that the

---

[10] Paragraph (a)(3) of the rule. It may be observed that without reference to the prohibition of the rule as it relates to aggregate indebtedness, the hypothecation of fully paid for customers' securities and the rehypothecation of margined securities for larger amounts than those owed by customers as to such securities has been held to constitute a fraudulent, manipulative, and deceptive practice in violation of Section 17(a)(3) of the Securities Act of 1933, *SEC* v. *Lawson*, 24 F. Supp. 360, 361-3 (D.M.D. 1938). See also *Investment Registry of America, Inc.*, 21 SEC 745, 752 (1946). In this connection, see the discussion below on this type of conduct as it relates to one aspect of the shingle theory. *Infra*, Sec. 16-9.

[11] Paragraph (b)(3) of the rule; and see SEC Securities Exchange Act Release No. 2690, Nov. 15, 1940, p. 10. In this way a broker-dealer is afforded a reasonable time between receipt of a check from a customer and its clearance in which he can effect a corresponding reduction in loans collateralized by securities of customers. *Ibid.*

[12] *Ibid.*

[13] *Ibid.*

broker-dealer owns or has received delivery of securities of like kind.[14] However, where the broker-dealer as principal has appropriated a security to a customer or has sold a security he owns to a customer, and the security is subject to a lien, it does not become a security "carried for the account of a customer" pending release from the lien, it being the broker-dealer's obligation, however, to release such lien as "promptly as practicable."[15] This latter proviso is best understood when it is appreciated that paragraph (a)(2) of the rule absolutely prohibits the commingling of securities owned by a broker-dealer under the same lien as a security "carried for the account of any customer." But, by definition[16] securities "carried for the account of any customer" include securities appropriated to a customer, or for which the customer has paid and which the broker-dealer owns or has received. If the securities in question were, at the time of appropriation or payment by the customer, subject to a lien securing a loan to the broker-dealer, the latter would then be commingling his own securities under the same lien as securities carried for the account of a customer and would be in violation of paragraph (a)(2) of the rule. To avoid this, the rule provides that, if the security owned by the broker-dealer for which the customer has paid or if the security appropriated to the customer, is subject to a lien, it is not regarded as a security carried for the account of a customer pending release from the lien as promptly as practicable.[17]

Sec. 11-4. Exemptions—miscellaneous. Consistent with the broad objectives of the rule as outlined, it contains a number of

---

[14] Paragraph (b)(2)(i)(ii) and (iii) of the rule. Apart from special arrangements which may govern special situations in the case of a dealer's transaction in which there is no agreement as to the time, method, and place of delivery, or in which prompt delivery is for some reason not contemplated, securities will be deemed "appropriated" to a customer, and therefore be securities carried for the account of the customer, "when the dealer segregates, identifies or otherwise earmarks the securities sold either by tagging them, by placing them in an envelope for the customer or by identifying them by some other means, such as a bookkeeping entry, in the customer's account, of the certificate numbers of the securities sold to him. . . ." SEC Securities Exchange Act Release No. 2822, March 17, 1941, p. 2.

[15] Subdivision (iii) of paragraph (b)(2) of the rule. SEC Securities Exchange Act Release No. 2690, Nov. 15, 1940, pp. 9-10. When the broker-dealer receives payment for the sale of, or has appropriated, the security, he must effectuate release of the lien "as soon as possible" in the light of all the surrounding facts and circumstances, such as the size of the firm and its staff, the scope of its operations, the volume of business and the physical, practical, and geographical limitations. *Idem.* at p. 11. See *Morrison Bond Co., Ltd.*, 11 SEC 125, 130-1 (1942); *W. F. Coley*, 31 SEC 722, 723-8 (1956); *Carl J. Bliedung*, 38 SEC 518. 522-3 (1958).

[16] Paragraph (b)(2)(ii) and (iii) of the rule. SEC Securities Exchange Act Release No. 2690, Nov. 15, 1940, pp. 9-10.

[17] *Ibid.*

exemptions and exceptions which take into account temporary exigencies which arise from the manner in which the business of a broker-dealer is normally conducted.

It has just been seen that, pending release from a lien collateralizing an obligation of a broker-dealer, a security is not carried for the account of a customer, despite either the appropriation of it by the broker-dealer to the customer or the payment by the customer in the case where the broker-dealer owns or has received delivery of a security of like kind.

In defining "aggregate indebtedness," the rule contains an exemption from the prohibition against hypothecating the securities of customers to secure a sum which exceeds the aggregate indebtedness of all customers in respect of securities carried for their accounts. This is to take care of the exceptional situation where customers' indebtedness is suddenly paid off in so great an amount as to use up the broker-dealer's normal "cushion"[18] and thus reduce the total of customers' debit balances below the broker-dealer's current borrowings on securities of customers. The exemption provides that the prohibition shall not be deemed violated by reason of an excess arising on any day through the reduction of the aggregate indebtedness of customers on that same day, provided that, as promptly as practicable after such reduction occurs, funds in an amount sufficient to eliminate the excess are paid or placed in transfer to pledgees to reduce the sum of the liens or claims to which securities carried for the account of customers are subjected.[19]

There is a "clearing house" exemption from the prohibitions

---

[18] ". . . Good brokerage practice alone would make it desirable for a broker to borrow substantially less on customers' securities than customers owe him. There should thus be a 'cushion' of his own capital between the amount of customers' debits and the amount of the broker's bank loans on customers' securities. This 'cushion' should be sufficient in size to absorb any reasonably anticipated reductions in customers' indebtedness." SEC Securities Exchange Act Release No. 2690, Nov. 15, 1940, p. 10.

[19] Paragraph (a)(3) of the rule. It has been seen that the term "as promptly as practicable" means as "soon as possible" in the circumstances. See *supra*, n. 15 and accompanying text. In any event, payments in reduction of the liens to proper size must be made before the lapse of one half hour on the next banking day at the place where the largest of the broker-dealer's loans are payable and, moreover, such payment must be made before the broker-dealer has obtained or increased any bank loan collateralized by securities carried for the account of customers. Paragraphs (a)(3) of the rule.

It may be noted that, in computing the sum of the liens or claims to which securities carried for the account of customers are subject, any rehypothecation by another broker-dealer who is subject to the rule may be disregarded. Paragraph (b)(4) of the rule.

of commingling broker-dealer securities with customers' securities under the same lien and of hypothecating customers' securities in excess of aggregate indebtedness. This relates only to the lien of a clearing corporation or similar department or association of a national securities exchange,[20] and it is limited to a loan made by the clearing house which is incidental to the clearing of transactions in securities, provided that the loan is to be repaid on the same calendar day.[21]

Sec. 11-5. Exemptions—transactions in special cash accounts.
The prohibition against the commingling, absent customers' written consents, of securities carried for the account of a customer under a lien covering securities carried for the account of any other customer has an exemption limited to the hypothecation of securities carried for the account of a customer in a special cash account within the meaning of Section 4(c) of Regulation T.[22] Such exemption arises if ". . . at or before the completion of the transaction of purchase of such securities for, or of sale of such securities to, such customer, written notice is given or sent to such customer disclosing that such securities are or may be hypothecated under circumstances which will permit the commingling thereof with securities carried for the account of other customers. . ."[23] The purpose of this exemption is to take care of

---

[20] Paragraph (d) of the rule.

[21] *Ibid.* This paragraph contains a proviso that the term "aggregate indebtedness" as defined in paragraph (a)(3) of the rule does not include indebtedness in respect of securities which are subject to a clearing house lien exempted by paragraph (d) of the rule. See also SEC Securities Exchange Act Release No. 2690, Nov. 15, 1940, p. 11.

[22] For a discussion of the Special Cash Account, see *supra*, Sec. 9-4.

[23] Paragraph (c) of the rule. It is provided that the term "the completion of the transaction" as used in this rule is to be given the same meaning as in Rule 15C1-1(b) which provides in substance that (1) where a customer purchases a security and makes payment before payment is requested or due, the completion of the transaction occurs when the broker-dealer delivers the security into the account of the customer; or (2) with the exception of the transaction just noted, a transaction is completed, in the case of a customer who purchases a security through or from a broker-dealer, when the customer pays the broker-dealer any part of the purchase price, or, if payment is effected by bookkeeping entry, when the entry is made for any part of the purchase price; or (3) where a customer sells a security through or to a broker-dealer and delivers it prior to the time when delivery is requested or has become due following notification, completion occurs at the time the broker-dealer makes payment to or into the account of the customer; and (4) where, apart from premature delivery of the security as noted, a customer sells a security to or through a broker-dealer (a) if the security is in the custody of the broker-dealer, completion occurs where the security is transferred out of the customer's account, or (b) if the security is not in the custody of the broker-dealer, completion occurs when it is delivered to the broker-dealer.

the need to borrow funds temporarily to finance the purchase for cash of securities purchased for or sold to customers and delivered into their special cash accounts.[24] A typical notice complying with the requirements of the paragraph (c) exemption is set out in the margin.[25] Of course, any lien for such loan may cover only securities carried for the account of customers.[26]

Sec. 11-6. Impact on banking practices—terms of rehypothecation. In discussing and explaining the impact of the rule, the Commission pointed out certain specific conditions existing at the time of its adoption which were intended to be outlawed by paragraphs (a)(2) and (a)(3) of the rule. It was noted that the then typical bank loan agreement contained a provision authorizing rehypothecation by the bank of any collateral deposited by the broker-dealer, alone or with other property, for an amount greater than the broker-dealer's borrowings from the bank. It was furthermore pointed out that upon the effectiveness of the rule such provisions would be outlawed by the paragraph (a)(2) prohibition against commingling under the same lien of securities carried for the account of a customer with securities carried for the account of any person other than a bona fide customer.[27] Such provisions

---

[24] National Association of Securities Dealers, *Explanatory Memorandum Re: SEC Rules X-8C-1 and X-15C2-1 Which Govern The Pledging of Securities as Collateral By Over-The-Counter Brokers and Dealers,* February 6, 1941 (NASD 2-6-41), pp. E-23 and E-24. The borrowing normally takes the form of a "day loan," the proceeds of which are used by the broker-dealer to pay for securities bought for several customers which in turn are delivered to the customers who make payment therefor. All of the securities become securities carried for the account of customers as soon as the broker-dealer receives them from the seller. Paragraph (b)(2)(i) of the rule. They are all also hypothecated or subjected to the lien of the day loan as soon as they are paid for with the proceeds of the day loan. The broker-dealer has therefore pledged and commingled securities carried for the account of several different customers under the same lien and would have to first receive the consent of each customer were it not for the fact that the securities will be placed in the special cash account for each customer, in which case, only proper notice need be given as set forth in the paragraph (c) exemption to the paragraph (a)(1) prohibition.

[25] "The securities above described are or may be hypothecated under circumstances that will permit the commingling thereof with securities carried for the account of other customers. Such hypothecation and commingling, however, shall cease or will have ceased upon payment by you for the above described securities in the amount indicated above and delivery of such securities to you, to your order, or into your account." This notice customarily appears as a printed or stamped legend on the confirmation to the customer which, as will be seen, must be sent to a customer at or before "the completion of the transaction." See *infra,* Sec. 12-2.

[26] Paragraphs (a)(1) and (2) and (c) of the rule.

[27] SEC Securities Exchange Act Release No. 2690, Nov. 15, 1940, pp. 11-13. Of course, the broker-dealer himself is not a bona fide customer. It was also pointed out by the Commission that such rehypothecation provisions would violate the paragraph (a)(3) prohibition against hypothecating securities carried for the account of customers for sums exceeding aggregate indebtedness of customers. *Ibid.*

and others in other blanket loan agreements which had provided for the commingling under the same lien of a broker-dealer's own securities with those carried for the account of any customer were all to be outlawed.[28] It was pointed out in this connection that broker-dealers who pledge customers' securities to refinance the sums as to which credit has been extended to or maintained for customers and who pledge with the same lender their own securities as collateral for their own borrowings must see to it that the pledgee, whether a bank or any other lender, does not have a "cross lien" on customers' securities, as additional collateral for other loans made to the broker-dealer on his own securities or those of other non-customers. In brief, with the minor exception noted directly below, the pledgee may not be given a lien upon customers' securities for any loans except those made against securities carried for the account of customers of the same broker-dealer.[29] However, in this connection, there is an exemption which provides that a broker-dealer's own securities may be subjected to a lien for a loan made against securities carried for the account of customers as additional collateral, provided that the pledgee agrees that the securities which it is informed are carried for the account of customers will be physically segregated from any other securities.[30] To qualify for the description in this exemption of a "loan made against securities for the account of customers," only securities carried for the account of customers may be used to obtain or increase the loan or to be substituted for other securities carried for the account of customers.[31]

Paragraph (e) provides an additional exemption from the paragraph (a)(2) prohibition of commingling securities of a broker-dealer under the same lien with securities carried for the account of a customer. This is simply that the prohibition does not extend "to a lien for a loan and to be repaid on the same calendar day."[32]

Sec. 11-7. Notice and certification requirements. The rule

---

[28] *Ibid.*

[29] *Idem.* at p. 12.

[30] Paragraph (e) of the rule.

[31] The additional collateral thus given by a broker-dealer to a pledgee would be in the nature of a "one way lien," as distinguished from the "cross lien" mentioned in the text.

[32] Subdivision (ii) of paragraph (e). This also gives effect to the practice of day-loan financing by brokers and dealers in the purchase of securities upon customers' orders where the transactions are to be reflected in the special cash accounts of customers. See *supra*, n. 24.

finally contains what is called "Notice and Certification Requirements." Apart from the occasion of day loans which are made and to be repaid on the same day, a broker-dealer may not hypothecate a security carried for the account of a customer unless, at or prior to the time of each such hypothecation, the broker-dealer gives written notice to the pledgee that the security pledged is carried for the account of a customer and that such hypothecation does not contravene any provision of the rule.[33] Exemption from this notice and certification requirement is provided for in the case of an omnibus account carried for the broker-dealer by another broker-dealer, if the broker-dealer for whom such account is carried has furnished a signed statement to the broker-dealer carrying the account, that all securities carried in that account will be carried for the account of customers and that the hypothecation of such securities by the broker-dealer for whom such account is carried will not contravene any provision of the rule.[34]

---

[33] Paragraph (f) of the rule.

[34] Paragraph (f) of the rule. We have seen that the omnibus account is one of the special accounts provided for by Regulation T. Section 4(b) of Regulation T. 12 CFR 220.4(b). See Sec. 9-3, *supra,* for discussion of the omnibus account. The signed statement is usually made in a form commonly in use known as the Omnibus Account Agreement made between the broker-dealer for whom the account is carried and the broker-dealer carrying the account.

Chapter 12

RULES OF CONDUCT BASED UPON FIDUCIARY RELATIONSHIP

Sec. 12-1. General observations of relationship. In the discussion of the credit restrictions imposed by Section 11(d)(1) of the Act, we noted the concern of Congress with the need for protecting public investors in dealing with a person who functions as both a broker and dealer.[1] In a number of rulings, the Commission has held that, if under all the circumstances a broker-dealer has the relationship of "agent" to his customers, he is a "broker" as to such customer.[2] The circumstances which result in the existence of an agency relationship may vary, but in essence, apart from explicit assumption by a broker-dealer of the obligations of agent, they add up to a course of dealings designed to engender trust and confidence in the broker-dealer and heavy reliance by customers on the broker-dealer's advice. This may be achieved, for example, by the assumption on the part of the broker-dealer of the role of investment adviser[3] or by conduct inducing feeble or unsophisticated customers to have "implicit," "blind," or "perfect" faith in the broker-dealer and his recommendations.[4] However the relationship may arise, the broker-

---

[1] *Supra*, Sec. 9-5, and see Sen. Rep. No. 792, 73rd Cong. 2d Sess. (1934), p. 11. In the Commission's 1936 *Report on the Feasibility and Advisability of the Complete Segregation of the Functions of Dealer and Broker,* the Commission advised against such complete segregation in favor of the imposition of controls to eliminate the evils of the commingling. *Idem.* at pp. 109-114. Consequently, all regulations of brokers and dealers are predicated on the assumption of such commingling of activities.

[2] See *Arleen W. Hughes,* 27 SEC 629 and 952 (1948); *Oxford Company, Inc.,* 21 SEC 681 (1946). *Investment Registry of America, Inc.,* 21 SEC 745 (1946); *Norris & Hirshberg, Inc.,* 21 SEC 865 (1946). *Investment Service Co.,* SEC Securities Exchange Act Release No. 6884, Aug. 15, 1962, pp. 8-9. It will be recalled *supra,* Sec. 1-1, that the definition of broker in Section 3(a)(4) of the Act refers to a "person engaged in effecting transactions in securities for the account of others. . ."

[3] *Arleen W. Hughes,* 27 SEC 629 and 952 (1948). And see SEC Investment Advisers Act Release No. 40, Feb. 5, 1945, p. 2.

[4] *Norris & Hirshberg, Inc.,* 21 SEC 865, 881-882 (1946). And see *Gill-Harkness & Co.,* 38 SEC 646, 650 (1958), where the trust and confidence engendered was such that customers made loans to the broker-dealer. And see *J. Logan & Co.,* SEC Securities Exchange Act Release No. 6848, July 9, 1962. p. 10 at n. 17. See also *Investment Service Co.,* SEC Securities Exchange Act Release No. 6884, Aug. 15, 1962, pp. 8-9,

dealer is regarded as having the obligations of a fiduciary;[5] he is precluded from assuming an adverse role in his dealings with the customer in the absence of consent following full disclosure of any adverse interest and of such other information possessed by the broker-dealer as the customer should have to make an informed determination with respect to such dealings. Thus, if the broker-dealer engages in a sale of securities he owns to a customer to whom he has a fiduciary obligation, he must inform the customer of the cost to the broker-dealer[6] and the best price at which the securities could be obtained with due diligence in the open market.[7] A broker-dealer having an agency relationship, moreover, must make specific disclosures of the nature already mentioned in connection with each separate transaction;[8] as ". . . only specific and informed consent of the customer prior to the completion of the transaction . . .";[9] or "explicit and informed ratification afterwards . . ."[10] can operate to discharge the fiduciary of full responsibility. Non-action by the customer is not such ratification, despite a claim that the broker-dealer's confirmation purported to show the adverse interest.[11]

In keeping with these basic tenets, Congress and the Commission adopted special provisions on the subject of confirmations of transactions by broker-dealers with their customers. In addition, the Commission has adopted special standards of conduct applicable to broker-dealers in the handling of discretionary accounts.

---

aff'd 319 F.2d 340 (8th Cir. 1963), where the agency relationship arose from actual assumption of that role by a broker agreeing to execute a customer's order.

5 *Ibid.*

6 It would not satisfy the fiduciary's obligation merely to disclose the prevailing price of the security. His own lower cost at an earlier date would still have to be disclosed.

7 *Oxford Company, Inc.*, 21 SEC 681, 692 (1946); *Hughes* v. *SEC*, 174 F.2d 969, 975-6 (DC. Cir. 1949); *Alm & Co.*, 36 SEC 279, 282-3 (1955); SEC Investment Advisers Act Release No. 40, Feb. 5, 1945, p. 2 (same as Securities Exchange Act Release No. 3653). In *Investment Service Co.*, SEC Securities Exchange Act Release No. 6884, Aug. 15, 1962, pp. 8-9, aff'd 319 F.2d 340 (8th Cir. 1963), the breach of fiduciary obligation arose from the failure of the broker to execute an order for a customer to sell a specified number of shares of stock at 50 cents a share "at the earliest possible date" when, shortly following receipt of the order, the broker sold shares of the same stock out of its inventory at prices higher than 50 cents a share, thus competing with its customer rather than giving precedence to the customer's order.

8 SEC Investment Advisers Act Release No. 40, *supra*, n. 7, at p. 3.

9 *Investment Registry of America, Inc.*, 21 SEC 745, 757 (1946).

10 *Oxford Company, Inc.*, 21 SEC 681, 692 (1946).

11 *Ibid.* and see *Hughes* v. *SEC*, 174 F.2d 969 (D.C. Cir. 1949).

Sec. 12-2. Confirmation requirements—in general. Under Section 11(d)(2) of the Act, a member of a national securities exchange who is both a broker and a dealer, or any person who transacts a business in securities as both a broker and dealer and transacts such business through the medium of such a member, is prohibited from using jurisdictional means to effect any transaction[12] with respect to any non-exempted security unless, if the transaction is with a customer, the broker-dealer discloses to the customer in writing at or before the completion of the transaction whether he is acting as a dealer for his own account, as a broker for such customer, or as a broker for some other person.

Rule 15c1-4 under the Act applies to transactions over-the-counter[13] by a broker-dealer; it prohibits any act on the part of a broker-dealer designed to effect with or for the account of any customer[14] any transaction in, or to induce the purchase or sale by such customer of any security without giving or sending to the customer at or before the completion of each such transaction a written notification containing specified disclosures. These are: (1) "whether he is acting as a broker for such customer, as a dealer for his own account, as a broker for some other person, or as a broker for both such customer and some other person;[15] and (2) in any case in which he is acting as a broker for such customer or for both such customer and some other person, either the name of the person from whom the security was purchased or to whom it was sold for such customer, and the date and time when such transaction took place or the fact that such information will be

---

[12] To "effect" a transaction includes any "participation in a transaction whether as principal, agent, or both." SEC Securities Exchange Act Release No. 605, April 17, 1936.

[13] The rule specifically excepts from its operation transactions in United States Tax Savings Notes, United States Defense Savings Stamps, and United States Defense Savings Bonds, Series E, F, and G.

[14] "Customer" refers to any one other than a broker or dealer, and would apply to a person to whom the broker-dealer, if a corporation, sells its own capital stock. See Rule 15c1-1(a) under the Act. Although a bank may perform functions similar to brokers and dealers, we have seen, *supra*, Sec. 1-1, that, by definition, a bank is neither a broker nor dealer. Hence, a bank is a "customer." SEC Securities Exchange Act Release No. 1462, Nov. 15, 1937. For the meaning of the term, "effect" a transaction, see n. 12, *supra*.

[15] [Author's note] When a broker-dealer is acting as agent for both buyer and seller, he must disclose that fact to each of them, and, as provided for by subdivision "(2)" of the rule set forth directly below in the text, the broker-dealer must disclose to each, the commissions received from both. *Mitchell & Company Inc.*, Securities Exchange Act Release No. 7109, Aug. 2, 1963, p. 1.

furnished upon the request of such customer, and the source and amount of any commission or other remuneration received or to be received by him in connection with the transaction."[16]

The written notice called for by Section 11(d)(2) and Rule 15c1-4 is called the "confirmation."[17] Collectively, these provisions are referred to as the "confirmation requirements." Although the information required by Rule 15c1-4 is somewhat more detailed than that called for by Section 11(d)(2), the basic disclosures required are the same in both cases, namely whether the broker-dealer is acting as a principal and thus reveals an adverse interest, or whether he is acting as agent for the customer.[18] If he acts as agent, he is under obligation, as a fiduciary, to secure the best possible price for the customer, he must confirm as agent, and he must divulge all profits obtained.[19] It has been seen that if the broker-dealer is in fact a fiduciary of the customer, he is an agent for the customer and he cannot convert his role into that of an independent principal[20] unless he receives specific, express, informed authorization from the customer as to each such transac-

---

[16] Rule 15c1-4.

[17] The caption employed in connection with Rule 15c1-4 is "Confirmation of Transactions."

[18] See *Fidelity Securities Corporation,* SEC Securities Exchange Act Release No. 6987, January 4, 1963, p. 1.

The Special Study Report recommends that additional information be disclosed in the confirmation such as the circumstances (if the facts warrant) that the broker-dealer is making the only market in the securities he is selling to the customer, that they are being sold out of the broker-dealer's inventory, that there is a spread of 20 percent or more in prevailing interdealer bids, and that (in the case of a sale of less than 100 shares or a sale at a price of less than $500 a share, or $1500 in the aggregate) the broker-dealer as principal will show the best interdealer bid on the opposite side of the transaction, and that representative bid quotations will be disclosed in principal transactions. *Special Study Report,* Pt. 2, Ch. VII, pp. 677-8. And see SEC Special Market Study Release No. 33, April 30, 1963, pp. 5-6.

[19] *Oxford Company, Inc.,* 21 SEC 681, 688-9 (1946).

[20] *Supra,* Sec. 12-1. ". . . it is fundamental that a broker cannot, by a mere form of words employed in a confirmation, transform himself at will into a principal. . ." *Investment Registry of America, Inc.,* 21 SEC 745, 757 (1946). And see *Oxford Company, Inc., supra,* 21 SEC at pp. 692-693; *Hughes* v. *SEC,* 174 F.2d 969 (D.C. Cir. 1949). In a given case, the circumstances may be such that a dealer, acting as principal in a transaction, affords the impression it is acting as agent and thus not only perpetrates a fraud upon the customer, but also violates the confirmation requirements by not confirming as agent. See, *SEC* v. *Rapp,* 304 F.2d 786 (2d Cir. 1962). See also *Looper & Company,* 38 SEC 294, 301 (1958); *J. Logan & Co.,* SEC Securities Exchange Act Release No. 6848, July 9, 1962, p. 10, n. 17. *Investment Service Co.,* SEC Securities Exchange Act Release No. 6884, Aug. 15, 1962, pp. 8-9.

tion with the customer prior to the completion of the transaction, or explicit and informed ratification afterwards.[21]

Sec. 12-3. Confirmation requirements—miscellaneous comments. Before terminating our discussion on the subject of confirmations, some relevant items are worth noting. One is that neither the confirmation nor any information contained in it may be employed as a device to defraud. For example, it is a violation of the anti-fraud provisions to use language on a confirmation which gives customers the impression that, in a special cash account transaction, it is the customer who violates Regulation T if he fails to make payment within the seven days. We have already seen that Regulation T is directed to the broker-dealer and delineates its obligations rather than those of its customers,[22] so that the failure of a customer to make payment within seven days places upon the broker-dealer the obligation of cancelling or liquidating purchase transactions.[23]

Similarly, a confirmation may not be used to convey false information, or employed as a basis for maintaining false records based on such false information on the confirmation.[24]

It may be furthermore noted that in the sale of mutual funds to the public through dealers, it is the practice of many underwriter-distributors or custodians to confirm sales directly to the customer of the dealers. If such confirmations meet the informational elements of the confirmation requirements and if they con-

---

[21] See SEC Investment Advisers Act Release No. 40, *supra*, n. 3, at p. 3; *Investment Registry of America, Inc.*, 21 SEC 745, 757 (1946); *Oxford Company, Inc.*, 21 SEC 681, 692 (1946).

The term "at or before the completion of the transaction" as used in Section 11(d)(2) means "at or before the time the customer parts with value in connection with the transaction." See SEC Securities Exchange Act Release No. 253 (Class A), March 31, 1935.

The definition of the term "completion of the transaction" in paragraph (b) of Rule 15c1-1 which governs the terms used in Rule 15c1-4 is substantially the same in that the term is defined, basically, as the occasion when the customer parts with value either by paying for a security purchased or delivering a security sold to the broker-dealer or sold by the broker-dealer for the account of the customer. Exceptions to this definition occur in situations when the customer has prematurely parted with value, in which case the transaction is completed by actions of the broker-dealer fulfilling his obligations of payment or delivery to the customer, as the case may be. See *supra*, Sec. 11-5, n. 23.

[22] *Supra*, Sec. 9-1. See *supra*, Sec. 11-5, n. 23.

[23] *Supra*, Sec. 9-4.

[24] See *Reilly, Hoffman & Co., Inc.*, SEC Securities Exchange Act Release No. 6924, October 29, 1962, p. 2.

tain a legend that they are being transmitted to the customer on behalf of the broker-dealer, it is of no significance that the confirmation was not prepared or transmitted to the customer directly by the broker-dealer.[25]

Sec. 12-4. Rules as to discretionary accounts-churning.

If a broker-dealer or his employee is vested by a customer with discretionary power to effect transactions with or for the account of the customer, it is quite plain that the relationship is one of trust and confidence and that the broker-dealer has assumed the role of agent with a fiduciary obligation to the customer.[26] Under applicable rules, immediately after he effects such a transaction for a customer, a broker-dealer must make a record of it, including the name of the customer, the name, amount, and price of the security and the date and time when the transaction occurred.[27] Additionally, the broker-dealer is prohibited from effecting in the customer's account ". . . any transactions of purchase or sale which are excessive in size or frequency in view of the financial resources and character of such account."[28] The basis for this prohibition against an excessive "rate of turnover" is plain, and it is manifestly declaratory of the obligation of a fiduciary which would exist absent specific rule.[29]

---

[25] In connection with our discussion on the bookkeeping and records maintenance requirements, we have seen that copies of such confirmations containing specified information, maintained by selling dealers would constitute compliance with applicable record requirements as to confirmations. See *supra,* Sec. 6-1.

It would appear that a confirmation not conforming to the provisions of the confirmation statute or rule might not involve a violation of such statute or rule if the confirmation is delivered locally by hand without use of jurisdictional means. See *Daniel & Co., Ltd.,* 38 SEC 912 at n. 9 (1957).

[26] See e.g., *Norris & Hirshberg,* 21 SEC 865, 883-5 (1946). We have seen, *supra,* that the fiduciary obligation remains even though the broker-dealer casts the transaction as a principal, or dealer, transaction rather than in the form of a broker's, or agency, transaction.

[27] Paragraph (b) of Rule 15c1-7.

[28] Paragraph (a) of Rule 15c1-7. Both paragraphs of Rule 15c1-7 are cast in terms of definitions of the term "manipulative, deceptive, or other fraudulent device or contrivance" as used in Section 15(c)(1) of the Act. That section prohibits the use of jurisdictional means on the part of a broker-dealer to purchase or sell or induce the purchase or sale of a non-exempted security over-the-counter "by means of any manipulative, deceptive, or other fraudulent device or contrivance," and it authorizes the Commission to adopt rules defining such devices or contrivances. A "customer" is anyone but another broker-dealer, Rule 15c1-1(a), and includes a bank. SEC Securities Exchange Act Release No. 1462, November 15, 1937.

[29] See *Norris & Hirshberg, Inc.,* 21 SEC 865 (1946) p. 890, n. 31.

Examples of excessive rate of "turnover" may be found in *Norris & Hirshberg, Inc.,* 21 SEC 865, 883-885 (1946), aff'd, 177 F.2d 228 (D.C. Cir. 1949); *R. H. Johnson &*

The term "churning" is applied to such excessive activity and its obvious purpose is to increase unduly the profits or commissions of the broker-dealer over the normal profits and commissions appropriate for the financial resources and character of the account. In addition to the rate of turnover,[30] other factors may lead to the conclusion that churning has taken place. Among them are a succession of purchases and sales in the account of the same security (designated as "in and out" transactions) within relatively brief periods of time between such purchases and sales.[31] Another is the frequent "switching" of funds in the account from one security to another following short intervals.[32] In short, the sale and repurchase of the same security and the switching of funds and securities in rapid succession without adequate rational basis other than the creation of commissions and profits for the broker-dealer may reasonably lead to the conclusion that churning has taken place in the account.[33]

It may be noted that churning can result in the absence of a discretionary power to effect transactions with or for an account, if the activity in the account results from advice given by the broker-dealer to the customer which results in the account being churned.[34]

From what has already been stated about the inadmissibility of permitting a broker-dealer who is an agent from shedding his role and becoming a principal, it follows that a broker-dealer effecting transactions for a discretionary account may not buy securities from or sell securities to that account.[35]

Company, 36 SEC 467, 471 (1955), *aff'd,* 231 F.2d 523 (D.C. Cir. 1956), *cert den* 352 U. S. 844; and *Reynolds & Co.,* 39 SEC 902, 905-7 (1960). The "turnover" rate is computed by dividing the aggregate amount of purchases by the average cumulative monthly investment. The average cumulative monthly investment is arrived at by accumulating the total of the net investment in the account after each month and dividing that sum by the number of months for which the turnover rate is being computed. *Reynolds & Co., supra* at p. 906, n. 10. See also *R. H. Johnson & Company, supra* at p. 471; *Looper and Company,* 38 SEC 294, 297 at n. 6 (1958); *J. Logan & Co.,* SEC Securities Exchange Act Release No. 6848, July 9, 1962, p. 6, n. 11.

[30] See n. 29, *supra.*
[31] *Reynolds & Co., supra,* n. 29.
[32] *Ibid.*
[33] *Ibid.*
[34] *Ibid.* and see *R. H. Johnson & Co., supra,* n. 29 at p. 471.
[35] *Supra,* Sec. 12-1. Of course, in a given transaction if the broker-dealer procures specific consent of the customer following full disclosure of the broker-dealer's adverse interest including the cost and current market price of the security, any profits to the broker-dealer from any source and the like, the transaction might not

It may also be observed that, what is prohibited in the way of conduct on the part of a broker in respect of a discretionary account is as much prohibited to a dealer who really has an agency relationship and effects excessive activities in the account of a customer.[36]

---

offend the anti-fraud rules of the Act, see SEC Investment Advisers Act Release No. 40, Nov. 15, 1945, pp. 2-3. This is the same as SEC Securities Exchange Act Release No. 3653.

[36] See *Norris & Hirshberg, Inc.*, 21 SEC 865, 885 (1946); *Reynolds & Co.*, 39 SEC 902, 905-907 (1960). The fact that the rule 15c1-7 prohibition against excessive turnover is by its terms directed against a "dealer" as well as a "broker" affords no basis for a claim that a broker-dealer may act as a principal with reference to a discretionary account. *Norris Hirshberg, Inc., supra* at p. 885. The fact that an account is not discretionary does not preclude a finding of excessive activity on the part of a broker-dealer, if, because of his relationship with the customer, he has induced the customer to engage in trading which is excessive in size or frequency in view of the financial resources and character of the customer's account. See *Samuel B. Franklin & Company*, SEC Securities Exchange Act Release No. 7407, Sept. 3, 1964, pp. 6-7; *E. H. Rollins & Sons, Inc.*, 18 SEC 347, 380 (1945).

CHAPTER 13

PROHIBITIONS AS TO SPECIAL TYPES OF ACTIVITY IN CONNECTION WITH DISTRIBUTIONS

Sec. 13-1. Distribution—in general. Certain practices engaged in by broker-dealers and others interested in distributions of securities have been found to be manipulative,[1] and the Commission has adopted rules to outlaw them.

A "distribution" has been held to include "the entire process by which in the course of a public offering the block of securities is dispersed and ultimately comes to rest in the hands of the investing public."[2] Thus, a distribution is not completed if any part of the offering remains in the hands of broker-dealers or in the hands of persons (such as, for example, officers, directors, partners, employees, and favored friends of broker-dealers, underwriters, or issuers) who are not genuinely members of the public.[3]

---

[1] Manipulative activity consists of the use of concealed and other fraudulent devices artificially to raise, maintain, or depress the price of a security for the purpose of inducing the purchase or sale of that security by others. Sen. Rep. No. 792, 73rd Cong. 2d Sess. (1934), pp. 7-9, 17; Sen. Rep. No. 1455, 73rd Cong., 2d Sess. (1934), pp. 31-36, 54. HR Rep. No. 1383, 73rd Cong., 2d Sess. (1934), pp. 21, 31; SEC Securities Exchange Act Release No. 605, April 17, 1936; 46 Yale L.J. 624, 635 (1937). Manipulation can assume an infinite variety of forms. Some of these are dealt with specifically in the Act. See e.g., Sections 9(a)(1), (2), (3), (4), and (5) of the Act. Others, it will be seen, are reached by the general anti-fraud provisions. See *infra*, Sec. 18-3.

[2] *Lewisohn Copper Corp.*, 38 SEC 226, 234 (1958), and cases there cited. Although the "distribution" concept was evolved under the Securities Act of 1933, the same basic approach is applied with reference to the Securities Exchange Act, as seen from authorities cited in n. 3 directly below.

[3] *Idem.* at p. 234, n. 7. And see *Lewis Wolf, Inc.*, SEC Securities Exchange Act Release No. 6949, Nov. 21, 1962, p. 2, and *Best and Garey Co., Inc.*, SEC Securities Exchange Act Release No. 6841, July 6, 1962, p. 2; *Reilly, Hoffman & Co., Inc.*, SEC Securities Exchange Act Release No. 6924, Oct. 29, 1962, p. 2. And see authorities cited at notes 4 to 8, directly below. See also SEC Securities Act Release No. 4401, Aug. 3, 1961, pp. 2-3; SEC Securities Act Release No. 4150 (same as SEC Securities Exchange Act Release No. 6097), Oct. 23, 1959, p. 3. Of course, with the specific, limited, exception noted below with respect to Rule 10 b-6, *infra*, Sec. 13-12, if a part of the block is to be offered is placed by an underwriter or selling dealer in his own "investment account" or in the "investment account" of an affiliate, that part is regarded as not having been distributed. *C. A. Benson & Co., Inc.*, SEC Securities Exchange Act Release No. 7044, March 26, 1963, pp. 1-2. See *First California Company*, 40 SEC 768, 771-3 (1961). So, also, the placing of part of the block in "controlled" accounts, and the further resale of those securities either directly out of the

For the purposes of the rules under discussion, moreover, the term "distribution" applies to any "intensive campaign,"[4] "major selling effort,"[5] or unusual marketing operation[6] in the sale of a number of units of a security, irrespective of whether the number involved is a small part of the total number of units outstanding[7] or whether or not the conventional procedure of utilizing an underwriter or selling group is employed.[8] In brief, the term "distribution" refers to any selling activity, based upon either the magnitude of the offering or the selling efforts and selling methods utilized, which constitutes a departure from casual trading.[9]

Sec. 13-2. Distributions—primary and secondary. In some of these rules, prohibitions are imposed on specified activities in connection with the "primary or secondary distribution" of a security. The use of the terms "primary" and "secondary" in these contexts is not for the purpose of recognizing any differentiation between them with regard to the application of the rule to the proscribed activity, but, rather, for the purpose of reaching the forbidden activity in the context of any distribution, whether primary or secondary.[10]

---

accounts or through the device of "repurchasing" these securities from the original buyers and reselling them, does not result in a completion of the distribution until the securities reach the hands of ultimate public investors. *Siltronics, Inc.,* SEC Securities Exchange Act Release No. 7158, Oct. 18, 1963, p. 2; *Batten & Co., Inc.,* SEC Securities Exchange Act Release No. 7086, May 29, 1963; *Advanced Research Associates, Inc.,* SEC Securities Exchange Act Release No. 7117, Aug. 16, 1963, pp. 22-3, 27.

[4] *Lawrence Rappee,* 40 SEC 607, 609-10 (1961).

[5] *Gob Shops of America, Inc.,* 39 SEC 92, 103, n. 25 (1959); *Theodore A. Landau,* 40 SEC 1119, 1120-25 (1962); *SEC* v. *Scott Taylor, Inc.,* 183 F.Supp. 904, 908, n. 8 (S.D.N.Y. 1960).

[6] For example, the making of a public offering over-the-counter of a security traded on a national securities exchange. *J. A. Latimer & Co., Inc.,* 38 SEC 790, 793 (1958); or the utilization of others to bid for the security which is the subject of sale; see e.g., *Theodore A. Landau, supra,* n. 5; *Lawrence Rappee, supra,* note 4.

[7] *Theodore A. Landau, supra,* n. 5.

[8] *Bruns, Nordeman & Company,* 40 SEC 652, 659-661 (1961).

[9] See authorities cited in notes 4 to 8 immediately above; and see SEC Securities Exchange Act Release No. 1411, October 7, 1937, p. 1, containing an opinion of the Commission's Director of the Trading and Exchange Division on Rule MC6 which has since been renumbered as Rule 15c1-6. In pertinent part, he contrasted a distribution from other selling activity by referring to non distributional activity as "the usual type of position trading."

In examining the magnitude of the offering it would appear relevant to consider the size of the offering in relation to (1) the number of units of the same class of securities outstanding, (2) the volume of trading in the security during the period when the selling occurred, and (3) the total dollar amount involved in the sales.

[10] Opinion of Director of the Commission's Division of Trading and Exchange, *supra,* n. 9. Normally the difference between a primary and a secondary distribution of a security is this: In a primary distribution the proceeds are received either

Sec. 13-3. Distribution—disclosure of interest. Any broker acting for a customer or for both such customer and another person, and any dealer receiving fees or promises of fees from a customer for advising the customer with respect to securities, is, with the exception noted below, prohibited from effecting with or for the account of such customer any transaction in, or inducing the purchase or sale over-the-counter of any non-exempted security "in the primary or secondary distribution of which such broker or dealer is participating or is otherwise financially interested."[11] The exception to this rule occurs if, at or before the completion of each such transaction, the broker or dealer provides the customer with written notification of the existence of such participation or interest.[12] The type of financial interest possessed by a broker-dealer in a distribution which would render the prohibition applicable to him is any financial stake in the success of the distribution. The happenstance that the broker-dealer might own some securities of the same class as the issue being distributed might not be regarded as that type of financial interest, if it is *de minimis*. So long as a financial interest does actually exist on the part of a broker-dealer in the effectuation of the distribution, it is nevertheless of no importance whether he "owns the security, has it under option, is acting as agent for some principal, or is merely a member of a selling group . . ."[13]

directly or indirectly (by firm commitment underwriting) by the issuer; and a secondary distribution is made by or on behalf of some person other than the issuer who receives no part of the proceeds of the offering. See SEC, *Report on the Feasibility and Advisability of Complete Segregation of the Functions of Dealer and Broker* (1936) p. 185. See also Special Study Report, Pt. 1, Ch. IV, p. 563, n. 197, where it is stated, among other things, that "A secondary distribution is generally understood to be the disposition of a block of securities by any person other than the issuer."

[11] Rule 15c1-6. A customer is any one other than a broker or dealer. Rule 15c1-1(a), and includes a bank. SEC Securities Exchange Act Release No. 1462, November 15, 1937. For the meaning of the term, "effect" a transaction, see *supra*, Sec. 12-2, n. 12.

[12] Rule 15c1-6. For the meaning of the term "completion of the transaction," see *supra*, Sec. 11-5, n. 3. As we have seen, the confirmation of a transaction for or with a customer must be provided by the broker-dealer "at or before the completion of the transaction." See *supra*, Sec. 12-2. Hence, the notification required by Rule 15c1-6 normally appears in the confirmation. It may furthermore be observed that Rule 15c1-6 is concerned with circumstances under which the broker-dealer has a fiduciary obligation to his customer either by admittedly acting as agent or by having built up a relationship of trust and confidence as an adviser of the customer, for compensation, as to securities. The disclosures required by Rule 15c1-6 are, of course, not all of the disclosures required. See *supra*, Sec. 12-1. It would appear that the Rule 15c1-6 requirement applies if a partner or principal of the broker-dealer is financially interested in the distribution.

[13] SEC Securities Exchange Act Release No. 1411, October 7, 1937, p. 1.

Sec. 13-4. Sales at the market. A representation by a broker-dealer that a security is being offered to a customer "at the market" is a representation that there exists an independent market price based upon the forces of supply and demand; in brief that the market price of the security results from free competitive forces representing the collective judgments of buyers and sellers, as distinguished from a price arrived at almost exclusively by the direct or indirect activity of the broker-dealer offering the security.[14]

The Commission adopted a rule respecting such a representation by a broker or dealer who is participating or otherwise financially interested in the distribution of a security not admitted to trading on a national securities exchange.[15] This rule provides that it is a "manipulative, deceptive, or other fraudulent device or contrivance," as that term is used in Section 15(c)(1) of the Act, for such a broker or dealer to make such a representation to a customer as to such a security, "unless such broker or dealer knows or has reasonable grounds to believe that a market for such security exists other than that made, created, or controlled by him, or by any person for whom he is acting or with whom he is associated in such distribution, or by any person controlled by, controlling, or under common control with him." Violations of this rule are viewed with utmost seriousness.[16]

Sec. 13-5. Inducing purchases on exchange to facilitate distribution. Irrespective of whether he is a broker or dealer, a person participating or otherwise financially interested in the primary or

---

[14] SEC Securities Release No. 4401, Aug. 3, 1961, p. 1; *Theodore A. Landau*, 40 SEC 1125-6 (1962); *Lawrence Rappee*, 40 SEC 607, 609 (1961); Associated Investors Securities, Inc., SEC Securities Exchange Act Release No. 6859, July 24, 1962, p. 9; *Sterling Securities Company*, 39 SEC 487, 492 (1959); *Norris Hirshberg, Inc.*, 21 SEC 865, 875-6, 881 (1946); *W. K. Archer Company*, 11 SEC 635, 645 (1942); see also, *Canusa Gold Mines Ltd.* 2 SEC 548, 552 (1937); *Rickard Ramone Gold Mines Ltd.*, 2 SEC 377, 385 (1937); *Unity Gold Corp.*, 3 SEC 618, 629-630 (1938); *Otis v. SEC*, 106 F.2d 579 (6th Cir. 1939); *Coplin v. U. S.*, 88 F.2d 652, 661 (9th Cir. 1937); *Floyd A. Allen & Co., Inc.*, 35 SEC 176, 185 (1953); *Thornton & Co.*, 28 SEC 208 (1948). Cf. *SEC v. C. H. Abraham & Co., Inc.*, 186 F. Supp. 19 (S.D.N.Y. 1960).

[15] Rule 15c1-8. As to what constitutes being "financially interested" in the distribution of a security, see *supra*, Sec. 13-3. As to a rule of the Commission designed to reduce the possibility of fictitious quotations by broker-dealers, see *infra*, Sec. 16-5.

[16] See e.g.,*Theodore A. Landau, supra*, n.14; 1962, pp. 6-7; *Lawrence Rappee, supra*, n. 14; *Associated Investors Securities, Inc.*, SEC Securities Exchange Act Release No. 6859, July 24, 1962, p. 9. *Advanced Research Associates, Inc.*, SEC Securities Exchange Act Release No. 7117, Aug. 16, 1963, p. 27; *Woods & Company, Inc.*, SEC Securities Exchange Act Release No. 7178, Nov. 29, 1963. And see SEC Securities Exchange Act Release No. 6097, October 3, 1959, p. 3 (same as SEC Securities Act Release No. 4150).

secondary distribution of any security of any issuer is, with exceptions to be noted below, prohibited from directly or indirectly paying or agreeing to compensate anyone for attempting to induce third persons to purchase the same or other security of the same issuer on a national securities exchange. He is also prohibited from directly or indirectly paying or agreeing to pay anyone for purchasing the same or other security of the same issuer on a national securities exchange for any account other than the account of the person paying or agreeing to pay the compensation.[17] In the event the person participating or financially interested in the primary or secondary distribution of such security should engage in such prohibited activity, he is furthermore prohibited from using jurisdictional means or the facilities of any national securities exchange in effecting sales or deliveries of such security.[18]

One objective of these provisions is to reach a fraudulent and manipulative practice in connection with distributions under which participants, principally brokers and dealers, and others financially interested in the distribution of a security, bribe the sales representatives of other broker-dealers, or provide special compensation to their own sales representatives, to recommend to their customers the purchase of the security on the exchange while the person making such payments is distributing the security off the exchange.[19] The manipulative effect of the prohibited activity on the price of the security under distribution is manifest when, as is not uncommon, a security traded on a national securities exchange is distributed over-the-counter at a price representing a discount from the market price on the exchange.[20] Additionally, this practice represents a fraud on the customers induced to make the purchases of the securities on the exchange.[21]

---

[17] Paragraphs (a)(1) and (b) of Rule 10b-2. See SEC Securities Act Release No. 4401, Aug. 3, 1961, p. 1.

[18] Paragraph (a)(2) of Rule 10b-2.

[19] See SEC Securities Exchange Act Release No. 1330, August 4, 1937, p. 2; and SEC Securities Exchange Act Release No. 1411, October 7, 1937, pp. 1-2, relative to Rule GB 2 which has since been redesignated as Rule 10b-2; and see 8 SEC Ann. Rep., p. 9.

[20] See e.g., *J. A. Latimer & Co., Inc.*, 38 SEC 790, 793 (1958).

[21] See *United States* v. *Brown*, 79 F.2d 321, 325 (2d Cir. 1935) where the court said: ". . . As to bribing the 'customers' men' the deceit consists of this: When a prospective buyer comes to a broker for advice he supposes that what he gets is an opinion unweighted by personal interest. To pay the broker to advise the purchase of a specified stock is to bribe him to misrepresent a fact, to wit, that his corrupted advice is not corrupted. . . ."

Another main objective of these prohibitions is to guard against the danger involved in an exchange market being subjected to "artificial activity generated by the extra selling effort involved in a distribution."[22]

The prohibitions just mentioned are so sweeping that they literally encompass the payment by a broker-dealer participating or otherwise financially interested in a distribution of the ordinary compensation given to his sales representatives whose ordinary duties include the solicitation or execution of brokerage orders on a national securities exchange, and who, in the regular course of their employment, recommend purchases of securities. Accordingly, the applicable rule contains an exception to cover that situation.[23]

There is another exception to this general prohibition. This relates to special plans of distribution filed with the Commission by a national securities exchange declared effective by the Commission.[24] A typical plan declared effective by the Commission under this proviso relates to the distribution of a block of securities on the exchange when the exchange determines that the regular auction market on the exchange cannot absorb the block within a reasonable time and within a reasonable range of prices. The plan would permit the person making the offering to pay a special commission which ordinarily exceeds the regular commission, to the brokers of the purchasing customers, but it would stipulate that such brokers may not receive compensation from their own customers and that appropriate disclosures describing the special character of the transaction be made to the broker's customers in the confirmation. Provision would also be made for appropriate designations on the exchange ticker tape of transactions effected as part of a special plan.[25]

---

22 Special Study Report, Pt. 1, Ch. IV, p. 562, note 189.

23 Paragraph (c) of Rule 10b-2. ". . . The rule, however, does not prohibit a broker-dealer from paying a salary to a person in his own regular employment whose ordinary duties include the solicitation or execution of brokerage orders on an exchange as long as the payment is not made to induce the purchase of a specific security." SEC Securities Exchange Act Release No. 1330, *supra,* n. 19 at p. 2, announcing the adoption of Rule GB 2 which has been redesignated as Rule 10b-2.

24 Subparagraphs (d)(1) and (2) of Rule 10b-2. The Commission's declaration of effectiveness is made with ". . . due regard for the public interest and for the protection of investors. . ." *Ibid.*

25 For a discussion of various kinds of these plans, see Special Market Study Report, Pt. 1, Ch. IV, pp. 560-564. For Commission action approving such plans, see e.g., *Action Declaring Effective Exchange Distribution Plan and Special Offering Plan of Pacific Coast Stock Exchange Under The Securities Exchange Act of 1934,* SEC

A person paying special compensation under a special offering plan must nevertheless cease doing so if he knows or has reasonable grounds to believe, at the time of payment or the agreement to pay, that transactions connected with the distribution are being carried out in violation of the plan.[26]

Sec. 13-6. Best efforts underwritings—all or none or similar conditions—misrepresentation as to type of offering. As distinguished from an arrangement by which an underwriter is committed to take and pay for all of the securities to be publicly offered ("firm commitment" underwriting), underwriting arrangements are frequently made between issuer (or selling security holder) and underwriter under which the underwriter's obligation is limited to using his "best efforts" to effectuate the distribution. Some best efforts underwritings contain arrangements for the return of funds to subscribers in the event a specified minimum number of units of the security are not sold by a specified time. This feature is sometimes called a "best efforts all or none" underwriting, or by an appropriate variation, depending on the minimum number of units which must be sold to avoid the return of funds to the subscriber.

The first observation which may be appropriate in this connection is that it is a violation of Rule 10b-9(a)(1)[27] to represent that a best efforts underwriting is an "all or none" offering unless prompt refunds must be made to purchasers in the event all of the offered units are not sold at a specified price within a specified time or if the total amount due to the seller is not received by him by a specified date. It is also fraudulent in a best efforts underwriting to represent that all or part of the consideration paid by purchasers will be refunded to them if all or some of the securities are not sold unless the security is part of an offering

Securities Exchange Act Release No. 5452, Feb. 14, 1957; *Action Declaring Effective Amended Special Offering Plan of American Stock Exchange Under the Securities Exchange Act of 1934*, SEC Securities Exchange Act Release No. 5800, Oct. 16, 1958. And see 8 SEC Ann. Rep. 9 (1942) and 9 SEC Ann. Rep. 13 (1943). See also SEC Securities Exchange Act Release No. 5238, Oct. 11, 1955. A "Special Offering Plan" is, in effect, a fixed price offering based on the market price. An "Exchange Distribution Plan" is a distribution "at the market." And the distribution of a block of listed securities off the exchange, in the "over-the-counter market," is called a "Secondary Distribution." SEC *Statistical Bulletin* Vol. 22, No. 5, May 1963, p. 11.

[26] Subparagraph (1) of paragraph (d) of Rule 10b-2.

[27] Since this rule is adopted under Section 10(b) of the Act, it applies to all persons, including broker-dealers. It is apt to be more applicable to broker-dealers than any other group of persons, however.

or distribution being made on the condition that all or a specified part of the consideration paid for such security will be promptly refunded to the purchaser if a specified number of the units of the security are not sold at a specified time or if the total amount due to the seller is not received by him by a specified date.[28]

The basic point of these anti-fraud provisions is to outlaw the masquerading of a mere "best efforts" underwriting as being "all or none" or "part or none" offerings when the terms of the underwriting contract are so vague as to permit it to be construed to be fulfilled if the underwriter merely gets persons to agree within the specified period to purchase the specified minimum units of the offered securities but has not within the specified period actually collected full payment for such securities.[29]

Sec. 13-7. Straight best efforts underwritings—broker-dealer's obligations. It is a fraudulent, deceptive, or manipulative act or practice for any broker-dealer participating in any distribution of securities the subject of a best efforts underwriting arrangement, unless the money or other consideration he receives for the securities is promptly transmitted to the persons entitled thereto.[30]

This means that the selling dealer must promptly transmit the proceeds to the underwriter, and that the underwriter must in turn promptly transmit the funds to the issuer (or selling security holder) or in accordance with the latter's instructions. Moreover, the term "promptly" envisions that, giving effect to the necessary time for checks to clear, no more than a maximum of four days will lapse between the receipt of funds and their transmittal.

The requirement for prompt transmittal, moreover, applies to principal underwriters and retail dealers who sell mutual fund securities since such securities are continuously the subject of distribution.

---

[28] Subdivision (2) of Rule 10b-9(a). It would also constitute a fraud for an underwriter who has not succeeded in selling the specified minimum number of units within the specified time to attempt to meet the "all or none" or "part or none" condition by selling the unsold portion to himself, directly or indirectly; and thus attempt to avoid the loss of underwriter's compensation.

[29] SEC Securities Exchange Act Release No. 6864, July 30, 1962.

[30] Subdivision (a)(1) of Rule 15c2-4. By its terms the rule applies to all underwriting arrangements except a "firm commitment underwriting." In general, this applies to "best efforts" underwritings, but it may also apply to arrangements under which underwriters take down options as they sell or when the underwriter may otherwise avoid any obligation to sell.

Sec. 13-8. Best efforts underwritings—"all or none" or similar contingency—special requirements. If the best efforts distribution be on an "all-or-none" basis or on any other basis which contemplates that payment is not to be made to the person on whose behalf the distribution is being made until a further event or contingency occurs, a broker-dealer participating in the distribution has two alternative requirements. First, he must promptly deposit the money or other consideration received in a separate bank account as agent or trustee for the persons who have the beneficial interests in the funds (the subscriber or the person on whose behalf the distribution is being made, as the case may be) until the appropriate event or contingency has occurred, when he must then promptly, in accordance with prescribed arrangements, transmit or return the consideration to the persons entitled thereto.[31]

In the alternative, the broker-dealer may promptly transmit the funds to a bank which has agreed in writing to hold all such funds in escrow for the persons who have the beneficial interest in the funds and to transmit or return such funds directly to the persons entitled to them when the appropriate event or contingency has occurred.[32]

The obligations of each broker-dealer participating in the distribution in this area are separate from those of other broker-dealer participants. Each participating broker-dealer is required to make his own arrangements, either for the separate agency or trust account envisioned by alternative "(A)" of Rule 15c2-4, or for an escrow agreement under alternative "(B)." Such arrangements can be made in participation with the underwriter, but not with the person on whose behalf the securities are being distributed.

Broker-dealers who utilize the alternative "(A)" separate agency or trust account, as distinguished from the escrow arrangement under alternative "(B)," are required under the bookkeeping rules to maintain a separate record containing the name and address of each subscriber, the amount received from each, and the date and amount of the deposits into the separate bank account. The distribution of the funds must be by checks drawn on the

---

[31] Alternative "(A)" of subdivision (2) of Rule 15c2-4(a).
[32] Alternative "(B)" of subdivision (2) of Rule 15c2-4(a).

separate agency or trust account directly to the issuer or sub-scribers entitled thereto. The use of alternative "(A)" will not serve to eliminate from a broker-dealer's liabilities the sums de-posited in the special accounts; hence his aggregate indebtedness[33] will continue to mount and his net capital will be adversely af-fected by this arrangement until the contingency occurs which permits him to dispose of the funds. His need for capital to meet net capital requirements will mount correspondingly.

The use of the escrow agreement with a bank as escrow agent, however, will enable a broker-dealer to dispose of the liabilities resulting from receipt of proceeds of sales of securities to the extent that he transmits such proceeds to the escrow agent. Thus, the special net capital problems arising from a best efforts "all-or-none" or "part-or-none" underwriting arrangement may be obviated by use of the escrow agreement[34] envisioned by alter-native "(B)" of Rule 15c2-4(a)(2).

Sec. 13-9. Equity-funding arrangements—special require-ments. Fairly recently, new types of investment plans have evolved, particularly in connection with the sales of mutual fund securities. Under these programs, the security sold to a customer by the broker-dealer is used as collateral for a loan whose proceeds are in turn used for payment of premiums on a life insurance policy sold to the customer as an integral part of the program. Arrangements of this type are known as "equity-funding" plans.[35] A special rule has been adopted to deal with the abuses which have arisen in connection with equity funding programs.[36] Under this rule the broker-dealer offering such a plan involving such an extending of or arranging for credit must, before any part of the transaction is entered into, deliver to the customer a statement in writing setting forth specified information with respect to the

---

[33] See *supra*, Sec. 8-4. Whether or not he holds the funds in an agency or trust capacity, as distinguished from commingling them in his working capital, the broker-dealer still must account for and pay the funds out to those ultimately entitled to them.

[34] A copy of a sample escrow agreement appears as appendix P, *infra*, Sec. 25-16. For reference to this subject in the discussion of the net capital rule, see *supra*, Sec. 8-4.

[35] Apart from the significance of these programs to the discussion of special anti-fraud provisions applicable to distributions, these arrangements are viewed as involving the offer and sale of a security, in the form of an "investment contract," in addition to the security which is being sold to serve as collateral for the loan for the life insurance premiums. See SEC Securities Act Release No. 4491, May 22, 1962.

[36] Rule 15c2-5. This is popularly termed the "equity-funding rule."

specific proposed arrangement;[37] which statement cannot be prepared until the broker-dealer first obtains from the customer details concerning the customer's financial situation and needs.[38] The statement must be based in part, moreover, upon a reasonable determination by the broker-dealer that the entire transaction, including the loan arrangement, is suitable for the customer.[39]

Accordingly, the written statement must set forth the basis on which the broker-dealer made his determination that the transaction is suitable for the customer in relation to his financial situation and needs.[40] Additionally, the statement must set forth the exact nature and extent of the customer's obligations under the particular loan arrangement, including, among other things, the specific charges which the customer will incur in each period during which the loan may continue or be extended.[41] Moreover, detailed information must be furnished in the statement as to the nature and extent of the risks and disadvantages the customer will incur in the entire transaction, including the loan arrangement.[42] For example, if the proposal contemplates the cancellation of any of the customer's existing life insurance policies, full disclosure of the impact of such a course must be brought home to the customer in the statement.[43] Finally, disclosure must be made in the statement of all remuneration, in the form of discounts, commissions or otherwise, received and to be received by

---

[37] The specific items of information required to be given are discussed directly below in the text. At this juncture, it is pertinent to observe that the particulars required to be furnished by the rule go beyond what is normally required in a Securities Act of 1933 prospectus. See SEC Securities Exchange Act Release No. 6851, July 17, 1962, p. 1.

[38] Subdivision (a)(2) of Rule 15c2-5.

[39] *Ibid.*

[40] *Ibid.* This aspect of the rule appears to draw in part on the principles enunciated in *Anderson* v. *Knox*, 297 F.2d 702 (9th Cir. 1961), a case involving the sale of only life insurance policies, in which it was held to be a fraud to propose a life insurance program as suitable to an insured, when, in fact, it was not.

[41] Subdivision "(A)" of Rule 15c2-5(a)(1).

[42] Subdivision "(B)" of Rule 15c2-5(a)(1).

[43] Such information would include whether the premium on the new insurance is higher than the old insurance, as well as a statement that "the purchaser may be incurring additional expense because he is paying the 'acquisition costs' twice— once when the cancelled policy was purchased and again to acquire the new policy— that it may take a specified additional period of time for the dividends or the cash value of the new policy to equal those under the old policy; and that under the new policy the prospect may lose the benefits of the 'contestability provision' because the period during which the insurer may contest the policy for specified reasons (e.g., certain medical disabilities) may have expired under the prospect's old insurance policy and he may be required to 'wait through' this period under the new policy." SEC Securities Exchange Act Release No. 6851, July 17, 1962, p. 2.

the broker-dealer, any person controlling, controlled by, or under common control with the broker-dealer, or by any other person participating in the transaction.[44]

Sec. 13-10. Equity-funding arrangements—extension of credit involved—exemptions. In our discussion of Regulation T, we have seen that its restrictions apply only to a broker-dealer who is a member of a national securities exchange or who transacts a business in securities through the medium of any such member.[45] We have also seen that the credit restrictions of Section 11(d)(1) of the Act apply to such member or such broker-dealer only if he is both a broker and a dealer.[46] Conceivably, if a broker-dealer is not a member of a national securities exchange and is not transacting a business in securities through the medium of such member, and if he transacts business only as a dealer at all times, such a person would not be governed by the restrictions of Regulation T or Section 11(d)(1) as regards the extension, maintenance, or arranging for credit for the purchase or carrying of securities. Such extension, maintenance, and arrangements for credit are involved in equity funding programs;[47] it may be that a dealer who sells only mutual fund securities may participate in such extension, maintenance, and arranging for credit without regard to the limitations and restrictions of Regulation T and Section 11(d)(1).[48] If, however, such a dealer be merely a specially formed instrumentality of a broker-dealer who transacts a business as both broker and dealer, it is not likely that the credit restrictions could be obviated by such a device.[49]

The equity-funding rule provides that its provisions do not apply to any credit extended or arranged by a broker-dealer subject

---

[44] Subdivision "(C)" of Rule 15c2-5(a)(1). The purpose of this provision in part is manifestly to make clear to the customer that if, for example, the broker-dealer is affiliated directly or indirectly with some one who will profit through a fee for the arranging or extending of credit or from commissions on the life insurance premiums, the recommendation to the customer may be motivated by such special gains which would otherwise be concealed. Of course, in addition to the life insurance commissions arising from the program, the commissions from the sale of mutual funds received by the broker-dealer, his affiliates and other participants must be disclosed. To satisfy subdivision "(B)" moreover, the entire sales load involved in the sale of the mutual fund securities sold in connection with the plan must be revealed.

[45] *Supra,* Sec. 9-1.

[46] *Supra,* Sec. 9-5.

[47] SEC Securities Exchange Act Release No. 6726 February 8, 1962, p. 1.

[48] *Ibid.*

[49] *Ibid.*

to Regulation T if the credit is extended or arranged, in compliance with Regulation T, only for the purpose of purchasing or carrying the security offered or sold.[50]

Sec. 13-11. Bidding for or purchasing a security while engaged in its distribution—general prohibitions. A manipulative device not infrequently engaged in by persons who participate or are otherwise interested in a distribution is the diminution of the existing "trading" or "floating" supply of the security being distributed.[51] This is accomplished by bidding for and buying securities of the same class and series as the security to be, and being, distributed.

To eliminate this manipulative device, the Commission adopted a rule defining such practice and activity as a ". . . 'manipulative or deceptive device or contrivance' as used in Section 10(b) of the Act. . . ." This is Rule 10b-6 under the Act.

Under the rule, a person connected with the distribution of a security who is specifically encompassed by the rule is prohibited, until completion of his participation in the distribution, from using jurisdictional means directly or indirectly to bid for or purchase any account in which he has a beneficial interest, "any security which is the subject of such distribution, or any security of the same class and series, or any right to purchase any security; or to attempt to induce any person to purchase any such security or right. . . ."[52]

The persons encompassed by the rule are: an underwriter

---

[50] Paragraph (b) of Rule 15c2-5.

[51] See *Barrett & Company*, 9 SEC 319, 327 (1941); *Halsey, Stuart & Co., Inc.*, 30 SEC 106, 125 (1949). The "floating" or "trading" supply of a security is ". . . that part of the issue which is outstanding and which is held by dealers and the public with a view to resale for a trading profit, as distinguished from that part of the stock held for investment." *Barrett & Company, supra* at p. 327; and see *Halsey, Stuart & Co., Inc., supra* at p. 125, and *Gob Shops of America, Inc.*, 39 SEC 92, 102-3 (1959). Manipulation of the market of a security in connection with a distribution has consistently been viewed as the perpetration of a fraud on the investing public. See *Rickard Ramore Gold Mines, Ltd.*, 2 SEC 377, 385-6 (1937); *Canusa Gold Mines Ltd.*, 2 SEC 548, 563 (1937); *Thompson Ross Securities Co.*, 6 SEC 1111, 1121-2 (1940); *Reiter Foster Oil Corporation*, 6 SEC 1028, 1048-9 (1940); *Adams & Co.*, 33 SEC 444, 457 (1952).

[52] Paragraph (a) of Rule 10b-6. The prohibition applies also to a security (1) which is convertible immediately into the security being distributed, or (2) which entitles the holder immediately to acquire the security being distributed. Paragraph (b) of Rule 10b-6. Unless the other security is immediately convertible into the security being distributed or the right to purchase the distributed security is immediately exercisable, the prohibition of the rule does not apply to such convertible security or right.

or prospective underwriter in a particular distribution of a security; the issuer or other person on whose behalf the distribution is being made; and a broker or dealer or other person who has agreed to participate or is participating in such a distribution.[53]

Sec. 13-12. Bidding for or purchasing a security—participation in distribution and completion. We have already explored the meaning of the term "distribution" in the context of the discussion on the general subject of rules prohibiting specified activities in connection with distributions. In that connection, we have seen that the term "distribution" encompasses every step in the process of the scatteration of a block of securities into the hands of ultimate investors who are members of the public. We noted that any part of an offering remaining in the hands of any broker-dealer or of other persons not genuinely members of the public has not been distributed.[54] It was also pointed out that, for the purposes of the rules in question, any intensive campaign, major selling effort, or unusual marketing operation employed in the sale of a number of units of a security constitutes a distribution, irrespective of whether the number being sold is a small part of the number of outstanding units, or whether or not conventional methods of distribution are utilized, such as an underwriter, underwriting syndicate, or selling group. Finally, it was observed that for the purposes of these rules the term "distribution" refers to any selling activity which is a departure from casual trading, either because of the magnitude of the offering or the selling efforts or methods utilized.[55]

It should be borne in mind that securities may be the subject of distribution even though they are not the subject of sale for cash. So, securities distributed as the result of merger, recapitalization, and the like may not be bid for or purchased by those engaged in furthering and carrying out the transaction until after all of the securities involved have been distributed.

According to the rule, an issuer or other person on whose behalf the distribution is being made shall be deemed to have completed his participation in the distribution when the entire

---

[53] Paragraph (a) of Rule 10b-6.

[54] But see the temporary exception noted below in this Section with respect to Rule 10b-6.

[55] *Supra*, Sec. 13-1.

distribution has been completed.[56] An underwriter will be re-garded as having completed his participation when (1) he has distributed his participation including all other securities of the same class acquired in connection with the distribution, and (2) when all stabilization arrangements and trading restrictions to which he is a party with respect to such distribution has been terminated.[57] As to any other person, the participation is com-pleted when he has distributed his participation in the distribu-tion.[58] Securities taken for investment by an underwriter or dealer or other person who participated in the distribution are regarded for the limited purpose of the rule as being no longer the subject of distribution; and the prohibition of the rule against bidding for or purchasing the securities in the open market are lifted, so long as the block taken for investment is not the subject of dis-tribution.[59] Whenever such securities taken for investment should later become the subject of a distribution, however, the prohibi-tions of Rule 10b-6 again become operative with reference to that distribution, just as they do in respect of any other distribution of securities.

It has already been noted in this connection that securities the subject of distribution which are allotted to "insiders," such as partners, officers, employees or relatives of underwriters or participant dealers will be regarded as not distributed within the purview of Rule 10b-6 until they have been resold to ultimate investors.[60] Additionally, if an underwriter or other person en-gaged in the distribution of a security sells some of it to brokers and dealers, either at a discount or at public offering price, to enable them to make an over-the-counter market for the security, this arrangement would render such brokers and dealers par-ticipants in the distribution while they are disposing of such securities. Accordingly, while so engaged, they are prohibited by Rule 10b-6 from bidding for or making purchases of the security.[61]

Moreover, if a broker-dealer bids for or purchases a security at the instance of another who is engaged or about to engage in its

---

[56] Clause A of paragraph (c)(3) of Rule 10b-6.

[57] *Idem.* at Clause B. See the reference *infra* at Sec. 13-18 to the subject of stabilization.

[58] *Idem.* at Clause C.

[59] *Ibid.*

[60] *Supra*, this Section and Sec. 13-1.

[61] SEC Securities Exchange Act Release No. 6097, October 23, 1959, p. 3. This is the same as SEC Securities Act Release No. 4150.

distribution, such broker-dealer is a participant in the distribution.[62] The person at whose instance the broker-dealer makes the bids violates the rule, since he is not only prohibited from engaging in such activities "indirectly," but is also forbidden to "induce any person to purchase any such security until after he has completed his participation in such distribution."[63] It would similarly appear plain that if a broker-dealer is prohibited by Rule 10b-6 from bidding for or purchasing a security, a partner, officer, director, or employee of the broker-dealer is also not permitted to engage in such activities.[64]

In connection with a rights offering, it is a common practice for a financial institution to be designated as agent for security holders for selling or purchasing rights for fractions of the underlying security particularly to enable those security holders owning fractions to purchase additional fractions to enable them to buy whole units, and, incidentally, to enable other stockholders, owning fractions and not desiring to buy whole units, to realize upon their rights. So long as the institution confines its activities in rights to persons who acquired them directly from the issuer as security holders of the issuer, the financial institution will be regarded as merely the agent of such security holders and not as a person participating in the distribution.

A person registered as a specialist in a particular security with a national securities exchange is, like anyone else, prohibited from bidding for or purchasing that security if he is in fact a participant in the distribution of other units of the same security by way of sales on the exchange. He cannot properly predicate or justify such bidding or purchasing on his obligation, as specialist, to maintain a "fair and orderly market" in the security on the excuse that there is too wide a spread between the public bid and offer.[65]

---

62 *Theodore A. Landau*, 40 SEC 1119, 1123-5 (1962). The Special Study Report, Pt. 2, Ch. VII, p. 675, item 3(a) recommended the adoption of a rule specifically requiring a dealer who enters quotations on behalf of another dealer to give specific disclosure of that fact. See the discussion, *infra* at Sec. 16-5, on Rule 15c2-7 embodying these recommendations.

63 Paragraph (a) of Rule 10b-6. And see *Lawrence Rappee*, 40 SEC 606, 609-10 (1961), and *Theodore A. Landau, supra*, n. 62.

64 It would appear for this reason that the Commission has seen no need to adopt a 1956 proposal which would have specifically expressed such prohibition. See SEC Securities Exchange Act Release No. 5415, Dec. 6, 1956.

65 See SEC Staff *Report On Organization Management, And Regulation of Conduct of Members Of the American Stock Exchange* (1962), p. 31 [hereinafter called "American Stock Exchange Report"]. And see *Re, Re & Sagarese*, SEC

In short, as a practical matter, a specialist cannot properly participate in a distribution, as underwriter, dealer, broker, or otherwise, of a security in which he is a specialist.[66]

Questions sometimes arise in connection with an underwriter or selling group member as to whether, having sold his entire participation or allotment and having otherwise completed his participation in the distribution, he is free to trade (bid for or purchase as well as sell) in the security prior to receiving payment for all of the units he distributed. In such a case, if some of the purchases should be cancelled and thus become unsold, the distribution will not have been completed until all of such units are resold; hence, unless a broker-dealer underwriter or selling group member can be absolutely certain that no such cancellations will occur, he risks violating Rule 10b-6 if he begins to trade in the security prior to receiving payment for all the units distributed.

However, a firm commitment underwriter need not wait for the settlement with the issuer before trading, if he has completed his participation as defined by the rule.

Other problems arise from the accumulation by a managing underwriter of a short position in the distributed security resulting from selling more units than the number being distributed. If such underwriter desires to begin trading in the security, he would be well advised to refrain from such activity until the short position has been covered. In the first place, the accumulation of a substantial short position may of itself constitute a distribution

---

Securities Exchange Act Release No. 6900, September 21, 1962, pp. 1-2. On the subject of the obligation of a specialist on the American Stock Exchange to engage in dealer transactions in a security to maintain a "fair and orderly market," see American Stock Exchange Report, *supra* at p. 22.

[66] However, the fact remains that under Section 11(b) of the Act, it is the responsibility of a national securities exchange through its specialists to maintain a fair and orderly market in the securities traded in on the exchange. See *Re, Re & Sagarese*, SEC Securities Exchange Act Release No. 6900, Sept. 21, 1962, p. 2. American Stock Exchange Report, p. 22. Consequently, if a specialist (or odd lot dealer) has no direct or indirect arrangement to participate in a distribution, is not otherwise connected with the distribution, and is simply performing his functions as a specialist (or odd lot dealer as the case may be), no question is likely to be raised if, while bidding for or purchasing a security, he may purchase for his own account for resale a modest number of units of the same security, or accept for a modest number of units of that security limited price or market orders, from, or as agent for, some broker or dealer participating in a secondary distribution, provided that priority is given to public bids at the same price. See American Stock Exchange, *Information Circular* No. 12-63, March 7, 1963. See also Special Offering and Distribution Plans under Rule 10b-2, discussed *supra* at Sec. 13-5; e.g., SEC Securities Exchange Act Release No. 5238, October 11, 1955, p. 5.

of the number of units in excess of the number originally sought to be distributed. Secondly, if the managing underwriter engages in transactions designed to depress the price of the security in order to cover the short position at a low cost, he may be engaged in a manipulation of the price of the security.[67] Finally, to avoid the possibility of manipulation in any event, the managing underwriter must purchase all unsold units of other underwriters before attempting to purchase any part of the security in the open market.[68]

Trading may not be commenced by an underwriter until he has distributed not only his participation, but all other securities of the same class acquired in connection with the distribution.[69] In general the securities so acquired would have resulted from stabilization purchases by the managing underwriter on behalf of all of the underwriters.[70] Consequently, no underwriter may begin trading so long as securities purchased in stabilization operations have not been sold by the managing underwriter. Of course, even if the syndicate stabilization long position be disposed of, an underwriter may not begin trading activities until he has fully completed his own participation in the distribution.

Some Rule 10b-6 problems arise in connection with "uncoordinated" or "uncontrolled" secondary distributions. These are popularly referred to as the *Hazel Bishop* type of distributions, and are most frequently met in situations under which a number of selling security holders, acting independently of each other, engage in distributing blocks of their own holdings from time to time on the market at market prices. While executing an order to sell by such a selling security-holder customer, a broker-dealer is a participant in the distribution. The broker-dealer is thus prohibited by Rule 10b-6 from trading in the security while any part of the customer's order to sell remains unexecuted.[71]

---

[67] See *infra*, Sec. 18-2. Moreover, as agent of all of the underwriters in the covering of the short position, the manager would violate the anti-fraud provisions of the federal securities laws if he failed to divide *pro rata* among all the underwriters any profits from short, covering transactions. For all of these reasons it is deemed not feasible for an underwriter to trade while covering a short position.

[68] This follows because, in covering the short position, the manager is agent for all of the underwriters; hence, he cannot buy on the market on their behalf while they are still engaged in the distribution.

[69] Subdivision (B) of paragraph (c)(3) of Rule 10b-6.

[70] For a discussion of stabilization see *infra*, Sec. 13-18.

[71] See SEC Securities Act Release No. 4401, August 3, 1961. This release points out that, in general, there are three different types of "uncontrolled" secondary

Sec. 13-13. Bidding for or purchasing a security—the "hot issue." The term "hot issues" has been used to refer to "those issues which on the first day of trading, frequently the offering date, sold at a substantial premium."[72] This is frequently brought about by allotment of a portion of the issue at the public offering price to so-called trading firms active in the over-the-counter market. Such firms not only sell their allotment at prices substantially higher than the public offering price, but also engage in bidding for and purchasing the security while disposing of their allotments.[73]

Another device frequently employed is to allot a substantial part of the offering among "insiders," such as partners, officers, employees or relatives, or favored customers of the broker-dealer participant in the distribution, or among other broker-dealers or "insiders" of such other broker-dealers.[74] We have seen that allotments to broker-dealers and to "insiders" of the type mentioned are not "distributed";[75] hence all of the prohibitions of Rule

---

distributions. One type involves selling stockholders who, though independent of each other, are interrelated by family, business, or contractual ties. As to this type, the release points out the feasibility of avoiding Rule 10b-6 violations by agreements between the issuer and the selling security holders at the time the issuer arranges to issue the securities (not infrequently in exchange for property as distinguished from cash). Apart from a commitment not to bid for or purchase securities of the same class, the selling stockholders would agree not to engage in stabilization activities and would report to the issuer all sales, pledges, or other dispositions by them of the issuer's stock. A second type of "uncontrolled" distribution involves selling security holders having no relationship with each other, each of whom has and intends to sell a substantial number of units of the security. As to these, the issuer at a minimum should direct attention to Rule 10b-6 prohibitions. A third type involves small unrelated security holders whose holdings are so small as not to constitute the subject of a "distribution."

[72] SEC Securities Act Release No. 4150, Oct. 23, 1959, p. 1 (same as SEC Securities Exchange Act Release No. 6097).

[73] *Ibid.*

[74] *Idem.* at p. 2. And see *Lewis Wolf, Inc.,* SEC Securities Exchange Act Release No. 6949, Nov. 21, 1962, p. 2; *Best and Gary Co., Inc.,* SEC Securities Exchange Act Release No. 6841, July 6, 1962, p. 2. See also Address by James C. Sargent, Commissioner, Securities and Exchange Commission: *Some Current Problems Of The Securities And Exchange Commission* before the 42nd Annual Convention of North American Securities Administrators, Atlantic City, New Jersey, September 10, 1959, pp. 2-3 on file at SEC, Washington, D. C., and New York, N. Y.

[75] *Supra,* Sections 13-1 and 13-12. And see *Valley Forge Securities Co., Inc.,* SEC Securities Exchange Act Release No. 7055, April 12, 1963, p. 3; *R. J. Hayes & Co., Inc.,* SEC Securities Exchange Act Release No. 7102, July 18, 1963, pp. 1-2; *Batten & Co., Inc.,* SEC Securities Exchange Act Release No. 7086, May 29, 1963, pp. 1-2; *Advanced Research Associates, Inc.,* SEC Securities Exchange Act Release No. 7117, Aug. 16, 1963, pp. 21-2, 27; *Siltronics, Inc.,* SEC Securities Exchange Act Release No. 7158, Oct. 18, 1963, p. 2. This practice is known as "free riding and withholding," and it involves resales by the "insiders" to the public at premium prices, *Special Study Report,* Pt. 1, Ch. IV, pp. 528-533.

10b-6 are applicable to the activities of such broker-dealers and "insiders."[76]

Another technique used in connection with the "hot issue" is the allotment by a broker-dealer participant in the distribution of a specified number of units to a customer at the public-offering price upon condition that additional purchases of a specified number of units of the same security will be made at the market by the customer from the broker-dealer after the issue is initially sold. This involves inducing a person to purchase a security of the class being distributed at a time when the broker-dealer participant had not completed his participation in the distribution. Such a "tie-in" arrangement therefore violates Rule 10b-6.[77]

In addition to the devices already mentioned for limiting the supply of a new security and thus creating a "hot issue," some broker-dealers (1) have imposed penalties on customers and salesmen if the security was resold within a specified time after original sale, (2) have refrained from delivering certificates to customers for unduly long periods after sale and thus restricted resales, and (3) have delayed notifying customers of allotments for several days after sale. Moreover, some broker-dealers would stimulate the so-called after market (and thus increase public interest and the price) by means of active publicity and other means of solicitation.[78]

The *Special Study Report* has recommended certain measures for coping with the "hot issue" type of problem, a number of which are under active consideration. For example, the Commission is considering the adoption of rules regarding new issues for (1) specifying minimum periods of time for broker-dealers to notify customers of allotments and to deliver certificates, and (2) requiring underwriters who receive options, warrants, or "cheap stock" as part of their underwriting compensation, to notify the Commission when they exercise such options or warrants or sell the options, warrants, "cheap stock," or securities obtained upon the exercise of the options or warrants.[79] Moreover, recent legisla-

---

[76] *Lewis Wolf, Inc., supra,* n. 74; *Best And Gary Co., Inc., supra,* n. 74.
[77] Paragraph (a) of the rule. See SEC Securities Act Release No. 4358, April 24, 1961 (same as SEC Securities Exchange Act Release No. 6536).
[78] All of these techniques are mentioned in the *Special Study Report,* Pt. 1, Ch. IV, pp. 525-35.
[79] See *Special Study Report,* Pt. 1, Ch. IV, pp. 557-558, items 1, 2, and 7, and see SEC Special Market Study Release No. 25, April 30, 1963, p. 6.

tion has been enacted in respect of new issues extending the period from the present 40 days to 90 days[80] during which a dealer, not a part of the underwriting or selling groups, must furnish prospectuses under the Securities Act of 1933.

The Commission has already dealt with the "hot issue" techniques of (1) delaying the beginning of the offering and (2) suspending the offering midstream, by the adoption of rules with respect to securities offered pursuant to a Securities Act registration statement or a notification under Regulation A under that Act. These rules provide for prompt notice to the Commission if the offering (1) is not commenced within three days of final Commission clearance of the filing or (2) is suspended within fifteen days after effectiveness of the filing.[81]

Sec. 13-14. Bidding for or purchasing a security—underwriter, prospective underwriter. An "underwriter" is defined in the rule as a person who has agreed with the issuer or other person on whose behalf the distribution is to be made either to purchase the securities for distribution, or to distribute them on behalf of the issuer or such other person, or to manage or supervise such distribution.[82] The term "underwriter" as here defined is thus not limited, as in the case of the Securities Act, to persons who fit the definition of Section 2(11) of that Act.[83]

A "prospective underwriter" means one who has agreed with the issuer, or other person on whose behalf the distribution is to be made, to submit a bid pursuant to public invitation, or one who has reached an understanding with the issuer or such other person that he will become an underwriter, whether or not the terms and conditions of the underwriting have been agreed upon.[84] Bearing in mind that the Rule 10b-6 prohibitions apply to a "prospective underwriter," this definition gives effect to the purpose of imposing the restrictions of the rule on those "who are participating or expect to participate in a distribution."[85]

---

[80] Section 4(3) of the Securities Act. Securities Acts Amendments of 1964, Sec. 12.

[81] See Rules 263 and 462 under the Securities Act.

[82] Paragraph (c)(1) of Rule 10b-6.

[83] *Gob Shops of America, Inc.*, 39 SEC 92, 103, n. 25 (1959). As pointed out in the *Gob Shops case, supra*, for Rule 10b-6 purposes one may be an underwriter as there defined without being a person who has purchased from or sells for an issuer, a controlling person, or from or for an underwriter for the issuer or controlling person.

[84] Paragraph (c)(2) of Rule 10b-6.

[85] SEC Securities Exchange Act Release No. 5040, May 18, 1954, p. 1.

A "broker, dealer, or other person who has agreed to participate or is participating" in a distribution is subject to Rule 10b-6
restrictions.[86] We have seen that such persons include "insiders"[87]
of broker-dealer participants, as well as persons who actually engage in activities in furtherance of the distribution, whether or
not they formalize arrangements respecting such activities.[88] By
reaching a person who has "agreed to participate in the distribution," the rule reaches the bidding for or purchasing of the security
by a person who has not yet actually engaged in the distribution.[89]

**Sec. 13-15. Bidding for or purchasing a security—excep-
tions and exemptions, in general.** To the sweeping prohibitions
of the rule, there are a number of exceptions designed to take out
of its scope certain restricted activities which would not be manipulative in effect and which, consistent with the objectives of the
rule, would in some instances preserve for public investors a
market with respect to securities of the same class and series being
or to be distributed.

For example, a most necessary exception relates to offers to
sell as well as the solicitation of offers to buy "the securities being
distributed."[90] Similarly, there is an exception which authorizes
the usual arrangements for the taking down by underwriters or
prospective underwriters of the securities from the issuer or other
person on whose behalf the distribution is being made; and, pursuant to an agreement among underwriters or selling group agreement, the making by the underwriters or prospective underwriters of allotments and reallotments among underwriters and
selling group members of portions of the issue being distributed.[91]

---

[86] Subdivision (3) of Rule 10b-6(a).

[87] *Supra,* Sections 13-1 and 13-12.

[88] *Ibid.*

[89] SEC Securities Exchange Act Release No. 5040, May 18, 1954, p. 1.

[90] Exception numbered "(6)" of paragraph (a) of Rule 10b-6. However, if the
security is to be distributed by sales on a national securities exchange, the prohibitions of Rule 10b-2 (see *supra,* Sec. 13-5) would specifically prohibit the giving of
compensation to persons to solicit the purchase of the security on the exchange.
Hence, exception numbered "(6)" has no application to a security traded on an
exchange unless the distribution is effected over the counter. As regards the
security distributed on the exchange, the only activity open to those distributing
the security is to make the offer on the exchange and wait until the offer is met,
or to meet the bids on the floor of the exchange. See SEC Securities Exchange Act
Release No. 4401, Aug. 3, 1961, p. 1.

[91] Exception numbered "(1)" of paragraph (a) of Rule 10b-6. It is this exception which permits an underwriter to solicit underwriting business and to make the
customary arrangements embodied in underwriting agreements as well as in agreements among underwriters and selling group agreements. For a discussion of the

There are also other exceptions to the absolute prohibitions in paragraph (a) of the rule which are not concerned with the preservation of an existing market in the securities. There is exception numbered "(2)" which permits an underwriter, absent solicitation, to privately purchase large blocks of the same security, not on an exchange and without the intervention of any broker or dealer, with the view, generally but not necessarily, of distributing all of such blocks in a single offering. Unlike exception "(1)" which may involve solicitation by the underwriter or prospective underwriter of the very block which he hopes to distribute, exception "(2)" becomes operative only if the purchase is not solicited by the underwriter or prospective underwriter. It may be noted, moreover, that the conditions of exception "(2)" may be met only if the purchase is made away from the market; hence the purchase may not be made on an exchange or with the intermediation of a broker-dealer. Moreover, each block purchased must, of course, be so substantial in size as to negate an evasion of the basic thrust of Rule 10b-6 which, as seen, is to preclude the use of the manipulative device in connection with distributions of sopping up existing floating supply.[92]

Exception numbered "(3)" permits purchases by an issuer more than forty days after the commencement of the distribution, if the purchases are made to satisfy sinking fund requirements. We have seen that exception numbered "(6)" is the one which authorizes solicitation of offers to buy "the securities being distributed."[93] It also permits sales and solicitations by a participating dealer as principal of orders to buy units of the same class as the security being distributed which the participant dealer had on hand in long position prior to becoming a participant in the distribution. Exception numbered "(7)" permits without limitation the acquisition of securities of the class being distributed if made through the exercise of any right or conversion privilege to acquire such securities. Exception numbered "(10)" relates to a plan of distribution adopted and effective under Rule 10b-2 under the Act.[94]

---

usual type of distributing arrangements, see *Brooklyn Manhattan Transit Corp.*, 1 SEC 147 (1935).

[92] See *supra,* Sec. 13-11.

[93] See *supra,* n. 90, where we have also noted the limitations on this exception in respect of securities distributed on a national securities exchange in cases where Rule 10b-2 would apply.

[94] For reference to such plans see Sec. 13-5, *supra.*

Apart from these "exceptions" to paragraph (a) of the rule, several "exemptions" from the operation of the rule are specified.[95] Additionally, in a given case the Commission may upon written request or its own motion exempt, unconditionally or on specified conditions, transactions, which would otherwise come within the purview of the rule, if it concludes that they would not constitute a manipulative or deceptive device or contrivance within the purpose of the rule.[96]

Certain types of bids and purchases may be made to facilitate the distribution. These consist of (a) stabilization transactions, provided they are made in conformity with Rule 10b-7 under the Act,[97] and (b) bids for as well as purchases of rights to purchase the security under distribution (or a security of the same class or series), provided such bids and purchases are made in compliance with the restrictions of Rule 10b-8 under the Act.[98]

Sec. 13-16. Bidding for or purchasing a security—exceptions and exemptions, to preserve existing market. The remaining exceptions are concerned with not depriving the public of a market in respect of securities of the same class and series as those being or to be distributed, under circumstances consistent with the basic anti-manipulative purpose of the rule. The exceptions involve the recognition that the brokers and dealers who make a market in a security are those who are very frequently invited to become underwriters or selling dealers.

Exception numbered "(5)" of Rule 10b-6(a) excludes from the prohibition of the rule "brokerage transactions not involving solicitation of the customer's order." This enables an underwriter or participating broker-dealer who makes a market in the security being or to be distributed to act as agent for a customer in buying or selling for the customer a security of the same class and series, provided the broker did not solicit the order. The absence of solicitation of the order is regarded as the factor militating against thwarting the anti-manipulative objective of the rule. A broker

---

[95] These include "exempted securities" as defined in Section 3(a)(12) of the Act, face amount certificates, and redeemable securities of investment companies under the Investment Company Act of 1940, and specified types of stock option and stock purchase plans. See paragraphs (d) and (e) of Rule 10b-6.

[96] Rule 10b-6, paragraph (f).

[97] Exception numbered "(8)" of Rule 10b-6(a). For a discussion of Rule 10b-7, see *infra*, Sec. 13-18.

[98] Exception numbered "(9)" of Rule 10b-6(a). For a discussion of Rule 10b-8, see *infra*, Sec. 13-22.

satisfying the exception may insert quotations in the sheets to enable him to execute the order. In general, this exception has no application to a situation where securities of the class being distributed have not previously had a market. In brief, a broker-dealer engaged in a distribution of a security for which there has been no market prior to the commencement of the distribution can hardly claim that his transactions are unsolicited when he is actively engaged in effecting the distribution among his customers.[99]

Another exception, with the same basic purpose and which is regarded as containing ample safeguards against its use as a manipulation, is exception numbered "(11)" of Rule 10b-6(a). Exception "(11)" provides, as to an underwriter, prospective underwriter, or participating dealer, that purchases or bids may be made by them over-the-counter up to ten or more business days prior to the proposed commencement of the distribution, and that thereafter, up to five or more business days prior to the anticipated commencement, they may make unsolicited purchases, provided that none of such bids or purchases "are for the purpose of creating actual, or apparent, active trading in or raising the price of such security. . ." Stated otherwise, in the absence of a manipulative purpose, an underwriter, prospective underwriter, or participating dealer may purchase over-the-counter securities of the same class to be distributed and place bids in the daily quotation sheets up to ten business days prior to the proposed commencement of the offering.[100] Between the tenth and fifth business day prior to such commencement, his activity, if any, must be limited to the making of purchases if he did not solicit the transaction with his customer. In that period, he may not insert bid quotations in the daily quotation sheets nor may he indirectly bid for the security by the device of having his name appear in the sheets "OW"[101] or "Name Only"[102] in connection with the security. In the five (business) day period prior to the commencement of the offering, he may not engage as principal in any purchase transaction.

---

[99] See *Sutro Bros. & Co.*, SEC Securities Exchange Act Release No. 7053, April 10, 1963, pp. 8-9.

[100] The exception specifically provides that, in the case of securities offered pursuant to an effective registration statement under the Securities Act of 1933, the distribution shall not be deemed to commence for the purposes of exception "(11)" prior to the effective date of the registration statement.

[101] Offer Wanted.

[102] Indication of an interest in buying or selling.

Some basic principles should be kept in mind with respect to exception "(11)". Exception "(11)" has no application with respect to transactions on an exchange; hence as to such transactions, an underwriter, prospective underwriter, or participating dealer is precluded from making any bid for or puchase of the security in question unless one of the other exceptions or exemptions is applicable.

Secondly, exception "(11)" applies to transactions only by an underwriter, prospective underwriter, or dealer participating (or who has agreed to participate) in the distribution. This gives effect to the purpose behind the exception not to deprive public investors of a market which would have existed for them except for the 10b-6 prohibitions applicable to those who make the principal market in the security. Accordingly, no other person subject to Rule 10b-6 restrictions, such as the issuer or other person on whose behalf the distribution is being made, may engage in transactions permitted to the underwriter, prospective underwriter, or participating dealer by exception "(11)."

Moreover, it will be recalled that if an underwriter or dealer places an unsold portion of a distribution with himself for investment, he will be free to trade in the security if he otherwise has completed his participation in the distribution. However, such trading may occur only so long as the block taken for investment is held by the underwriter or dealer.[103] Once the underwriter or dealer intends to dispose of that unsold block, all of the Rule 10b-6 restrictions again come into force, and, to the extent that exception "(11)" may be applicable, all of its conditions must be met with respect to bid quotations and purchases.

Finally, the exception by its terms does not permit it to be used as a cloak for "creating actual or, apparent active trading in or raising the price" of the security. Where that manipulative purpose lies behind activities which come within the technical framework of exception "(11)," the activities are nevertheless manipulative and in violation of Rule 10b-6.[104]

There is one other exception concerned with maintenance of existing markets. That is exception numbered "(4)" which permits transactions of purchase by a participant in the distribution if

---

[103] *Supra*, Sec. 13-12.
[104] *Bruns, Nordeman & Company*, 40 SEC 652, 660-1 (1961).

he is an odd lot dealer on a national securities exchange and effects odd lot transactions (together with offsetting round lot transactions) for the purpose of effecting or executing odd lot orders for the security, provided the odd lot transactions are offset by round lot transactions as promptly as possible.

Sec. 13-17. Bidding for or purchasing a security—conclusions. Rule 10b-6 is only one of the anti-manipulative tools employed by the Commission within statutory grant. Others will be discussed elsewhere in this work.[105] It should be emphasized here that the rule does not purport to cover every possible manipulative activity; and the fact that a particular activity is not specifically dealt with or prohibited by the rule does not necessarily mean that it is not unlawful under the Act or other rules of the Commission.[106]

It may be noted that, apart from the circumstance that transactions claimed to come within exception "(11)" may not be engaged in at the same time as stabilizing is being effected,[107] if more than one exception to Rule 10b-6(a) be applicable to the same person in connection with the same distribution, such person may bid for and purchase securities of the same class under each applicable exception.

It should finally be observed, moreover, that the Commission considers with utmost seriousness violations of Rule 10b-6.[108]

Sec. 13-18. Bidding for or purchasing a security—stabilization transactions, basic concepts. Exception numbered "(8)" of

---

[105] *Infra*, Sec. 18-2.

[106] SEC Securities Exchange Act Release No. 5194, July 5, 1955, p. 3; and see SEC Securities Exchange Act Release No. 5040, May 18, 1954, pp. 1-2.

[107] See the discussion at Sec. 13-19, *infra*, as to the incompatibility of bids and purchases under exception "(11)" with stabilizing bids and purchases made pursuant to Rule 10b-7 as provided for by exception "(8)" of Rule 10b-6.

[108] See e.g., *Theodore A. Landau*, 40 SEC 1119 (1962); *Lawrence Rappee*, 40 SEC 607 (1961; *Bruns, Nordeman & Company*, 40 SEC 652 (1961); *Best & Garey Co., Incorporated*, SEC Securities Exchange Act Release No. 6841, July 6, 1962, p. 2; *Michael J. Bogan, Jr.*, SEC Securities Exchange Act Release No. 6810, May 23, 1962; *Reynolds & Co.*, SEC Securities Exchange Act Release No. 6978, Dec. 20, 1962, p. 2; *C. A. Benson & Co., Inc.*, SEC Securities Exchange Act Release No. 7053, April 10, 1963, pp. 8-9; *Batten & Co., Inc.*, SEC Securities Exchange Act Release No. 7086, May 29, 1963, p. 2; *P. deRensis & Co.*, SEC Securities Exchange Act Release No. 7114, Aug. 9, 1963, p. 2; *Advanced Research Associates, Inc.*, SEC Securities Exchange Act Release No. 7117, Aug. 16, 1963, p. 27; *Harwyn Securities, Inc.*, SEC Securities Exchange Act Release No. 7153, Oct. 4, 1963, p. 2; *Siltronics, Inc.*, SEC Securities Exchange Act Release No. 7158, Oct. 18, 1963, p. 2. And see *SEC* v. *Electronics Security Corp.*, 217 F. Supp. 831 (D. Minn. 1963).

Rule 10b-6(a) excludes from the prohibition of that rule ". . . stabilizing transactions not in violation of Rule 10b-7; . . ."

"Stabilizing" is a technique employed in facilitating a distribution which consists of the buying of a security for the limited purpose of preventing or retarding a decline of the price of the security in the open market.[109] This is regarded as permissible, and even necessary, to enable underwriters to protect themselves against the risk of a break in the market which would be a normal result of the selling pressure involved in a distribution, such protection being deemed desirable in the public interest generally in order to preserve the machinery for the flotation of securities so vital to the national interest.[110]

It should be emphasized that trading activity in connection with a distribution which raises the price of a security or is greater than necessary to prevent or retard a decline in the market price of the security would not constitute stabilization; it would be manipulation.[111] In adopting Rule 10b-7, the Commission has delineated the type of activity which, if followed in the context of a distribution, would result in conduct recognized as stabilization as distinguished from manipulation.[112] Stabilizing activities which are not in conformity with Rule 10b-7 constitute unlawful manipulation.[113]

Initially, the rule sets out its basic limits by providing that: "No stabilizing bid or purchase shall be made except for the purpose of preventing or retarding a decline in the open market price of a security."[114] Thus, stabilizing transactions[115] may not be

---

[109] SEC Securities Exchange Act Release No. 2446, March 18, 1949, p. 3; SEC Securities Exchange Act Release No. 6127, November 30, 1959, p. 1.

[110] SEC Securities Exchange Act Release No. 2446, *supra*; 6 SEC Ann. Rep. 97-100 (1940); SEC Securities Exchange Act Release No. 6127, *supra* n. 109, at p. 2.

[111] SEC Securities Exchange Act Release No. 3505, Nov. 16, 1943 (same as SEC Securities Act Release No. 2955).

[112] See paragraph (a) of Rule 10b-7.

[113] *Ibid.*

[114] Paragraph (c) of the rule.

[115] The term "transaction" includes a bid or a purchase. Rule 10b-7(b)(2). The term "stabilize," "stabilizes," "stabilizing," or "stabilized" means the placing of any bid or the effecting of any purchase for the purpose of pegging, fixing, or stabilizing the price of any security, but a bid is not a stabilizing bid unless shown on the market. Rule 10b-7(b)(3). Bids actually placed with dealers are deemed shown on the market even though not placed in the quotation sheets. The term "pegging, fixing, or stabilizing" is a tautological expression for the concept of bidding for or purchasing a security in order to prevent or retard a decline in the open market price of a security being distributed or for the purpose of pegging or fixing the price of a security. SEC Securities Exchange Act Release No. 2446, March 18,

effected to facilitate any "offering at the market."[116] And no stabilizing may "be initiated at a price which the stabilizer knows or has reason to know is the result of activity which is fraudulent, manipulative, or deceptive under the Act or any rule or regulation thereunder."[117]

Apart from these broad prohibitions, the remainder of the rule is concerned with the bounds of activity which would sustain the claim that particular transactions constitute stabilization rather than manipulation.

To debar activity greater than that necessary to prevent or retard a decline in the market price, the rule provides that any person who places a stabilizing bid or effects a stabilizing purchase on a securities exchange must grant priority to any independent bid at the same price irrespective of the size of such independent bid or the time when it is entered.[118] Similarly, if a person places a stabilizing bid or effects a stabilizing purchase over-the-counter, he must grant priority to any independent bid at the same price placed with or transmitted to him irrespective of the size of such independent bid or the time when it is entered.[119] In order

1940, pp 3-4; HR Rep. No. 1383, 73rd Cong., 2d Sess. (1934), pp. 21, 31; Sen. Rep. No. 792, 73rd Cong., 2d Sess. (1934), p. 17. See also Rule 17a-2(a); and see SEC Securities Exchange Act Release No. 6127, Nov. 30, 1959.

[116] "Offering at the market" is defined as an offering in which it is contemplated that any offering price set in any calendar day will be increased more than once during such day. Rule 10b-7(b)(1). Although the Commission adopted former Rule X-9A6 in 1940 to permit stabilizing in offerings stated to be "at the market," it repealed that Rule when it adopted Rules 10b-6, 7 and 8. SEC Securities Exchange Act Release No. 5194, July 5, 1955, pp. 2-3. Thus the Commission came around to the recognition of the validity of the view expressed in 1940 by Commissioner Robert E. Healy that a purported stabilization of an offering at the market was necessarily manipulative. *Dissenting Opinion*, Commissioner Healy, SEC Securities Exchange Act Release No. 2446, March 18, 1940, and see SEC Securities Exchange Act Release No. 5040, May 18, 1954, p. 1. Although stabilizing may be engaged in on the basis of existing market prices or bids in contemplation of an offering prior to the time the public offering price is fixed, the actual offering, when made, must not be an "offering at the market" as that term is defined in the rule.

[117] Paragraph (f) of Rule 10b-7. See *Michael J. Meehan*, 2 SEC 588, 628 (1937).

[118] Paragraph (d) of Rule 10b-7.

[119] *Ibid.* To implement these requirements, paragraph (d) of the rule also provides that: "Any person placing or transmitting a bid which he knows is for the purpose of stabilizing the price of any security shall disclose the purpose of such bid to the person with whom it is placed or to whom it is transmitted . . .". This requirement does not extend to the placement of bid quotations in the daily quotation sheets. However, the required disclosure must be made to a broker or dealer who communicates with the bidder in response to the quotation. It may be noted that as regards an over-the-counter transaction, the priority given is to the independent bid or purchase order placed with the stabilizer. The stabilizer is under no obligation to send his customers to other broker-dealers, but merely to give them priority over his own transactions.

further to eliminate the possibility of excess activity, the rule additionally provides that control of stabilizing operations be placed so that there shall be maintained no more than one stabilizing bid in any one market at the same price at the same time.[120] Quotations in the over-the-counter market, however, may be maintained by any number of broker-dealers for the account of the stabilizer so long as they are maintained at the same bid.[121]

Sec. 13-19. Bidding for or purchasing a security—stabilization transaction levels. In prescribing the levels at which stabilizing transactions may be made, the design of the rule is to guard against the raising of prices under the guise of stabilization.

In the first place, it concerns itself with the highest price at which a stabilizing bid or purchase may be made initially. With certain exceptions, the initial stabilizing bid or purchase price for a security may not be higher than "the highest current independent bid price for such security."[122] In the absence of a market, such as with a new security, stabilizing may be initiated at any price "not in excess of the public offering price."[123] Under specified circumstances, if a market does exist for the security and the principal market is a securities exchange, the initial stabilizing bid or purchase may be made up to the level of the last independent sale price on the exchange, even though that be higher than the highest current independent bid price.[124] The circumstances are (1) that the security was traded either on the day stabilizing is begun, or had been traded on either of the two preceding calendar days or, in the event of an intervening week-end or holiday, on

---

[120] Paragraph (e) of Rule 10b-7. If a stabilizing bid is made by the managing underwriter or other person selected for the purpose, neither the underwriter nor any broker-dealer participant may make bids or purchases in the open market under claim of the application of exception numbered "(11)" of Rule 10b-6(a). In brief, exception "(11)" must be interpreted in light of paragraph (e) of Rule 10b-7; the latter paragraph would be thwarted if exception "(11)" bids or purchases were permitted at a time when stabilizing is being engaged in. However, acquisitions, bids, and purchases under any of the other exceptions under paragraph (a) of Rule 10b-6 may be made while stabilizing is being effected.

[121] Paragraph (e) of Rule 10b-7.

[122] Rule 10b-7 at paragraph (j)(1).

[123] *Ibid.* and see *Idem.* at paragraph (j)(5) which provides that the stabilizing price may never exceed the public offering price. Special prices available to special groups or class of persons, including employees or holders of warrants or rights are not to be regarded as the public offering price and therefore do not set the limit of the stabilizing price. *Ibid.* and see paragraph (j)(3).

[124] *Idem.* at paragraph (j)(3).

the last preceding business day; and (2) that the current asked price is equal to or above the last independent sale price.[125]

The manifest reason for the imposition of these conditions is that stabilizing should not be permitted on the basis of a sale price which has become either stale by lapse of time, or obsolete as a measure for a stabilization level, as evidenced by the fact that the current asked price is below the last sale price. In the event the last sale price has thus become stale or obsolete, the stabilizing bid or purchase may be no higher than the highest current independent bid price, except that, if the first sale after the entering of the stabilizing bid is an independent sale at a higher price, the security may be stabilized at a price not in excess of that independent sale price.[126]

If stabilizing was begun before determination of the initial public offering price, and if the offering price is higher than the stabilizing bid or purchase price, then, after determination of the public offering price, stabilizing may be resumed at the price at which it could be initiated at the time of the determination of the public offering price.[126] A stabilizing bid properly made initially may be reduced at any time. It may be maintained at that level, moreover, irrespective of changes in the independent asked or sale price of the security, with the proviso that in no event may stabilizing be engaged in at a level higher than that at which stabilizing is being effected in the principal market for the security.[128] If stabilizing bids and purchases be discontinued for a period of less than three business days, they may be resumed in connection with the same distribution only at the level of, whichever is the lower, the last lawful stabilizing price, or the price at which stabilizing could then be initiated.[129] If stabilization purchases are not made for three consecutive business days or more,

---

[125] Paragraph (j)(2) of Rule 10b-7.

[126] *Ibid.*

[127] Paragraph (j)(4) of Rule 10b-7. It should be noted when the public offering price is ascertained, the raising of the stabilizing price may be made only to the price at which stabilizing could be initiated at that time, in accordance with the criteria for the proper price levels discussed immediately above in the text. And, where the public offering price is higher than such levels, stabilizing may not be engaged in at prices as high as the public offering price.

[128] *Ibid.* It must always be borne in mind, however, that the stabilizing activity may in no event be designed to raise the price of a security. See paragraph (c) of Rule 10b-7. And see *Associated Investors Securities Inc.*, SEC Securities Exchange Act Release No. 6859, July 24, 1962, pp. 9-10.

[129] Paragraph (j)(4) of Rule 10b-7.

however, even though stabilizing bids had been made in that period, stabilizing may be continued or resumed at the price at which it could then be initiated.[130]

A security being called or redeemed may not be stabilized at a level higher than the call or redemption price plus dividend or interest accruals, unless such security is convertible immediately into another security, in which case stabilizing may be at a price lawful for the security for which the distributed security is exchangeable or convertible.[131] Also, if the stabilized security goes "ex-rights," "ex-dividend," or "ex-distribution," the stabilizing level must be reduced by the value of the rights, dividend, or distribution.[132] When two or more securities are being offered as a unit, the component securities may not be stabilized at prices, the sum of which exceeds the offering price of the unit.[133]

In case a security is traded in on more than one market, the proper level for the initiation of stabilizing is that which would be lawful in the principal market for the security in the United States open for trading when stabilization is initiated.[134] If such principal market be a securities exchange which is closed when stabilizing is initiated, then stabilizing may commence at a level which would have been proper if it had been initiated at the close of such principal market.[135] No person may place a stabilizing bid on a securities exchange prior to the time the opening quotations for the security on such exchange are available, unless he has been and is lawfully stabilizing such security at such price,

---

[130] *Ibid.*

[131] Paragraph (j)(8) of Rule 10b-7.

[132] Paragraph (j)(6) of Rule 10b-7. There is a provision in this paragraph to the effect "that if the dividend, right, or distribution has a value of not more than 50 percent of the minimum price differential, the stabilizing price need not be reduced."

[133] Paragraph (j)(7) of Rule 10b-7. Care must be taken, moreover, that bids for or purchases of any component security of the unit should not be at prices which would be the equivalent of giving a premium on another component. Special prices available to special groups such as employees or holders of warrants or rights are not to be taken as the public offering price. *Ibid.*

[134] Paragraph (h) of Rule 10b-7. The net effect of this is to permit stabilizing on the basis of current prices on an exchange other than the principal market, if the principal market is closed and the other exchange is open.

[135] *Ibid.* This provision comes into force only if all of the exchange markets on which the security is traded are closed. It is subject to the condition that the person stabilizing does not know and has no reason to know that other persons have offered or sold such security at a lower price after such close. *Ibid.* Special prices to special groups, such as employees or holders of warrants or rights, are not taken into account for this purpose. *Ibid.*

except that, immediately prior to the opening of a securities exchange, a stabilizing bid may be made at a price not in excess of the level at which he could have initiated stabilizing on that exchange at the previous close of the exchange.[136]

Sec. 13-20. Bidding for or purchasing a security—stabilization transactions, notice and reporting requirements.

Apart from the necessity for complying with the restrictions and limitations as to extent of activity and prices laid down by Rule 10b-7, the conditions of the rule are not satisfied until its disclosure and reporting requirements have been fulfilled.

A person whose activity renders him subject to the rule and who sells to, or purchases for the account of, any person, any security where the price of such security, right, or warrant has been stabilized, is required to give or send to such second person, at or before the completion of each transaction entered into while the distribution is in progress, a written notice that stabilizing purchases may be or have been effected.[137] This can be satisfied by the placing of a legend provided for by Rule 426 under the Securities Act of 1933 on a prospectus, offering circular, confirmation, or other writing, received by the purchaser at or before the completion of the transaction.[138]

Rule 17a-2 under the Act requires notices and reports in connection with stabilizing transactions to be made by a member of a national securities exchange, a broker or dealer who transacts a business in securities through the medium of any such member, and by a registered broker-dealer. Rule 10b-7(e) makes the re-

---

[136] Paragraph (i) of Rule 10b-7. However, the paragraph contains the condition that the person stabilizing does not know and has no reason to know that other persons have offered or sold such security at a lower price after such close. Special prices to special groups, such as employees or holders of warrants or rights, are not taken into account for this purpose. *Ibid.*

[137] Paragraph (k) of Rule 10b-7.

[138] *Ibid.* The Rule 426 legend is as follows: "In Connection With This Offering. The Underwriters May Overallot or Effect Transactions Which Stabilize Or Maintain The Market Price Of (identify each class of securities in which transactions may be effected) At A Level Above That Which Might Otherwise Prevail In The Open Market. Such Transaction May Be Effected On (identify each exchange on which stabilizing transactions may be effected. If none, omit this sentence.) Such Stabilizing, If Commenced, May Be Discontinued At Any Time."

The term "completion of the transaction" is not defined for the purposes of this rule, but, in light of its use here in an anti-manipulative context, the definition of the term in Rule 15c1-1 would appear applicable. See *supra*, Sec. 11-5 n. 23, and Sec. 12-2.

quirements of Rule 17a-2 applicable to any other person whose activities render him subject to Rule 10b-7.

The initial obligation as regards notification is that of the manager who effects one or more stabilizing purchases for his sole account or for the account of a syndicate or group.[139] He must promptly notify the Commission of the name and class of the security being stabilized, and the price, date, and time at which the first stabilizing purchase was effected. In addition, the manager must supply the names and addresses of the syndicate members, and their respective commitments if the syndicate has already been formed; if not, such information must be supplied as soon as the syndicate is formed.[140] In addition, the manager must promptly inform each member of the syndicate respecting the name and class of the security being stabilized and the date and time at which the first stabilizing purchase was effected.[141] Moreover, when stabilizing has been terminated, the manager must promptly notify the Commission and the syndicate members of the date and time of termination.[142]

The remaining obligations under Rule 17a-2 relate to the filing of reports with the Commission. These requirements refer to those who are managers, and also to any person who has a participation in an account for which a stabilizing purchase is effected.[143] The reports must be filed on Form X-17A-1.[144] There are requirements for the filing of reports "as manager"[145] and reports "not as manager."[146] The reports "as manager" are filed by those who effect stabilizing purchases. The reports "not as

---

[139] The term "manager" is defined as "the person stabilizing for his sole account or for the account of a syndicate or group of which he is a participant." Rule 17a-2(b)(1). As stated in Rule 17a-2(a), the requirements of the rule relate to stabilizing in connection with securities registered under the Securities Act of 1933 or offered under Regulation A under that Act as well as to all offerings in excess of $300,000.

[140] Paragraph (c)(1) of Rule 17a-2. In the case of a standby or contingent underwriting, information should be supplied as to the percentage participation of each syndicate member; in the case of a best efforts underwriting only the total amount offered need be stated. *Ibid.* If the information as to the composition of the syndicate and the respective commitments of the group members have been furnished in a Securities Act of 1933 registration statement or in a Notification filed pursuant to Regulation A under that Act, such information need not be included in the notice of stabilization. Also, if such information has been otherwise filed with the Commission, it may be incorporated by reference. *Ibid.*

[141] Paragraph (c)(2) of Rule 17a-2.

[142] Paragraph (e)(3) of Rule 17a-2.

[143] See the last sentence of paragraph (a) of Rule 17a-2.

[144] A copy of SEC Form X-17A-1 appears as Appendix Q, Sec. 25-17, *infra.*

[145] Paragraph (d) of Rule 17a-2.

[146] Paragraph (e) of Rule 17a-2.

manager" are made by those who only have a participation in the account for which stabilizing is effected.[147]

A report "as manager" may include only such transactions as are effected for the syndicate or group if the manager is stabilizing for the account of such syndicate or group.[148] The first of such reports "as manager" must be filed not later than three business days following the day upon which the first stabilizing purchase was effected. It must contain information as to all purchases, sales, and transfers[149] in the stabilized and offered securities[150] (and in the rights if the offering is a rights offering) during the period beginning on the ninth business day prior to the first day on which the offering was made or beginning on the business day prior to the day on which the first stabilizing purchase was effected—whichever date is earlier—and ending on the day upon which the first stabilizing purchase was effected.[151]

Until stabilizing is terminated, the report "as manager" must continue to be made thereafter and must contain information with reference to all purchases, sales, and transfers for the syndicate account effected on the previous business day in the stabilized and offered securities and in the rights.[152] And if the manager has a short position in the stabilized or offered security when stabilizing is terminated, he must continue to report "as manager" not later than the next business day, all purchases, sales, and transfers effected on any day in such security until such short position is covered.[153]

---

[147] Paragraph (d) and (e) of Rule 17a-2.

[148] Paragraph (d)(4) of Rule 17a-2.

[149] The term "transfer" means any change in the control of a position in a security unaccompanied by a change in ownership. Rule 17a-2(b)(2).

[150] "Offered security" is defined to include any security of the same class and series. Rule 17a-2(b)(3).

[151] Paragraph (d)(1) of Rule 17a-2. A prospective underwriter who engaged in stabilizing activities in anticipation of becoming an underwriter must file a report on Form X-17a-2 as manager, even though it turns out that he is not selected as the underwriter.

In the case of securities offered pursuant to an effective registration statement under the Securities Act of 1933, the distribution is deemed not to commence prior to the effective date of the registration statement. *Ibid.*

[152] Paragraph (d)(2) of Rule 17a-2.

[153] Paragraph (d)(3) of Rule 17a-2. It may be appropriate here to note that purchases to cover a syndicate short position at the completion of a distribution resulting from over-allotment does not normally come within the purview of the concept of a stabilizing purchase. See Rule 17a-2(a). However, the covering of such syndicate short position by open market purchases would be regarded as manipulative if any member of the underwriting syndicate or selling group is long by reason of being left with an unsold portion of the original offering. Since over-allotment is

Reports "not as manager" are made by all persons having an interest in the account for which stabilizing purchases are made. This report is made only once not later than five business days following the day of the termination of stabilization. It must reflect all purchases, sales, and transfers in the stabilized and offered securities (and in the rights in the case of a rights offering). The period covered by the report commences with the ninth business day prior to the first day upon which the offering was made, or on the business day prior to the day upon which the first stabilizing purchase was effected—whichever date is earlier—and ending on the day stabilizing was terminated.[154] This report "not as manager" must also be filed by the manager to reflect all of his purchases, sales, and transfers not effected for the syndicate or group account. Thus, the manager must file the "not-as-manager" report to reflect his own underwriting transactions. Other participants in the syndicate account who report "not as manager" should report only their own transactions.

Form X-17A-1 has been revised from time to time. In its present state, it calls for the lumping of all transactions effected by the reporting person as broker for another at the same price on the same day. It elicits information as to the position in the security at the beginning of the reporting period and at the end of the period. It also calls for each transaction as dealer in the stabilized or offered security (or in the rights in an appropriate case) by the reporting person in the reporting period. By reference to appropriate symbols on the form, the items reported

---

effected to facilitate an offering, the covering of the short position is regarded as being made with the manipulative purpose of inducing others to purchase the offered security unless there exist such factors as, (1) no syndicate or group member is long the offered security, (2) reasonable efforts are made by the manager to acquire the securities away from the market in negotiated transactions, (3) the manager is not concurrently making additional short sales, (4) the independent market price is higher than the fixed offering price, (5) there is a reasonable time lapse following termination of distributive efforts, (6) the underwriting group holds no options on securities of the same class, and (7) all agreements restricting sales have been terminated. SEC Securities Exchange Act Release No. 3506, Nov. 16, 1943 (same as SEC Securities Act Release No. 2956). For the same basic reasons, a managing underwriter may not cover a syndicate short position by open market purchases resulting from bids or prices not limited by Rule 10b-7 if, at the same time, he is maintaining a stabilized bid. Subdivision (B) of Rule 10b-6(c)(3) specifically provides that a distribution by an underwriter is not completed while stabilizing arrangements have not terminated.

[154] Paragraph (e) of Rule 17a-2. This paragraph provides, also, that the effective date of a Securities Act of 1933 registration statement shall be the earliest date on which an offering pursuant to such statement may be deemed to commence.

reflect not only a purchase or sale, as the case may be, but also some description as to the type of person with whom the transaction was engaged in. For example, the letters RET adjacent to an entry showing a sale reflects a retail sale;[155] the letters MGR adjacent to an entry showing a purchase would reflect the taking of an allotment from the manager; and a transfer of stock to the manager in fulfillment of an obligation as selling group member to do so upon demand would be reflected as a sale with the letters MGR adjacent to the item. In all, there are ten such symbols designed to provide the required information in appropriate detail. Data as to purchases, sales, and transfers required by the form include dates, amounts, prices, and times. Dates supplied should be the actual dates on which the transactions occurred.[156]

One final observation with respect to the filing of reports on Form X-17A-1 should be made. If no stabilization purchases were made, even though stabilization bids were placed, no report need be filed.

Sec. 13-21. Bidding for or purchasing a security—stabilization transactions, miscellaneous matters. Neither the stabilization rule nor the reporting rule apply to transactions in exempted securities as defined in Section 3(a)(12) of the Act, including securities issued or guaranteed as to both principal and interest by the International Bank for Reconstruction and Development.[157] Additionally, the restrictions of the stabilization rule would not apply to such transactions as the Commission upon written request or its own motion may exempt, with or without conditions, from the operation of the rule as not constituting a manipulative or deceptive device or contrivance comprehended within the purpose of the rule.[158] Finally, the stabilization rule provides that, if a violation by a person would be involved purely as the result of the previous act or omission on the part of someone else, the person would not be chargeable with such violation unless he knew or had reason to know of such previous act or omission.[159]

---

[155] A broker or dealer who places in his investment account any unsold part of the distribution should report the transaction as a retail sale to itself.

[156] Such dates are referred to as "trade dates" in contra-distinction from "settlement dates" which represent in the trade the dates when delivery and payment are to be effected. In a sale, "regular way," payment, and delivery occur four days after the trade date. See CCH *N. Y. Stock Exchange Guide* ¶ 2064, Rule 64.

[157] Rule 10b-7(n); Rule 17a-2(b)(4).

[158] Rule 10b-7(c).

[159] Rule 10b-7(m).

A discussion of the subject of stabilizing would not be complete without pointing out that stabilizing is permissible in the absence of rules. Hence, so long as activity which does not raise or depress the price of a security is engaged in for a purpose other than to induce the purchase or sale of the security by others, such activity is not prohibited if not outlawed by rule.[160] It has been seen that stabilizing activity to facilitate a distribution must be in compliance with Rule 10b-7. However, the stabilizing of the price of a security to maintain its value as collateral and for other purposes apart from facilitating a distribution are not uncommon practices. There is pending a Commission proposal to outlaw these practices by prohibiting all stabilizing activity except in connection with a distribution.[161]

Sec. 13-22. Bidding for or purchasing a security—rights offerings, background and general considerations. It has been seen that, as a person subject to Rule 10b-6, an underwriter, prospective underwriter, issuer, or other person on whose behalf a distribution of securities is being made, as well as a broker, dealer, or other participant in the distribution, may not use jurisdictional means to bid for or purchase for any account in which he has a beneficial interest "any right to purchase" the security being or to be distributed.[162] It has also been seen that exception numbered "(9)" of Rule 10b-6(a) exempts from this prohibition "bids for or purchases of rights not in violation of Rule 10b-8. . . ."[163]

Rule 10b-8 concerns itself with distributions by jurisdictional means of securities offered through rights on a pro rata basis to security holders.[164] This type of offering has come into prominence in recent years. Apart from the circumstance that a number of such offerings are made in the common stock of an issuer to

---

[160] See SEC Securities Exchange Act Release No. 605, April 17, 1936, and SEC Securities Exchange Act Release No. 6127, Nov. 30, 1959. Activity which raises or depresses the price of a security for the purpose of inducing other persons to buy or sell the security is manipulative. See Sections 9(a)(2), (3), (4), and (5) of the Act. Persons engaged in the distribution of a security are presumed to have the purpose of inducing others to buy the security when such persons pursue a course of conduct designed to facilitate the distribution. SEC Securities Exchange Act Release No. 3505, Nov. 16, 1943, p. 4; SEC Securities Exchange Act Release No. 3506, Nov. 16, 1943, p. 2.

[161] SEC Securities Exchange Act Release No. 6127, Nov. 30, 1959.

[162] Rule 10b-6(a).

[163] *Supra,* Sec. 13-15.

[164] Rule 10b-8(a).

satisfy the preemptive rights of stockholders, many of them are floated among existing security holders because they represent a favorable market for the raising of additional desired capital. In some rare cases in which the issuer is confident that its security holders will subscribe in sufficient quantities to satisfy its needs, it will not engage an underwriter. Most rights offerings, however, involve a "stand-by" arrangement with an underwriter under which the underwriter agrees to purchase for resale the unsubscribed portion of the issue. Moreover, even though an underwriter be not obtained by an issuer for a standby underwriting, the issuer frequently enlists the assistance of brokers and dealers in bringing about the exercise of the rights, and, on occasion, may make arrangements with a particular broker-dealer to manage such a program.

For the "standby" underwriter, a rights offering poses the special problem that he has no idea as to the size of his commitment, and, throughout the entire rights period, he is in a highly exposed position, subject to the fluctuations of the market. The standby underwriter will therefore want to purchase as many outstanding rights as possible. The more rights he purchases, the more control he has over his commitment. Accordingly, he goes into the market to acquire rights. He then exercises the rights and arranges for "layoffs" of the offered security among brokers and dealers. In turn, they will dispose of the securities to their customers.[165]

Sec. 13-23. Bidding for or purchasing a security—rights offerings, permissible activities. To meet the manipulative possibilities inherent in this type of conduct and in practices of issuers in conjunction with brokers and dealers relative to dealings in the rights and the underlying security, Rule 10b-8 has two basic restrictions applicable to persons within its purview. The rule provides for limits as to (1) the prices at which the underlying security may be sold and (2) the prices at which the rights may be purchased.

By its terms, the rule outlaws as a "manipulative or deceptive device or contrivance" the use of jurisdictional means by any person participating in a distribution of securities being offered

---

[165] This method of dealing with rights by the underwriter is called the "Shields Plan."

through rights to perform any act prior to the expiration of the rights which the rule prohibits.[166] Specifically excluded from the rule, however, is a person whose role in the course of the offering is limited strictly to receiving compensation from the issuer for obtaining exercises of rights by security holders to whom the rights were originally issued.[167] As a participant in the distribution of the underlying security, this dealer is subject to the prohibitions of Rule 10b-6 which preclude him from bidding for or purchasing the underlying security, although, under Rule 10b-8, he is free to buy and sell rights as well as to sell the underlying security without conforming to the limitations and restrictions of Rule 10b-8.[168]

Sec. 13-24. Bidding for or purchasing a security—rights offerings, price limitations on sales of underlying securities. A person covered by Rule 10b-8 may not offer or sell the underlying security (or a security of the same class and series) at a price higher than the last price fixed by the manager of the distribution or fixed by a formula prescribed in an agreement with the manager. If the principal market for the security is a securities exchange, the price when fixed may not exceed the price at which the security last sold on the exchange (plus an amount equal to an exchange commission) or the current asked price on the exchange (plus such commission), whichever is higher.[169] If the principal market for the security is not a securities exchange, the sale price when set may not be higher than the highest price at which a dealer not participating in the distribution is offering the security at the time to other dealers (plus an amount equal to a dealer's concession).[170] There are stated exceptions to these

---

[166] Rule 10b-8(a).

[167] *Ibid.* If the offering has an oversubscription feature under which existing security holders are entitled to subscribe not only for their pro rata share but also for securities as to which other security holders failed to exercise their rights, a person may still come within this exclusion and receive compensation from the issuer for inducing such oversubscriptions, provided of course the right to oversubscribe is exercised by an original holder with oversubscription rights.

[168] Indeed, any other participant in the rights distribution is subject to all of the prohibitions of Rule 10b-6 except as to dealings in the rights which satisfy the limitations of Rule 10b-8. This is the purport of exception numbered "(9)" of Rule 10b-6(a).

[169] Paragraph (b) of Rule 10b-8.

[170] *Ibid.* These pricing limitations relate principally to "layoffs" of stock acquired by the underwriter following his having purchased rights and having exercised them. If no offers are being made of the underlying security and its principal market is not on a securities exchange, the price restrictions of Rule

price restrictions relative to offers and sales of the distributed security. They are set forth in the margin.[171]

Sec. 13-25. Bidding for or purchasing a security—rights offerings, price limitations on purchases. The price restrictions relative to the purchase of rights apply to all bids and purchases of rights on behalf of a sole distributor or a "syndicate or group" participating in the distribution or any member or members of such a syndicate or group.[172]

It may be observed initially that, unless the price of the offered security is being stabilized, there are no price restrictions as to the purchase of rights by such distributor, syndicate, group, or member thereof, if such purchaser of rights is short the securities on balance; that is, if all of the rights bought by him as principal are necessary to acquire offered securities previously sold by him.[173] Stated otherwise, the price restrictions as to the purchase of rights are applicable, with certain exceptions, to such person if either (1) the price of the security is being stabilized, or (2) such person, having acquired as principal any right not necessary to procure securities previously sold by him in connection with the distribution, has not sold the securities which have been or can be acquired through such rights.[174]

10b-8(b) do not apply. The amount of any accrued dividends or interest may be added to such prices. *Ibid.*

It may be observed that paragraph (b) of Rule 10b-8 contains the provision that, although the price fixed for the offer or sale of the distributed security may be set from time to time, a price set on one calendar day may not be increased more than once during that day. The obvious purpose of this provision is to prevent the offering from becoming an "offering at the market" as defined in Rule 10b-7(b)(1); thus, stabilizing activities in connection with the offered security would be permissible.

[171] These are: (1) privately negotiated transaction effected otherwise than on a securities exchange, among persons participating in the distribution; (2) odd lot transactions (and the off-setting round-lot transactions) by a person registered as an odd lot dealer on a national securities exchange who offsets such odd-lot transactions by round-lot transactions as soon as possible; (3) brokerage transactions not involving solicitation of the customer's order; (4) offers and sales at the subscription price to the holders of rights; (5) offers and sales to members of any group or class entitled to a special price; and (6) offers and sales of securities owned beneficially on the record date for the rights or acquired through the exercise of rights issued in respect of securities so owned. See paragraph (c) of Rule 10b-8.

[172] Rule 10b-8(d).

[173] *Ibid.*

[174] Paragraph (d) of Rule 10b-8. The term "syndicate or group" as used in that paragraph includes (1) any person who has agreed to purchase from the issuer of rights any of the securities offered through but not purchased upon the exercise of the rights; (2) any person other than the issuer who, as "dealer-manager," manages a distribution of a rights offering involving "soliciting dealers"; (3) any person

Thus, the pricing limitations laid down in the rule to be followed in the bids for and purchases of rights are applicable to the "Shields Plan" type of distribution as distinguished from the "Columbia Gas Plan."[175]

Here follow the conditions and restrictions which are applicable to the Shields Plan: On an exchange market, not more than one bid to purchase rights may be maintained in any one market at the same price at the same time; and, as respects a security traded only over-the-counter, more than one bid for the rights may be maintained by or for the account of a sole distributor or syndicate or group so long as they are all maintained at the same price.[176] If trading has not begun on the business day on which trading in the rights could lawfully have begun, and a theoretical value of the rights can be ascertained by a generally accepted mathematical formula, then the rights may be thereafter bought at a price not in excess of such theoretical value.[179] Absent such special circumstances, no bid for or purchase of rights may be made until an independent market for the rights has been established.[178] As to rights traded in the United States only over-the-counter the initial bid or purchase price may be no higher than the highest current independent bid price.[179] If the principal market for the rights in the United States is a securities exchange open for trading at the time of the initial bid or purchase, then such bid or purchase may be made in any market at the last independent sale price on the exchange if the last sale price is not stale or obsolete as defined by the rule. If the last sale price should thus be stale, then the initial bid or purchase may be at a price

---

who, as "soliciting dealer" is entitled to receive, directly or indirectly, from the issuer of the rights, compensation for obtaining exercises of such rights; and (4) all persons who have agreed with the issuer of rights, or with each other, that they will engage in the purchase of rights and the sale of the securities which may be acquired through the exercise of rights. *Ibid.*

175 See *supra*, n. 165 and accompanying text. Under the "Columbia Gas Plan," there is generally no underwriter or manager. Under the usual arrangements, there is no stabilization and rights may not be bought unless the dealer has previously sold the offered security.

176 Paragraph A of Rule 10b-8(d).

177 *Idem.* at paragraph (B). Where the subscription price is lower than the market price of the offered security, it is a relatively simple matter to compute the theoretical value of the right. In the absence of a market price and of an independent market, no bid for or purchase may be made as to the rights. However, if a "layoff" of the underlying security occurs, the "layoff" price can be used as a basis for computing the theoretical value for the rights.

178 *Idem.* at paragraph (B).

179 *Idem.* at paragraph (C).

no higher than the highest current independent bid price on the exchange.[180] In the event the initial bid or purchase is made after the close of the exchange, such bid or purchase may be made at the price which could have been set at the close of the exchange, unless the bidder or purchaser knows or has reason to know that other persons have offered or sold the right at a lower price after such close.[181]

Subject to the *caveat* that purchases of rights must be limited to the number necessary to acquire the securities which the sole distributor or syndicate or group members have previously sold or expect to be able to sell within five business days after the expiration of the rights, a bid lawful when initiated may be continuously maintained or reduced, irrespective of changes in the independent bid, asked or sale price of such right.[182] Apart from transactions specifically exempted from the price restrictions relative to the purchase of rights,[183] bid and purchase prices of rights by a person subject to the price restrictions may not be increased unless either no rights have been purchased by him as principal for a full business day, or the independent bid price in the principal market for such rights in the United States has exceeded such price for a full business day.[184] In that event the bid or purchase price may be increased to such level as would be applicable if it were the initial bid or purchase.[185]

The rule envisions the possibility that events may arise which would render the price restrictions as to the purchase of rights inapplicable and that later events may occur to make such restrictions operative. In such a case the first bid for or purchase of rights after the restrictions have become applicable shall be treated as though it were the initial bid governed by conditions at the time restrictions are resumed.[186]

---

[180] *Idem.* at paragraph (C). The last sale price on the exchange would be stale if the right was not traded on the exchange on the day of the initial bid or purchase or on the preceding business day; and the last sale price would be obsolete if the current asked price is below the last sale price at the time of the initial bid or purchase. *Ibid.*

[181] *Ibid.*

[182] *Idem.* at paragraphs (E) and (G).

[183] These exemptions are set forth in paragraph (H) of Rule 10b-8(d). See n. 187, *infra.*

[184] Rule 10b-8(d) at paragraph (E). For the purpose of this paragraph a "full business day" means a period beginning any time on one business day and extending to the same time of day the next business day. *Ibid.*

[185] *Ibid.*

[186] Rule 10b-8(d) at paragraph (F). The situation under which the restrictions as to the bid and purchase price for rights by a person within the purview of the

The price restrictions do not in any event apply to purchases of rights specified as exempt from their application. These are set forth in the margin.[187]

Absent such exemption the price restrictions of the rule relative to bidding for and purchasing rights are of such a nature that a broker-dealer subject to such restrictions cannot possibly make a market in the rights.

Sec. 13-26. Bidding for or purchasing a security—rights offerings, miscellaneous matters. As in the case with the related rules, 10b-6 and 7, the Commission, with or without conditions, may exempt any transaction upon written request or its own motion if it is convinced that the transaction would not constitute a "manipulative or deceptive device or contrivance" comprehended within the purpose of the rule.[188] Additionally, if a person performs or omits an act which would involve a violation only if someone else had previously done or omitted to do some other act, such person is not regarded as having violated the rule by his act or omission unless he knew or had reason to know about the other person's act or omission.[189]

---

rule might be lifted might occur in the typical Columbia Gas Plan distribution in which no underwriter is involved and no stabilizing is effected in the offered security, and where the persons coming within the restrictions (such as a "dealer manager" who is managing the distribution for the issuer, or a "soliciting dealer" who receives compensation, directly or indirectly from the issuer for obtaining exercises of rights) shift from a long position on balance to a short position on balance in the offered security vis a vis the rights. *Idem.* at paragraph (d), and see *supra*, notes 165 and 175 over accompanying text.

[187] All of these are provided for in paragraph (H) of Rule 10b-8(d), and refer to transactions (1) by or through a manager of a distributing group in a privately negotiated transaction off the market without the intervention of a broker-dealer, a transaction enabling large rights holders who do not want to exercise them, to sell to the underwriters; (2) by an underwriter or dealer directly from a retail customer in an unsolicited privately negotiated transaction; (3) which are stabilizing transactions; (4) by and between persons participating in the distribution; (5) by an odd-lot dealer in the rights; (6) to enable a customer who wants to exercise the rights to round out enough for the purpose; (7) by an issuer who offers to security holders to whom the rights are originally issued to buy back the rights, so long as the security holder has sold neither the right nor the offered security, this being the so-called G.P.U. (General Public Utilities) Plan; and (8) by a "dealer-manager," as defined, who has no standby commitment and who manages a distribution involving the services of a "soliciting dealer," as defined.

[188] Rule 10b-8(f).

[189] Rule 10b-8(e).

CHAPTER 14

PROHIBITIONS RELATING TO SHORT SALES

Sec. 14-1. Background discussion. The Commission defines a "short sale" as "any sale of a security which the seller does not own or any sale which is consummated by the delivery of a security borrowed by or for the account of the seller." [1]

In the enactment of the Securities Exchange Act of 1934, Congress recognized and evidenced concern with certain basic manipulative and other destructive potentials in short selling practices.[2] With minor exceptions, Congress prohibited an officer, director, or beneficial owner of more than ten percent of any class of any equity security of an issuer registered for listing on a national securities exchange from selling short any equity security of the issuer of the listed security.[3] Additionally, it prohibited the use of jurisdictional means by any one to effect a short sale in a security registered for listing on a national securities exchange in contravention of such rules and regulations as the Commission may prescribe as necessary or appropriate in the public interest or for the protection of investors.[4]

Continuing studies by the Commission between 1935 and 1938 led to the conclusion that in a declining market in securities listed on an exchange, the trend is accentuated to the detriment of the public by activity of a comparatively few professionals in not only liquidating long positions in "market leaders" but in creating additional selling pressure by extensive short sales of such stocks and thus bringing about a condition of acute distress in the market generally.[5]

---

[1] Rule 3b-3.

[2] See Sen. Rep. No. 792, 73rd Cong., 2d Sess. (1934), p. 9.

[3] Section 16(c) of the Act. The term "equity security" is defined in Section 3(a)(11) of the Act.

[4] Section 10(a) of the Act.

[5] SEC Securities Exchange Act Release No. 1548, January 24, 1938, pp. 3-8. It is thus seen that the concern as to the impact of short selling was not confined to its fraudulent aspects, but included as well the broader consideration that "in a declining market certain types of short sales are seriously destructive of stability." *Idem.*

It is manifest that short selling under such conditions, when not thoroughly demoralizing of the market, has, at a minimum, the effect of enabling the short seller to drive the price of the security he has sold to a price substantially lower than the sales price and thereby to reap a profit. It was to curb the depressing effect of short sales on the prices of listed securities that the Commission adopted a set of rules with provisions designed to minimize such effect.

Sec. 14-2. Short sales rules—basic price restrictions, implementing provisions, definitions. The short selling rules are composed of basic prohibitions, together with some implementing provisions as well as specified exemptions to cover situations in which the dangers of short selling are not inherent. The basic prohibitions are that: "No person shall for his own account or for the account of any other person, effect on a national securities exchange a short sale of any security (1) below the price at which the last sale thereof, regular way, was effected on such exchange, or (2) at such price unless such price is above the next preceding different price at which a sale of such security, regular way, was effected on such exchange. . . ."[6] This formula was explained in these simple terms at the time of its adoption: "[the rule] permits short sales at the *same* price as the last sale, provided the last sale price was higher than the last *different* price which preceded it."[7]

---

at p. 8. The term "market leaders" is applied to stocks which, by virtue of prominence and popularity, enjoy a large volume of trading. *Idem.* at p. 6. This Commission study confirmed the criticism in respect of short sales which impelled Congress to place the entire subject under Commission regulation by rule. See Sen. Report No. 792, 73rd Cong., 2d Sess. (1934), p. 9. See also *Special Study Report,* Pt. 2, Ch. VI, p. 292.

[6] Rule 10a-1(a). It may be noted from the text directly above that the short sales rules by their terms refer only to such sales effected on a national securities exchange. In determining the price at which a short sale may be effected, all prices as to securities going "ex-dividend, ex-right, or ex-any other distribution" may be reduced by the value of such distribution prior to the "ex" date. *Ibid.* However, prices at which short sales may be made are not reduced by the amount of taxes required to be paid as the result of the transaction.

The term "regular way" refers to the type of sale calling for delivery of and payment for the security at the expiration of a specified period which, in accordance with the custom or rule of the exchange, is the time in which payment and delivery must be made in the absence of special agreement calling for earlier or later settlement. On the New York Stock Exchange, "regular way" calls for settlement on the fourth business day after the transaction. See CCH *N. Y. Stock Exchange Guide* ¶ 2064, Rule 64.

[7] SEC Securities Exchange Act Release No. 2039, March 10, 1939, p. 1. Emphasis in original. Prior to the adoption of the rule in its present form, the rule requirement was that a short sale could be effected only at a price higher than the last

To implement this basic prohibition is a provision which precludes any member of a national securities exchange from executing, through any facility of the exchange, any sell order unless the order is marked "long" or "short."[8] And he may not mark a sell order "long" unless the security to be delivered in consummation of the sale is carried in the account for which the sale is to be effected, or he is informed that the seller owns the security ordered to be sold and will deliver that security to the account for which the sale is to be effected, as soon as possible without undue inconvenience or expense.[9] Additionally, a member may not fail to deliver a security on the date delivery is due, nor may he lend, nor arrange for the loan of, any security for delivery after sale to the purchaser's broker, if the member knows or has reason to believe that the sale was or will be effected pursuant to an order marked "long"; unless the member knows or has been informed by the seller either that the security sold has been forwarded to the account for which the sale was effected or that the seller owns the security, that it is then impracticable for the seller to deliver it to such account, and that the seller will deliver it as soon as is possible without undue inconvenience or expense.[10] These restrictions as regards lending or failing to deliver a security are subject to modification by the exchange upon which the sale was effected upon a finding by the exchange, after application prior to any such loan or failure to deliver, that the sale resulted from a mistake made in good faith following the use of due diligence to ascertain whether the seller was indeed "long" the security, and an additional finding, either that the condition of the market at the time of the discovery of the mistake was such that, to cover by purchase for cash would result in undue hardship, or that the mistake was made by the seller's broker and the sale was at a price permissible for a short sale.[11]

---

sale price. *Ibid.* and see SEC Securities Exchange Act Release No. 1548, January 24, 1938, p. 3.

[8] Paragraph (b) of Rule 10a-1. The symbols "1" or "S" would satisfy this requirement. SEC Securities Exchange Act Release No. 1571, February 5, 1938, p. 3. The requirement as to marking an order "long" or "short" applies not only to the memorandum handed by a member to its floor partner, but also to the memorandum of each brokerage order required by the bookkeeping rules to be maintained by the broker. See *supra,* Sec. 6-1.

[9] Paragraph (c) of Rule 10a-1.

[10] Paragraph (a) of Rule 10a-2.

[11] Paragraph (b) of Rule 10a-2. Absent such special relief, if the member has not received the security from the seller by the due date of delivery pursuant to a

It should be kept in view that a sell order may not be marked "long" unless (a) the customer owns the security and it is already carried in the account he has with the member, the account being the one from which delivery after sale is to be effected, or (b) the member is informed that the seller owns the security, and will deliver it to the account for which the sale is to be effected, as soon as possible without undue inconvenience and expense.[12] For the purposes of the rule, a person is deemed to "own" a security only to the extent that he has a net long position in that security. Thus, if a person maintains two accounts, one of which is short 1000 shares, and the other, long 1000 shares, such person does not "own" the security and hence any sell order by him must be marked "short" and be subject to the pricing restrictions as to short sales.[13] A person will be deemed to own a security "if (1) he or his agent has title to it; or (2) he has purchased or has entered into an unconditional contract, binding on both parties, to purchase it but has not received it; or (3) he owns a security convertible into or exchangeable for it and has tendered such security for conversion or exchange; or (4) he has an option to purchase or acquire it and has exercised such option; or (5) he has rights or warrants to subscribe to it and has exercised such rights or warrants."[14] A person is deemed to "own" a "when issued" security "if he has entered into a contract to purchase the same binding on both parties and subject only to the condition of issuance or, by virtue of his ownership of an issued security will be entitled to receive, without the payment of consideration, the 'when issued' security, to the extent that he has not already disposed of such 'when issued' security."[15]

---

sell order marked "long," the member must cover by purchasing it for cash for the account of the customer. See SEC Securities Exchange Act Release No. 1571, February 5, 1938, p. 5.

[12] Paragraph (e) of Rule 10a-1.

[13] SEC Securities Exchange Act Release No. 1571, February 5, 1938, p. 4. As seen, if the security is not already in the customer's account, the member must ascertain the actual net position of the seller. Hence if accounts maintained by the seller with the member reflect an even position in the security, the customer must show that he otherwise owns enough of the security to cover the "long" sale.

[14] Idem. at pp. 3-4. "He is not deemed to own a security if he owns securities convertible into or exchangeable for it but has not tendered such securities for conversion or exchange, or if he has an option or owns rights or warrants entitling him to such security, but has not exercised them."

[15] Idem. at p. 5. The same principle would apply to a "when distributed" security; namely, if a person has an absolute right to receive it he is regarded as owning it and his sell order may be marked "long."

A representation by a seller that he "owns" a security which it is then impracticable for him to deliver but which will be delivered as soon as possible without undue inconvenience or expense may be in the form of a written agreement with the member that such will be the case with respect to any sell order designated as "long"; the agreement also containing a commitment of the seller that when placing a "short" sell order he will designate it as such.[16]

Sec. 14-3. Short sales rules—exemptions from price restrictions. There are a number of exemptions from the pricing restrictions as to designated types of short sales, but none of these are exempt from the requirement that the sell order be marked "short."[17] The most significant of these, relating to certain types of arbitrage transactions, will be mentioned here. The others are noted in the margin.[18]

Although it is a "short sale," a transaction will be exempt from the pricing restrictions of the rule if it is the "sale of a security for a special arbitrage account by a person who then owns another security by virtue of which he is, or presently will be, entitled to acquire an equivalent number of securities of the same class as the securities sold, provided such sale, or the purchase which such sale offsets, is effected for the bona fide purpose of

---

[16] See SEC Securities Exchange Act Release No. 1571, February 5, 1938, p. 2.

[17] All of the exemptions are set forth in paragraph (d) of Rule 10a-1 which provides that paragraph (a), the pricing provisions of the rule, shall not apply to the transactions specified in paragraph (d). Exempt short sales orders are marked "short exempt." See *Special Market Study Report*, Pt. 2, Ch. VI, p. 294.

[18] These include (a) the sale of an odd lot and certain related transactions by an odd lot dealer; (b) a sale on an exchange effected with the approval of the exchange for the purpose of equalizing the price of the security on that exchange with the price of the security on another exchange which is the principal exchange market for the security; (c) the sale of a security on an exchange effected for a special international arbitrage account for the purpose of profiting from the current difference between the price on that exchange and the price of the same security on a market outside the jurisdiction of the United States, provided the seller knows or has reason to believe that a corresponding offer is available on such foreign market and he intends to accept that offer immediately, a depositary receipt for a security being deemed the security represented by the receipt; and (d) the sale of a security on an exchange under a special offering plan declared effective under Rule 10b-2(d) under the Act. It may be noted that in the case of a security which is traded in on two exchanges, if there be a difference in the prices on the two exchanges, the price on the particular exchange on which the order is executed is the one which determines the proper level, rather than a lower price on the other exchange. The only exception to this arises if the first exchange is not the principal exchange market and a sale is effected on the first exchange with the approval of that exchange for the purpose of equalizing the price with that on the principal exchange market for the security. Subdivision (d)(6) of Rule 10a-1.

profiting from a current difference between the price of the security sold and the security owned and that such right of acquisition was originally attached to or represented by another security or was issued to all the holders of any class of securities of the issuer."[19]

The elements of this exemption are (a) the securities sold must be securities of like number and class as the seller is, or presently will be,[20] entitled to acquire by virtue of securities he owns; (b) such right to acquire the securities sold was a right originally attached to or represented by the security owned or was a right issued to all holders of the class of securities of the issuer owned by the seller;[21] (c) the sale, or the purchase which such sale offsets, is effected for the bona fide purpose of profiting from a current difference between the price of the security sold and the price of the security owned;[22] and (d) the sale must be for a special arbitrage account of the seller.[23]

Sell orders for transactions which come within this exemption are commonly marked "Short Exempt (d)(7)" or "Short Exempt—7."[24]

Sec. 14-4. Short sales rules—miscellaneous observations. As will be developed at a later point, a national securities exchange

---

[19] Paragraph (d)(7) of Rule 10a-1.

[20] "Presently" is nowhere defined, but custom has it that, if the new securities (sold short) become exchangeable for the old securities (owned by the seller) within sixty days, the requirement that the seller "presently will be entitled to acquire an equivalent number of securities of the same class as the securities sold" will be satisfied.

[21] A right to a new security by virtue of a merger or consolidation is, of course, a right issued to all holders of the same class of securities of the issuer. It is sometimes thought to include an offer by another company to exchange its shares for shares of a specified class of the issuer, if the offer is made unconditionally to all holders of the specified class.

[22] If the short seller fails to exercise the subscription or conversion privilege, as the case may be, but covers his short position in other ways, such as by borrowing, or purchasing the security in the market, he does not have the requisite "*bona fide*" purpose.

[23] A "Special arbitrage account," is one of the special accounts provided for by Regulation T in which are reflected transactions not subject to the credit restrictions of Regulation T. See *supra,* Sec. 9-3. Transactions which may be effected in such an account include, among others: "xx a purchase of a security which is, without restriction other than the payment of money, exchangeable or convertible within a reasonable time into a second security together with an offsetting sale at or about the same time of such second security, for the purpose of taking advantage of a disparity in the prices of the two securities." Sec. 4(d) of Regulation T; 12 CFR 220.4(d).

[24] The reason for this designation is that the exemption is provided for by paragraph (d)(7) of Rule 10a-1.

has the obligation to discipline its members for violations of provisions of the Act and the rules thereunder.[25] Provisions of Rule 10a-1 implementing the price restrictions of the rule are directed specifically to members of national securities exchanges;[26] and relief in the case of mistakes made in good faith after use of due diligence is afforded under the rule through the exchange on which the sale is effected. For these reasons, most problems relative to the short sales rules are dealt with by the exchanges. However, the Commission retains full jurisdiction over all matters arising under its rules, and in a given appropriate case will deal with a violation of the short sales rule by a member of an exchange irrespective of whether the exchange takes action.[27]

[25] See *Infra*, at Sec. 23-2.

[26] See e.g., paragraph (b) and (c) of Rule 10a-1.

[27] See e.g., *Re, Re, & Sagarese*, SEC Securities Exchange Act Release No. 6900, September 21, 1962, p. 2.

As the result of the Special Study, moreover, the Commission has under consideration the adoption of pricing rules which would be designed to minimize the depressing effect on the market of short sales of "trading favorites," and "market leaders" by prohibiting short sales of a particular security when its market is under extraordinary selling pressure. *Special Study Report* Pt. 2, Ch. VI, pp. 292-3-4, item "3"; SEC Special Market Study Release No. 33, July 23, 1963, p. 4.

Chapter 15

OTHER ANTI-FRAUD AND ANTI-MANIPULATIVE PROVISIONS

Sec. 15-1. Failure to disclose control relationship with issuer. If a broker or dealer is "controlled by, controlling, or under common control" with an issuer, he would be perpetrating a "manipulative, deceptive or other fraudulent device or contrivance" if he should fail to make timely disclosure of such relationship to a customer he induces to buy or sell, or for or with whom he effects any transaction in, the security of that issuer over-the-counter.[1] Such disclosure must be made before the broker-dealer enters into any contract with the customer respecting the purchase or sale of the security. Moreover, if it was made orally prior to that time, it must be given or sent in writing to the customer "at or before the completion of the transaction."[2]

A problem which may arise in connection with the application of this provision may occur when a broker-dealer, or a partner or corporate officer of a broker-dealer, is a director or has some other relationship with the issuer which the broker-dealer, partner, or officer, may feel does not render him a person "controlled by, controlling, or under common control with," the issuer. A question as to the existence of such a control relationship with an issuer in any given case would be a question of fact.[3] A tribunal which may be called upon to decide the matter might well draw a conclusion different from that of the person concerned. Accordingly, such a broker-dealer, partner, or officer would be well advised to disclose

---

[1] Section 15(c)(1) and Rule 15cl-5. See *Graham & Co.*, 38 SEC 809, 810-811 (1959); *Dennis Securities Corp.*, 39 SEC 364, 366 (1959); *Security Enterprises, Inc.*, SEC Securities Exchange Act Release No. 6314, July 11, 1960, p. 3; *J. J. Magaril Company, Inc.*, SEC Securities Exchange Act Release No. 6997, January 21, 1963, p. 1.

[2] Rule 15cl-5. The term "completion of the transaction" is defined in Rule 15cl-1. For the meaning of the term as there defined, see *supra*, Sections 11-5 and 12-2. Since a confirmation of a transaction must be given or sent to a customer at or before the completion of the transaction (see *supra*, Sec. 12-2) the written disclosure is customarily given in the confirmation.

[3] See SEC Securities Exchange Act Release No. 1330, August 4, 1937.

the facts as to the relationship with the issuer, and, acting in good faith, he may disclaim the existence of a control relationship.[4]

Sec. 15-2. Commission action suspending trading on exchange and over-the-counter. Section 19 (a)(4) of the Act empowers the Commission summarily to suspend for a period of ten days trading on any national securities exchange in any security registered for listing on an exchange. This power has been most often exercised in connection with the pendency of a proceeding before the Commission under Section 19(a)(2) of the Act to determine whether to deny, suspend, or withdraw the registration of a security for listing on a national securities exchange for failure to comply with provisions of the Act or its rules and regulations. Its exercise most generally occurs "where sudden changes of circumstances make it appear that the information available to the public about the security is misleading or inadequate to permit investors to make an informed judgment with respect to the purchase or sale of the security so that there is a possibility for fraud, and it appears that the additional necessary information can be obtained and made available to investors . . ."[5]

In the past, when the Commission adopted an order under Section 19(a)(4) suspending trading on a national securities exchange and announced that the order was promulgated "to

---

[4] There is no express provision for such a disclaimer in this context. However, the acceptance by the Commission of this technique in other areas in which disclosure of a control relationship is required renders it reasonable that it would be acceptable here. For example, in another, but somewhat comparable connection, Rule 12b-22 provides: "If the existence of control is open to reasonable doubt in any instance, the registrant [of securities on a national securities exchange] may disclaim the existence of control and any admission thereof; in such case, however, the registrant shall state the material facts pertinent to the possible existence of control." See also, Rule 410 under the Securities Act of 1933. And *cf*. Rule 16a-3(d) under the Act for another example of resort to the disclosure and disclaimer technique in a different but comparable context for present purposes.

[5] *Securities Acts Amendments, 1959*, HR 86th Cong., 1st Sess. (1959), p. 163. See e.g., SEC Securities Exchange Act Release No. 6827, June 13, 1962; SEC Securities Exchange Act Release No. 6747, March 6, 1962; SEC Securities Exchange Act Release No. 6800, May 10, 1962. The Commission has also exercised the Section 19(a)(4) suspension power during the pendency of administrative proceedings under the Securities Act of 1933 relative to information publicly available in a Securities Act of 1933 registration statement which appears to the Commission to be false and misleading. See e.g., SEC Securities Exchange Act Release No. 6182, February 12, 1960; SEC Securities Exchange Act Release No. 6973, December 17, 1962.

Additionally, the Commission has consistently construed its summary suspension power to extend to the making of successive ten day orders throughout the pendency of the Section 19(a)(2) or other administrative proceeding; and that has been its practice. *Securities Act Amendments 1959, supra* at p. 163. This interpretation has been recognized by Congress Sen. Rep. No. 379, 88th Cong., 1st Sess. (1963), p. 66.

prevent fraudulent, deceptive or manipulative acts or practices," a broker-dealer was thereupon prohibited from using jurisdictional means to engage in any over-the-counter activity designed to effect, with or for the account of a customer, any transaction in, or to induce the purchase or sale by such customer of, such suspended security. This power has now been codified into the Act.[6]

Troublesome questions arise in connection with the application of this rule in cases where the suspension occurs after a transaction with a customer in the security has been initiated, but before consummation of the transaction. The prohibition precludes any act on the part of any broker or dealer designed to effect, with or for the account of a customer, any transaction in the suspended security. Consequently, "any act" engaged in to effectuate the transaction is prohibited. If the suspension is initiated following the customer's order but prior to payment, the broker-dealer may not accept payment, whether by bookkeeping entry or otherwise. On the other hand, if payment had been made prior to the initiation of suspension so that the only remaining acts on the part of a broker-dealer to effectuate physical delivery of the securities to which the customer is entitled are basically mechanical, such acts are not prohibited, and delivery may be made to the customer.

If a customer owns a "put" [7] which, by its terms must be exercised by a date prior to the expiration of an outstanding suspension order, he may stand to lose money if the put could be exercised profitably and the suspension prohibited such exercise. The purpose of the suspension is to protect public investors against fraud which may be exercised in the context of absence of accurate information concerning the security. It was not intended by the suspension to penalize investors and deprive them of the benefit of their contract rights, if appropriate effect can be given to its basic purpose. Accordingly, in the absence of special circumstances such as may arise from the identity of the customer or the customer's relationship with the issuer and control persons of the issuer, a broker-dealer may assist a customer to exercise a

---

[6] Section 15(c)(5) on the Act.

[7] A "put" is an option given to a person to sell to the maker a specified amount of securities at a stated price within a specified period. See SEC *Report On Put And Call Options* (1961), p. 9.

put in respect of a suspended security. In other cases in which the transaction did not have the fraudulent or manipulative purpose aimed at by the suspension and the persons involved have no relationship with the issuer or control persons of the issuer, broker-dealers have been invited to present the facts to the appropriate Commission staff for consideration of a "no-action" request.

A suspension of trading as to one class of security of an issuer does not affect trading in any other class of the issuer's securities, unless the other class is convertible into the suspended class. Whether or not trading in such convertible security is effected to evade the prohibitions of the suspension is a matter which can be decided only on the facts of a given case.[8]

It may be noted that Section 15(c)(5) prohibits the effecting of transactions and the consummation of transactions over-the-counter. A Section 19(a)(4) suspension order, however, is directed only against "trading" on the exchange. Hence if a transaction has been effected on an exchange prior to the entry of a Section 19(a)(4) suspension order, it may be consummated by payment and delivery thereafter should the rules of the exchange so permit.

It may also be observed that the Section 15(c)(5) suspension is directed by its terms against brokers and dealers. Thus the prohibitions of that Section do not apply to a "bank" as defined in the Act, because, as we have seen, a "bank" is by definition not a broker or dealer.[9] On the other hand, the section prohibits a broker or dealer from engaging in any act designed to effect a transaction in the security with anyone, including a bank.

Finally, since this prohibition is directed only to brokers and dealers, it would not apply to transactions directly between persons who are not broker-dealers. Of course, a broker-dealer may take no hand in bringing such persons together.[10]

---

[8] Even if it be assumed in a specified situation that the transaction in the convertible security is not to evade the impact of Section 15(c)(5), a broker-dealer would be obligated to inform purchasers of the convertible security that, if it be converted, the underlying security thus obtained would be subject to the rule regarding suspension of trading.

[9] See *supra*, Sec. 1-1.

[10] The Commission might lift the suspension upon termination of the proceeding in connection with which it effected the suspension. See e.g., (re: *Black Bear Industries, Inc.*), SEC Securities Exchange Act Release No. 6975, December 18, 1962. Or, without reference to the underlying proceeding, the Commission may decide to

Sec. 15-3. Commission action suspending trading in any security. It has been already noted directly above in the text that, in addition to its power to suspend trading on an exchange, the Commission now has the same power with respect to a security not traded on an exchange. And, in the face of such suspension, a broker-dealer is prohibited from effecting or inducing a transaction in the suspended security with any one.[11]

Sec. 15-4. Misrepresentation as to effect of registration. It would be a "manipulative, deceptive or other fraudulent device or contrivance" as that term is used in Section 15(c)(1) of the Act for a broker or dealer to represent that the fact of his registration as a broker-dealer or the fact that the Commission has not denied or revoked his registration "indicates in any way that the Commission has passed upon or approved the financial standing, business, or conduct of such registered broker or dealer or the merits of any security or any transaction or transactions therein."[12]

---

lift the suspension because accurate information as to the security has become publicly available. See e.g., SEC Securities Exchange Act Release No. 6937, Nov. 14, 1962, and SEC Securities Exchange Act Release No. 6973, Dec. 17, 1962; and SEC Securities Exchange Act Release No. 7263, March 6, 1964. In other cases, the suspension has been lifted because the exchange delisted the security. See e.g., SEC Securities Exchange Act Release No. 6926, Oct. 30, 1962.

See *Sadif* v. *Burnham & Co.*, 243 N.Y.S. 2d 822 (1963), an action for damages for non-delivery of securities, where the court refused to strike a defense based on the prohibition of former Rule 15c2-2 which has been replaced by Section 15(c)(5).

[11] Section 15(c)(5) of the Act. Securities Acts Amendments of 1964, Sec. 6(c). As is the case with the power under Section 19(a)(2) of the Act, each suspension may be for a period not exceeding ten days. Section 15(c)(5) of the Act is in essence a codification of former Rule 15c2-2 which has accordingly been abrogated as superseded by that section. See SEC Securities Exchange Act Release No. 7408, Sept. 1, 1964, p. 1.

[12] Section 15(c)(1) and Rule 15c1-3. It is permissible for a broker-dealer to state orally or on his stationery that he is registered, so long as it is not done with misleading effect.

Part V

FRAUDULENT PRACTICES OUTLAWED BY GENERAL ANTI-FRAUD PROVISIONS

CHAPTER 16

SHINGLE THEORY

Sec. 16-1. In general. It has just been seen that the fact of registration cannot be pointed to as an indication that the Commission has placed its stamp of approval on the manner in which a broker-dealer conducts his business. Nevertheless, the solicitation and acceptance by a broker-dealer of orders from customers and the confirmation of transactions do constitute a representation by the broker-dealer that he will deal fairly with his customers and that such transactions will be handled promptly in the usual manner, in accordance with trade custom.[1]

Stated otherwise, by mounting his "shingle," the broker-dealer makes this broad, basic representation to the public at large. This fundamental standard of conduct has thus become known as the "shingle theory."[2] It should be emphasized that the application of the shingle theory to a given transaction is not predicated upon the existence of a fiduciary obligation by the broker-dealer to his customer. These criteria are applied to all transactions by a broker-dealer including those engaged in as "dealer" or principal.[3] In brief they represent standards of professional conduct.[4]

It is not possible to set limits on the variety of ways in which the sweeping representation implied by his shingle may be rendered false by a broker-dealer. Because of certain recurring tech-

---

[1] E.g., SEC Securities Exchange Act Release No. 6778, April 16, 1962, p. 1; *Lawrence Rappee,* 40 SEC 607, 610 (1961); *Sol T. Pfeffer,* 40 SEC 612, 615 (1961); *Harvey H. Shields, Jr.,* 39 SEC 608, 609 (1959); *William Harrison Keller, Jr.,* 38 SEC 900, 905 (1959); *Batkin & Co.,* 38 SEC 434, 446 (1958); *Gill Harkness & Co.,* 38 SEC 646, 651 (1958); *Lewis H. Ankeny,* 29 SEC 514, 516 (1949).

". . . His solicitation and acceptance of orders constituted representations that he would deal fairly with his customers in the usual manner in accordance with trade custom . . . ." *Harvey H. Shields, Jr.,* 39 SEC at 609. See also *Charles Hughes & Co., Inc.* v. *SEC,* 139 F.2d 434 (2d Cir. 1943).

[2] *Ibid.* and see concurring opinion of Clark, J., in *Kahn* v. *SEC,* 297 F.2d 112 at 115 (2d Cir. 1961).

[3] *Ibid.* and see *G. Alex Hope,* 7 SEC 1082, 1084 (1940), as well as the other cases cited below as illustrations of the application of the shingle theory to transactions by broker-dealers as principals for their own account.

[4] ". . . the relationship of a securities dealer to his clients is not that of an ordinary merchant to his customers. . . ." *William Harrison Keller, Jr.,* 38 SEC 900, 905 (1959).

171

niques employed by fringe elements in transactions with customers, however, the instances of the application of the shingle theory have tended to fall into several categories. These are: (1) the failure to disclose the charging or paying of a price for a security not reasonably related to the prevailing market price for the security; (2) the failure to pay for securities sold and delivered by a customer to a broker-dealer, the failure to make timely delivery of a security sold to and paid for by a customer, and the hypothecation or other conversion to the broker-dealer's own use of fully-paid-for securities of customers held by the broker-dealer for safe-keeping; (3) the transaction of business with customers at a time when the broker-dealer is either insolvent or his liabilities exceed his current assets, or he is unable to meet his current obligations as they arise; and (4) the sale of large blocks of securities to strangers through numerous salesmen over the long-distance telephone and by use of flamboyant literature, under circumstances calculated to cause customers to make hasty decisions on the basis of oral, undocumented, unfounded representations, and the use of other high pressure "boiler room" tactics.

Such conduct is viewed as being in violation of the general anti-fraud provisions of the federal securities laws typified by Section 15(c)(1) of the Act as implemented by Rule 15c1-2.[5] Each of these categories will be discussed in turn.

Sec. 16-2. Price not reasonably related to market price. The mere quotation to a customer of a price for a security contains the implied representation that the price bears a reasonable relationship to the prevailing market price. Consequently, a broker-dealer makes a false representation if he fails to disclose that the price charged or paid to a customer for a security is not reasonably related to the prevailing market price.[6] To ascertain whether

---

[5] See *supra*, Chapter 10, and *infra*, Sec. 18-3, for references to Section 15(c)(1) of the Act and Rule 15c1-2, as well as to other anti-fraud provisions of the Act and the Securities Act.

[6] *E.g., Investment Service Co.*, SEC Securities Exchange Act Release No. 6884, August 15, 1962, pp. 7-8. *Theodore A. Landau*, 40 SEC 1119, 1126-7 (1962); *Lawrence Rappee*, 40 SEC 607, 610 (1961); *Sol T. Pfeffer*, 40 SEC 612, 615 (1961); *Fidelity Securities Corporation*, SEC Securities Exchange Act Release No. 6987, January 4, 1963, p. 1; *George Wales Allen*, 39 SEC 297, 299-300, 302 (1959); *Gregory & Company, Inc.*, 38 SEC 304, 307-8 (1958); *Jack Goldberg*, 10 SEC 975, 980 (1942); *G. Alex Hope*, 7 SEC 1082, 1084 (1940). See also *Charles Hughes & Co., Inc.* v. *SEC*, 139 F.2d 434 (2d Cir. 1943); and *Associated Securities Corporation* v. *SEC*, 293 F.2d 738 (10th Cir. 1961).

The quotation of a price [by a broker-dealer] is also a representation that the

this false representation has been made in a given case it is necessary initially to examine into how the prevailing market price is determined; and, secondly, to consider what constitutes a reasonable relationship to the prevailing market price.

Sec. 16-3. Over-the-counter market—prices. The market price at any given time for a security traded in on an exchange is in general readily ascertainable. Transactions effected on an exchange occur at a particular place where a concentration of buyers and sellers participate in making a public auction market. The prices of actual transactions are publicly reported on a current basis.[7]

On the other hand, over-the-counter transactions are negotiated privately; and the prices involved in actual transactions are normally not available to public investors who have no information as to either actual sales prices or sales volume of given securities.[8]

"market is a free and independent market insofar as that broker-dealer is concerned." *Lawrence Rappee, supra,* SEC Securities Exchange Act Release No. 6504 at p. 4. And see the authorities cited at Sec. 13-4, n. 14, *supra,* relative to the discussion of "Sales At The Market."

[7] See SEC Report *On the Feasibility and Advisability of the Complete Segregation of the Functions of Dealer and Broker* (1936), pp. 65-66. As a rule, problems do not arise with respect to the charging of prices for listed securities not reasonably related to the market price, since most transactions in such securities are executed by brokers as agents for their customers where the prices charged or paid to the customer are exactly the same at which the broker purchased or sold the security on behalf of the customer. In such case, the broker charges a commission which is generally a percentage of the price of the security. It has been seen, *supra,* Sec. 12-2, that such compensation must be separately stated in the confirmation.

It is true though that broker-dealers will trade as principals over-the-counter in listed securities. This has been characterized as the "third market" by the Special Study Report, which makes a number of recommendations for its regulation still under study by the Commission. Special Study Report, Pt. 2, Ch. VIII, pp. 910-11; SEC Special Market Study Release No. 33, July 23, 1963, p. 7. At the present writing, the Commission has proposed a rule which would require broker-dealers who trade over-the-counter in common stocks traded on a national securities exchange to file periodic reports as to their activities in that regard. Proposed Rule 17a-9, SEC Securities Exchange Act Release No. 7360, July 8, 1964. The proposed rule provides for one type of report to be filed by a "market maker," and another type, by any other broker dealer. Paragraphs (a) and (b) of Proposed Rule 17a-9. Additionally, separate reports would be required of market makers and other broker dealers with regard to their trading over-the-counter in common stocks traded on the New York Stock Exchange. Paragraphs (c) and (d) of Proposed Rule 17a-9. A "market maker" is defined as a "dealer who, with respect to a particular security, holds himself out (by entering indications of interest in purchasing and selling in an inter-dealer-quotation system or otherwise) as being willing to buy and sell for his own account on a continuous basis otherwise than on a national securities exchange." Paragraph (f)(1) of Proposed Rule 17a-9.

[8] ". . . . Unlike listed securities, there is no central trading place for securities traded over-the-counter. The market is established by traders in the numerous firms all over the country through a process of constant communication to one another of

Nevertheless, there are a number of ways in which over-the-counter market prices may be ascertained. As a preliminary to such discussion, a brief explanation of the over-the-counter market may be helpful.

Sec. 16-4. Over-the-counter market—quotation sheets. Most brokers and dealers subscribe to the service of the National Quotation Bureau, Inc., a private organization which publishes and circulates each day among its subscribers loose-leaf sheets which contain quotations as to over-the-counter securities inserted for that day by subscribers.[9] Bids and offers are additionally often made directly between brokers and dealers who generally know the firms which specialize in the securities in which they have an interest.[10]

Bids and offers in respect of a security represent the range within which it is believed that business may be transacted. Stated otherwise, the function of a quotation is to invite negotiations between broker-dealers revolving around the quoted price as a starting point. The bid quotation represents the lowest price at which the bidding dealer thinks other dealers may be induced to negotiate a sale to him; the "offer" or asked quotation represents the highest price at which the offering dealer feels he can induce other dealers to negotiate a purchase from him.[11]

It may be observed that in most cases bids and offers as to over-the-counter securities are communicated within the broker-dealer community and that they represent prices around which broker-dealers propose to negotiate with one another, as distinguished from members of the public. The published quotations, therefore, represent what is known as the "wholesale," "inside," or dealers' market, as distinguished from the "outside" or public market. Prices paid to the public for securities are apt to

---

the latest offers to buy and sell. . . ." *Silver v. N. Y. Stock Exchange,* 373 U. S. 341, 83 S. Ct. 1246, 1252 (1963).

[9] *Special Study Report,* Pt. 2, Ch. VII, pp. 552-3, 570-1. See *Halsey Stuart & Co., Inc.,* 30 SEC 106, 113 at n. 1 (1949). And see *New York Times,* Oct. 23, 1960, Sec. 3, p. F3. These quotation sheets are published in three editions: (1) the "pink sheets" or Eastern Section, (2) the "green sheets" or Western Section, and (3) the "white sheets" or Pacific Coast Section. The respective colors given to the names of these sheets represent the color of the paper used. *Special Study Report,* Pt. 2, Ch. VIII, pp. 596-7. Broker-dealers from any section of the country are able to insert quotations in any of the three editions. *Ibid.*

[10] *Special Study Report,* Part 2, Ch. VII, pp. 558-62.

[11] *Samuel B. Franklin & Company,* 38 SEC 908, 911-12 (1959), aff'd 290 F.2d 719 (9th Cir. 1961).

be somewhat less than prices paid or quoted for such securities on the inside market, whereas prices charged to the public for securities sold to them tend to be somewhat higher than the asked prices of the inside market.[12]

Under arrangements with the National Quotation Bureau Inc., broker-dealer subscribers who publish bids and offers are required to honor their quotations, unless their needs have already been filled or some changes have occurred so that they no longer need to buy or sell, as the case may be, the securities which they quoted.[13] In general, moreover, apart from securities in which there are no regular indications of dealer trading interest, and, apart from relatively new speculative issues, the prices quoted in the daily quotation sheets in respect of a security on a given day tend to fall within a definite range because of competition, trade custom, general adherence to standards of fair dealing, and the impact of federal and state regulation.[14]

For these reasons, in the absence of more persuasive evidence relative to specific situations or transactions, the quotations in the National Daily Quotation Sheets, if genuine,[15] are regarded as furnishing *prima facie* evidence of prevailing market prices.[16] It

---

[12] *Special Study Report*, Pt. 2, Ch. VII, pp. 552-3. And see *Barrett & Company, Inc.*, 9 SEC 319 323, 325, 327, 328 at n. 10 (1941); *Richard A. Holman*, SEC Securities Exchange Act Release No. 6931, Nov. 6, 1962, p. 3.

Retail quotations published in newspapers, although based on wholesale quotations and reflecting a theoretical differential in price, do not provide indications as to the identities of interested dealers. Such quotations are supplied by local and regional committees of the National Association of Securities Dealers, Inc. ("NASD"). *Special Study Report*, Pt. 2, Ch. VII, pp. 533, 633.

[13] *Halsey Stuart & Co., Inc.*, 30 SEC 106, 126 at n. 30 (1949). However, the practice of "backing away" from quotations is not uncommon even in the face of rules of governing professional associations. *Special Study Report*, Pt. 2, Ch. VII, pp. 572-4. For these reasons, the *Special Study Report* (Pt. 2, Ch. VII, p. 674, Item 2) recommends that a broker-dealer inserting a quotation be obliged to buy or sell (depending on the quotation) at least 100 units of the quoted security. The Commission has this under consideration. SEC Special Market Study Release No. 33, July 23, 1963, p. 5.

[14] *Halsey Stuart & Co., Inc., supra*, 30 SEC at 129, n. 33. In the case of inactively traded issues and of relatively new speculative issues, it is not uncommon for inter-dealer quotations to turn out to be illusory. See *Naftalin & Co., Inc.*, SEC Securities Exchange Act Release No. 7220, January 10, 1964, p. 5.

[15] That actual contemporaneous transactions may be more persuasive than the quotations in the sheets may be seen in the discussion, *infra* at Sec. 16-6. See also the discussion directly below in the text on the subject of "Genuineness of Quotation."

[16] *Charles Hughes & Co., Inc., v. SEC* 139 F.2d 434, 438 (2d Cir. 1943); *Charles M. Weber d/b/a Weber-Millican & Co. v. SEC* 222 F.2d 822 (2d Cir. 1955); *Indiana State Securities Corp.*, 38 SEC 118, 120-1 (1957); *Maryland Securities Co., Inc.*, 40 SEC 443, 446, n. 9 (1960); *Richard A. Holman*, SEC Securities Exchange Act Release No. 6931, Nov. 6, 1962, p. 3.

may be noted that both the bid and asked prices as to a security at a given time must be taken into account in determining the market price, "since transactions will usually be effected at a price somewhere between the bid and ask—more normally closer to the dealer's bid if the other dealer takes the initiative to sell, and closer to the ask if such other dealer takes the initiative to buy."[17]

Sec. 16-5. Over-the-counter market—genuineness of quotation. As seen, the quotations in the sheets will be accepted as reflecting market prices in the absence of other, more convincing evidence. However, the quotations must be genuine, for if fictitious they will not in fact represent the market prices. For example, quotations in the sheets will not be taken as the measure of the market if they do not truly reflect the collective judgment of buyers and sellers in an open market. Thus, quotations as to a particular security will not be given weight if the market in that security is created or controlled by a broker-dealer and he places or causes the quotations to be placed in the sheets. Such quotations would represent an artificial rather than an independent market.[18]   In this connection, however, it may be observed that merely because a broker-dealer is "making a market" in an actively traded security, this does not of itself establish the absence of an independent market.

In "making a market" in a security, a broker-dealer specializes in it to the extent that he holds himself out within limits to buy or sell it from or to dealers and other persons. The result is that he may effect a high percentage of the transactions in the securities, and he is apt to be the principal buyer and seller. By the same token, the quotations by such "primary market maker" are apt to reflect rather narrow spreads between the "bid" and "ask" prices

---

[17] *Richard A. Holman,* SEC Securities Exchange Act Release No. 6931, Nov. 6, 1962, p. 5. When the transaction is one of sale, the asked quotations are taken as the market price. See *Mitchell Securities, Inc.,* 37 SEC 178, 181, 182 (1956).

[18] SEC Securities Act Release No. 4401, Aug. 3, 1961, p. 1; *Lawrence Rappee,* 40 SEC 607, 609-10 (1961); *D. Earle Hensley Co., Inc.,* 40 SEC 849, 852 (1961); *Palombi Securities Co., Inc.,* SEC Securities Exchange Act Release No. 6961, Nov. 30, 1962, pp. 5-6; *Sterling Securities Company,* 39 SEC 487, 492 (1959). See also *W. K. Archer Company,* 11 SEC 635, 645 (1942); *SEC v. C. H. Abraham & Co., Inc.,* 186 F. Supp. 119 (S.D.N.Y. 1960); and Cf., *Canusa Gold Mines Ltd.,* 2 SEC 548, 552-5 (1937); *Unity Gold Corp.,* 3 SEC 618, 629-30 (1938); *Floyd A. Allen & Company, Inc.,* 35 SEC 176, 185 (1953). Cf. also Rule 15c1-8 under the Act discussed *supra* at Sec. 13-4 and cases there cited at n. 14 in connection therewith.

and serve as reliable guides for market prices.[19] Moreover, if his dealings are with other dealers or with sophisticated public investors who have access to quotations and information as to the issuer, such dealers and investors have the opportunity to weigh investment in the particular security as against investment in others, and, consequently, there actually is the possibility of an independent market subject to free and competitive forces. If in fact, then, there be such an independent market for a security, the circumstances that a broker-dealer is "making a market" in that security will not prevent the quotations in the National Daily Quotation sheets as to such security from constituting evidence of the market price.[20]

Registered securities associations have now been given specific responsibility to adopt procedures relating to quotations and their dissemination designed to produce fair and informative wholesale and retail quotations and to prevent fictitious or misleading quotations.[21]

Additionally, as a measure to guard against fictitious quotations of a specified character, the Commission has adopted a new rule respecting the furnishing of quotations to an "inter-dealer-quotation-system."[22] Under this rule, a correspondent broker or dealer who submits to an inter-dealer-quotation-system a quotation on behalf of another broker or dealer must furnish the name of the other broker or dealer to the inter-dealer-quotation-system. Moreover, if a broker or dealer submits to an inter-dealer-quotation-system a quotation in futherance of any arrangement between or among brokers and dealers (such as a joint account, guarantee of profit, guarantee against loss, commission, markup, markdown, indication of interest, and accommodation arrangement), the broker or dealer submitting the quotation must identify each

---

[19] Such a broker-dealer has recently been characterized as a "primary market maker." *Special Study Report*, Pt. 2, Ch. VII, p. 675, Items 4 and 5. For a discussion on this subject, see *Naftalin & Co., Inc.,* SEC Securities Exchange Act Release No. 7220, January 10, 1964, pp. 5-7.

[20] See *Norris & Hirshberg*, 21 SEC 865, 875-6 (1946).

[21] Section 15A(b)(12) of the Act. Securities Acts Amendments of 1964, Sec. 7(a)(7). See *infra*, Chapter 24, for discussion of such associations generally.

[22] Rule 15c2-7. SEC Securities Exchange Act Release No. 7381, Aug. 6, 1964. An "inter-dealer-quotation-system" is defined as, "any system of general circulation to brokers and dealers which regularly disseminates quotations of identified brokers or dealers but shall not include a quotation sheet prepared and distributed by a broker or dealer in the regular course of his business and containing only quotations of such broker or dealer." Paragraph (c)(1) of Rule 15c2-7.

broker and dealer participating in such arrangement. In connection with such arrangement, however, the identities of the other brokers and dealers need not be furnished if only one of the brokers or dealers participating in the arrangement submits the quotation. What is aimed at here are multiple expressions of the same market.[23]

The rule furthermore prohibits a broker or dealer from entering into a correspondent or other arrangement of the type indicated, in furtherance of which two or more brokers or dealers furnish or submit quotations with respect to a particular security unless such broker or dealer informs all brokers or dealers furnishing or submitting such quotations of such correspondent and other arrangements and the identities of the parties thereto.[24]

In implementation of these requirements, brokers and dealers are prohibited from furnishing or submitting a quotation for a security to an inter-dealer-quotation-system unless the system makes it a general practice to disclose with each published quotation, by appropriate symbol or otherwise, the information conveyed to it pursuant to the rule, respecting the correspondent or other arrangement of the kind indicated, and respecting the identities of all other brokers or dealers whose identities are required by the rule to be furnished to the inter-dealer-quotation-system.[25]

The term "correspondent" means a "broker or dealer who has a direct line of communication to another broker or dealer in a different city or geographic area";[26] the term "quotation" is defined as "any bid or offer or any indication of interest (such as OW or BW) in any bid or offer."[27]

The rule was adopted on the basis of an analysis of the principal inter-dealer-quotation-system by the Special Study.[28]

Sec. 16-6. Over-the-counter market—dealers' contemporaneous cost or sales price. In general, the most satisfactory measure of the market price of a security sold to or brought from a cus-

---

[23] SEC Securities Exchange Act Release No. 7381, Aug. 6, 1964, p. 2.
[24] Subdivision (b) of Rule 15c2-7.
[25] Paragraph (a)(2) of Rule 15c2-7.
[26] Paragraph (c)(1) of Rule 15c2-7.
[27] Paragraph (c)(2) of the rule. "OW" stands for offer wanted; and "BW" means bid wanted.
[28] Special Study Report Pt. 2, Ch. VII, pp. 595-609.

tomer is the price involved in a contemporaneous offsetting transaction by the broker-dealer with a third person. Thus, the market price to be used as a measure for a proper sales price to a customer is the price paid for the security by the dealer on the same day of, or shortly before, the sale to the customer, if in fact the dealer made purchases of the security for his own account within such period.[29] Similarly, in measuring the market price of securities purchased by a dealer from his customer, the dealer's own contemporaneous or nearly contemporaneous sales to others provide the best guage.[30] However, if there has been a lapse of time between the transaction in the security which the dealer had with others and the transaction with the customer, the dealer's cost or sales prices (as the case may be) are of little weight as against current quotations in the National Daily Quotation Sheets.[31]

Sec. 16-7. Over-the-counter market—other guides. In a case where neither quotations in the sheets nor an actual contemporaneous transaction by the broker-dealer are available as guides to the market price of a security, resort may be had to other relevant evidence of market value, such as evidence of quotations in foreign markets or actual current quotations given to the broker-dealer upon his request by other broker-dealers.[32]

---

[29] *Sol T. Pfeffer,* 40 SEC 612, 615 (1961); *Lawrence Rappee,* 40 SEC 607, 609 (1961); *Investment Service Co.,* SEC Securities Exchange Act Release No. 6884, Aug. 15, 1962, p. 7; *Boren &Co.,* 40 SEC 217, 220 (1961); *W. T. Anderson Co., Inc.,* 39 SEC 630, 636 (1960); *Paul Carroll Ferguson,* 39 SEC 260, 263 (1959); *Samuel B. Franklin & Co.,* 38 SEC 908, 911-12 (1959), aff'd 290 F.2d 719 (9th Cir. 1961); *William Harrison Keller, Jr.,* 38 SEC 900, 905 (1959). And see *Associated Securities Corporation* v. *SEC,* 293 F.2d 738 (10th Cir. 1961). Where cost to the dealer is incurred contemporaneously or nearly contemporaneously with the sale to the customer, the transaction is characterized as riskless. *See W. T. Anderson Co., Inc.,* 39 SEC 630, 636 (1960). The *Special Study Report* (Pt. 2, Ch. VII, p. 676, item 7, and Ch. VIII, p. 911, item 4) recommends that such riskless transactions be required to be engaged in on an agency basis only, in respect of broker-dealers who are not "market makers." This is under active Commission consideration. SEC Special Market Study, Release No. 33, July 23, 1963, pp. 5, 7.

[30] *Samuel B. Franklin & Company,* 38 SEC 908, 910 (1959), aff'd 290 F.2d 719 (9th Cir. 1961).

[31] *Maryland Securities Co., Inc.,* 40 SEC 443, 446 (1960); *Boren & Co.,* 40 SEC 217, 221-2 (1960). And see *G. Alex Hope,* 7 SEC 1082, 1084 (1940), where the Commission said: ". . . It is not, of course, the amount of profit *per se* which we condemn. A change in market conditions may increase the market price of a security over the amount paid for it by the dealer to a point where he can fairly sell it to his customer at a substantial increase over the purchase price. . ."

[32] See *Special Study Report,* Pt. 2, Ch. VII, pp. 569-70; and see e.g., *Gregory & Company, Inc.,* 38 SEC 304, 307-8 (1958). See also, SEC Report on *The Feasibility and Advisability of the Complete Segregation of the Functions of Dealer and Broker* (1936), pp. 65-66. Such evidence as to market value may be taken into account in

Sec. 16-8. Reasonable relationship to market price. The market price of a security having been arrived at in a given transaction between a broker-dealer and his customer, adherence to the standards imposed by the broker-dealer's "shingle" is then to be determined by the relationship between the price paid by or to the customer and the market price. We have seen that the broker-dealer represents that the price to the customer is reasonably related to the market price. There is no hard and fast rule as to a reasonable "mark-up."[33] However, the 5 percent mark-up policy which the National Association of Securities Dealers, Inc. (NASD) adopted in 1943[34] is employed as a practical guide by the Commission.[35] Under this policy, mark-ups in dealer transactions should normally not exceed 5 percent of current quotations and should possibly be less.[36] A somewhat higher percentage is regarded as appropriate in the case of low priced securities selling below $10 a share.[37] In the case of so-called "penny stocks," if the transaction is small the percentage mark-up may be less significant than the dollar mark-up.[38] And, in addition to the dollar amounts, the number of transactions and unit prices should also be taken into account in relation to testing the reasonableness of mark-ups on so-called penny stocks.[39]

---

determining whether the price paid by a broker-dealer to a customer for a security is reasonably related to the market price. *Gregory & Company, Inc., supra.*

[33] The term "mark-up" is employed in referring to the percentage or amount above the market at which the broker-dealer sells the security to his customer; see e.g., *Managed Investment Programs,* 37 SEC 783, 786 (1957). The term "spread" represents the gap between the bid and offer quotations. See *Special Study Report,* Pt. 2, Ch. VII, pp. 552-3.

[34] See *Management Investment Programs, supra,* n. 33, at p. 786, n. 6.

[35] See, e.g., *Maryland Securities Co., Inc.,* SEC Securities Exchange Act Release, No. 7232, Feb. 4, 1964; *William Harrison Keller, Jr.,* 38 SEC 900, 905-6 (1959). *Investment Service Co.,* SEC Securities Exchange Act Release No. 6884, Aug. 15, 1962, p. 8. And see *Sol T. Pfeffer,* 40 SEC 612 (1961); *Lawrence Rappee,* 40 SEC 607 (1961). See also, *Associated Securities Corporation,* 293 F.2d 738 (10th Cir. 1961).

[36] *Ibid.* and see *Managed Investment Programs,* 37 SEC 783, 787 (1957). *National Association of Securities Dealers, Inc.,* 17 SEC 459, 472 (1934).

[37] *Ibid.* and see *Carl J. Bliedung,* 38 SEC 518 at pp. 520-1 note 10 (1958). Special expenses or special services might also justify a higher than usual mark-up. *Ibid.* But compare, *Midland Securities Inc.,* 40 SEC. 333, 338 (1961), where the Commission pointed out that excessive expenses, such as very high commissions paid to salesmen, do not justify excessive mark-ups. Also, the fact that a dealer made a short sale to the customer of the security in question does not justify an excessive mark-up. *Investment Service Co., supra,* SEC Securities Exchange Act Release No. 6884 at p. 8. And see, *Arthur J. Decker, Jr., Trustee,* SEC Securities Exchange Act Release No. 7068, April 26, 1963, pp. 2-3.

[38] *Samuel B. Franklin & Company,* 38 SEC 908, 911 (1959) aff'd 290 F.2d 719 (9th Cir. 1961) Penny stocks are those which sell for less than $1.00 a share.

[39] *Alfred D. Laurence & Co.,* 38 SEC 223 (1958) at p. 225, n. 4.

The *Special Study Report* (Pt. 2, Ch. VII, pp. 676-7, item 8) recommends greater

The amount by which the asked quotations exceed the bid quotations on a given day does not constitute a reasonable mark-up over a broker-dealer's actual cost in a transaction involving his purchase of the security and the sale of it to his customer on that same day. This difference merely represents the area within which it is believed that business between dealers may be transacted.[40]

Sec. 16-9. Failure to make timely delivery of securities or timely payment for purchased securities—conversion of customers' securities or funds to use of broker-dealer. Trade custom requires a dealer to consummate transactions with customers promptly; a dealer makes an implied representation that this will be done by the mere fact that he engages in business.[41] Failure to consummate transactions promptly in accordance with trade custom therefore constitutes a course of business which operates as a fraud and deceit upon customers.[42] It is accordingly a violation of the anti-fraud provisions for a dealer to accept an order and payment for a security without filling the order promptly, and to divert the proceeds of payment to his other business activities.[43] It is similarly a fraud on customers to purchase securities from them and fail promptly to pay them for the securities.[44]

Additionally, for the same basic reasons, it is a fraudulent and deceptive act, practice, and course of business, which operates as a fraud and deceit on a customer, for a broker-dealer to hypothecate or otherwise convert to his own use customers' funds or fully-paid-for securities of customers held by the broker-dealer for safekeeping.[45]

---

flexibility in mark-up policy to fit varying situations in other than riskless transaction. The Commission is considering appropriate action in that regard. SEC Special Market Study Release No. 33, July 23, 1963, p. 5.

[40] *Samuel B. Franklin & Company,* 38 SEC 908, 911-912 (1959), aff'd 290 F.2d 719 (9th Cir. 1961).

[41] SEC Securities Exchange Act Release No. 6778, April 16, 1962; *Vincent Associates Ltd.,* SEC Securities Exchange Act Release No. 6806, May 16, 1962, p. 1. Carl J. Bliedung, 38 SEC 518, 521 (1958); *Batkin & Co.,* 38 SEC 436, 446 (1958); *Bryan Halbert Kyger Jr.,* 38 SEC 433, 434 (1958).

[42] *Ibid.* A copy of SEC Securities Exchange Act Release No. 6778, *supra,* n. 41, is attached as appendix R. See Sec. 25-18, *infra.*

[43] *Ibid.* and see *Gabriel Sanders,* 37 SEC 165, 166 (1956); *C. J. Montague, Inc.,* 38 SEC 462, 463 (1958); *William Rex Cromwell,* 38 SEC 913, 915 (1958); *Sills and Company,* 38 SEC 931, 933 (1959); *Arkansas Securities Corporation,* 39 SEC 536, 538 (1959); *T. J. Campbell Investment Company, Inc.,* 39 SEC 940, 942 (1960); *Filosa Securities Company,* 39 SEC 896, 898 (1960); *Frank S. Kelly,* 32 SEC 636, 637-8 (1951); *Sam Belofsky,* 36 SEC 214, 215 (1955).

[44] *Ibid.*

[45] See e.g., *Thompson & Sloan, Inc.,* 40 SEC 451, 454 (1961); *Sherwood and Company,* SEC Securities Exchange Act Release No. 6876, Aug. 10, 1962, p. 1; *Florida*

Sec. 16-10. Engaging in business while insolvent, while liabilities exceed current assets, or while unable to meet current obligations when due. The acceptance by a broker-dealer of orders from customers and the confirmation of transactions with customers constitute representations that the broker-dealer is solvent,[46] that his liabilities do not exceed his current assets,[47] and that he is able to meet his current obligations as they become due.[48] Accordingly if, in such circumstances a broker-dealer is in fact insolvent or has liabilities exceeding current assets or is not able to meet his current obligations when due, he is engaged in fraudulent conduct as to his customers.[49]

Sec. 16-11. Engaging in boiler room activity. "Boiler room" activity consists essentially of offering to customers securities of particular issuers in large volume by means of an intensive campaign through numerous salesmen by telephone or direct mail without regard to the suitability to the needs of the customer in such manner as to induce a hasty decision to buy the security,

Underwriting and Securities Services Corp., SEC Securities Exchange Act Release No. 6789, April 24, 1962, p. 1; *Aldrich, Scott & Co., Inc.*, 40 SEC 775, 776 (1961); *First Idaho Corporation*, 40 SEC 668, 669-70 (1961); *SEC v. C. H. Abraham & Co. Inc.*, 186 F. Supp. 119 (S.D.N.Y. 1960). See also, *SEC v. Lawson*, 24 F. Supp. 360, 361-3 (D.Md. 1938); and see, SEC Litigation Release No. 1525, Nov. 24, 1959; and SEC Litigation Release No. 1781, September 16, 1960; *Investment Registry of America, Inc.*, 21 SEC 745, 752 (1946).

[46] *Invesco Inc.*, SEC Securities Exchange Act Release No. 6993, Jan. 21, 1963, p. 2; *Sanders Investment Company, Inc.*, SEC Securities Exchange Act Release No. 6942, Nov. 20, 1962; *Aldrich, Scott & Co., Inc.*, 40 SEC 775, 776-7 (1961); *Thompson & Sloan, Inc.*, 40 SEC 451, 454 (1961); *Alan Associates Securities Corp.*, SEC Securities Exchange Act Release No. 6434, Dec. 16, 1960, p. 3; *Earl L. Robins*, 39 SEC 847, 849 (1960); *Milton R. Aronson*, 39 SEC 839, 841 (1960); *Harvey H. Shields, Jr.*, 39 SEC 608, 609 (1959); *Abraham Rosen*, 39 SEC 268, 270 (1959); *John D. Ferris*, 39 SEC 116, 119 (1959). *Gill-Harkness & Co.*, 38 SEC 646, 650-2 (1958); *Batkin & Co.*, 38 SEC 436, 446 (1958).

[47] *Ibid.* and see *M. Posey Associates Ltd.*, SEC Securities Exchange Act Release No. 6947, Nov. 21, 1962, p. 1; *State Securities Corporation*, SEC Securities Exchange Act Release No. 7120, Aug. 20, 1963, p. 2; *SEC v. C. H. Abraham & Co., Inc.*, 186 F. Supp. 119 (S.D.N.Y. 1960).

[48] *Ibid.* and see *J. I. Magaril Company, Inc.*, SEC Securities Exchange Act Release No. 6997, Jan. 21, 1963, p. 2; *D. Earle Hensley Co.*, 40 SEC 849, 852 (1961); *Jay Morton & Company, Inc.*, SEC Securities Exchange Act Release No. 7037, March 20, 1963, p. 1; *Investment Brokers of N. J., Inc.*, SEC Securities Exchange Act Release No. 7017, Feb. 7, 1963; *Wakefield, Carder & Holt, Inc.*, 40 SEC 675, 678 (1961).

[49] See authorities cited in notes 46, 47 and 48, immediately above. It may be noted that, if in fact a broker-dealer is insolvent or his liabilities exceed his current assets, the mere fact that some of the liabilities are the subject of a satisfactory subordination agreement for net capital purposes (see, *supra*, Sec. 8-6) does not negate violation of the anti-fraud provisions if he transacts business with customers, since all liabilities are taken into account for anti-fraud purposes.

although (a) the broker-dealer has little or no knowledge of the financial condition of the issuer, the broker-dealer having made no effort to obtain such information, or (b) he fails in any event to disclose the absence of any reasonable basis for optimistic predictions or statements made, or to furnish any known adverse information.[50]

It is neither fair nor in accordance with the standards of the profession (and it is therefore fraudulent conduct) for a broker-dealer to engage in boiler room tactics.[51]

In recognition of the fact that boiler room tactics are frequently practiced on strangers,[52] the Commission has proposed the adoption of a rule which, in broad outline, would prohibit the offer or sale of any equity security of certain types of issuers at a price of $10.00 or less a share by telephone to a person that is not a "regular customer."[53]

---

[50] See e.g., *Harold Grill*, SEC Securities Exchange Act Release No. 6989, Jan. 8, 1963, p. 4; *Banner Securities Inc.*, SEC Securities Exchange Act Release No. 6985, Dec. 28, 1962, p. 3; *Palombi Securities Co., Inc.*, SEC Securities Exchange Act Release No. 6961, Nov. 30, 1962, p. 4; *Nance-Kieth Corporation*, SEC Securities Exchange Act Release No. 6946, Nov. 21, 1962, p. 2; *Security Adjustment Corporation*, SEC Securities Exchange Act Release No. 6943, Nov. 20, 1962, p. 1; *J. Logan & Co.*, SEC Securities Exchange Act Release No. 6848, July 9, 1962, p. 2; *A. J. Caradean & Co.*, SEC Securities Exchange Act Release No. 6903, Oct. 1, 1962, pp. 2-5; *Mac Robbins & Co., Inc.*, SEC Securities Exchange Act Release No. 6846, July 11, 1962, pp. 4-5; *Alexander Reid & Co., Inc.*, 40 SEC 986, 990 (1962); *Best Securities Inc.*, 39 SEC 931, 933-4 (1960). See also, *B. Fennekohl & Co.*, SEC Securities Exchange Act Release No. 6898, Sept. 18, 1962, pp. 2-7; *R. B. Michaels & Co.*, 40 SEC 492, 494-5 (1961); *Midland Securities Inc.*, 40 SEC 635, 640 (1961); *Berko v. SEC*, 316 F.2d 137 (2d Cir. 1963); *Ross Securities, Inc.*, SEC Securities Exchange Act Release No. 7069, April 30, 1963, pp. 6-7; *Norman Joseph Adams*, SEC Securities Exchange Act Release No. 7072, April 30, 1963, p. 3; *John J. Cravin Co., Inc.*, SEC Securities Exchange Act Release No. 7064, April 22, 1963, p. 2; *Herring v. Hendison*, 218 F. Supp. 419 (S.D.N.Y. 1963).

[51] *Ibid.* and see *J. H. Lederer Co., Inc.*, 38 SEC 794, 796-7 (1958); *Barnett & Co., Inc.*, SEC Securities Exchange Act Release No. 6310, July 5, 1960, p. 4.

[52] See e.g., *A. G. Bellin Securities Corp.*, 39 SEC 178, 180 (1959).

[53] *Proposal To Adopt Rule 15c2-6 Under The Securities Exchange Act of 1934*, SEC Securities Exchange Act Release No. 6885, Aug. 15, 1962. The proposed rule would not apply to offers and sales to institutional customers (bank, trust company, insurance company, pension, welfare, profit sharing or similar fund, or registered investment company) or to other broker-dealers. A "regular customer" is defined in the proposed rule. The definition would result in prohibiting telephone contact of total strangers. By its terms, the proposed rule would not apply to a security registered under the Securities Act or of issuers required by the Exchange Act or other Acts to file financial statements with the Commission, or of issuers whose certified financial statements reveal net income for the most recent fiscal year or, in some circumstances, the last preceding fiscal year, or of issuers which have specified characteristics published in recognized securities manuals. For other details of the proposed rule, see SEC Securities Exchange Act Release No. 6885, *supra*.

Other improvements in selling practices are suggested in the *Special Study Report*, Pt. 1, Ch. III, pp. 328-30.

CHAPTER 17

OTHER OUTLAWED FRAUDULENT PRACTICES

Sec. 17-1. In general. There are several other types of activities practiced by fringe element broker-dealers (usually but not necessarily in the context of boiler room practices) which have been condemned as fraudulent. These activities include (1) the making of recommendations to customers not suited to their needs, (2) the making of flamboyant, unbalanced representations and predictions without knowledge of the facts, without foundation, and without independent investigation, (3) the confirming of sales to customers of securities not ordered, (4) the making of a number of recurring types of miscellaneous misrepresentations, some of which will be mentioned below,[1] and (5) in general, engaging in a course of business which operates as a fraud or deceit upon customers.

Sec. 17-2. Non-suitable recommendations. In *Anderson* v. *Knox,*[2] an insurance salesman represented that he would arrange a suitable insurance plan for the plaintiff in light of plaintiff's special circumstances and needs. When he arranged the plan and sold plaintiff the insurance and other features that made up the plan, however, it turned out, as the court later found, that the salesman acted in complete disregard of the client's needs to the substantial damage of the client, who was accordingly awarded appropriate damages.

The type of representation as to suiting the client's needs that was expressly made by the salesman in *Anderson* v. *Knox* appears to be implicit in the recommendations made by a broker-dealer to his customer.[3] In any event, where, as frequently happens, securities are sold to customers on the representation that

---

[1] *Infra*, Sections 17-5 to 17-10.
[2] 297 F.2d 702 (9th Cir. 1961).
[3] See *Address Presented At The Seminar On The Management Functions In The Investment Banking Industry, Sponsored By Education Committee, New York Group, Investment Bankers Association Of America* by Commissioner Manuel F. Cohen, Rye, New York, Oct. 25, 1962, p. 5, on file at SEC, Washington D. C. and New York, N. Y.

they are appropriate for the customer's needs and circumstances, *Anderson* v. *Knox* appears to provide ample authority not only for serving as the basis for civil remedies to the customer, but for appropriate enforcement action, as well, if in fact no effect was given to the client's needs.[4]

Sec. 17-3. Unfounded representations or predictions. Where there is no reasonable basis for making a representation or prediction to a customer to induce a transaction in a security, a broker-dealer making such recommendation or prediction violates the anti-fraud provisions of the federal securities laws.[5]

Thus, predictions that there is a likelihood of a price rise or future profits or dividends imply adequate foundation for the predictions and that there are no known facts which would make the predictions dangerous and unreliable.[6] And a statement as to a company's financial condition may not be made if such condition is not in fact known.[7] A prediction as to forthcoming listing on an exchange must have a basis.[8]

A claim that a representation or prediction was mere "puffing" does not justify its being made.[9] The fact is, a broker-dealer owes his customer the duty to investigate into the facts in respect

---

[4] Cf. *Boren & Co.*, 40 SEC 217, 222 (1960). The *Special Study Report* (Pt. 1, Ch. III, p. 329, item 4) recommends the adoption of appropriate rules setting standards of suitability. These are under consideration by the Commission. SEC Special Market Study Release No. 25, April 30, 1963, p. 4.

[5] The provisions which are violated are, among others, Section 15(c)(1) of the Act as defined by Rule 15c1-2 as well as other, similar anti-fraud provisions discussed *infra*, at Sec. 18-3. See *Reilly Hoffman & Co., Inc.*, SEC Securities Exchange Act Release No. 6924, Oct. 29, 1962, p. 1; *A. J. Caradean & Co., Inc.*, SEC Securities Exchange Act Release No. 6903, Oct. 1, 1962, p. 5; and see SEC Securities Act Release No. 4445, Feb. 2, 1962, p. 3. See also authorities cited at notes 6 to 13 directly below.

[6] See *A. J. Caradean & Co., Inc.*, SEC Securities Exchange Act Release No. 6903, Oct. 1, 1962, pp. 4-5; *Irving Grubman*, SEC Securities Exchange Act Release No. 6546, May 5, 1961, p. 3; *R. B. Michaels & Co.*, SEC Securities Exchange Act Release No. 6461, Feb. 6, 1961, p. 3; *B. Fennekohl & Co.*, SEC Securities Exchange Act Release No. 6898, Sept. 18, 1962, pp. 5-6; *Pilgrim Securities, Inc.*, 39 SEC 172, 175 (1959); *Leonard Barton Corporation*, 39 SEC 211, 214 (1959); *Best Securities, Inc.*, 39 SEC 931, 933 (1960); *Barnett & Co., Inc.*, SEC Securities Exchange Act Release No. 6310, July 5, 1960, p. 4; *Shelley Roberts & Co., of California*, 38 SEC 744, 749 (1958); *L. D. Friedman & Co., Inc.*, 37 SEC 795, 798-9 (1957). *A. G. Bellin Securities Corp.*, 39 SEC 178, 180-1 (1959).

[7] *A. G. Bellin Securities Corp.*, *supra*, 39 SEC at 183; *J. H. Lederer & Co., Inc.*, 38 SEC 794, 796-7 (1958).

[8] *L. D. Friedman & Co., Inc.*, 37 SEC 795, 798-9 (1957); *Shelley Roberts & Co., of California*, 38 SEC 744, 749 (1958).

[9] *B. Fennekohl & Co.*, SEC Securities Exchange Act Release No. 6898, Sept. 18, 1962, pp. 5-6.

of which he makes predictions or representations.[10] He cannot hide behind the claim that the representations he made were based on information transmitted to him by the issuer or its officials.[11]

Nor is sincere enthusiasm and genuine faith in the issuer's success a proper basis for making predictions which lack foundation.[12] The broker-dealer is additionally under obligation to make his customer aware of known adverse factors and to direct attention, if such be the case, to the "lack of pertinent information necessary to reach an informed judgment as to the value of the securities" being offered or sold to the customer.[13] Moreover, when making representations or predictions as to prospective profits, a broker-dealer is obligated to inform a customer of the risk of loss and of facts relating to the risk of loss.[14]

---

[10] *Banner Securities Inc.,* SEC Securities Exchange Act Release No. 6985, Dec. 28, 1962, p. 2; *Brown, Barton & Engel,* SEC Securities Exchange Act Release No. 6821, June 8, 1962, p. 4; *Best and Garey, Inc.,* SEC Securities Exchange Act Release No. 6841, July 6, 1962, p. 2. And see, SEC Securities Act Release No. 4445, Feb. 2, 1962, p. 3; *SEC v. Brown, Barton & Engel,* Civil Action No. 363-72 (D.N.J., Aug. 16, 1962). *SEC v. F. S. Johns & Co.,* 207 F. Supp. 566 (S.D.N.J. 1962). The *Special Study Report* recommends that broker-dealers be obligated at a minimum to consult officially filed material relating to the companies whose securities are the subject of recommendation. Pt. 1, Ch. III, p. 329, item 5, and p. 387, item 4.

[11] *Investment Service Co.,* SEC Securities Exchange Act Release No. 6884, Aug. 15, 1962, p. 7; *Keith Richard Securities Corp.,* 39 SEC 231, 236 (1959). Such self-serving declarations by issuers and officials may, of course, not be taken at face value. *Ibid.*

The practice on the part of some broker-dealers to send out under their own names material prepared on behalf of issuing companies has been adversely commented upon in the *Special Study Report,* Pt. 3, Ch. IX, pp. 78-86.

[12] *D. F. Bernheimer & Co., Inc.,* SEC Securities Exchange Act Release No. 7000, January 23, 1963, pp. 3-4.

[13] SEC Securities Act Release No. 4352, April 12, 1961 (same as SEC Securities Exchange Act Release No. 6525). And see SEC Securities Exchange Act Release No. 6926, Oct. 30, 1962, where the Commission said: ". . . it should be recognized that there is serious question as to the accuracy and adequacy of financial and other information heretofore filed with the Commission by Industrial Enterprises, nor is current information available about the operation and earnings of the company from which an informed evaluation of its stock may be made. Accordingly, brokers and dealers should exercise extreme care in effecting transactions in the stock with and for public investors." See also SEC Securities Act Release No. 4445, Feb. 2, 1962, p. 3.

[14] *Shelley Roberts of California,* 38 SEC 744, 749 (1958); *Leonard Burton Corporation,* 39 SEC 211, 214 (1959). And see SEC *Statement of Policy* (as amended Nov. 5, 1957), items (b)(2) and (c). At the instance of the *Special Study Report,* Pt. 3, Ch. IX, p. 102, item 1, the New York Stock Exchange revised its advertising rules governing advertising and publicity, through market letters and otherwise, of its members. These rules are designed to eliminate flamboyant, unsupported, and unbalanced statements in such literature. *N. Y. Stock Exchange* Rules 471, 472, 473, Par. 2474A.

For other examples of the effectiveness with which the "prediction" type of fraud is dealt with under the federal securities laws, see e. g., *U. S. v. Grayson,* 166 F.2d 863, 866 (2d Cir. 1948); *Oklahoma Trust Co. v. SEC,* 100 F.2d 888, 894 (10th

Sec. 17-4. False confirmations. We have seen in connection with our discussion of the Bookkeeping Rules that the confirmation of sales of securities not ordered violates the requirement that a broker-dealer's records must be accurate.[15] The practice of sending out, wholesale, confirmations to persons who never ordered the securities confirmed is also a fraudulent technique designed to bewilder public investors and, some times, to cow them into paying for such securities. Such practice is accordingly prohibited.[16]

Sec. 17-5. Miscellaneous misrepresentations. The number of fraudulent representations which may be possible in any given situation may be infinite. Experience has shown that, apart from false representations or misleading statements as to the facts surrounding the security itself which may be relevant to a decision to the purchase of such security, some of the less reputable broker-dealers tend to make recurring types of false or misleading material statements to induce customers to purchase. The variety of these could also be infinite, but a few of the most glaring examples merit special mention.

Sec. 17-6. Miscellaneous misrepresentations—regarding investment company securities. As the result of a number of recurrent types of misrepresentations used in the sale of investment company securities, the Commission has adopted a Statement of Policy as a guide for persons selling such securities, pointing out a number of misrepresentations in their offer and sale which should be avoided because of violations of the anti-fraud provisions of the federal securities laws.[17]

Sec. 17-7. Miscellaneous misrepresentations—comparison advertising. One of the more common types of misrepresentation is the use of "comparison" advertising with reference to a security. Thus, if a broker-dealer is offering life insurance stocks to customers, he may not predicate his inducement on the assumption

---

Cir. 1939); *Stone v. U. S.,* 113 F.2d 70, 75 (6th Cir. 1940). *Corporate Leaders Securities Co.,* 2 SEC 667 (1937). Cf *Rudd v. U. S.,* 178 F.2d 656, 660 (9th Cir. 1949).

[15] *Supra,* Sec. 6-2.

[16] *J. I. Magaril Company, Inc.,* SEC Securities Exchange Act Release No. 6997, Jan. 21, 1963, p. 2; *Thompson & Sloan, Inc.,* SEC Securities Exchange Act Release No. 6443, Jan. 3, 1961, p. 4. And see *Palombi Securities Co., Inc.,* SEC Securities Exchange Act Release No. 6961, Nov. 13, 1962, p. 4.

[17] SEC *Statement of Policy* as amended (November 5, 1957). Excerpts from the *Statement of Policy* are attached as Appendix S. See Sec. 25-19, *infra.*

that all life insurance stocks are safe and profitable investments, arising from the reference to only selected life insurance stocks which have had a favorable history.[18] The use of such selected list is fraudulent and misleading in the absence of qualifications and explanations pointing out (1) the material differences which exist between the securities on the list and the security being offered and (2) that there are no assurances that the past performances of the selected companies would be mirrored by the company whose security is being offered.[19]

Sec. 17-8. Miscellaneous misrepresentations—as to capacity. In connection with the discussion of the confirmation requirements, it was seen that at or before the completion of a transaction with a customer, a broker-dealer must confirm in writing whether, among other things, he is acting as broker (agent) for the customer or as dealer for his own account.[20] It sometimes happens that a broker-dealer who confirms a transaction with a customer as dealer for his own account will falsely convey the impression that he is the customer's agent in inducing the customer to purchase securities. This is done in a context in which the broker-dealer is attempting to convey to the customer that he is getting a bargain since the broker-dealer is not charging any commissions. The fact is, of course, that this is a misleading statement.[21]

Sec. 17-9. Miscellaneous misrepresentations—manipulation of the market. In selling securities, some unscrupulous broker-dealers appeal to customers by representing or promising that the price of the security will rise because of the market activity by such broker-dealers in the security. This flies in the face of the anti-fraud provisions because, of course, it cannot be lawfully done. The ignorant customer should be informed that such market ac-

---

[18] *G. J. Mitchell Jr., Co.,* SEC Securities Exchange Act Release No. 6433, Dec. 13, 1960, p. 4.

[19] *Ibid.* and see *Kay Brunell,* SEC Securities Exchange Act Release No. 6913, Oct. 15, 1962, p. 3; *Irving Grubman,* SEC Securities Exchange Act Release No. 6546, May 5, 1961, p. 3; *The Whitehall Corporation,* 38 SEC 259, 266-7 (1958); *Life Shares Trading Corporation,* SEC Securities Exchange Act Release No. 7211, January 8, 1964.

[20] *Supra,* Sec. 12-2.

[21] "The representation that no commission was being charged on the sales to Miss W., which were effected on a principal basis, was materially misleading. That representation was designed to make the customer believe that *Randall & Co.* was acting as agent entitled to charge a commission, rather than as principal and that the customer was receiving favored treatment by not being charged a commission in addition to the sales price, when in fact a commission charge is, of course, improper in a principal transaction. . ." *Leonard Burton Corporation,* 39 SEC 211, 213-14 (1959). And see, *SEC v. Rapp,* 304 F.2d 786 (2d Cir. 1962).

tivity would be illegal.[22] And the venal customer who knows better is thus illegally invited to become a participant in the broker-dealer's violation.[23] On either basis such representations are prohibited.

Sec. 17-10. Miscellaneous misrepresentations—use of hedge clause. Rights which investors or other persons may have by virtue of the provisions of the Act or of the Securities Act cannot be waived.[24] Accordingly, the use of any language in his literature by a broker-dealer which conveys the notion that the broker-dealer cannot be held accountable for otherwise actionable conduct is regarded as false and misleading, in violation of the general antifraud provisions.[25]

Sec. 17-11. Course of business which operates as a fraud or deceit upon customers—in general. Each of a number of antifraud provisions of the federal securities laws prohibits a broker-dealer (among others) from engaging in a "course of business which operates or would operate as a fraud or deceit" upon a customer.[26]

When apparently separate activities, conducted with frequency, contribute to an over-all fraudulent result, they may be viewed as a "course of business" amounting to a system of unlawful conduct, or an unlawful scheme.[27] It would therefore appear that a number of violations of law perpetrated by a broker-dealer having the ultimate effect of defrauding or deceiving his customers, constitutes such a prohibited course of business. Similarly,

---

[22] *Shelley Roberts & Co. of California,* 38 SEC 744, 749 (1958). See Sections 9(a)(3) and (5) of the Act, discussed, *infra* at Sec. 18-2.

[23] *Associated Investors Securities, Inc.,* SEC Securities Exchange Act Release No. 6859, July 24, 1962, p. 9. See the discussion, *infra,* at Sec. 18-2, of Sections 9(a)(3) and (5) of the Act.

[24] Section 29(a) of the Act and Section 14 of the Securities Act. See *Wilko v. Swan,* 346 U. S. 427 (1953).

[25] SEC Securities Act Release No. 3411 April 10, 1951.

[26] See Paragraph (a) of Rule 15c1-2 defining the term "manipulative, deceptive or other fraudulent device or contrivance" as used in Section 15(c)(1) of the Act which prohibits such activity on the part of a broker-dealer in connection with purchases or sales over-the-counter. Rule 10b-5(3) adopted under Section 10(b) of the Act outlaws such activity on the part of any one in connection with the purchase or sale of a security either over-the-counter or on the exchange. Section 17(a)(3) of the Securities Act contains similar prohibitions, applicable to any one in connection with the offer or sale of a security, whether over-the-counter or on an exchange.

[27] *Braatelein v. U. S.,* 147 F.2d 888, 895 (8th Cir. 1945). And see *Isaacs v. U. S.,* 301 F.2d 706, 725, 727-8 (8th Cir. 1962); *Pinkerton v. U. S.,* 328 U. S. 640, 644, 647 (1946); *U. S. v. Palladino,* 203 F. Supp. 35, 39-40 (D. Mass. 1962); *Aiken v. U. S.,* 108 F.2d 182, 183 (4th Cir. 1939); *Holmes v. U. S.,* 134 F.2d 125, 134 (8th Cir. 1943), cert. den. 319 U. S. 776 (1943).

it would appear that recurrence of the same type of violation by a broker-dealer over an extended period having the effect of defrauding or deceiving his customers, would constitute such a prohibited course of business.

In the context of broker-dealer activity, a course of business which operates or would operate as a fraud or deceit can assume myriads of forms. However, in a recent Commission opinion,[28] a few examples of such prohibited courses of business were furnished, and they are therefore worthy of special note. These were stated to be: (a) the execution of transactions not authorized by customers, (b) the sale to customers of securities which are subject to a third party's lien, (c) the failure to execute orders or deliver securities promptly, and (d) the acceptance of customers' funds while the broker-dealer is insolvent, or his liabilities exceed its current assets, or he is unable to meet his current obligations. It would also appear to be plain that the practice of converting customers' funds or securities to the broker-dealer's own use is a prohibited course of business. In fact, as stated, a combination of violations of law contributing to an overall fraudulent result, as well as the repetition by a broker-dealer with regularity of a single prohibited activity would result in the carrying on of a business which operates as a fraud or deceit on customers.

Another practice which may pervade a broker-dealer's operations with ultimate harmful effect on public investor customers is perhaps worthy of special mention. This relates to the careless hiring practices of some broker-dealers and to the failure of some broker-dealer to provide proper direction and supervision over employees.

Sec. 17-12. Careless hiring practices—failure to exercise proper supervision. We have seen that a broker-dealer is fully accountable for all acts of his employees in carrying on the broker-dealer business and that he has a basic responsibility for their direction and supervision.[29]

It would appear plain, therefore, that a broker-dealer engages in a prohibited course of business when, over an extended period, he carelessly hires salesmen without sufficient and proper inquiry,

---

[28] *MacRobbins & Co., Inc.*, SEC Securities Exchange Act Release No. 6846, July 11, 1962, pp. 3-4 at nn. 12, 13, 14, and 15.
[29] *Supra*, Sec. 5-2.

particularly if it turns out they have records indicating that their employment would expose customers to danger.[30] Surely, such a practice is calculated to operate as a fraud and deceit upon customers.

Similarly, a broker-dealer would appear to be engaged in a prohibited course of business if he fails to assume his obligation of direction and supervision over his employees and, if as a result, his customers suffer.[31]

---

[30] See, *SEC* v. *Rapp*, 304 F.2d 786 (2d Cir. 1962); *J. Logan & Co.*, SEC Securities Exchange Act Release No. 6848, p. 11. And see *Boruski* v. *SEC*, 289 F.2d 738 (2d Cir. 1961). *Vickers Christy & Co., Inc.*, SEC Securities Exchange Act Release No. 6872, Aug. 8, 1962, pp. 2-6; *Midas Management Corp.*, SEC Securities Exchange Act Release No. 6569, May 25, 1961, p. 3.

[31] *Reilly, Hoffman & Co., Inc.*, SEC Securities Exchange Act Release No. 6924, Oct. 29, 1962, p. 2; *J. Logan & Co., supra; Reynolds & Co.*, 39 SEC 902, 916-17 (1960); *Best Securities Inc.*, 39 SEC 931, 934 (1960); *Sterling Securities Company*, 39 SEC 487, 492 (1959). And see *Address Presented at the Seminar on the Management Function in the Investment Banking Industry Sponsored by Education Committee, New York Group, Investment Bankers Association of America* by Commissioner Manuel F. Cohen, Rye, New York, October 25, 1962, pp. 6-7, on file at SEC, Washington D. C., and New York, N. Y. See also *Leonard H. Zigman*, SEC Securities Exchange Act Release No. 6701, Jan. 5, 1962, p. 3. *Alexander Reid & Co., Inc.*, SEC Securities Exchange Act Release No. 7016, Feb. 7, 1963, p. 5; *Sutro Bros. & Co.*, SEC Securities Exchange Act Release No. 7052, April 10, 1963, p. 19; *Sutro Bros & Co.*, SEC Securities Exchange Act Release No. 7053, April 10, 1963, pp. 10-11; *John G. Cravin Co., Inc.*, SEC Securities Exchange Act Release No. 7064, April 22, 1963, p. 2; *McClane & Co., Inc.*, SEC Securities Exchange Act Release No. 7163, Nov. 1, 1963, p. 3; *Lawrence Securities Inc.*, SEC Securities Exchange Act Release No. 7146, Sept. 23, 1963, p. 3.

This principle is now codified in the Act. Section 15(b)(5)(E) of the Act. Securities Acts Amendments of 1964, Sec. 6(b).

CHAPTER 18

ANTI-MANIPULATIVE AND ANTI-FRAUD PROVISIONS OF EXCHANGE ACT

Sec. 18-1. In general. Thus far, our discussion as to anti-fraud and anti-manipulative provisions has been limited to activities of broker-dealers having specific relation to the conduct of a business as broker-dealer. It has been mentioned that, as regards securities transactions, the variety of forms which fraud, deception, or manipulation can assume is infinite.[1] And fraudulent and manipulative practices in connection with securities transactions may involve activity by a broker-dealer that is not unique to the conduct of the business of a broker-dealer. It will be seen that, in connection with transactions in securities, all manner of fraud, deceit, and manipulation is outlawed, irrespective of who may engage in such conduct. The broad provisions of the Act and the Rules therefore encompass broker-dealers among others. It will be noted though that activity of a broker-dealer which violates general anti-fraud and anti-manipulative provisions involves for him the violation of other provisions on the same subject which, by their terms, are limited in application to broker-dealers.

Sec. 18-2. Provisions relating to specific types of market manipulation. Generally stated, manipulation of the market in a security consists of the use of concealed and other fraudulent devices employed to raise, maintain, or depress the price of the security artificially for the purpose of inducing the purchase or sale of that security by others.[2]

A number of specific manipulative techniques are recognized

---

[1] *Supra*, Chapter 10. See *Archer* v. *SEC*, 133 F.2d 795, 803 (8th Cir. 1943); *Hughes* v. *SEC*, 174 F.2d 969 (D.C. Cir. 1949).

[2] See Sen. Rep. No. 792, 73rd Cong., 2d Sess. (1934), pp. 7-9, 17; Sen. Rep. No. 1455, 73rd Cong., 2d Sess. (1934) 31-6, 54; HR Rep. No. 1383, 73rd Cong., 2d Sess. (1934), pp. 21, 31. And see SEC Securities Exchange Act Release No. 6127, Nov. 30, 1959, pp. 1-2.

and dealt with by the Act and rules, in addition to those already mentioned in the discussion on Rule 10b-6.[3]

Section 9(a)(1) of the Act prohibits the use of jurisdictional means to effect "wash sales"[4] or "matched orders"[5] in respect of securities registered for listing on a national securities exchange. These and other manipulative practices specifically dealt with in Section 9(a) of the Act as relating to a listed security are viewed as prohibited in relation to a non-exempted, unlisted security by the general anti-fraud and anti-manipulative provisions of the Act and the rules.[6] Section 9(a)(2) of the Act prohibits any one from effecting alone or with others a series of transactions in a security "creating actual or apparent active trading in such security

---

[3] *Supra,* Sec. 13-11.

[4] A "wash sale" of a security is a sale engaged in to create a false or misleading appearance of active trading, or a false or misleading appearance with respect to the market for the security, which sale "involves no change in the beneficial ownership" of the security. Sec. 9(a)(1)(A). See *J. A. Latimer & Co., Inc.,* 38 SEC 790, 792 (1958). "Wash sales are a deceit because they broadcast the fact that a buyer and seller have agreed to exchange the shares at the purchased price, when they have not done so. . . ." *U. S. v. Brown,* 79 F.2d 321, 325 (2d Cir. 1935).

[5] A "matched order" as to a security is a transaction engaged in to create a false or misleading appearance of active trading or a false or misleading appearance with respect to the market for the security, when the transaction involves (a) the entering of orders for the purchase of the security with the knowledge that an order or orders to sell such security of substantially the same size, at substantially the same time and price has been or will be entered by or for the same or different parties, or (b) the entering of an order or orders for the sale of the security with the knowledge that an order or orders to buy the security of substantially the same size at substantially the same time and price has been or will be entered by or for the same or different parties. Sec. 9(a)(1)(B) and (C). It appears that frustration of this specific prohibition can be accomplished by use of orders not substantially of the same size despite the fact that exchange rules and practices normally result in orders being executed in 100 share lots, irrespective of the overall size of the buy and sell orders. *Wright* v. *SEC,* 112 F.2d 89 (2d Cir. 1940); *Securities Acts Amendments* (1959), 86th Cong., 1st Sess. (1959), p. 158.

[6] See SEC Securities Exchange Act Releases No. 1925, Nov. 1, 1938, No. 1689, May 3, 1938, and No. 1680, April 29, 1938. Specifically, these include Sections 10(b) and 15(c)(1) of the Act and the rules thereunder. See also *Halsey Stuart & Co., Inc.,* 30 SEC 106, 112-114, 123-4, 127 (1949); *Kidder Peabody & Co.,* 18 SEC 559, 569-570 (1945); *Barrett & Company,* 9 SEC 319, 328 (1941); SEC Securities Exchange Act Release No. 3505, Nov. 16, 1943, p. 2 (same as Securities Act Release No. 2955). See also *Gob Shops of America Inc.,* 39 SEC 92, 101 at n. 20 (1959). And see the reference to Sec. 15(c)(1) of the Act and Rule 15c1-2, *supra,* Chapter 10, as well as the references there to Section 10(b) of the Act and Rule 10b-5 and to Section 17(a) of the Securities Act of 1933.

Rule 10b-1 under the Act renders the provisions of Section 9(a) applicable to a non-exempted security which, under Section 12(a) and the rules thereunder, is permitted to be listed and traded on a national securities exchange without being registered for listing on the exchange. Rule 10b-3 is also a rule adopted under Section 10(b) of the Act. This rule merely incorporates Section 15(c)(1) of the Act and all the rules adopted under that section of the Act. Rule 10b-3 is accordingly confined in its application to broker-dealers and to over-the-counter transactions.

or raising or depressing the price of such security for the purpose of inducing the purchase or sale of such security by others." As used in the Act, a series of transactions encompasses a number of transactions so related in time and circumstances as to have the effect of "creating actual or apparent active trading in such security or raising or depressing the price of such security."[7] The term "apparent" as used in Section 9(a)(2) has the meaning of "open to view."[8] The effecting of "transactions" embraces the placing or the quotation of bids, even though the bids do not result in actual sales.[9] And the term "effect" in relation to effecting a transaction means to participate in some way in the transaction, whether as principal, agent, or both.[10] The manipulative purpose[11] is inferred from the circumstances of the case,[12] such as the making of a series of purchases having the effect of increasing the market price, and selling the acquired securities without permitting time to lapse to afford the market to find its own, independent level.[13] Similarly, a manipulative purpose will be inferred with reference to the distribution of a security if those interested in the distribution engage in activities which either raise the price or create excessive trading activity in the security.[14]

---

[7] See e. g., *Michael J. Meehan*, 2 SEC 588, 617 (1937); *Charles C. Wright*, 3 SEC 190, 196 (1938), and, on review, *Wright v. SEC*, 112 F.2d 89, 92 (2d Cir. 1940); *United States v. Minuse*, 114 F.2d 36, 38 (2d Cir. 1940) [conviction finally affirmed *U. S. v. Minuse*, 142 F.2d 338 (2d Cir. 1944)]; and see *Barrett & Company*, 9 SEC 319, 326, 328 (1941); See also *Gob Shops of America, Inc.*, 39 SEC 92, 101-3 (1959); *Bruns, Nordeman & Company*, SEC Securities Exchange Act Release No. 6540, April 26, 1961, p. 8 at n. 11. The more detailed rules of the Commission under Section 10(b) would apply to individual manipulative transactions without requiring proof of a "series" of such transactions. See *Securities Acts Amendments 1959*, 86th Cong., 1st Sess. (1959), p. 159.

[8] *Halsey Stuart & Co.*, 30 SEC 106, 127 (1949).

[9] *Kidder Peabody & Co.*, 18 SEC 559, 569-570 (1945); *Halsey Stuart & Co.*, 30 SEC 106, 127 (1949); *Adams & Co.*, 33 SEC 444, 450 n. 7 (1952). In the over-the-counter market, it is a common manipulative device to insert bids in the quotation sheets at increasingly higher prices. This activity tends to create a price at an inflated level. *SEC v. Gob Shops Of America, Inc.*, 39 SEC 92, 101 (1959). *C. A. Benson & Co., Inc.*, SEC Securities Exchange Act Release No. 7044, March 26, 1963, p. 2; *Advanced Research Associates, Inc.*, SEC Securities Exchange Act Release No. 7117, Aug. 16, 1963, p. 25 and n. 54; *A. T. Brod & Company*, SEC Securities Exchange Act Release No. 7139, Sept. 11, 1963, p. 2.

[10] SEC Securities Exchange Act Release No. 605, April 17, 1936.

[11] *I.e.* the purpose of inducing others to buy or sell. See SEC Securities Exchange Act Release No. 3056, Oct. 27, 1941, p. 2.

[12] *Ibid.* and see *Halsey Stuart & Co.*, 30 SEC 106, 123-4 (1949).

[13] SEC Securities Exchange Act Release No. 3056, Nov. 16, 1943, p. 3.

[14] SEC Securities Exchange Act Release No. 3505, Nov. 16, 1943, pp. 2-4 (same as SEC Securities Act Release No. 2955); SEC Securities Exchange Act Release No. 3506, Nov. 16, 1943, pp. 1-2 (same as SEC Securities Act Release No. 2956). And see *The S. T. Jackson & Company, Inc.*, 36 SEC 631, 653 (1950); *Adams & Co.*, 33 SEC 444,

Another outlawed manipulative device relates to a person offering to sell or selling, or offering to purchase or purchasing a security. Such a person is prohibited from making a statement for the purpose of inducing the purchase or sale of such security, if the statement was at the time and in the light of the circumstances under which it was made, false or misleading with respect to any material fact, and the statement was one which he knew or had reasonable ground to believe was so false and misleading.[15] Thus, if a person having a substantial short position in a security disseminates information tending to depress the price he would be making a misleading statement if, irrespective of the truth of that information, he failed at the same time to disclose the existence and extent of the short position; and he would therefore be engaged in prohibited manipulative conduct.[16]

Apart from this disclosure requirement, the specific provisions outlawing manipulation of the market are operative irrespective of whether or not disclosure of such activity is made in advance. In fact, the dissemination of advance information that manipulative activity will take place is itself prohibited as a manipulation.[17]

Sec. 18-3. General anti-fraud and anti-manipulative provisions. Mention has already been made of Section 15(c)(1) of the Act, implemented by Rule 15c1-2, as being typical of the all inclusiveness of the anti-fraud provisions of the federal securities

---

451 (1952). *Gob Shops of America, Inc.,* 39 SEC 92, 101 (1959); *Bruns, Nordeman & Company,* SEC Securities Exchange Act Release No. 6540, April 26, 1961, pp. 5-6; *Halsey Stuart & Co., Inc.,* 30 SEC 106, 124 (1949); *The Federal Corporation,* 25 SEC 227, 230 (1947). See also, *Re, Re & Sagarese,* SEC Securities Exchange Act Release No. 6900, Sept. 21, 1962, p. 2 ("closing transactions on the uptick"). *Reynolds & Co.,* SEC Securities Exchange Act Release No. 6978, Dec. 20, 1962, p. 2 item "2."

[15] Section 9(a)(4) of the Act.

[16] See e.g., *SEC v. Wolfson* (S.D.N.Y. Civ. Action No. 135-30 Order Dated August 1, 1958); Also, on the same case see SEC Litigation Release No. 1315, August 1, 1958.

[17] Sections 9(a)(3) and (5) of the Act prohibit anyone engaged in offering to sell, selling, offering to purchase, and purchasing, a security (or any one who receives consideration for the purpose from the offeror, seller or purchaser, as the case may be) from circulating or disseminating information to the effect that the price of the security will rise or fall because of the market operations of any one or more persons engaged in to raise or depress the price of the security. See also, *Associated Investors Securities, Inc.,* SEC Securities Exchange Act Release No. 6859, July 24, 1962, p. 9. And see, *Shelley Roberts & Co. of California,* 38 SEC 744, 749 (1958). As we have seen, however, the failure to disclose manipulative activity in connection with a distribution is in itself a violation of the anti-fraud provisions. See *supra,* Sec. 13-1. And see e.g., *Theodore A. Landau,* SEC Securities Exchange Act Release No. 6792, April 30, 1962, pp. 7-8 at n. 13.

laws.[18] Although the reach of these provisions is sufficiently extensive to encompass every conceivable type of fraud and deception which might be practiced in effecting transactions in or inducing the purchase or sale of securities, these measures are restricted by their terms to over-the-counter transactions by brokers and dealers in non-exempted securities.

Rule 10b-5, based on Section 10(b) of the Act, is just as far reaching as Section 15(c)(1) and Rule 15c1-2 in coverage with regard to the types and varieties of fraud and deception it outlaws; it applies moreover to any person, whether or not a broker-dealer, and refers to listed as well as unlisted non-exempted securities.[19] Here follow the provisions of Rule 10b-5:

> It shall be unlawful for any person, directly or indirectly, by the use of any means of instrumentality of interstate commerce, or of the mails, or of any facility of any national securities exchange,
>> (1) to employ any device, scheme or artifice to defraud,
>> (2) to make any untrue statement of a material fact or to omit to state a material fact necessary in order to make the statements made, in the light of the circumstances under which they were made, not misleading, or
>> (3) to engage in any act, practice, or course of business which operates or would operate as a fraud or deceit upon any person,
> in connection with the purchase or sale of any security.[20]

This rule, like the other anti-fraud provisions of the federal securities laws,[21] is consonant with the objective of Congress to forbid not only the telling of purposeful falsity but also the telling of half-truths and the failure to tell the whole truth. Accordingly, the restrictions and limitations of common law fraud have no relevance to an inquiry into the scope of the anti-fraud provisions

---

[18] *Supra,* Chapter 10.

[19] Section 10(b) of the Act provides in pertinent part: "It shall be unlawful for any person, directly or indirectly, by use of any means or instrumentality of interstate commerce or of the mails, or of any facility of any national securities exchange—(a). . . . (b) to use or employ, in connection with the purchase or sale of any security registered on a national securities exchange or any security not so registered, any manipulative or deceptive device or contrivance in contravention of such rules and regulations as the Commission may prescribe as necessary or appropriate in the public interest or for the protection of investors." The anti-manipulative provisions of Rule 10b-6 discussed *supra,* 13-11, are also based in part on Section 10(b) of the Act.

[20] Section 17(a) of the Securities Act of 1933 is as effective as Rule 10b-5 in reaching offers to sell or sales of securities; but it has no application to the purchase or offer to purchase securities.

[21] See e.g., Section 15(c)(1) of the Act and Rule 15c1-2 and Section 17(a) of the Securities Act of 1933. Cf. Sections 11(a) and 12(2) of the Securities Act.

of the federal securities laws.[22] Thus, it need not be established
that persons who engaged in transactions in the security did so in
reliance upon the false or misleading statements which were
made to induce transactions,[23] or that investors have actually incurred loss or damage.[24] All that need be shown is (a) that, in
the offer to sell, sale, offer to purchase or purchase, of a security,
there has been a false statement of a material fact,[25] or (b) that
there has been an omission to state a material fact necessary in
order to make the statement in light of the circumstances under
which they were made, not misleading,[26] or (c) that there has
been the use of any device, scheme or artifice to defraud, or (d)
that there was employed any act, practice, or course of business
which operates as a fraud or would operate as a fraud or deceit
upon any person.[27] In brief, the anti-fraud provisions are designed to reach any manifestation of fraud or deception em-

---

[22] *Hughes* v. *SEC*, 174 F.2d 969, 976 (D.C. Cir. 1949); *Charles Hughes & Co.* v.
SEC, 139 F.2d 434, 437 (2d Cir. 1943), and see *Norris & Hirshberg* v. *SEC*, 177 F.2d
228, 233 (D.C. Cir. 1949) where the court said: ". . . To say as petitioner does, that
every element of common law fraud must be proven in order to validate the revocation of a broker-dealer registration is to say that Congress had no purpose in
enacting regulatory statutes in this field and that its legislation in the field is
meaningless. . . ." See also *Associated Investors Securities Inc.*, SEC Securities
Exchange Act Release No. 6859, July 24, 1962, p. 8, where the Commission noted
that ". . . it is immaterial whether violations of the anti-fraud provisions of the
securities acts constitute fraud at common law or under another statute." The
"other" statute to which the Commission was referring in that case was the Mail
Fraud Statute. The Commission also pointed out that the circumstance that a
customer of a broker-dealer has the right under the particular arrangement to a
return of his money or to obtain more information does not negate violations of
the anti-fraud provisions.

[23] *A. J. Caradean & Co.*, SEC Securities Exchange Act Release No. 6903, Oct. 1,
1962, p. 5 at n. 10; *B. Fennekohl & Co.*, SEC Securities Exchange Act Release No.
6898, Sept. 18, 1962, pp. 5-6; *D. H. Victor & Company, Inc.*, SEC Securities Exchange Act Release No. 6562, p. 3; *N. Sims Organ & Co., Inc.*, SEC Securities Exchange Act Release No. 6495, March 14, 1961, p. 3. And see *Wilko* v. *Swan*, 346
U. S. 427 (1953).

[24] See *Russell Maguire & Company, Inc.*, 10 SEC 332, 351 (1941).

[25] According to Restatement of Torts §538 (2), a fact is material if ". . . its
existence or non-existence is a matter to which a reasonable man would attach
importance in determining his course of action in the transaction in question.
. . ." and, also, if ". . . the maker of the representation knows that its recipient
is likely to regard the fact as important although a reasonable man would not so
regard it. . . ." For the disclosure requirements in applications and reports required to be filed under the registration for listing and reporting requirements of
the Act, Rule 12b-2 defines "material" thus: "The term 'material' when used to
qualify a requirement for the furnishing of information as to any subject, limits
the information required to those matters as to which an average prudent investor
ought reasonably to be informed before buying or selling the security registered."

[26] The "half truth" specifically condemned in such cases as *Hughes* v. *SEC*,
174 F.2d 969, 976 (D.C. Cir. 1949).

[27] See the discussion, *supra*, on this topic at Sec. 17-11.

ployed in connection with any securities transaction. Thus in a related context, the Supreme Court of the United States has recently made it abundantly clear that the anti-fraud provisions of all of the federal securities laws, including such provisions in the Exchange Act, have as their fundamental purpose to substitute a philosophy of full disclosure for the philosophy of *caveat emptor* and thus to achieve a high standard of business ethics in the securities industry by eliminating all manner of fraud and deceit. In this connection, the court held that failure to disclose material facts was but one variety of fraud and deceit.[28]

[28] *SEC* v. *Capital Gains Research Bureau Inc.,* U. S. (Decided December 9, 1963).

PART VI

PENALTIES FOR VIOLATIONS;
ENFORCEMENT PROCEEDINGS

CHAPTER 19

CENSURE, DENIAL, SUSPENSION, AND REVOCATION OF REGISTRATION

Sec. 19-1. In general—classes of persons whose designated activities at any time may be grounds for sanctions against broker-dealers. Section 15(b)(5) of the Act provides that the Commission shall, after appropriate notice and opportunity for hearing, by order censure, deny registration to, or suspend for not more than twelve months, or revoke the registration of any broker or dealer if it finds that such sanction is in the public interest and that acts or circumstances specified in the section[1] have occurred or exist with reference to or have been committed by such broker or dealer, whether prior to or subsequent to becoming such a broker or dealer or by any person associated with such broker or dealer, whether prior or subsequent to becoming so associated."

The definition of a "person associated with a broker or dealer" is set out in the margin.[2] Such persons include, among others, those who are "controlled by," including employees of such applicant or registrant. It has already been seen that any person not a registered broker-dealer who effects or induces transactions in securities on behalf of an applicant for broker-dealer registration or of a registrant is a person "controlled by" the applicant or registrant, irrespective of how the relationship may be characterized as between the parties.[3] By rule and regulation,

---

[1] These acts and circumstances have come popularly to be termed "statutory grounds," and they will hereafter be collectively referred to by that term. The statutory grounds will be discussed below, *infra,* at Sections 19-4 to 19-10.

[2] These are specified in Section 3(a)(18) of the Act as ". . . any partner, officer, director or branch manager of such broker or dealer (or any persons occupying a similar status or performing similar functions) or any person directly or indirectly controlling or controlled by such broker or dealer, including any employee of such broker or dealer, except that for the purposes of Section 15(b) of this title (other than paragraph (7) thereof), persons associated with a broker or dealer whose functions are clerical or ministerial shall not be included in the meaning of such term. . . ." For the purposes of the Act, the Commission may classify employees and others controlled by a broker or dealer. *Ibid.*

[3] See, *supra,* Sec. 5-2; and see *National Association of Securities Dealers, Inc.,* 20 SEC 508, 516 (1945). See also SEC Securities Exchange Act Release No. 3674, April 9, 1945, pp. 1-2; and see, e.g., *Bond & Goodwin, Inc.,* 15 SEC 584, 599, 601 *et seq.* (1944); *E. H. Rollins & Sons, Inc.* 18 SEC 347, 390 *et seq* (1945); *Kidder,*

the Commission may classify persons, including employees, who are "controlled" by a broker or dealer.[4]

It is repeated for emphasis that, as to statutory grounds for censure, denial, suspension, or revocation which exist with reference to an applicant, registrant, or associated person, it does not matter whether the grounds existed or occurred prior or subsequent to the making of the application or to registration, or, as regards an associated person, whether prior or subsequent to the commencement of the association.[5] Accordingly, grounds which might serve as a basis for denial prior to the effectiveness of an application for registration may be employed as a basis for the specified sanctions after registration has been permitted to become effective. The Commission is not estopped by the fact that it dismissed denial proceedings without prejudice as moot from using the same charges as a basis for revocation.[6]

Since the Commission must conclude, in any event, that censure, denial, suspension or revocation is in the "public interest," that subject will be treated first. This will be followed by a reference to the concept of the term "willful" as it relates to certain of the statutory grounds for the specified sanctions. The several statutory grounds which serve as a basis for sanctions upon a finding of public interest will then be taken up in turn followed by a brief reference to procedural matters.

Sec. 19-2. Public interest—proceedings not penal, standards and considerations. Whatever may be the statutory grounds which serve as the basis for charges against a broker-dealer in a Section 15(b)(5) proceeding, the Commission may not impose the sanction unless "it finds that such censure, denial, suspension or revocation

---

Peabody & Co., 18 SEC 559 (1945); Allen Russel Securities, Inc., 38 SEC 599 (1958); Reynolds & Co., Inc., 39 SEC 902, 916-17 (1960); R. H. Johnson & Co. v. SEC, 198 F.2d 690 (2d Cir. 1952).

[4] Section 3(a)(18) of the Act.

[5] Section 15(b)(5). See Peoples Securities Co. v. SEC, 289 F.2d 268 (5th Cir. 1961); N. Sims Organ & Co., Inc., SEC Securities Exchange Act Release No. 6495, March 14, 1961, pp. 5-6, aff'd 293 F.2d 78 (2d Cir. 1961). Union Securities Corporation, SEC Securities Exchange Act Release No. 6749, March 7, 1962. Edmund S. Reed, SEC Securities Exchange Act Release No. 6877, Aug. 10, 1962, p. 1. And see Batten & Co., Inc., SEC Securities Exchange Act Release No. 6734, pp. 3-4. Haley & Company, 37 SEC 100, 107 (1956); Ramey Kelly Corporation, 39 SEC 756, 762 at n. 12; Realty Securities Inc., SEC Securities Exchange Act Release No. 7271, March 20, 1964.

[6] See N. Sims Organ & Co., Inc., supra, n. 5, and, on review, 293 F.2d 78 (2d Cir. 1961).

is in the public interest." It is plain from this as well as from the form of remedy that, upon the application of appropriate public interest standards discussed directly below, the imposition of the sanction is not a penalty, but a measure taken by the Commission to protect the public against future danger of exposure to the type of conduct which impelled the Commission to order the sanction.[7]

If the particular conduct of an applicant, registrant, or associated person which would serve as a basis for sanction indicates that it would be a hazard to the investing public to permit the applicant to do business, or a registrant to continue his business as a broker-dealer unchecked, the Commission could then find it in the public interest to impose the sanction it deems appropriate.[8] Thus, where the statutory grounds in a denial or revocation proceeding involve persistent violations by the broker-dealer, or associated person, of the same basic character, it is reasonable for the Commission to act on the assumption that, if registration be permitted or continued, the same types of violations will be perpetrated on the public.[9]

Additionally, a finding that particular disciplinary action is in the public interest may be predicated on a prior history of disciplinary action taken against the broker-dealer or associate by the Commission or other authority with jurisdiction to discipline the broker-dealer or associate for conduct in such capacity, or with other jurisdiction in relation to their securities transactions.[10] So,

---

[7] *Blaise D'Antoni & Associates* v. *SEC*, 289 F.2d 276, 277 (5th Cir. 1961); *Pierce* v. *SEC*, 239 F.2d 160, 163 (9th Cir. 1956). See *Wright* v. *SEC*, 112 F.2d 89, 94 (2d Cir. 1940). See also *Mutual Fund Distributors, Inc.*, SEC Securities Exchange Act Release No. 6862, July 25, 1962, p. 7. *Kimball Securities, Inc.*, 39 SEC 921, 924-5 (1960).

[8] *Ibid.* See *Associated Securities Corp.* v. *SEC*, 293 F.2d 738 (10th Cir. 1961). See also, *Schuck* v. *SEC*, 264 F.2d 358, 363 (D.C. Cir. 1958); *Brown Barton & Engel*, SEC Securities Exchange Act No. 6821, June 8, 1962, pp. 5-6. And see *J. Logan & Co.*, SEC Securities Exchange Act Release No. 6848, July 9, 1962, p. 11, *Alexander Reid & Co., Inc.*, SEC Securities Exchange Act Release No. 7016, Feb. 7, 1963, p. 6.

[9] *Ibid.* And see *Midas Management Corporation*, SEC Securities Exchange Act Release No. 6569, May 25, 1961, p. 2; *A. J. Caradean & Co., Inc.*, SEC Securities Exchange Act Release No. 6903, Oct. 1, 1962, p. 6. See also in another, but closely comparable context, *D. H. Victor & Company, Inc.*, SEC Securities Exchange Act Release No. 6562, May 17, 1961, p. 3. And see *Harold Grill*, SEC Securities Exchange Act Release No. 6989, Jan. 8, 1963, pp. 4-5.

[10] See *Gibbs & Company*, SEC Securities Exchange Act Release No. 6717, Jan. 29, 1962, p. 3; *Reynolds & Co.*, 39 SEC 902, 918 at n. 31 (1960). And see e.g., *Brown Barton & Engel*, SEC Securities Exchange Act Release No. 6821, June 8, 1962, pp. 5-6; *Theodore A. Landau*, SEC Securities Exchange Act Release No. 6792, April 30, 1962, p. 8 at n. 14; *Morris J. Reiter*, SEC Securities Exchange Act Release No. 6849, July 13, 1962, p. 7; *Irving Grubman*, SEC Securities Exchange Act Release No. 6546, May

too, the conviction of a broker-dealer or associate of a crime involving fraud will be taken into account as a public interest factor, even though the crime does not involve securities in any way.[11]

Moreover, for the purpose of applying the public interest standard, an injunction which may serve as a statutory ground for the institution of a Section 15(b)(5) proceeding will be examined to the extent of taking into account relevant parts of the injunction suit record.[12] By the same token, where violations have been found to be willful in the context of a broker-dealer disciplinary proceeding, the fact of willfulness may be taken into account on the question of public interest, even though such willfulness be itself an integral element of the statutory ground involved in the proceeding.[13] And the fact that the applicant, registrant, or associate has misled the Commission's staff in matters within the ambit of staff inquiry is also a matter quite relevant to the question of public interest.[14]

The alleged youth and comparative innocence of the applicant, registrant, or associate will not establish that the imposition of sanctions is not in the public interest, in the face of highly fraudulent activities on the part of such person and the fact that he had extensive experience in the field with other broker-dealers against whom disciplinary measures had been taken.[15]

The mere fact that the customers who testified in the proceeding had not complained to the applicant, registrant, or associate

---

5, 1961, p. 4 at n. 10. See also *Edward J. Carroll*, 39 SEC 777, 779 (1960); *Whitney & Company*, SEC Securities Exchange Act Release No. 7165, Nov. 6, 1963, p. 5.

11 See *Irving Grubman, supra*, SEC Securities Exchange Act Release No. 6546, at p. 4.

12 As to injunctions serving as a statutory ground, see discussion of Ground "(C)" *infra* at Sec. 19-6. See *Kimball Securities Inc.*, 39 SEC 921, 923-4 (1960). *The Western Trader Inc.*, 37 SEC 792, 794 (1957); *Kaye Real & Co., Inc.*, 36 SEC 373 (1958); *Schuck v. SEC*, 264 F.2d 358 (D.C. Cir. 1958). See also, in another but closely comparable context, *Ralph Harold Siepel*, 38 SEC 256, 258 (1958). See also *Brown Barton & Engel*, SEC Securities Exchange Act Release No. 6821, June 8, 1962, p. 6.

13 See *Schuck v. SEC, supra.*, n. 12,264 F.2d at 362. The discussion on the subject of willfulness as an element in specified statutory grounds for denial or revocation is found shortly below at Sec. 19-3.

14 *James H. Drass, Inc.*, 39 SEC 368, 371 (1959); *J. D. Creger & Co.*, 39 SEC 165, 170-1 (1959). See *F.C.C. v. W.O.K.O., Inc.*, 329 U. S. 223, 227 (1946). And, cf. *Gregory & Company, Inc.*, 38 SEC 304, 306 (1958).

15 See e.g., *Harold Grill*, SEC Securities Exchange Act Release No. 6989, Jan. 8, 1963, pp. 4-5.

is not persuasive on the point of public interest.[16] And, although the circumstance that a registrant's, applicant's, or associate's innocent stockholders will be adversely affected by the disciplinary measure may be considered on the public-interest issue,[17] it will not be given determinative, or even important, weight.[18]

Similarly, although the claimed reliance on counsel is a factor to be considered on the question of public interest, it is not taken as determinative, but as only one of the factors bearing on the question as to whether the violation is likely to be repeated.[19]

On the other hand, the Commission has held it not to be in the public interest to impose sanctions where there is no danger of public exposure to hazard, either because the violation was isolated and committed in the absence of bad faith,[20] or because, irrespective of the seriousness of the violation there, was no longer a possibility that the applicant, registrant, or associate would engage in business as or be employed by a broker-dealer and that therefore nothing could be accomplished on behalf of public investors by a disciplinary order.[21]

Sec. 19-3. Willfulness. Among the statutory grounds for disciplinary action is that the applicant, registrant, or associated person "willfully" made or caused to be made a false or misleading statement in any application for broker-dealer registration or in any report required to be filed under the Act or in any proceeding

---

[16] "The customers who testified made no complaint about the treatment afforded them by respondent or about the royalties they had purchased. Customers, however, need protection although they may not understand how they have been injured or even realize that advantage has been taken of them. . . ." *Lawrence R. Leeby* 13 SEC 499 (1943) at 511 [footnotes omitted].

[17] See *Pioneer Enterprises, Inc.*, 36 SEC 199 (1955).

[18] *Ibid.* And Cf. *FCC v. WOKO* 329 U. S. 223, 227 (1946), where the argument was made that non-renewal of a radio license would be hurtful to the applicant's stockholders, and where the Court said: ". . . . But as a matter of law, the fact that there are innocent stockholders can not immunize the corporation from the consequences of . . . [its] deception. . . . But in this as in other matters, stockholders entrust their interests to their chosen officers. . . ." See also, *A. G. Bellin Securities Corp.*, 39 SEC 178, 184-5 (1959), where, in a comparable context, the claim was made that the Commission's order would result in hardship to employees, and where the public interest was held to outweight such considerations.

[19] *The Whitehall Corporation*, 38 SEC 259, 273-4 (1958); *H. Carroll & Co.*, 39 SEC 780, 787 (1960). And see, *Brown Barton & Engel*, SEC Securities Exchange Act Release No. 6751, March 9, 1962, p. 4.

[20] See e.g. *Bristol Securities Inc.*, SEC Securities Exchange Act Release No. 6964, Nov. 30, 1962; *Vranken Investors Corporation*, SEC Securities Exchange Act Release No. 7237, Feb. 12, 1964.

[21] See e.g., *Benjamin Zwang & Co., Inc.*, SEC Securities Exchange Act Release No. 7001, Jan. 23, 1963. SEC Securities Exchange Act Releases Nos. 6722, Feb. 1,

before the Commission with respect to broker-dealer registration.[22] Other statutory grounds with a component of willfulness are, that the applicant, registrant, or associated person has willfully violated any provisions of specified statutes administered by the Commission, or of any rule or regulation under those Acts.[23]

For the purposes of denial or revocation proceedings under Section 15(b) of the Act, the term "willful" characterizes an act as being neither unintentional or inadvertent. In brief, it refers merely to a conscious, intentional act, and does not embrace knowledge that the conscious, intentional act constitutes a violation of law.[24] Indeed, the fact that the person committing the act does so because he believes it is lawful does not negate willfulness.[25] This is especially the case where the person commits an act after he has notice of the view of the Commission's staff that the proposed conduct would violate the law.[26] Moreover, the omission of an act will be regarded as willful if the person responsible was guilty of gross negligence or indifference; that is, of such a gross disregard of his obligations that his acts amount to intentional conduct.[27]

Although the claim that the advice of counsel was sought and followed may be relevant on the question of public interest,[28] it has no defensive impact on the issue of willfulness.[29]

Where the Commission obtained an injunction against the applicant, registrant, or associated person prior to the Section 15(b)(5) proceeding, the finding of the Court that the person en-

---

1962; 6919, Oct. 22, 1962; *Mineo & Co.*, SEC Securities Exchange Act Release No. 6917, Oct. 22, 1962.

[22] Section 15 (b)(5)(A) of the Act.

[23] Section 15(b)(5)(D). These will be discussed *infra* at Sec. 19-7.

[24] See *Shuck* v. *SEC, supra*, n. 12, 264 F.2d at p. 363, n. 18 where the Court said: "In *Hughes* v. *SEC*, 85 U. S. App. D.C. 56, 64, 174 F.2d 969, 977 (1949), we held that willfulness for purpose of Section 15(b)(D) means 'no more than that the person charged with the duty knows what he is doing. It does not mean that, in addition, he must suppose that he is breaking the law.' "

[25] *Halsey Stuart & Co., Inc.*, 30 SEC 106, 126 (1949).

[26] *Ibid.* And see *Makris Investment Brokers*, SEC Securities Exchange Act Release No. 6509, March 24, 1961, p. 3.

[27] See *John Munroe*, 39 SEC 308, 311 (1959); *Charles E. Bailey & Company*, 35 SEC 33, 41-2 (1953); *Sidney Ascher*, 31 SEC 753 (1950); *David Brody*, 31 SEC 757,758 (1950); *Lawrence Steele Costelle*, 31 SEC 759, 760 (1950); *Rudolph* v. *Klein*, SEC Securities Exchange Act Release No. 6415, Nov. 17, 1960, p. 5; *Barnett* v. *SEC*, 319 F.2d 340 (8th Cir. 1963).

[28] See *supra*, Sec. 19-2.

[29] See e.g., *David Joel Benjamin*, 38 SEC 614, 618-19 (1958); *Herman Bud Rothbard*, 39 SEC 253, 257 (1959); *H. Carroll & Co.*, 39 SEC 780, 784-5 (1960).

joined was aware of his actions and that they were done intentionally may be taken as *res adjudicata* in the Section 15(b)(5) proceeding and serve as an adequate basis in the latter proceeding for a finding of willfulness.[30]

The claim by an associate of inexperience in the securities business will not, even if true, negate willfulness in the face of particularly unconscionable conduct on his part.[31]

It may finally be observed on the subject of willfulness that, if it is an element in a statutory ground for disciplinary action, the proceeding is not subject to the condition precedent set forth in Section 9(b) of the Administrative Procedure Act[32] that, prior to the institution of a proceeding to suspend or revoke a license, the licensee must be afforded an opportunity to take corrective steps following written notice of the facts or conduct which may warrant disciplinary action.[33]

Sec. 19-4. Statutory ground "(A)"—false or misleading statements in application, report, or section 15(b)(5) proceeding. It has already been seen that an applicant for broker-dealer registration must provide accurate information in his application,[34] and that a registered broker-dealer is obliged to amend his application promptly whenever information contained in the application or amendments thereto becomes inaccurate.[35] Willful

---

[30] *Rudolph* v. *Klein,* SEC Securities Exchange Act Release No. 6415, Nov. 17, 1960, pp. 4-5.

[31] See *J. Logan & Co.,* SEC Securities Exchange Act Release No. 6848, July 9, 1962, p. 13; *Fidelity Securities Corporation,* SEC Securities Exchange Act Release No. 6987, Jan. 4, 1963, p. 2.

[32] 5 U.S.C. §1008(b). This section provides in pertinent part: "Except in cases of willfulness or those in which public health, interest, or safety requires otherwise, no withdrawal, suspension, revocation or annulment of any license shall be lawful unless, prior to the institution of agency proceedings therefor, facts or conduct which may warrant such action shall have been called to the attention of the licensee by the agency in writing and the licensee shall have been accorded opportunity to demonstrate or achieve compliance with all lawful requirements."

[33] *Shuck* v. *SEC, supra,* n. 12, 264 F.2d at p. 362, n. 14, and see *Sterling Securities Company,* 37 SEC 837 (1957), where the Commission held, also, that the necessity for a finding (based on an adequate record) that revocation is in the "public interest" provides an additional reason for lack of application of Section 9(b) of the Administrative Procedure Act to broker-dealer revocation proceedings, even in cases where willfulness is not an element in the particular statutory ground. It has been seen that the conditions of Section 9(b) are not applicable in cases ". . . in which public . . . interest or safety requires otherwise. . ."

[34] See the discussion, *supra* at Sec. 3-3, on Accuracy of Information In Application.

[35] See the discussion, *supra* at Sec. 5-3, under the item "Amendment of Application By Registered Broker-Dealer."

violation of these obligations by an applicant, registrant, or associate provides statutory grounds for sanctions if such action be found in the public interest.[36]

The willful making or causing to be made of a false or misleading statement or omission of a material fact in any other application for registration or any report required to be filed under the Act, or in a proceeding in respect of registration under Section 15(b)(5) is also included in the same statutory ground.[37]

Sec. 19-5. Statutory ground "(B)"—conviction for crimes involving purchase or sale of a security or arising out of conduct of investment adviser or broker-dealer business or for other specified crimes. Ground "(B)" of Rule 15(b)(5)[38] relates to an applicant, registrant, or associate who has been convicted within ten years preceding the filing of any such application for broker-dealer registration or at any time thereafter or any felony or misdemeanor which the Commission finds:

"(i) involves the purchase or sale of any security.

"(ii) arises out of the conduct of the business of a broker, dealer, or investment adviser.

"(iii) involves embezzlement, fraudulent conversion, or misappropriation of funds or securities.

"(iv) involves the violation of Section 1341, 1342, 1343 of Title 18, United States Code."[39]

A reference to the indictment or information and the judgment of conviction will readily disclose whether ground "(B)" exists as a basis for appropriate sanction upon a finding of public interest.[40]

---

[36] For application of Ground "(A)," see e.g., *Samuel Janov*, SEC Securities Exchange Act Release No. 7005, Jan. 25, 1963, p. 1; *Midas Management Corporation*, SEC Securities Exchange Act Release No. 6569, May 25, 1961, p. 3; *Edna Campbell Markey*, 39 SEC 274 (1959); *Herman Bud Rothbard*, 39 SEC 253, 258 (1959); *Peoples Securities Company*, 39 SEC 641, 646 (1960); *Talmage Wilcher Inc.*, 39 SEC 936 (1960); *Gregory & Company, Inc.*, 38 SEC 304, 306 (1958);*Joe Bert Sissom*, SEC Securities Exchange Act Release No. 7021, Feb. 11, 1963, p. 1; *Security Service Inc.*, SEC Securities Exchange Act Release No. 7127, Aug. 27, 1963, p. 1.

[37] Section 15(b)(5)(A). This would include false or misleading statements or omissions of material fact in any number of applications for registration and reports required to be filed by various provisions of the Act, such as Sections 12(a), 12(g), 13(a), 16(a), and 17(a) of the Act.

[38] Section 15(b)(5)(B).

[39] These are the mail fraud and wire, radio, and television fraud statutes.

[40] See e.g., *Bankers Securities, Incorporated*, SEC Securities Exchange Act Release No. 6878, Aug. 10, 1962, p. 1.

Convictions by a court of competent jurisdiction of a foreign country are within ground "(B)." *R. P. Clarke & Co., Ltd.*, 10 SEC 1072 (1942). Convictions based upon

Willfulness is not an essential element of Ground (B), although, presumably, it was an essential element for the conviction.

Sec. 19-6. Statutory ground "(C)"—injunction against acting in certain capacities or against engaging in or continuing any conduct or practice in connection with specified activities or with the purchase or sale of a security. Ground "(C)" of Section 15(b)(5) relates to an applicant, registrant, or associated person who "is permanently or temporarily enjoined by order, judgment, or decree of any court of competent jurisdiction from acting as an investment adviser, underwriter, broker or dealer, or as an affiliated person or employee of any investment company, bank or insurance company, or from engaging in or continuing any conduct or practice in connection with such activity, or in connection with the purchase or sale of any security."[41]

Willfulness is not an element of Ground (C). The existence of the injunction is enough to support a sanction upon a finding of public interest.[42] The fact that the injunction was not violated does not remove it as a statutory ground.[43]

Where personal jurisdiction of an applicant, registrant, or associated person is obtained by the Court, it is of no consequence that he is not named in the injunction if he was an officer of a corporation whose activities as to the sale of securities were enjoined along with those of the corporation's "agents, employees, brokers, partners, officers, directors and shareholders."[44] Moreover, if the injunction is binding on a person, he cannot go behind

a plea of guilty or of *nolo contendere* are as effective for ground "(B)" as a conviction following trial. See e.g., *Leo G. Siegfield*, 11 SEC 746, 747-9 (1942); *Jesse S. Locaby*, 29 SEC 271, 272 (1949); *Wendell M. Weston*, 30 SEC 296, 312-313 (1949). The granting of a pardon in respect of a conviction which occurred within ten years may be taken into account on the question of public interest. *Norvin T. Harris, Jr.*, 29 SEC 519, 520 (1949).

[41] Section 15(b)(5)(C). Injunctions for violation of net capital requirements and the bookkeeping rules fall within the type of injunction which serves as a basis for Ground "(C)." See *Market Securities Inc.*, SEC Securities Exchange Act Release No. 7107, Aug. 2, 1963, p. 2.

[42] *Shuck* v. *SEC*, 264 F.2d 358, 362 (D.C. Cir. 1958).

[43] See *Frank Payson Todd*, SEC Investment Advisers Act Release No. 109, Oct. 31, 1960, p. 4; *Ralph Harold Siepel*, 38 SEC 256, (1958); *Kaye, Real & Company Inc.*, 36 SEC 373 (1955); *J. D. Creger & Co.*, 39 SEC 165, 169-70 (1959); *Kimball Securities Inc.*, 39 SEC 921, 924 at n. 4 (1960).

[44] *Oil Royalties Investment Trust Ltd.*, 4 SEC 529, 531-2 (1939). In the absence of proof to the contrary, it will be presumed that the Court obtained such personal jurisdiction. *Ibid.*

it for the purpose of relitigating the issues already resolved against him by the Court.[45] Additionally, the Commission will take official notice of the entry of an injunction.[46]

Presumably, if an outstanding injunction serving as the basis for ground "(C)" were duly abrogated by subsequent order of a court having jurisdiction so to act, ground "(C)" would no longer be applicable.[47]

For the purposes of ground "(C)," moreover, an injunction entered prior to the passage of the Act is regarded as having equal force as an injunction entered on a statutory ground after the Act's enactment;[48] a consent decree stands on the same footing as any other injunction.[49] "Cease and Desist" orders of state administrative officials are not normally regarded as court orders and hence would not normally be regarded as injunctions.[50]

Sec. 19-7. Statutory ground "(D)"—willful violations of specified statutes administered by the commission or of rules or regulations thereunder. Ground "(D)" applies to an applicant, registrant, or associated person who has willfully violated any provision of the Securities Act of 1933, of the Investment Advisers Act of 1940, of the Investment Company Act of 1940, or of the Securities Exchange Act of 1934, or of any rule or regulation under those statutes.[51]

It is of course not feasible to make reference to every provision of the specified statutes and rules which could serve as the basis for disciplinary action under ground "(D)." As to the provisions of the Securities Exchange Act of 1934 and the rules thereunder to which this book makes specific reference, attention

---

[45] See *Gibbs & Company*, SEC Securities Exchange Act Release No. 6717, Jan. 29, 1962, p. 5. We have seen, though, that the record of the injunction proceeding may be examined for such light as it may shed on the issue of "public interest." See *supra*, Sec. 19-2.

[46] See *Frederick Securities Corporation*, 38 SEC 801, 802 (1959).

[47] However, courts will not lift an injunction merely because, by passage of time, the conditions which prompted its being granted no longer exist. See *Wirtz* v. *Graham Transfer & Storage Co.*, 322 F.2d 650 (5th Cir. 1963). See also, *People* v. *Scanlon*, 180 N. Y. S. 2d 93 (1958), appeal dismissed 6 N. Y. 2d 185; and *People* v. *Scanlon* (N. Y. App. Div. Dec. 27, 1961).

[48] *M. Paul Conant & Co., Inc.*, 39 SEC 511, 512-13 (1959).

[49] See, *Frank Payson Todd*, SEC Investment Advisers Act Release No. 109, Oct. 31, 1960, p. 4; and see also *James F. Morrisey*, 25 SEC 372, 381 (1947) which also holds that an injunction may not be attacked collaterally.

[50] It appears, however, that in some states, such as Virginia and Oklahoma, "cease and desist" orders are deemed to be court orders.

[51] Section 15(b)(5)(D).

is directed to them as provisions which have served as the basis for sanctions on various occasions under Ground "(D)."

With respect to the Securities Act of 1933 and its rules, the violations of which are most commonly designated as rendering ground "(D)" applicable are the violations of the anti-fraud provisions of that Act and of the registration requirements of Section 5 of that Act. As regards the anti-fraud provisions of Section 17(a) of that Act relative to offers and sales of securities by jurisdictional means, it has been seen that, in practical effect, Section 17(a) of that Act has substantially the same sweep as the anti-fraud provisions of the Securities Exchange Act of 1934 discussed in this chapter.[52]

An injunction against a registrant or applicant obtained upon complaint of the Commission which is sustained upon a finding of a violation of a provision of one of the statutes or rules specified in ground "(D)" may be taken in a revocation or denial proceeding as *res adjudicata* upon the issue of such violation.[53]

Some special mention should be made, however, of the participation by a broker or dealer in an illegal distribution in violation of Section 5 of the Securities Act of 1933 as an element in ground "(D)."

Sec. 19-8. Statutory ground "(D)"—participation in illegal distribution. It is not within the scope of this book to provide a detailed analysis of the requirements of Section 5 of the Securities Act of 1933 or of the various provisions of that Act as to exemptions from such requirements. For the purposes of discussing a type of willful violation of the provisions of the Securities Act of 1933 which not infrequently serves as a basis for revocation upon a finding of public interest, it will suffice to refer to this summarization of the registration requirements of Section 5 of the Securities

---

[52] See *supra*, Sec. 18-3. Witness this typical statement appearing in opinions of the Commission: "The anti-fraud provisions alleged to have been violated are Section 17(a) of the Securities Act and Sections 10(b) and 15(c)(1) of the Exchange Act and Rules 10b-5 (17 CFR 240.10b-5) and 15cl-2 (17 CFR 240.15cl-2) thereunder. The composite effect of these provisions as applicable to this case is to make unlawful the use of the mails or means of interstate commerce in connection with a purchase or sale of any security by the use of a device to defraud, an untrue or misleading statement of a material fact, or any act, practice, or course of business which operates or would operate as a fraud or deceit upon a customer." *Batkin & Co.,* 38 SEC 436, 437 at n. 2 (1958).

[53] *Rudolph* v. *Klein,* SEC Securities Exchange Act Release No. 6415, Nov. 17, 1960, p. 4 at n. 6, and cases there cited, including *James F. Morrisey,* 25 SEC 372, 381 (1947).

Act of 1933 frequently employed in Commission opinions in Commission disciplinary proceedings; "Section 5 of the Securities Act prohibits the use of the mails or the facilities of interstate commerce to offer to sell securities unless a registration statement has been filed or to sell or deliver after sale securities unless a registration statement is in effect as to such securities."[54] It may be observed initially that the terms of Section 5 are absolute. They refer to any offer or sale by any person of any security through jurisdictional means.

The burden of establishing the availability of any exemption is on the one who claims it.[55] Consequently, unless a broker or dealer is in a position to establish the existence of an exemption by evidence of probative value, he will be in violation of the registration requirements of the Securities Act of 1933. Whether or not it would be in the public interest to revoke the registration of a broker-dealer for such a violation may depend upon whether he participated in a distribution of securities under circumstances which should have placed him on notice that a distribution was taking place and whether he should consequently have refrained from engaging in it because he was in no position to establish the existence of an exemption. A broker or dealer who relies, for example, upon the exemption that his transaction is by one who is not an underwriter must be prepared to trace the securities he is selling to a source which is neither the issuer, a person in a control relationship with the issuer, nor an underwriter for any of them.[56]

It has been pointed out that a broker-dealer has the responsibility of acquainting himself with the requirements of the federal securities laws which relate to the conduct of his business.[57] Among the most important of these are the registration requirements of Section 5 of the Securities Act of 1933.

---

[54] This is the summarization appearing in *Battery Securities Corporation,* 38 SEC 89, 91 note 4. See also the Commission's release on the subject of *Distribution By Broker-Dealers Of Unregistered Securities,* SEC Securities Act Release No. 4445, Feb. 2, 1962 (same as SEC Securities Exchange Release No. 6721).

[55] *Idem.* at p. 1; *SEC v. Sunbeam Gold Mines Co.,* 95 F.2d 699, 701 (1938); *SEC v. Ralston Purina Co.,* 346 U. S. 119, 126 (1953); *Ira Haupt & Co.,* 23 SEC 589, 595 (1946); *SEC v. Culpepper,* 270 F.2d 241 (2d Cir. 1959); *Gilligan, Will & Co. v. SEC,* 267 F.2d 461 (2d Cir. 1959), *cert den* 361 U. S. 896.

[56] See, *SEC v. Culpepper,* 270 F.2d 214 (2d Cir. 1959); *SEC v. Chinese Consolidated Benevolent Ass'n.,* 120 F.2d 738 (2d Cir. 1941); *The S. T. Jackson & Company, Inc.,* 36 SEC 631, 648-9 (1950).

[57] *Supra,* Sec. 5-1.

It is, therefore, incumbent upon a broker-dealer to know that "a distribution of securities comprises the entire process by which in the course of a public offering the block of securities is dispersed and ultimately comes to rest in the hands of the investing public."[58] He must also know that he is a participant in an illegal distribution if the unregistered security he sells comes from the issuer, or a person in a control relationship with the issuer or an underwriter for any of them, and it has not previously reached the hands of a member of the investing public.[59] He must know that in such circumstances he is an "underwriter" because he is engaged in steps necessary to the distribution of the securities to the investing public, and that he is therefore in violation of Section 5.[60]

It has been held by the Commission that where the volume of transactions in a security is out of the ordinary and the security emanates from relatively few persons, the circumstances are such as to place a broker-dealer on notice that a distribution is taking place.[61]

In its release on the subject of *Distribution By Broker-Dealers Of Unregistered Securities*,[62] the Commission has furnished guide

[58] *Lewisohn Copper Corporation*, 38 SEC 226, 234 (1958).

[59] *Idem.* at p. 234 n. 7; and see *Brooklyn Manhattan Transit Corporation*, 1 SEC 147 (1935); *The S. T. Jackson & Company, Inc.*, 36 SEC 631, 648-9 (1950).

[60] *SEC* v. *Culpepper*, 270 F.2d 241 (2d Cir 1959); *SEC* v. *Chinese Consolidated Benevolent Ass'n.*, 120 F.2d 738 (2d Cir. 1941).

[61] *The S. T. Jackson & Co., Inc.*, 36 SEC 631, 648 (1950). And witness this language from the Commission's release on *Distribution By Broker-Dealers of Unregistered Securities Supra* (SEC Securities Act Release No. 4445, at p. 2): "The amount of inquiry [into the ultimate source of the security] called for necessarily varies with the circumstances of particular cases. A dealer who is offered a modest amount of a widely traded security by a responsible customer, whose lack of relationship to the issuer is well known to him, may ordinarily proceed with considerable confidence. On the other hand, when a dealer is offered a substantial block of a little-known security, either by persons who appear reluctant to disclose exactly where the securities came from or where the surrounding circumstances raise a question as to whether or not the ostensible sellers may be merely intermediaries for controlling persons or statutory underwriters, then searching inquiry is called for." A copy of SEC Securities Exchange Act Release No. 4445 is attached as Appendix T. See Sec. 25-20, *infra*.

[62] SEC Securities Act Release No. 4445, Feb. 2, 1962 (same as Securities Exchange Act Release No. 6721). Attached as Appendix T. Sec. 25-20, *infra*.

A broker-dealer engages in an illegal distribution when he sells to persons not residents of the same state of the issuer which did not register its securities because it was ostensibly confining its distribution to residents of that state in order to avail itself of the so-called "intra-state" exemption provided for by Section 3(a)(11) of the Securities Act of 1933. *J. A. Hogle & Co.*, 36 SEC 460, 463, 464 (1955). Also, if a broker-dealer engages in the distribution of a security offered pursuant to claim of an exemption under Regulation A under the Securities Act of 1933, he engages in an illegal distribution if the terms and conditions of Regulation A are not complied with. *Charles E. Bailey & Co.*, 35 SEC 33, 43-44 (1953). Suspension pro-

posts on the subject of illegal distribution to assist broker-dealers in avoiding that type of violation.

Another service provided by the Commission to brokers and dealers to assist them in avoiding participation in an illegal distribution is the publication of the "Canadian Restricted List" containing the names of Canadian issuers. "The primary purpose of the restricted list is to put brokers and dealers on notice of the fact that securities of Canadian companies named thereon appear to be the subject of illegal distribution in this country, because of non-registration. . . ."[63] Before executing transactions in securities on the restricted list, brokers and dealers should satisfy themselves that any such security purchased by them for resale or acquired in the execution as broker of a customer's order is not a part of the illegal distribution, since otherwise the broker or dealer himself may be regarded as participating in an unlawful distribution in violation of the Securities Act. . . ."[64] Brokers and dealers have been cautioned by the Commission, moreover, that the list does not necessarily contain the names of all securities of Canadian issuers which are the subject of an illegal distribution; and they are told that they should refrain from engaging in activities which might make them participants in a distribution if they are "otherwise on notice of facts indicating the existence of an unlawful distribution."[65]

Sec. 19-9. Statutory ground "(E)"—willfully participating in violations of specified statutes and rules, failure to supervise. By recent enactment, ground "(E)" has been added to the statutory grounds for Commission disciplinary action.[66] Ground "(E)" applies to a broker-dealer or associated person who has willfully aided, abetted, counseled, commanded, induced, or procured the violation by any other person of the Securities Act of 1933, the Investment Advisers Act of 1940, the Investment Company Act

---

ceedings under Regulation A are not a condition precedent to the revocation of broker-dealer registration on this ground. *Ibid.* and see *Justin Steppler, Inc.,* 37 SEC 252, 255-6 (1956).

[63] *Canadian Restricted List,* SEC Securities Act Release No. 4689, May 8, 1964, p. 1.

[64] *Ibid.*

[65] *Ibid.* The power and authority of the Commission to publish the *Canadian Restricted List* was upheld in *Kukatush Mining Corp.* v. *SEC,* 309 F.2d 647 (D.C. Cir. 1962).

[66] Section 15(b)(5)(E). Securities Acts Amendments of 1964, Sec. 6(b).

of 1940, or the Securities Exchange Act of 1934, or of any rule or regulation thereunder.

In addition, ground "(E)" refers to a broker-dealer or associated person who "has failed reasonably to supervise, with a view to preventing violations of such statutes, rules and regulations, another person who commits such a violation if such other person is subject to his supervision."[67] For the purpose of ground "(E)," a broker-dealer or other supervisor shall not be deemed to have failed reasonably to supervise any person if (1) there have been established procedures, and a system for applying such procedures, which would reasonably be expected to prevent and detect, insofar as practicable, any such violation by a supervised person, and (2) the broker-dealer or other supervisor has reasonably discharged the duties and obligations incumbent upon him by reason of such procedures and system without reasonable cause to believe that such procedures and system were not being complied with.[68]

Sec. 19-10.   Statutory ground "(F)"—being subject to a bar order or suspension order.   As will be seen, the Commission is empowered under specified circumstances to enter an order barring or suspending a person from being associated with a broker or dealer.[69] Under ground "(F),"[70] if a broker-dealer or associated person is subject to an order barring or suspending his right to be associated with a broker or dealer, this may serve as a ground for disciplinary action against the broker-dealer under Section 15(b)(5) of the Act if the Commission finds such step to be in the public interest.

Sec. 19-11.   Some procedural considerations—in general.   It

---

[67] We have seen, *supra*, Sec. 17-12, that failure to supervise an employee, controlled person, or other person subject to a broker-dealer's supervision is a violation by the broker-dealer and its supervisory personnel of the anti-fraud provisions of the Act. Now, under ground "(E)," failure to supervise serves as an express, independent statutory ground for Commission disciplinary action.

[68] Section 15(b)(5)(E). Securities Acts Amendments of 1964, Sec. 6(b). On this subject, it may be helpful to refer to the booklet entitled *Supervision and Management of Registered Representatives and Customer Accounts*, published by the New York Stock Exchange. Subdivision (E) of Section 15(b)(5) does not limit the power of the Commission to discipline a broker or dealer for conduct of any associated person which would constitute a basis for a disciplinary order against the broker dealer on grounds "(A)," "(B)," "(C)," and "(D)" discussed above in this chapter. Sen. Rep. No. 379, 88th Cong., 1st Sess. (1963), p. 76.

[69] Section 15(b)(7) of the Act. See the discussion of this provision, *infra* at Sec. 21-2.

[70] Section 15(b)(5)(F) of the Act.

has been seen that a disciplinary order can be made only "after appropriate notice and opportunity for hearing."[71] Consequently, the institution and course of a broker-dealer disciplinary proceeding are governed by the Rules Of Practice Of The Securities And Exchange Commission.[72] No attempt will be made here to delve into the Rules Of Practice whose provisions embrace the procedural steps which must or may be taken from the time a proceeding is initiated until it is ultimately concluded. A few of such matters, particularly some of those relating to the initiation of the proceeding and certain provisions specially applicable to broker-dealer proceedings, appear to be worth mentioning, however.

Sec. 19-12. Some procedural considerations—initiation of proceeding. A proceeding is initiated by *ex parte* order of the Commission, of which notice is given to each party and other person entitled to notice, or to the person designated by any such party or person as being authorized to receive on his behalf notices issued by the Commission.[73] Among other things, the notice informs such party or person in timely fashion of the time, place, and nature of any hearing and the legal authority and jurisdiction under which the hearing is to be held, and includes a short, and simple statement of the matters of fact and law to be considered and determined.[74] Proceedings may be public or private.[75] If public, the Commission will publish in the Federal Register, and will circulate, a release on the subject summarizing the order initiating the proceeding.[76] Of course, no such release is issued when the proceeding is private. However, hearings in a proceeding initiated as a private proceeding will be made public upon request of all respondents.[77] The notice of proceedings not infrequently provides that the time and place of hearing are to be

---

[71] *Supra*, Sec. 19-1. See Section 15(b)(5) of the Act.

[72] Hereinafter called SEC Rules Of Practice, 17 CFR 201.1-201.26 (1960). Particular reference is made to Rule 1, SEC Rules of Practice, 17 CFR 201.1.

[73] SEC Rules of Practice, Rule 6(a), 17 CFR 201.6(a). In our discussion on the subject of registered securities associations relative to certain disqualifications for membership, reference will be made in that context to certain classes of persons who may be affected by a disciplinary proceeding and are given the right to notice and hearing. See, *infra*, Sections 21-2 and 24-9.

[74] SEC Rules Of Practice, Rule 6(a); *supra*.

[75] *Idem*. at Rule 11(b), 17 CFR 201.11(b), and see Section 22 of the Act.

[76] SEC Rules of Practice, Rule 6(b), 17 CFR 201.6(b). See e.g., SEC Securities Exchange Act Release No. 6838, July 3, 1962.

[77] *Idem*. at Rule 11(b), 17 CFR 201.11(b).

later announced,[78] in which case a separate announcement of hearing is released.[79] The notice of hearing must be given a reasonable time in advance of the hearing and may be given by personal service, by confirmed telegraphic notice, or by registered or certified mail, addressed to the last known business or residence address of the party or other person entitled to notice, or to the address of his agent for service. As stated, once initiated, the course of the proceeding will be governed by the Commission's Rules of Practice.

Sec. 19-13. Some procedural considerations—effect of dissolution of corporate broker-dealer. We have seen that disciplinary action may be based not only on the past activities of the applicant, but on those of any associated person.[80] Because of the future impact of Commission findings as to associated persons, the dissolution of a corporate broker-dealer will not serve to render moot a disciplinary proceeding in which the actions of an associated person may serve as a basis for disciplinary action.[81]

---

[78] See e.g., SEC Securities Exchange Act Release No. 6863, July 26, 1962.
[79] See e.g., SEC Securities Exchange Act Release No. 6840, July 5, 1962.
[80] *Supra*, Sec. 19-1.
[81] *W. T. Anderson Company, Inc.*, 39 SEC 630, 633 (1960); *Peoples Securities Co. v. SEC*, 289 F.2d 268 (5th Cir. 1961).

CHAPTER 20

DEFERMENT, POSTPONEMENT, SUS-PENSION OF APPLICATION, WITH-DRAWAL AND CANCELLATION

Sec. 20-1. Deferment. It has been seen that Section 15(b)(1) of the Act provides that an application for registration shall become effective, with stated exceptions, thirty days after the filing of the application.[1] An amendment to a pending application filed prior to the effective date will normally be treated as though it had been filed simultaneously with and as part of the application.[2] Consequently, the application would normally become effective on the thirtieth day after filing, irrespective of when amendments to it had been filed prior to effectiveness. The Commission, however, has the discretion to defer the effective date until the thirtieth day after the filing of the last amendment, if it deems such deferment to be necessary or appropriate in the public interest or for the protection of investors.[3]

Sec. 20-2. Postponement and suspension. In the course of a proceeding to deny registration, the Commission, in its absolute discretion, may postpone the effective date of the registration for a specified period not exceeding fifteen days.[4] Should the Commission desire to postpone effectiveness indefinitely until final determination of the denial proceeding, however, it may do so only after appropriate notice and opportunity for hearing (which may consist solely of affidavits and oral argument), upon a finding that such postponement is "necessary or appropriate in the public interest or for the protection of investors."[5] Similarly, during the

---

[1] *Supra*, Sec. 3-8.
[2] Section 15(b)(3) of the Act.
[3] Section 15(b)(3).
[4] Section 15(b)(6).
[5] *Ibid.* If the postponement and the denial proceedings have not been determined prior to the time the registration becomes effective (thirty days after the filing of the application), they must be dismissed as moot, but the charges upon which the denial proceeding was based may be used in a disciplinary proceeding. See *N. Sims Organ & Co., Inc.*, SEC Securities Exchange Act Release No. 6495, March 14, 1961, pp. 5-6, aff'd 293 F.2d 78 (2d Cir. 1961).

pendency of a revocation proceeding, the Commission may, after notice and opportunity for hearing, suspend the registration upon a finding that such suspension is "necessary or appropriate in the public interest or for the protection of investors."[6]

The considerations for the exercise of the Commission's discretion are substantially the same on the question of postponement of the effective date of registration in the course of a denial proceeding as on the question of suspension of registration pending the outcome of a revocation proceeding. In essence, they are these: For the limited purpose contemplated by the suspension and postponement provisions of Section 15(b)(6), postponement or suspension of registration, as the case may be, will be ordered if the evidence is sufficient to warrant a finding that the privilege of engaging in the securities business should be withheld or withdrawn, as the case may be, pending final determination of whether registration should be denied or revoked.[7] In weighing that privilege against potential danger to the public if the privilege is exercised in the interim, the primary considerations are the public interest and protection of public investors.[8] Thus, in the context of a postponement or suspension proceeding, postponement or suspension will be ordered if there is a preliminary showing that serious misconduct of such a nature as would appear to warrant denial or revocation has occurred; and that, upon broad considerations supported by the record, public investors would be exposed to danger if the applicant or registrant were permitted to deal with them during the extended interval that may be required for a determination of the issue of denial or revocation.[9] It is not an

---

[6] Section 15(b)(6).

[7] See *Biltmore Securities Corporation,* SEC Securities Exchange Act Release No. 6394, Oct. 17, 1960, p. 5. See also, *A. G. Bellin Securities Corp.,* 39 SEC 178, 185 (1959).

[8] *Ibid.* And see *D. H. Victor & Company, Inc.,* SEC Securities Exchange Act Release No. 6562, May 17, 1961, p. 3; *Lloyd Miller and Company,* SEC Securities Exchange Act Release No. 6883, Aug. 15, 1962, p. 5 at n. 5; *Peerless-New York, Incorporated,* 39 SEC 712, 715-16 (1960).

[9] *Ibid.* And see (as to postponement) *Bristol Securities Inc.,* SEC Securities Exchange Act Release No. 6860, July 20, 1962, p. 2; *Arthur Liebowitz,* SEC Securities Exchange Act Release No. 6714, Jan. 23, 1962; *John G. Cravia Co., Inc.,* SEC Securities Exchange Act Release No. 6693, Dec. 28, 1961; *Kay Brunnell,* SEC Securities Exchange Act Release No. 6580, June 23, 1961, p. 3; *Harold Grill,* SEC Securities Exchange Act Release No. 6568, May 24, 1961, p. 3; *H. N. Cooper & Company, Inc.,* SEC Securities Exchange Act Release No. 6564, May 22, 1961, p. 3; *Irving Grubman,* SEC Securities Exchange Act Release No. 6385, Oct. 6, 1960, p. 2; *M. Paul Conant & Co., Inc.,* 39 SEC 511, 513 (1959). And as to suspension, see *Lloyd Miller and Company,* SEC Securities Exchange Act Release No. 6883, Aug. 15,

essential element in support of a suspension or postponement order that the precise activities upon which denial or revocation is sought will be continued. Thus, it is no defense to point out that a particular violation charged has been completed and there is no danger that it will continue.[10] If indicated, willfulness will be taken into account.[11] But it is not essential that willfulness be found.[12]

Sec. 20-3. Special suspension procedure. The hearing in the suspension proceeding may consist solely of affidavits and oral arguments.[13]

Before leaving this subject, it should be mentioned that, with reference to suspension proceedings, there are special provisions in the Rules of Practice as regards post hearing procedures which require steps to be taken at considerably shorter time intervals than is normally the case.[14]

Sec. 20-4. Withdrawal of registration. Withdrawal from broker-dealer registration by filing a written notice of withdrawal is authorized by the Act upon such terms and conditions as may be adopted by the Commission in the public interest and for the protection of investors.[15]

1962, p. 5; *Brown, Barton & Engel*, SEC Securities Exchange Act Release No. 6821, June 8, 1962, p. 6; *Alexander Reid & Co., Inc.*, SEC Securities Exchange Act Release No. 6496, March 13, 1961, p. 4; *Barnett & Co., Inc.*, SEC Securities Exchange Act Release No. 6310, July 5, 1960, p. 5; *Alexander Dvoretsky*, 39 SEC 125, 128 (1959); *International Investments Inc.*, 39 SEC 339, 341 (1959); *Philip Newman Associates, Inc.*, 38 SEC 798, 800 (1959); *Norman Joseph Adams*, SEC Securities Exchange Act Release No. 7072, April 30, 1963, p. 3. *Albion Securities Company, Inc.*, SEC Securities Exchange Act Release No. 7259, March 4, 1964; *Financial Counsellors Inc.*, SEC Securities Exchange Act Release No. 7296, April 22, 1964, pp. 3-4.

[10] *A. G. Bellin Securities Corp.*, 39 SEC 178, 184-5 (1959).

[11] As to postponements, see *S. A. E. Corporation*, SEC Securities Exchange Act Release No. 6577, June 9, 1961, p. 3; *Irving Vincent Powell*, SEC Securities Exchange Act Release No. 6517, March 31, 1961, p. 3; *Irving Grubman*, SEC Securities Exchange Act Release No. 6385, Oct. 6, 1960, p. 2. As to suspensions, see *Alexander Dvoretsky*, 39 SEC 125, 128 (1959); *Philip Newman Associates Inc.*, 38 SEC 798, 800 (1959).

[12] *N. Sims Organ & Co., Inc.*, SEC Securities Exchange Act Release No. 6495, March 14, 1961, p. 6 at n. 16, aff'd 293 F.2d 78 (2d Cir. 1961) (postponement); *Biltmore Securities Corporation*, SEC Securities Exchange Act Release No. 6394, Oct. 17, 1960, p. 5; *Barnett & Co., Inc.*, SEC Securities Exchange Act Release No. 6310, July 5, 1960, p. 5; *A. G. Bellin Securities Corp.*, 39 SEC 339, 341 (1959); *M. Paul Conant & Co., Inc.*, 39 SEC 511, 513 (1959).

[13] Section 15(b)(6).

[14] See SEC Rules of Practice, Rule 19 (17 CFR 201.19). Cf. SEC Rules of Practice, Rules 16-18 inclusive. 17 CFR 201.16-18, inclusive.

[15] Section 15(b)(6) of the Act. Apart from specific exceptions, documents required to be filed under the Act are not filed until actually received by the Commis-

These terms and conditions are embodied in a rule[16] which provides that a notice to withdraw shall become effective on the thirtieth day after filing, unless, prior to its effective date the Commission institutes a disciplinary proceeding pursuant to Section 15(b).[17] If the Commission institutes a disciplinary proceeding against a broker-dealer within thirty days after he files a notice of withdrawal, or if such a proceeding is pending against a broker-dealer when a notice to withdraw is filed, the withdrawal does not become effective and cannot become effective, except on such terms and conditions as the Commission may deem necessary in the public interest or for protection of investors.[18] Thus, following the institution of a disciplinary proceeding, withdrawal can be had only upon application, which the Commission usually decides upon a consideration of the entire record of the proceeding after the hearing upon the merits.[19] If the Commission ultimately decides not to take disciplinary action, it will grant the application for withdrawal.[20] And, on such occasion when it concludes that

---

sion at its headquarters office in Washington D.C. Rule 0-3 under the Act, and see *Looper and Company*, 38 SEC 291, 292-3 (1957). Accordingly, a notice of withdrawal claimed to have been mailed to the Commission at its headquarters office but which was not received by the Commission will not be regarded as having been filed. *Looper and Company, supra.*

[16] Rule 15b-6.

[17] *Ibid.*

[18] *Ibid.* And see *Harold Gersten*, SEC Securities Exchange Release No. 7007, Jan. 25, 1963, p. 2.

[19] See the following cases in which the application for withdrawal was denied because the Commission, on the merits, decided that the imposition of appropriate sanctions better served the public interest: *Harry George Arness*, SEC Securities Exchange Act Release No. 7004, Jan. 24, 1963; *Michael L. Spano*, SEC Securities Exchange Act Release No. 7003, Jan. 24, 1963, p. 1; *Pickman Investment Company*, SEC Securities Exchange Act Release No. 6984, Dec. 28, 1962, p. 2; *Investment Service Co.*, SEC Securities Exchange Act Release No. 6884, Aug. 15, 1962, p. 9; *H. Carroll & Co.*, 39 SEC 780, 787-8 (1960); *Edna Campbell Markey*, 39 SEC 274, 276 (1959); *Jefferson Associates, Inc.*, 39 SEC 271, 273 (1959); *M. J. Shuck Company*, 38 SEC 69, 70-1, 74 (1957), aff'd 264 F.2d 358 (D.C. Cir. 1958); *Battery Securities Corp.*, 38 SEC 89, 90 (1957); *Owen & Co.*, 38 SEC 918, 920 (1959).

[20] See e.g., where the Commission found statutory grounds to exist but concluded that revocation was not in the public interest: *George Frederick Wheeler*, 38 SEC 403, 404 (1958). See e.g., where withdrawal was permitted upon condition that the record of the proceeding may be received in evidence in any future disciplinary proceeding: *Perkins and Company, Inc.*, 39 SEC 615, 616 (1959); *Gaylord J. Case*, 38 SEC 253, 254-5 (1958). And see e.g., where the Commission did not sustain the basic charges against the registrant and the other relatively minor violations did not result in public harm: *Investment Bankers of America, Inc.*, SEC Securities Exchange Act Release No. 6994, Jan. 21, 1963, p. 2; *Robert E. Sechler & Associates, Inc.*, SEC Securities Exchange Act Release No. 7012, Feb. 1, 1963. *Selected Securities Incorporated*, SEC Securities Exchange Act Release No. 7025, Feb. 19, 1963; *Carol, Finch, Hazel & Co.*, SEC Securities Exchange Act Release No. 7022, Feb. 11, 1963. See, also, e.g., *Solomon J. Bolder*, SEC Securities Exchange

a disciplinary order is not necessary because the registrant or associates have already been effectively dealt with in the public interest, it may discontinue the proceeding and grant withdrawal.[21]

Sec. 20-5. Withdrawal of application. It has already been noted that a denial order may have consequences for associated persons in connection with a later association with another broker-dealer registrant.[22] For this reason, the Commission takes the view that a plea for withdrawal of an application for registration should not be granted as of right, and that, when made in the context of denial proceedings involving serious charges, the withdrawal of the application should be denied until the Commission shall have disposed of the denial proceeding on the merits.[23] Despite the circumstance that there is no provision in the Act or by rule relative to the withdrawal of applications, this view of the Commission has been sustained by the Courts.[24] If, upon the merits, denial is not ordered, the application for withdrawal will be granted.[25]

Sec. 20-6. Cancellation. Section 15(b)(6) of the Act provides that the Commission "shall" cancel the registration or application, as the case may be, of a broker-dealer who is no longer in existence or has ceased to do business as a broker or dealer.

Despite the use of the term "shall," the function of cancella-

---

Act Release No. 7224, January 22, 1964, where the Commission granted request for withdrawal where, although registrant failed to file a financial report under Rule 17a-5, he was not engaged in the securities business and did not owe money or securities to customers.

[21] Thus, where the associates were already under disqualification from acting in the securities business by reason of an outstanding injunction and of Commission findings in another broker-dealer revocation proceeding, and where the registrant itself had been out of business for more than five years, the Commission saw no point in processing the revocation proceeding under consideration, and granted withdrawal. *Benjamin Zwang & Co., Inc.*, SEC Securities Exchange Act Release No. 7001, Jan. 23, 1963. And see SEC Securities Exchange Act Release No. 6722, Feb. 1, 1962, for another example of the granting of withdrawal on similar considerations.

[22] *Supra,* Section 19-1.

[23] *R. D. French & Co.*, 39 SEC 946, 947, 948 (1960); *Peoples Securities Company,* 38 SEC 186, 188 (1958); *A. J. Caradean & Co., Inc.*, SEC Securities Exchange Act Release No. 6903, Oct. 1, 1962, p. 6 and p. 6 at n. 12. *Arthur Leibowitz,* SEC Securities Exchange Act Release No. 7057, April 12, 1963, p. 2; *H. N. Cooper & Co., Inc.*, SEC Securities Exchange Act Release No. 7018, Feb. 7, 1963, p. 2.

[24] *Peoples Securities Co.* v. *SEC,* 289 F.2d 268 (5th Cir. 1961); *Blaise D'Antoni & Associates* v. *SEC,* 289 F.2d 276 (5th Cir. 1961), rehearing denied 290 F.2d 688 (1961).

[25] See e.g., *R. D. French & Co.*, 39 SEC 946, 947, 948, 949 (1960).

tion is not mandatory, and, where grounds for disciplinary action exist, such action cannot be thwarted by the expedient on the part of the applicant or registrant of dissolving or otherwise ceasing to exist or do business.[26] The necessity for going ahead with such disciplinary proceedings stems, of course, from the impact of findings as regards the registrant's or applicant's associates on subsequent associations with other broker-dealers.[27] The cancellation provision is not designed to impede that type of administration, since, in appropriate cases, the disciplinary order may be necessary in the public interest. Instead, it is merely designed for "getting rid of 'dead wood' in the Commission's files,"[28] and thus relieve it of the unnecessary administrative burden of inspections,[29] surveillance with reference to such matters as the filing, and certification of Annual Statements, Reports of Financial Condition,[30] and the like.

Thus, if it learns that a broker-dealer is no longer engaged in business, the Commission may notify the registrant that his registration will be cancelled unless he advises the Commission that he wishes to be heard. If the registrant fails to respond or otherwise fails to make a showing why cancellation should not be ordered, the Commission will cancel the registration.[31]

Moreover, consistent with its policy as to withdrawal already noted[32] the Commission may in certain cases dismiss pending disciplinary proceedings against a broker-dealer registrant and cancel the registration, if it is no longer in business and its associates have already otherwise been dealt with so as to effectively

---

[26] *Peoples Securities Co.* v. *SEC,* 289 F.2d 268, 275 (5th Cir. 1961), affirming *Peoples Securities Company,* 38 SEC 186, 189 (1958). And see *Mutual Fund Distributors, Inc.,* SEC Securities Exchange Act Release No. 6862, July 25, 1962, p. 6; *W. T. Anderson Company, Inc.,* 39 SEC 630, 632-3 (1960). *The Whitehall Corporation,* 38 SEC 259, 274 at n. 34 (1958); *Giles Edward MacQueen, Jr.,* 35 SEC 275 (1953); *Irving A. Shayne,* 30 SEC 665 (1949); *W. H. Bell & Co., Inc.,* 29 SEC 709, 722 at n. 20 (1949); *Russell Maguire & Co., Inc.,* 10 SEC 332, 352 (1941).

[27] *Peoples Securities Co.* v. *SEC,* 289 F.2d 268, 275 (5th Cir. 1961).

[28] *Ibid.*

[29] See *supra,* Sec. 6-5.

[30] See *supra,* Sec. 7-1.

[31] See e.g., *R. A. J. Dawson,* SEC Securities Exchange Act Release No. 6939, Nov. 16, 1962. There is no procedure prescribed for cancellation either by statute or rules. How the Commission will proceed in a given case depends on the circumstances.

[32] See *supra,* Sec. 20-4.

disqualify them from being employed or engaged in the business in the future.[33]

---

[33] See SEC Securities Exchange Act Release No. 6919, Oct. 22, 1962, Item (b); *R. A. J. Dawson* SEC Securities Exchange Act Release No. 6939, Nov. 16, 1962; *Mineo & Co.*, SEC Securities Exchange Act Release No. 6917, Oct. 22, 1962. And see SEC Securities Exchange Act Release No. 6936, Nov. 14, 1962; SEC Securities Exchange Act Release No. 6950, Nov. 20, 1962; SEC Securities Exchange Act Release No. 6979, Dec. 31, 1962; SEC Securities Exchange Act Release No. 6698, Jan. 2, 1962; SEC Securities Exchange Act Release No. 6871, Aug. 17, 1962, Item (b); *Peerless— New York Incorporated*, SEC Securities Exchange Act Release No. 7097, July 10, 1963. See also SEC Securities Exchange Act Releases Nos. 7023(a) (Feb. 11, 1963), 7040(a) (March 20, 1963), 7099(a) (July 12, 1963), and 7161(b) (Oct. 8, 1963).

CHAPTER 21

OTHER REMEDIES FOR VIOLATIONS

Sec. 21-1. Against broker-dealers. Any discussion of the remedies available to the Commission for violations of the federal securities laws by a broker-dealer would not be complete without mentioning that, under Section 19(a)(3) of the Act, the Commission has the power after notice and opportunity for hearing to suspend for a period not exceeding twelve months or expel a broker-dealer or any other member, including an associate, from membership in a national securities exchange, upon a finding that he violated any provision of the Act or rule, thereunder, or effected any transaction for a person who he had reason to believe was violating a provision of the Act or such a rule in connection with that transaction.[1]

Additionally, Section 15A (l)(2) empowers the Commission after notice and opportunity for hearing to suspend for a period not exceeding twelve months or to expel a broker-dealer from membership in a registered securities association, or to bar any person from being associated with a member thereof, upon a finding (a) that he violated any provision of the Act or rule thereunder or effected any transaction for a person who he had reason to believe was violating any such provision in connection with that transaction, or (b) that he willfully violated a provision of the Securities Act of 1933 or any rule thereunder, or effected any transaction for any person who he had reason to believe was willfully violating any such provision in connection with that transaction.[2]

---

[1] See e.g. *Bruns, Nordeman & Company*, SEC Securities Exchange Act Release No. 6540, April 26, 1961, p. 12. *Wright* v. *SEC*, 112 F.2d 89 (2d Cir. 1940). For additional observations on the subject of remedies available against a member of a national securities exchange for such violations, see *infra*, Sec. 23-5.

[2] See e.g., *Bruns, Nordeman & Co., supra*, SEC Securities Exchange Act Release No. 6540 at p. 11; *D. F. Bernheimer & Co., Inc.*, SEC Securities Exchange Act Release No. 7000, Jan. 23, 1963, p. 7; *Brown, Barton & Engel*, SEC Securities Exchange Act Release No. 6751, March 9, 1962, p. 5; *Reynolds & Co.*, 39 SEC 902, 919-20 (1960). And see SEC Securities Exchange Act Release No. 6971, Dec. 17, 1962. For additional discussion as to remedies available against members of registered securities associations, see *infra*, Sec. 24-8.

Other measures which may be taken by the Commission with respect to violations by a broker-dealer of the federal securities laws are the institution of an action for an injunction,[3] or the reference after investigation of any matter to the Attorney General of the United States for possible criminal prosecution.[4] These steps are available to the Commission with regard to any one who violates those laws, irrespective of whether or not he be a broker-dealer.[5] Consequently, these subjects are not within the fields covered by this book. However, with reference to the remedy of injunction a few observations may be appropriate. The trend of judicial opinion appears to be to the effect that, in injunction actions authorized by statute to be instituted by a government agency, such as the Commission, injunctive relief will be granted if the court finds that unquestionable violations of law have been recently committed; an affirmative showing of threat of continuation or of irreparable injury not being essential.[6] Moreover, in actions against broker-dealers, the Commission has had occasion to suggest to the court that public interest would best be served in the circumstances by the appointment of a receiver. These suggestions have been accepted by the courts.[7]

It may finally be observed on the subject of remedies that the Commission has complete discretion not only as to the choice of one of several remedies in a given case,[8] but also, if the situation

---

[3] Section 21(e) of the Act. And see Section 20(b) of the Securities Act.

[4] *Ibid.*

[5] *Ibid.*

[6] See *SEC* v. *Boren*, 283 F.2d 312, 313-14 (2d Cir. 1960) and cases there cited; *Mitchell* v. *Pidcock*, 299 F.2d 281 (5th Cir. 1962); *Bradford* v. *SEC*, 278 F.2d 566, 567 (9th Cir. 1960); *SEC* v. *Mainland Securities Corp.*, 192 F. Supp. 862 (S.D.N.Y. 1961).

[7] See e.g., *SEC* v. *Barrett Herrick Co., Inc.* (S.D.N.Y. Civ. No. 112-396, 1956); *SEC* v. *Adams & Co.* (N.D. Ill., No. 49C 1145); *SEC* v. *Zipkin & Co.*, (N.D. Ill. 53C 53); *SEC* v. *Investment Brokers of New Jersey* (D.N.J. 1960); *SEC* v. *Arthur C. Costello* (E.D. Mo. 1960); *SEC* v. *N. R. Henipstead* (D.R.I. 1944); *SEC* v. *Woodman* (D. Mass. 1944); *SEC* v. *Lubbe* (S.D. Ill., 1943); *SEC* v. *H. S. Simmons & Co., Inc.*, 190 F. Supp. 432 (S.D.N.Y. 1961). And see, in the context of violations of federal securities laws by persons other than broker-dealers: *SEC* v. *Los Angeles Trust Deed & Mortgage Exchange*, 285 F.2d 162 (9th Cir. 1960); *Aldred Investment Trust* v. *SEC*, 151 F.2d 254 (1st Cir. 1946); *SEC* v. *Fiscal Fund*, 48 F. Supp. 712 (D.Del. 1943). See also SEC Litigation Release No. 2491, Jan. 25, 1963, reflecting the "freezing" of a broker-dealer's assets.

[8] ". . . [S]everal sanctions may be available for the same act or series of acts. If a broker-dealer engages in manipulation in violation of Section 9 of the Exchange Act, for example, the Commission may either proceed administratively to expel or suspend him from a national exchange if he is a member thereof, or to revoke his registration or could go into the appropriate federal court for an injunction, or could refer the matter to the Department of Justice for criminal proceedings. . . ."

be appropriate to pursue several different remedies either at one time[9] or successively.[10]

Sec. 21-2. Against existing and future associated persons. Prior to recent amendments of the Act, an associated person could not be made a party initially to any Commission disciplinary proceeding involving his conduct and, in any event, not against his will.[11] It had been indicated, however, that he might nevertheless be adversely affected by such non-participation.[12] The Commission accordingly adopted a rule providing for notice of the proceeding against the broker-dealer to be given, in addition, to "any person associated with him whose interests may be affected by the proceedings."[13] The rule further provided that, if the associated person participated generally in the proceeding or filed a notice of appearance, he would be deemed a party of record entitled to notice of all intermediate developments in the proceeding. It afforded him in any event the privilege of attending the hearings or examining the record or making appropriate arrangements with a party of record, and thus of informing himself of intermediate developments and determining for himself whether he desired to be heard at any time.[14] The Commission took the position that such notice and opportunity to be heard furnished a basis for a holding that there was a binding effect on the associated person of any findings as to him.[15]

Administrative Procedure In Government Agencies The Securities and Exchange Commission, Sen. Doc. No. 10, 77th Cong., 1st Sess. (1941), Part 13, pp. 8-9.

[9] "The injunction and administrative remedies pursued by us are compatible and are designed to serve different purposes, the one to restrain further sales of a particular security in violation of anti-fraud and registration provisions of Acts we administer, and the other to determine whether registrant should be permitted to continue to do business as a registered broker and dealer. An injunction not only does not preclude action by us with respect to the registration, but is expressly made a ground for revocation. . ." *A. G. Bellin Securities Corp.,* 39 SEC 178, 186 (1959). See also Sen. Doc. No. 10, *supra* n. 8, at pp. 8-9.

[10] Sen. Doc. No. 10, *supra* n. 8, at pp. 8-9.

[11] *Wallach* v. *SEC,* 202 F.2d 462 (D.C. Cir. 1953).

[12] *Ibid.*

[13] Rule 9(b), SEC Rules of Practice. 17 CFR 201.9(b). And see the companion provisions of Rule 15b-9 under the Act. The provisions and procedures set forth in these rules are applicable to other proceedings relative to broker-dealers in which an associated person may be involved. See *infra,* Sections 23-5 and 24-8.

[14] *Ibid.* Because of these special provisions inviting an associated person to become a party or otherwise to participate in the proceeding, Rule 15b-9 under the Act provides that SEC Rules of Practice Rules 9(c) to 9(h) inclusive, 17 CFR 221.9(c) to 9(h), inclusive on the subjects of, leave to be heard, intervention, and the like, do not apply to broker-dealer proceedings.

[15] See *Mason, Moran & Co.,* 35 SEC 84, 86 at n. 6 (1953); *R. H. Johnson & Co.,* 35 SEC 110, 112 (1953). And see *Security Investment Corporation,* 39 SEC 885, 891

Now, the Commission is empowered to deal directly with an associated person with regard to his own conduct.

Pursuant to Section 15(b)(7) of the Act,[16] the Commission may, after appropriate notice and opportunity for hearing, issue an order censuring "any person" or barring him from being associated with a broker-dealer, or suspending for not more than twelve months his association with any broker-dealer, if the Commission finds such action in the public interest after a finding that:

> 1. Such person has committed or omitted any act or omission enumerated in grounds "(A)", "(D)", or "(E)" which would serve as the basis for Commission disciplinary action against a broker-dealer under Section 15(b)(5);[17] or
>
> 2. Such person has been convicted, within ten years of the Section 15(b)(7) proceeding against him, of any offense specified in ground "(B)" which would serve as the basis for Commission disciplinary action against a broker-dealer[18] under Section 15(b)(5); or
>
> 3. Such person is enjoined from any action, conduct or practice encompassed in ground "(C)" which would serve as the basis for Commission disciplinary action against a broker-dealer under Section 15(b)(5).[19]

It is unlawful for a person who is thus barred or suspended by Commission order from association with a broker-dealer to willfully become or be so associated without the consent of the Commission. Concomitantly, it is unlawful for a broker-dealer to permit such person to become or remain associated with him without the consent of the Commission, if the broker-dealer knew, or, in the exercise of reasonable care, should have known of such order.[20]

(1960), where Commission held over objection that an associated person who received notice may be named a cause for revocation. See also *Freedman* v. *SEC*, 146 F. Supp. 9 (S.D.N.Y. 1956), where the Court overruled the contention of an associated person that the effect of the special procedural rule as to associates is to render nugatory the ruling of *Wallach* v. *SEC, supra*. In the *Freedman* case the court noted that the question of the binding effect on an associate of a denial or revocation order against his broker-dealer cannot be decided except in the context of another proceeding in which such binding effect is claimed to be determinative.

[16] Securities Acts Amendments of 1964 Sec. 6(b).

[17] For a discussion of grounds "(A)," "(D)," and "(E)" with respect to broker-dealer disciplinary proceedings, see *supra, Sections* 19-4, 19-7 and 19-9.

[18] For a discussion of Ground "(B)," see, *supra*, Sec. 19-5.

[19] See *supra*, Sec. 19-6, for a discussion of Ground "(C)."

[20] We have seen *supra*, Sec. 19-10, that if a broker-dealer is subject to such a bar or suspension, this serves as a basis for Commission disciplinary action under ground "(F)" under Section 15(b)(5).

PART VII

SELF-REGULATION UNDER
COMMISSION SUPERVISION

CHAPTER 22

GENERAL OBSERVATIONS ON SELF-REGULATION

Sec. 22-1. Enforcement responsibilities—in general. An integral part of the Congressional design for regulation of brokers and dealers in the interest of public investors is the utilization for that purpose of certain types of organized bodies whose memberships are composed of brokers and dealers. Granting special privileges to these organizations, Congress at the same time imposes upon them important enforcement responsibilities. The law envisions that memberships in these organizations carry with them important prerogatives. The organizations are endowed with disciplinary powers which would deprive members of part or all of such benefits either temporarily, by suspension, or permanently, by expulsion. The Commission remains in the background with what has been termed, "reserved control,"[1] pursuant to which it has the power not only to deal with the organizations, themselves, but also to discipline their members by taking appropriate measures of either a temporary or permanent nature.

This technique of self-regulation under broad Commission supervision is employed partly to afford the financial community the opportunity on its own initiative to clean house and carry on its functions within the framework of the federal securities laws,[2] and partly to avoid the necessity for expanding the organization of the Commission to the mammoth proportions which would otherwise be necessary to enable it to perform its responsibilities under those laws.[3]

The first of these types of organizations subjected to this Congressional treatment were the exchanges. They were already in existence when the Act was adopted and were recognized as being "affected with a public interest in the same degree as any

---

[1] HR Rep. No. 1383, 73rd Cong., 2d Sess. (1934), p. 15.
[2] *Ibid.* and HR Rep. No. 2307, 75th Cong., 3rd Sess. (1938), pp. 4-5; Sen. Rep. No. 1455, 75th Cong., 3rd Sess. (1938), pp. 3-4.
[3] *Ibid.*

other great utility."[4] The techniques employed were necessarily experimental and were adopted in the face of determined opposition.[5] And, when legislation was enacted in 1938 with respect to registered securities associations, the supervisory role given to the Commission was much more pervasive and direct.

The ensuing discussion will deal with only those activities of the national securities exchanges and associations which relate to their enforcement responsibilities under the federal securities laws.

---

[4] HR Rep. No. 1383, *supra* at p. 15.

[5] See, Schlesinger, *The Coming of the New Deal* (1959), pp. 456-470.
The self-regulatory scheme as to exchanges is discussed in SEC *Staff Report On Organization, Management And Regulation of Conduct Of Members Of the American Stock Exchange* (1962), p. 47, as well as in the *Special Study Report*, Pt. 4, Ch. XII. See also, *Cooperative Regulation*, Address by SEC Commissioner Manuel F. Cohen, *Institute of Investment Banking* meeting, Philadelphia, Pa., March 10, 1964. On file at SEC Washington D.C., and New York, N.Y.

CHAPTER 23

NATIONAL SECURITIES EXCHANGES

Sec. 23-1. Definitions and registration. An "exchange" means any "organization, association, or group of persons, whether incorporated or unincorporated, which constitutes, maintains, or provides a market place or facilities for bringing together purchasers and sellers or for otherwise performing with respect to securities the functions commonly performed by a stock exchange as that term is generally understood, and includes the market place and the market facilities maintained by such exchange."[1] The Act makes it unlawful for any broker, dealer, or exchange to make use of the mails or any means or instrumentality of interstate commerce for the purpose of using any facility of any exchange within or subject to the jurisdiction of the United States to effect any transaction in a security, or to report any such transaction unless such exchange is registered as a "national securities exchange," or is an "exempted exchange."[2]

Registration as a national securities exchange is effected by the filing of an application called a "registration statement" which must be the subject of an order of the Commission within thirty days thereafter either granting or denying registration. Denial may result only after notice and opportunity for hearing.[3] Regis-

---

[1] Section 3(a)(1) of the Act. The term "facility" of an exchange includes, among other things, the premises, the tangible and intangible property whether or not on the premises, any right to the use of such premises, property or any service thereof for the purpose of effecting or reporting a transaction on the exchange, and any right of the exchange to the use of any property or service; and it includes, among other things, any system of communication to or from the exchange, by ticker or otherwise, maintained by or with the consent of the exchange. Section 3(a)(2).

[2] Section 5 of the Act. An exchange may be "exempted" upon the granting of an application for the purpose by the Commission upon a finding that "by reason of the limited volume of transactions effected on such exchange, it is not practicable and not necessary or appropriate in the public interest or for the protection of investors to require such registration."

As of June 30, 1962, there were fourteen registered exchanges and four exempted exchanges, 28 SEC Ann. Rep. 40 (1963).

[3] Section 6(e). The exchange may prior to the expiration of the thirty days withdraw its application, or consent to deferment of Commission action for a stated longer period after the date of filing. *Ibid.*

tration as a national securities exchange may be granted if the application conforms to specified requirements and contains specified commitments, and if it appears to the Commission that the exchange is so organized as to be able to comply with the provisions of the Act and the rules under the Act, and that the rules of the exchange are just and adequate to insure fair dealing and to protect investors.[4] The registration statement must contain an agreement by the exchange to comply with the provisions of the Act and the rules under the Act, and, so far as is within its powers, to enforce compliance with the Act and rules thereunder by its members.[5] It must contain such data as to its organization, rules of procedure and membership, as well as such other information, as the Commission may prescribe by rule in the public interest or for public investor protection.[6] Additionally, there must be included a copy of the "rules of the exchange" which, by definition, comprises the constitution, articles of incorporation with all amendments, and existing by-laws or rules or "instruments" corresponding thereto[7] and there must be attached an agreement by the exchange to furnish the Commission with copies of any amendments to the "rules of the exchange" forthwith upon their adoption.[8]

Sec. 23-2. Powers and duties—enforcement of acts and rules. The Act provides that no registration as a national securities exchange shall be granted or remain in force unless the rules of the exchange include provision for the expulsion, suspension, or disciplining of a member for conduct or proceeding inconsistent with just and equitable principles of trade and declare that the willful violation of any provision of the Act of any rule or regulation thereunder shall be considered conduct or proceeding incon-

---

[4] Sections 6(a), 6(b) and 6(d). The Commission's findings as to the American Stock Exchange on these subjects are referred to in SEC Staff Report, *supra*, Sec. 22-1, n. 5, at p. 47. And see, as to the National Stock Exchange, SEC News Digest, Aug. 16, 1960, p. 2.

[5] Section 6(a)(1). A member of an exchange includes the firm of which a member is a partner as well as any other partner of the firm. The term "member" means "any person who is permitted either to effect transactions on the exchange without the services of another person acting as broker, or to make use of the facilities of an exchange for transactions therein without payment of a commission or fee or with the payment of a commission or fee which is less than that charged the general public. . ." Section 3(a)(3).

[6] Section 6(a)(2).

[7] Section 6(a)(3).

[8] Section 6(a)(4).

sistent with just and equitable principles of trade.[9] Moreover, there is express provision in the Act for Commission sanction following appropriate administrative proceedings for the failure of a national securities exchange so far as is within its power to enforce compliance by a member with the provisions of the Act and the rules under the Act.[10] The net purport of these provisions is that a national securities exchange has an affirmative responsibility to enforce such provisions against its members. And, for this purpose, the Act has been construed as, *pro tanto* but within limits, the lifting of the antitrust ban of the Sherman Act,[11] with respect to a national securities exchange, whether the exchange enforcement action in that area relates to a member's activities on the exchange or over-the-counter.[12]

Exchanges may be liable in damages for failure to enforce its rules. Thus, it has been held that to the extent a person has been damaged by such failure of enforcement, a cause of action would lie against the exchange for recovery of such damages.[13]

The obligation on the exchange to enforce the Act and rules thereunder carries with it the obligation to have and maintain an organization adequate to the effective assumption of such responsibilities.[14]

---

[9] Section 6(b) of the Act. An exchange is not prohibited from adopting and enforcing any rule not inconsistent with the Act or any rule thereunder or with applicable state law. Section 6(e).

[10] Section 19(a)(1) of the Act provides that, after notice and opportunity for hearing the Commission may suspend up to twelve months or withdraw completely the registration of a national securities exchange if the Commission finds that the exchange has violated any provision of the Act or rule thereunder or that it has failed to enforce against a member so far as is within its power, compliance with the Act or any rule thereunder, or against an issuer of a security registered on the exchange. See the comment on this subject at pp. 47, 53-4 of the SEC Staff Report, *supra*, Sec. 22-1, n. 5. See also the notice of Proceedings to withdraw registration of the San Francisco Mining Exchange SEC Securities Exchange Act Release No. 6865, July 30, 1962.

[11] Particular instances of Exchange self regulation which fall within the scope and purposes of the Securities Exchange Act may be regarded as justified in answer to the assertion of an antitrust claim. See *Silver* v. *New York Stock Exchange*, 373 U. S. 341, (1963).

[12] *Ibid.*

[13] *Baird* v. *Franklin*, 141 F.2d 238, 239, 240-1, 244 (2d Cir. 1944). And see *Silver* v. *New York Stock Exchange, supra*, n. 11.

[14] Section 6(d) provides that, as a condition of registration, an exchange must be "so organized as to be able to comply with the provisions of this title and the rules and regulations thereunder. . . ." See also the comments in SEC Staff Report, *supra*, note 10, at pp. 47, 53-4. The responsibilities and functions of national securities exchanges under Regulation T and in connection with the provisions of the "short sales" rule have already been mentioned. See Sec. 9-4 and Sec. 14-3, *supra*.

Sec. 23-3. Powers and duties—maintaining fair and orderly market, the specialist. In addition to its other duties and responsibilities it is a function of a national securities exchange through its specialists "to maintain a fair and orderly market."[15] Specialists are registered as such with the exchange to specialize in specific securities.[16] In general, a specialist is required to "inject himself into the market on either the bid or offer side, or both, if in his judgment there is too wide a spread between the public bid and offer."[17] He must thus be prepared to engage in transactions as a dealer for his own account in the securities as to which he is a specialist.[18] In engaging in such activities, however, the specialist must "restrict his dealings so far as practicable to those reasonably necessary to maintain a fair and orderly market and/or those necessary to permit him to act as an odd lot dealer if the rules of the exchange permit him to act as an odd lot dealer."[19] The main concern, of course, is the possible manipulation of the market by a person having the unique advantages of a specialist, and from the conflict arising out of acting as both broker and dealer.[20] He may also permit himself to be used as a vehicle for illegal distributions.[21] Within these anti-manipulative and other limits, however, we have seen that the specialist may and should engage in such

---

[15] See Section 11(b) of the Act. And see SEC Staff Report, *supra*, Sec. 22-1, n. 5, at pp. 22-23.

[16] See Section 11(b) of the Act; and see "Ninth Rule" of SEC *Rules For The Regulation Of Trading On Exchanges Recommended By The Securities And Exchange Commission For Adoption By National Securities Exchanges*, April 17, 1935.

[17] SEC Staff Report, *supra*, Sec. 22-1, n. 5 at p. 22.

[18] *Ibid.*

[19] Section 11(b) of the Act.

[20] SEC Securities Exchange Act Release No. 7432, Sept. 24, 1964, proposing Rule 11b-1. See *Special Study Report*, Pt. 2, Ch. VI-D, pp. 57-171, and see SEC Staff Report, *supra*, Sec. 22-1, n. 5, at pp. 22-3. See also SEC Securities Exchange Act Release No. 1117, March 30, 1937. Section 11(b) also provides in this connection that, with stated exceptions, a specialist may not disclose information in regard to orders placed with him unless such information be available to all members of the exchange. Additionally, the section states: "It shall also be unlawful for a specialist acting as a broker to effect on the exchange any transaction except upon a market or limited order." For the meaning of these terms, see *The Language of Investing— A Glossary*, New York Stock Exchange, December, 1957.

[21] See *United States* v. *Re*, 336 F.2d 306 (2dCir. 1964), and see *supra*, Sec. 13-12, where the role of specialists was discussed in the context of the anti-manipulative provisions of Rule 10b-6.

The *Special Study Report*, Pt. 2, Ch. VI, pp. 166-161, makes recommendations for the adoption of exchange rules calling for higher capital requirements for specialists and a number of rules that would guard against manipulation and disorderly markets. These have in the main been concurred in by the Commission. Special Market Study Release No. 33, July 23, 1963, pp. 2-3.

activities in the security as will make for a fair and orderly market for the security on the exchange.

Sec. 23-4. Commission's supervision powers over exchanges directly. As already indicated, the Commission may suspend or withdraw the registration of an exchange for failure to enforce against members, and issuers of securities registered on such exchange so far as is within its power, the provisions of the Act and rules thereunder.[22]

Following the taking of certain prescribed preliminary steps, moreover, if the Commission determines that changes in the rules of a national securities exchange are necessary or appropriate for the protection of investors or to insure fair administration of the exchange, the Commission is empowered to adopt rules and regulations altering or supplementing the rules of the exchange or ordering the exchange so to alter or supplement its rules in respect of specified matters.[23] To implement the exercise of these powers, the Commission has adopted a rule calling for advance notice to it of an exchange proposal to adopt or amend any of its rules.[24]

The Commission additionally has the power to promulgate

---

[22] *Supra*, Sec. 23-2, Section 19(a)(1) of the Act. See the notice of *Proceedings Instituted to Determine Whether Registration of San Francisco Mining Exchange Should Be Withdrawn*, SEC Securities Exchange Act Release No. 6865, July 30, 1962.

[23] Initially, the Commission must make an appropriate request in writing addressed to the exchange that the exchange effect on its own behalf specified changes in its rules and practices within limits specified by statute. If the exchange does not make the requested changes, the Commission may then institute hearings upon notice to determine whether, under the statutory criteria, the changes should be effected or ordered. Section 19(b) of the Act.

The specified matters are: "(1) safeguards in respect of the financial responsibility of members and adequate provision against the evasion of financial responsibility through the use of corporate forms or special partnerships; (2) the limitation or prohibition of the registration or trading in any security within a specified period after the issuance or primary distribution thereof; (3) the listing or striking from listing of any security; (4) hours of trading; (5) the manner, method, and place of soliciting business; (6) fictitious or numbered accounts; (7) the time and method of making settlements, payments, and deliveries and of closing accounts; (8) the reporting of transactions on the exchange and upon tickers maintained by or with the consent of the exchange including the method of reporting short sales, stopped sales, sales of securities of issuers in default, bankruptcy or receivership, and sales involving other special circumstances; (9) the fixing of reasonable rates of commission, interest, listing and other charges; (10) minimum units of trading; (11) odd-lot purchases and sales; (12) minimum deposits on margin accounts; and (13) similar matters." Section 19(b) of the Act. For examples of the exercise of this power by the Commission, see e.g., *Rules of New York Stock Exchange*, 10 SEC 270 (1941); and see SEC Securities Exchange Act Release No. 5981, June 5, 1959 (floor trading on American Stock Exchange); SEC Securities Exchange Act Release No. 5889, Feb. 20, 1959 (increase in commission rates established by New York Stock Exchange).

[24] Rule 17a-8, SEC Securities Exchange Act Release No. 7253, March 3, 1964.

rules regulating floor trading by members of national securities exchanges, as well as excessive trading by members for their own account on the exchange but off the floor.[25] In exercise of this power and on the recommendation of the Special Study, it has recently adopted a rule requiring exchanges to submit plans which would in effect compel floor traders to act as auxiliary specialists and, in that connection, to have and maintain specified minimum capital.[26]

In national emergencies, the Commission with the approval of the President has the power summarily to suspend all trading on any national securities exchange for a period not exceeding ninety days.[27]

Sec. 23-5. Commission's supervisory powers over members and officers of exchange. The Commission has the power after notice and opportunity for hearing to issue an order suspending up to twelve months or expelling from a national securities exchange any member or officer who the Commission finds has

---

[25] Section 11(a)(1) of the Act. Trading by members on the floor of exchanges has been the subject of adverse criticism from time to time. In recommending the adoption of Section 11(a) of the Act, the House Committee report pointed out that the activity of floor traders tends to run with the tide and thereby to accentuate the moves of the market and stimulate undue speculation. HR Rep. 1383, 73rd Cong., 2d Sess. (1934), p. 14. A softer version of this criticism was echoed a few years later by the Commission following a partial study on the subject. SEC *Report On The Feasibility And Advisability Of The Complete Segregation Of The Functions Of Dealer And Broker* (1936), pp. 24-25. In 1945, the Commission concluded after further study that floor trading as then conducted gave undue advantages to floor traders, accelerated market movements, and accentuated fluctuations in particular securities or groups of securities. SEC Securities Exchange Act Release No. 3727, Aug. 28, 1945. The most recent review of floor trading activities on behalf of the Commission is reflected in the Special Study Report, Pt. 2, Ch. VI, pp. 203-242, in which it is suggested that probably the only justifiable function of a floor trader is that of an "auxiliary specialist" and, therefore, that appropriate capital and other requirements be imposed on his activities to curb disruptive market tendencies. *Idem.* at pp. 241-2, items 1 and 2.

Attached as Appendix U is SEC Securities Exchange Act Release No. 7290, April 9, 1964, entitled, *Proposed Rule Restricting Floor Trading*. This release contains a concise, informative discussion on the subject of floor trading. See Sec. 25-21, *infra.*

[26] Rule 11a-1, SEC Securities Exchange Act Release No. 7330, June 10, 1964. See in this connection the plan of the New York Stock Exchange mentioned in Release No. 7330, the plan of the American Stock Exchange, SEC Securities Exchange Act Releases Nos. 7359 and 7374, dated June 30 and July 23, 1964, respectively, and the *Amendments To Floor Trading Plans Filed By The New York And American Stock Exchanges Under The Securities Exchange Act Of 1934,* SEC Securities Exchange Act Release No. 7375, July 23, 1964.

[27] Section 19(a)(4) of the Act. Mention has been made previously in another connection of the power granted to the Commission by Section 19(a)(4) to suspend trading in a particular security on a national securities exchange for successive ten-day periods. See *supra*, Sec. 15-2.

violated any provision of the Act or rule thereunder, or has effected any transaction for any other person who, he has reason to believe, is violating in respect of such transaction any provision of the Act or rule thereunder.[28]

In summary, membership in a national securities exchange carries with it important economic advantages resulting from the right to effect transactions on the exchange without utilizing the services of another person acting as broker, or the right to make use of the facilities of the exchange for transactions on it without payment of a commission or fee or with payment of a commission or fee which is less than that charged the general public.[29] An exchange is permitted to give members these advantages so long as the exchange complies with the Act and rules thereunder and, having a proper organization as well as appropriate rules to insure fair dealings and protect investors, enforces such compliance as respects its members.[30] A member is permitted to avail himself of these advantages so far as the Act is concerned so long as he complies with the Act and the rules thereunder, and has not effected any transaction for any other person who, he has reason to believe, is violating in respect of that transaction any provision of the Act or any rule thereunder.[31]

---

[28] Section 19(a)(3) of the Act. And see, e.g., *Charles C. Wright*, 12 SEC 100, 105-6 (1942), aff'd *Wright* v. *SEC*, 134 F.2d 733 (2d Cir. 1943); *Kidder Peabody & Co.* 18 SEC 559, 573 (1945); *Bruns, Nordeman & Company*, SEC Securities Exchange Act Release No. 6540, April 26, 1961, p. 12; *Reynolds & Co.*, SEC Securities Exchange Act Release No. 6978, Dec. 20, 1962, p. 3. This power to discipline members or officers is not limited to registered broker-dealers. It will be recalled that a broker or dealer whose activities and transactions in non-exempted securities are carried out only on a national securities exchange need not be registered. See *supra*, Sec. 2-2; and see Section 15(a) of the Act. We have seen *supra*, Sec. 21-1, that the remedy of suspension or expulsion from membership is not exclusive and that other remedies may be availed of by the Commission. Sometimes the remedy of temporary suspension is applied when more drastic measures are not called for. See *Kidder Peabody & Co.*, *supra*.

[29] See Section 3(a)(3), definition of "member."

[30] Section 19(a)(1). The exchange is also under obligation to enforce the Act and rules thereunder against issuers of securities registered on the exchange insofar as it is within the power of the exchange. *Ibid.*

[31] Section 19(a)(3). Of course, a member can be disciplined by the exchange for violation of exchange rules not involving a violation of the Act or rules thereunder. See Section 6(c). Against arbitrary or excessively harsh rules, the Commission has the reserved power under Section 19(b) to compel the alteration or supplementation of such rules if such action is necessary or appropriate "to insure fair administration" of the exchange. See *supra*, Sec. 23-4.

CHAPTER 24

REGISTERED SECURITIES ASSOCIATIONS

Sec. 24-1. Scope of chapter. This chapter discusses the background, purposes, and responsibility of a registered securities association.

Sec. 24-2. Background. The overhanging threat of the important economic sanctions involved in suspension or expulsion from an exchange was recognized by Congress as a valuable enforcement tool. Thus it was that a few years after the Act became law the same basic enforcement idea was extended to the over-the-counter market in connection with legislation providing for "registered securities associations."[1] The legislation was enacted in 1938 as an amendment to the Act by the addition of a new Section 15A of the Act.[2] This section provides for the regulation by a registered securities association of its member broker-dealers subject to Commission supervision.

The instrument which renders a registered securities association so effective is the provision of Section 15A(i)(1) of the Act that the rules of such an association may provide that no member may deal with a non-member broker or dealer except at the same prices, for the same commissions or fees and on the same terms

---

[1] "Thus it is contemplated that exclusion from membership in a registered securities association will be attended and implemented by economic sanctions. In this respect exclusion from such an association would be comparable in effect to expulsion from a national securities exchange. It is these economic sanctions which would make possible effective discipline within the association." Sen. Rep. No. 1455, 75th Cong., 3rd Sess. (1938), p. 8; HR Rep. No. 2307, 75th Cong., 3rd Sess. (1938), p. 9. The statute which was enacted was Public Law No. 719, 75th Cong., app'd. June 25, 1938. It is known as the Maloney Act. See 10 SEC Ann. Rep. 76 (1944).

[2] The basic idea for such an association had its genesis in the industry code for brokers in the over-the-counter market, established under the National Industrial Recovery Act. This code was in effect at the time of the enactment of the Securities Exchange Act of 1934, but the National Industrial Recovery Act was declared unconstitutional in 1935. Thereafter, industry representatives took up with the Commission the concept of an organization of over-the-counter brokers and dealers to take part in regulation of such brokers and dealers comparable to the regulation by exchanges of its members. The ultimate result of these discussions was the enactment of Section 15A. See, 10 SEC Ann. Rep. 76-77 (1944); 4 SEC Ann. Rep. 32-33 (1938).

and conditions as are accorded by the member to the general public.[3] Only one association has become registered with the Commission. Its name is the National Association of Securities Dealers, Inc.[4] And, by virtue of Section 15(A)(i)(1), it has been observed that it is virtually impossible for a non-member dealer to participate in a distribution of important size.[5]

A registered securities association is thus endowed with these and other effective disciplinary powers which, it will be seen, it is required to exercise in enforcement of its rules. These privileges, powers, and responsibilities[6] will now be examined together with the role of the Commission within the framework of Section 15A.

Sec. 24-3. Registration—rules and organization required. Registration of a securities association is accomplished by the filing of an application, called a "registration statement," containing such information as the Commission may prescribe and accompanied by a copy of the "rules of the association" composed of its constitution, charter, and articles of incorporation or association, together with all amendments and all existing by-laws or any rules or instruments corresponding to any of them. It must be accompanied also by such data as to its organization, membership, and rules of procedure, as well as other information, as the Commission may by rules and regulations require as necessary or appropriate in the public interest or for the protection of investors.[7]

---

[3] Section 15A(n) provides that if any provision of Section 15A is in conflict with any provision of federal law in effect at the time Section 15A becomes effective, the provisions of Section 15A shall prevail. Thus, Section 15A(i)(1) has the effect of repealing *pro tanto* the provisions of the Sherman Act, (15 U.S.C. § 1) which may have prohibited such a rule by such an association. See *U. S.* v. *Socony Vacuum Oil Co.,* 310 U. S. 150, 227 at n. 60 (1940). However, in other aspects, the Sherman Act may have application to such rules and to the conduct of such an association. See *National Association of Securities Dealers, Inc.,* 19 SEC 424, 446-464 (1945).

See *Boruski, Jr.* v. *National Securities & Research Corporation,* 237 N.Y.S. 2d 772 (1962).

[4] *National Association of Securities Dealers, Inc.,* 5 SEC 627 (1937).

[5] *National Association of Securities Dealers, Inc.,* 19 SEC at p. 441.

[6] By the enactment of the Investment Company Act of 1940 Sections 22(a) and (b) 15 U.S.C. 80a-22(a) and (b) (1958), a registered securities association was given added powers to adopt rules regulating the conduct of its members in connection with transactions in redeemable securities of open-end investment companies.

[7] Section 15A(a)(1) and (2). These provisions, together with Section 15A(c) and (d), envision and authorize the creation and existence of an "affiliated securities association" which must be affiliated with a "national securities association." Section 15A(d)(1) and (e). No registration has occurred with reference to an "affiliated securities association." The form of application and number of copies are prescribed by Rule 15aa-1 and Form X-15AA-1.

The Commission may grant the application for registration if satisfied that the requirements of the Section have been met. It may deny an application only after notice and opportunity for hearing. No time limit is placed on the granting or denying of the application.[8] The conditions for the granting of an application are that the "rules of the association" embody the principles set forth in the section, and that (1) by reason of the number of its members, the scope of their transactions, and the geographical distribution of its members, the association will be able to comply with the provisions of the Act and the rules thereunder and to carry out the purposes of the section,[9] and (2) the association is so organized and is of such a character as to be able to comply with the provisions of the Act and the rules thereunder and to carry out the purposes of the Section.[10]

Except for a broker or dealer excluded from membership by the provisions of Sections 15A(b)(4) and (5), any broker or dealer who uses jurisdictional means in engaging in over-the-counter transactions in securities must, by rule, be eligible for membership.[11] The rules must also assure a fair representation of members in the adoption of any rule or amendment and in the selection of officers and directors, as well as in all other phases of administration of the affairs of the association.[12] Moreover, they must provide for equitable allocation of dues among members to defray reasonable administration expenses.[13] They must be designed, furthermore, to prevent fraudulent and manipulative acts and practices, to promote just and equitable principles of trade, to provide safeguards against unreasonable rates of commission or other charges and, in general, to protect investors and the public interest and to remove impediments to and perfect the mechanism of a free and open market.[14]

---

[8] Section 15A(e). There is provision for withdrawal of registration. Section 15A(f).

[9] Section 15A(b)(1). This requirement applies only to a "national securities association" as distinguished from an "affiliated securities association." Section 15A (d)(1).

[10] Section 15A(b)(2). This provision permits an association, however, to make appropriate restrictions as to membership such as on a geographical basis or on the basis of the types of business being done, so long as it appears to the Commission that such restrictions are necessary and appropriate in the public interest or for the purposes of the section.

[11] Section 15A(b)(3).

[12] Section 15A(b)(6).

[13] Section 15A(b)(7).

[14] Section 15A(b)(8). We have seen, *supra*, Sec. 2-7, that, with respect to registered broker-dealers who are not members of a registered securities association, the

Conversely, the rules may not include such provisions as are designed to permit unfair discrimination between customers or issuers, or brokers or dealers, or to fix minimum profits, to impose any schedule of prices, or to impose any schedule or fix minimum rates of commissions, allowances, discounts or other charges.[15] Furthermore, the rules must provide that members and persons associated with members shall be appropriately disciplined by expulsion, suspension, fine, censure, or being suspended or barred from being associated with all members, or any other fitting penalty, for any violation of the association's rules.[16]

The rules also must set forth disqualifications which prohibit the association from accepting or continuing a person in membership with such disqualifications. Thus a broker or dealer cannot be admitted to or continued in membership, if he (a) has been and is suspended or expelled from a registered securities association or from a national securities exchange, or has been and is barred from being associated[17] with all members of such association or from being associated with all brokers or dealers who are members of such exchange, for a violation of any rule of such association or exchange which prohibits any act or transaction constituting conduct inconsistent with just and equitable principles of trade, or requires any act the omission of which constitutes conduct inconsistent with just and equitable principles of trade;[18] or (b) is subject to an order of the Commission denying, suspending for

---

Commission is empowered to adopt rules and regulations designed "to promote just and equitable principles of trade, to provide safeguards against unreasonable rates of commissions or other charges, and in general, to protect investors in the public interest and to remove impediments to and perfect the mechanism of a free and open market." Section 15(b)(10).

[15] Section 15A(b)(8). See *National Association of Securities Dealers, Inc.*, 19 SEC 424 (1945), where the Commission reversed the disciplinary action taken by the National Association of Securities Dealers, Inc. against members who, as parties to an underwriting syndicate agreement, refused to adhere to the contract schedule of prices and discounts. The association had taken the disciplinary action on the ground that the conduct of the members was in violation of the rule prohibiting conduct inconsistent with just and equitable principles of trade. However, the Commission held that this was but an indirect method of imposing upon members a fixed schedule of prices and discounts, and that the disciplinary action was therefore based upon a rule which was being interpreted in a manner as to make it violate Section 15A(b)(8) (formerly 15A(b)(7)).

[16] Section 15A(b)(9). Securities Acts Amendments of 1964, Sec. 7(a)(5).

[17] The term "associated person," as defined in Section 3(a)(21) of the Act, means a person registered with the association pursuant to its rules or a person associated with a broker dealer member of the association. We have already discussed the meaning of a person associated with a broker dealer as defined in Section 3(a)(18) of the Act. See *supra*, Sec. 19-1.

[18] Section 15A(b)(4)(A).

a period not exceeding twelve months, or revoking his registration pursuant to Section 15 of the Act or barring or suspending him from being associated with a broker or dealer, or expelling or suspending him from membership in a registered securities association or a national securities exchange,[19] or (c) whether, prior or subsequent to becoming a broker-dealer, by his conduct while associated with a broker or dealer he was a cause of any order of suspension or expulsion from an association or exchange of the type just mentioned above, or of any such Commission bar order or order of denial, revocation, expulsion or suspension, which is in effect with respect to such broker or dealer,[20] or (d) has associated with him any person who is known, or in the exercise of reasonable care should be known to him to be a person, who, if such person were a broker or dealer would be ineligible for admission to or continuance in membership upon the grounds just above set forth.[21] In the face of the existence of a designated disqualification, the broker or dealer may nevertheless be admitted or continued in membership if the Commission so approves or directs in cases in which the Commission finds it appropriate in the public interest.[22]

Based on recent amendments to the Act, a registered securities association now may, unless the Commission otherwise directs in the public interest, adopt rules denying admission to a broker-dealer or refusing to continue him in membership of such broker-dealer, whether prior or subsequent to becoming such, or if any associated person of such broker-dealer, whether prior or subsequent to becoming so associated, has been or is suspended or expelled from a national securities exchange and is barred or suspended from being associated with all members of such exchange, for violation of any rule of such exchange.[23] We have just seen that an association must deny membership to a broker-dealer if he, prior or subsequent to becoming a broker-dealer (or a person associated with him, whether prior or subsequent to becoming so associated), has been and is barred from being associated with

---

[19] Section 15A(b)(4)(B). Securities Acts Amendments of 1964, Sec. 7(a)(3).

[20] Section 15A(b)(4)(C). For a discussion of matters relative to the finding of the Commission in a disciplinary order that a person is a "cause" of such order, see *infra*, Sec. 24-9.

[21] Section 15A(b)(4)(D).

[22] Section 15A(b)(4).

[23] Section 15A(b)(3).

all members of such exchange, and if such suspension, expulsion or bar results from violation by the broker-dealer or associated person of a rule of the exchange which prohibits any act or transaction constituting conduct inconsistent with just and equitable principles of trade, or which requires any act, the omission of which constitutes conduct inconsistent with just and equitable principles of trade.[24]

Difficulties of applying this provision in given instances arise in circumstances where the exchange made no specific finding that the particular rule violated is one which prohibits an act practice or omission constituting conduct inconsistent with just and equitable principles of trade.[25] To eliminate this cloudy area, Section 15A(b)(3) now provides that a registered securities association may adopt rules making ineligible for membership or continuation in membership a broker-dealer who (or whose associated person) has been and is suspended or expelled from a national securities exchange or has been and is barred from association with all members of the exchange, by reason of the violation of any rule of the exchange, irrespective of whether that rule prohibits an act or transaction constituting conduct inconsistent with just and equitable principles of trade. If adopted, such eligibility rules would not serve as a bar to membership in a registered securities association unless the grounds for the disciplinary action by the exchange involved serious misconduct of a nature affecting the public interest and protection of investors.[26]

Subject to the approval or direction of the Commission, no person may become a member of a registered securities association, and no natural person may be associated with a member, unless such person is qualified to become a member or an associated person in conformity with specified and appropriate standards of training and experience adopted by the association, and such other qualifications as it may deem necessary or desirable, including, in the case of a member, standards of financial responsibility.[27]

The rules adopting such qualifications and standards may (A) appropriately classify prospective members, taking into account such matters as, type of business done, nature of securities

---

[24] Section 15A(b)(4)(A).
[25] Sen. Rep. No. 379, 88th Cong., 1st Sess. (1963), pp. 79-80.
[26] Idem. at p. 80.
[27] Section 15A(b)(5).

sold, and persons proposed to be associated with members; (B) specify that all or any part of such standards shall apply to any such class; (C) require persons in any class to pass prescribed examinations; (D) provide as to associated persons other than prospective members and partners, officers and supervisory employees (which may by definition include branch managers and others), that such associated persons may be qualified solely on the basis of compliance with specified standards of training and other appropriate qualifications;[28] (E) provide that applicants to become a member or an associated person shall set forth such facts as to training, experience (and in the case of a membership applicant, his financial responsibility), and other qualifications of the applicant as the association may prescribe, and in this connection, the association may adopt procedures for verification of the qualifications of the applicant; and (F) require any class of persons associated with a member to be registered with the association in accordance with procedures specified by rules.[29]

Additionally, the rules of the association must include provisions governing the form and content of quotations relating to securities sold over-the-counter which may be disseminated by any member or associated person, and prescribing the persons to

---

[28] We have seen, *supra*, Sec. 2-7, that registered broker-dealers who are not members of a registered securities association, as well as natural persons associated with them, must "meet such specified and appropriate standards with respect to training, experience, and such other qualifications as the Commission finds necessary or desirable." See Section 15(b)(8). In this connection, the Commission also is authorized to (A) appropriately classify brokers, dealers, and associated persons, taking into account the type of business done and nature of securities sold, (B) specify which standards are applicable to each class, (C) require persons in any such class to pass prescribed examinations, and (D) provide that any such person in any such class other than a broker or dealer or partner, officer or supervisory employee (including any branch manager) may be qualified on the basis of compliance with such specified standards of training and such other qualifications as the Commission finds appropriate. See Section 15(b)(8)(A), (B), (C), and (D). As regards examinations, the Commission may provide that they be administered by a registered securities association or a national securities exchange and may require the registrant or associate, as the case may be, to pay reasonable fees or charges for the administration of the examination. Similarly, reasonable fees or charges may be imposed by the Commission when it administers the examination directly. *Ibid.* In addition, the Commission may by rules and regulations fix reasonable fees and charges to be paid by a non member registered broker dealer "to defray the costs of additional regulatory duties required to be performed by the Commission because such broker or dealer is not a member of such a securities association." Section 15(b)(9).

[29] *Ibid.* And Section 15A(b)(5) also provides that any application or supplemental document required by association rules to be filed by an applicant shall be deemed an application required to be filed under the Act for the purposes of Section 32 of the Act which prohibits false or misleading statements in any document required to be filed under the Act.

whom such quotations may be supplied. Such rules must be designed to produce fair and informative quotations, both at the wholesale and retail level, and to prevent fictitious or misleading quotations, as well as to promote orderly procedures for collecting and publishing quotations.[30]

Finally, the rules of the association must provide for a fair and orderly procedure with respect to the disciplining of members and persons associated with members or to the denial of membership to a broker or dealer applicant or the barring of any person from being associated with a member. Under the rules, the association may not deny membership except upon notice and opportunity to be heard upon the specific grounds for denial under consideration; and the determination must set forth the specific basis for denial. A record must be made of the hearing and proceeding.[31] As to disciplinary proceedings against a member or other person, the rules must provide for specific charges to be made, and for notice to the member or other person and an opportunity to defend; a record of the proceeding and hearing must be kept. The determination must contain written statements setting forth (A) the act, practice or omission which the member or other person is found to have committed or omitted, (B) the specific rules which were found to have been violated by such act, practice or omission, (C) whether the act, practice or omission is "deemed to constitute conduct inconsistent with just and equitable principles of trade" and (D) the penalty imposed.[32]

As stated, if the association has the requisite rules and if it appears to the Commission that the association also has the type of membership and organization prescribed by the Section, registration may be granted.

Sec. 24-4. Registration—responsibilities. We have seen that approval of an application for registration as a national securities association is conditioned, among other things, upon its having the requisite rules and that an organization of such a character as

---

[30] Section 15A(b)(12). Securities Acts Amendments of 1964, Sec. 7(a)(7).

[31] Section 15A(b)(10). Securities Acts Amendments of 1964, Sec. 7(a)(6).

[32] *Ibid.* The requirements as to the specific finding on whether the conduct found was such as to be inconsistent with just and equitable principles of trade ties in with the disqualification in Section 15A(b)(4) resulting from expulsion or suspension from a national securities association for violation of a rule prohibiting conduct inconsistent with just and equitable principles of trade.

to enable it to comply with the Act and the rules thereunder and to carry out the purposes of Section 15A of the Act.[33]

As is the case with the exchanges, the adoption of the required rules and the acceptance of the powers and privileges accorded to a national securities association[34] places upon the association the responsibility for enforcing such rules.[35] In this connection, it may be observed that the rule of the National Association of Securities Dealers Inc. requiring members to observe high standards of commercial honor and just and equitable principles of trade[36] is applied by it to enforce the Act and rules thereunder and the Securities Act and rules thereunder against its members.[37] This basic rule is also applied by the association to the conduct of members contrary to just and equitable principles of trade, apart from whether or not such conduct may involve violations of the federal securities laws.[38]

Sec. 24-5. Supervisory powers of commission—adoption of rules by association. Copies of each proposed change in or addition to the rules of an association must be filed with the Com-

---

[33] Sections 15A(b)(1) and (2).

[34] See e.g., Section 15A(i)(1), discussed *supra*, at Sec. 24-2, authorizing the association to compel its members to discriminate against non-members.

[35] See *National Association of Securities Dealers, Inc.*, 20 SEC 508, 512-13 (1945). Cf. *Baird v. Franklin*, 141 F.2d 238, 244 (2d Cir. 1944); *Silver v. New York Stock Exchange*, 373 U. S. 341 (1963).

[36] Rules of National Association of Securities Dealers Inc., Sec. 1, Article III. We have seen, *supra*, Sec. 24-3, that a registered securities association, in conformity with Section 15A(b)(8), must adopt rules to promote just and equitable principles of trade.

[37] See e.g., the following review proceedings by the Commission which involved such enforcement by the association: *Palombi Securities Co., Inc.*, SEC Securities Exchange Act Release No. 6961, Nov. 30, 1962 (false confirmations, improper extension of credit, failure to maintain records, manipulation of market); *Joseph Blumenthal*, SEC Securities Exchange Act Release No. 6847, July 12, 1962 (net capital deficiency, failure to maintain records); *Robert H. Davis*, SEC Securities Exchange Act Release No. 6730, Feb. 12, 1962 (failure to maintain records). *Richard A. Holman*, SEC Securities Exchange Act Release No. 6931, Nov. 6, 1962 (net capital deficiency, inability to meet current obligations); *Ernest F. Boruski Jr.*, SEC Securities Exchange Act Release No. 6376, Oct. 7, 1960 (failure to adhere to SEC Statement of Policy, Nov., 1957, with respect to false and misleading representations in the offer and sale of securities of investment companies). *Metropolitan Securities Inc.*, SEC Securities Exchange Act Release No. 7010, Jan. 31, 1963 (net capital deficiency).

[38] An important example is afforded by *First California Company*, SEC Securities Exchange Act Release No. 6586, July 6, 1961, which involved disciplinary proceedings for violation of the association's anti-"free riding" rule by a member participating in a distribution by withholding from the public in excess of 25 percent of the member's allotment and dividing such percentage among accounts in which officers and employees of the member had an interest. See also, the "Hot Issue" release SEC Securities Exchange Act Release No. 4150, Oct. 23, 1959, pp. 2, 3-4.

mission.[39] Such change or addition becomes effective automatically on the thirtieth day after filing or such earlier date as the Commission may determine, unless the Commission enters an order disapproving the change or addition as not consistent with the requirements applicable to an association's rules required to be adopted as a condition precedent to original registration.[40]

A mere statement of policy as to the interpretation of a rule is not a change or addition to the rules. Thus the National Association of Securities Dealers, Inc. was held not to have adopted a rule merely because it had circulated among members a statement of policy by which it would be guided, as the result of a then recent survey, with reference to what constitutes a reasonable differential between the price charged by a member to a customer and the prevailing market price.[41] On the other hand, the interpretation of a rule will not be countenanced which results in the rule's having a meaning specifically prohibited by the Act.[42] An example of a rule which was disapproved is one which attempted under prior legislation to impose minimum capital re-

---

[39] Section 15A(j). This section also requires adherence to Commission rules calling for the filing of information and documents to keep current or supplement the registration statement and accompanying documents. See Rule 15a-j.

[40] Section 15A(j). The Commission does not approve any proposed rule, but will institute a proceeding on the question of disapproval, upon its own motion if it has question, or at the instance of a complaining party. See e.g., *National Association of Securities Dealers, Inc.*, 9 SEC 38 (1941), and *National Association of Securities Dealers, Inc.*, 17 SEC 459 (1944).

[41] *National Association of Securities Dealers, Inc.*, 17 SEC 459 (1944). This related to the so-called 5 percent mark-up policy announced at that time by the association. The Commission examined the association's statement in light of the results of the study theretofore made by the association and in light of the association rule which provides: "It shall be deemed conduct inconsistent with just and equitable principles of trade for a member to enter into any transaction with a customer in any security at any price not reasonably related to the current market price of the security." The Commission noted that the association stated it would take into account not only the percentage mark-up but also such factors as market conditions, dollar amounts, the fact that a member is entitled to a profit, and any unusual circumstances. *Idem.* at pp. 469-470.

In the discussion of the *Shingle Theory, supra,* at Sections 16-1 to 16-8, it was pointed out that the violation of the Act consisted of the failure to disclose the absence of such reasonable relationship to the market price. In the enforcement of its rule, however, the association depends only on the excessive mark up and not the absence of disclosure. See e.g., *Midland Securities, Inc.*, SEC Securities Exchange Act Release No. 6413, Nov. 16, 1960, pp. 2-6; *Samuel B. Franklin & Co.*, 38 SEC 908 (1959); *Graham & Co., Inc.*, 38 SEC 314, 315-318 (1958); *Management Investment Programs*, 37 SEC 783, 786-7 (1957).

[42] *National Association of Securities Dealers, Inc.*, 19 SEC 424 (1945). See discussion of this case *supra,* at Sec. 24-3, n. 15.

quirements as a condition of membership.[43] And an example of a rule which the Commission has declined to disapprove is the one requiring members of the association to register its representatives who, as a condition of registration, must agree to be bound by the articles of incorporation, by-laws, rules and rulings of the association.[44]

After notice and hearing, the Commission may by order abrogate a rule if it appears to the Commission that such step is necessary or appropriate to assure fair dealing by the members of the association, to assure fair representation of its members in the administration of its affairs, or otherwise to protect investors or effectuate the purposes of the Act.[45] Additionally, the Commission may request in writing that the association adopt any specified alteration or supplement to its rules with respect to (A) the basis for and procedure in connection with the denial of membership or the barring from being associated with a member, or the disciplining of members or associated persons, or the qualifications required for members or natural persons associated with members or any class thereof; (B) the method for adoption of any change in or addition to the rules of the association; (C) the method of choosing officers and directors; and (D) affiliation between registered securities associations.[46] Upon failure of the

---

[43] *National Association of Securities Dealers, Inc.*, 12 SEC 322 (1942). This rule was held to be inconsistent with the requirements of former provisions of Sections 15A(b)(1) and (2) which require an association to have sufficient number of members and that it be so organized and of such a character as to comply with and carry out the provisions of the Act. *Idem.* at p. 326. By recent enactment, however, a registered securities association is given the authority and responsibility to impose standards of financial responsibility on its members. Section 15A(b)(5).

[44] *National Association of Securities Dealers, Inc.*, 20 SEC 508 (1945). This power to require registration of associated persons is now codified in Section 15A(b)(5)(F) of the Act. In the cited case, the Commission pointed out that the rules in question were not inconsistent with any of the provisions of Section 15A(b) and were affirmatively designed to meet the requirements of former Section 15A(b)(7) (now Section 15A(b)(8)) which calls for rules to protect investors and the public interest. Hence it was held to be a reasonable requirement that registration of representatives be a condition of membership. *Idem.* at pp. 512-513. The views there expressed are based on the premise that improper supervision of employees by a member is contrary to just and equitable principles of trade. See *Leonard H. Zigman*, SEC Securities Exchange Act Release No. 6701, Jan. 5, 1962, p. 3; *Vickers, Christy & Co., Inc.*, SEC Securities Exchange Act Release No. 6872, Aug. 8, 1962; See also *Gordon M. Copp*, SEC Securities Exchange Act Release No. 6644, Oct. 11, 1961; *Palombi Securities Co., Inc.*, SEC Securities Exchange Act Release No. 6961, Nov. 30, 1962, pp. 8-9. See also *National Association of Securities Dealers, Inc.*, 9 SEC 38 (1941), for another example of rules which the Commission declined to disapprove.

[45] Section 15A(k)(1).

[46] Section 15A(k)(2).

association to comply with such request within a reasonable time, the Commission is authorized by order to alter or supplement the rules of the association in the manner requested, or in modified form, after appropriate notice and opportunity for hearing upon a finding that such alteration or supplementation or modification is necessary or appropriate in the public interest or for the protection of investors or to effectuate the purposes of the section with reference to one of the enumerated subject matters.[47]

Sec. 24-6. Supervisory powers of commission—review of association proceedings. If an association disciplines a member or an associated person, or denies admission to a broker or dealer seeking to become a member or bars any person from becoming associated with a member, the Commission may on its own motion subject such action to its review.[48] Any person aggrieved by such association action may file an application for review within thirty days thereafter, or within such longer period as the Commission may determine.[49] Institution of review proceedings either by the Commission or an aggrieved person operates as a stay of association action until an order is issued following review, unless, after notice and opportunity for hearing (which may consist of only affidavits and oral argument on the question of the stay), the Commission decides to lift the stay.

A proceeding for review must be on notice with opportunity for hearing upon a consideration of the record of the association hearing[50] and such other evidence as the Commission may deem

---

[47] *Ibid.*

[48] Section 15A(g). Securities Acts Amendments of 1964 Sec. 7(c).

[49] *Ibid.* And see Rule 15 ag-1.

[50] Section 15A(g). The provision for review set forth in Section 15A(g) refers to disciplinary action and denial of membership for reasons apart from the statutory disqualifications as to membership set forth in Section 15A(b)(4) which provides that the enumerated disqualifications should serve as an automatic bar to the admission or continuing of a broker-dealer in membership. See e.g., *Norris & Hirshberg, Inc,* 21 SEC 865 (1946); *Junger Anderson & Co.,* 31 SEC 747, 752 (1950). Provision for the lifting of the bar of Section 15A(b)(4) and lifting of a restriction prescribed by association rule under Section 15A(b)(3), is a matter separate and apart from the procedure specified for review of association action by Section 15A(g). For one thing, Section 15A(b)(4) contains separate authority for Commission action, and this is cast in terms of the granting of relief from the bar rather than the review of association action. In recognition of this distinction, the Commission has adopted separate rules governing the respective procedures. The procedural rule for relief under Sections 15A(b)(3) and (4) is Rule 15ab-1. (See SEC Securities Exchange Act Release No. 7408, Sept. 1, 1964). It provides, *inter alia,* for an application for the relief to be filed either by the association or the interested member. The procedure for review of association action under Section 15A(g) is

relevant.[51] In the case of review of an order denying membership or barring a person from being associated with a member, the Commission must determine that the ground for such order exists in fact and that such grounds are valid under Section 15A of the Act.[52] If it finds otherwise, the Commission's order must require the association to admit the applicant broker or dealer to membership or permit such person to be associated with a member.[53]

If, upon review of disciplinary action, the Commission finds that any penalty imposed upon a member or associated person is excessive or oppressive, having due regard to the public interest, the Commission is empowered to cancel, reduce or require remission of the penalty.[54]

In all disciplinary review proceedings the Commission must dismiss the proceeding, except for modification of penalty, if it finds that the the member or associated person has engaged in acts and practices as found or has omitted to take action as found, and that the acts and practices or omission are in violation of the rules of the association which the association had designated in its determination as having been violated.[55] The Commission

governed by Rule 15ag-1. By the nature of the relief which may be sought by an aggrieved person under Section 15A(g), that rule envisions applications only by aggrieved persons.

Rule 15ag-1 sets forth the precise procedures which must be followed, and it provides at paragraph "(g)" that the Rules of Practice also apply.

[51] This power of review given to the Commission is regarded as a *de novo* proceeding. Accordingly, in a court proceeding to review an order of the Commission as provided for by Section 25(a) of the Act, the Court of Appeals will not delve into the record made at the association's hearings, but will consider only the record before the Commission. *R. H. Johnson & Co. v. SEC*, 198 F.2d 690, 695 (2d Cir. 1952), *cert den* 344 U. S. 855. Such power of review together with the Commission's power to disapprove association rules saves the regulatory scheme of Section 15A from being unconstitutional as an improper delegation of power to a non governmental body. *Ibid.* And see *Silver* v. *New York Stock Exchange*, 373 U. S. 341 (1963) at n. 12.

The Commission will only very rarely receive additional evidence on review. Rule 15ag-1(e). See *Herrick, Waddell & Co.*, 23 SEC 301, 303 (1946); *Gerald M. Greenberg*, 39 SEC 601 (1959); *Richard A. Holman*, SEC Securities Exchange Act Release No. 6631, Sept. 21, 1961.

[52] Section 15A(h)(3).

[53] *Ibid.* For an example of where the Commission ordered the National Association of Securities Dealers Inc. to admit a broker-dealer to membership, see *John Munroe*, SEC Securities Exchange Act Release No. 6513, March 24, 1961.

[54] Section 15A(h)(2). See e.g., *Gilbert Parker*, 34 SEC 385 (1952); *Standard Bond and Share Co.*, 34 SEC 208 (1952); *Peter Widdershoven*, SEC Securities Exchange Act Release No. 6767, March 29, 1962; *Robert H. Davis*, SEC Securities Exchange Act Release No. 6730, Feb. 12, 1962. *Naftalin & Co., Inc.*, SEC Securities Exchange Act Release No. 7220, January 10, 1964, pp. 11-12; *Bailey & Co.*, SEC Securities Exchange Act Release No. 7241, Feb. 14, 1964.

[55] Section 15A(h)(1). See e.g., *F. R. Gentry & Co., Inc.*, SEC Securities Exchange Act Release No. 6986, Jan. 2, 1963; *Palombi Securities Co., Inc.*, SEC Securities

must also determine whether the acts, practices or omission in question constitute conduct inconsistent with just and equitable principles of trade, and must make an appropriate declaration.[56]

If the Commission finds, conversely, that the member or associated person did not commit or omit the act or practice found, or that such act or omission is not prohibited or required by rule, the Commission must set aside the action of the association.[57]

Sec. 24-7. Supervisory powers of commission—revocation and suspension of registration of association. After appropriate notice and hearing, if the Commission finds that the association has violated any provision of the Act or of any rule thereunder or has failed to enforce compliance with its own rules, or has engaged in other activity tending to defeat the purposes of the section, the Commission may suspend up to twelve months or revoke the registration of the association if it finds that such action is necessary or appropriate in the public interest or for the protection of investors or to carry out the purposes of the section.[58]

Sec. 24-8. Supervisory powers of commission—suspension or expulsion of member, officer, or director. A member may be suspended up to twelve months or expelled from membership in an association or a person may be barred from being associated with a member, by Commission order upon notice and hearing if the Commission finds that he (A) has violated any provision of the Act or rule thereunder, or has effected any transaction for any

---

Exchange Act Release No. 6961, Nov. 30, 1962; *Vickers, Christy & Co., Inc.*, SEC Securities Exchange Act Release No. 6872, Aug. 8, 1962; *Joseph Blumenthal*, SEC Securities Exchange Act Release No. 6847, July 12, 1962; *Bennett-Manning Company*, SEC Securities Exchange Act Release No. 6632, Sept. 26, 1961. For dismissal of review proceedings by registered representatives upon sustaining the ruling of the National Association of Securities Dealers, Inc., see e.g., *Gordon M. Copp*, SEC Securities Exchange Act Release No. 6644, Oct. 11, 1961; *Leonard H. Zigman*, SEC Securities Exchange Act Release No. 6701, Jan. 5, 1962; *Richard A. Holman*, SEC Securities Exchange Act Release No. 6931, Nov. 6, 1962; *Valley Forge Securities Company Inc.*, SEC Securities Exchange Act Release No. 7055, April 12, 1963.

[56] The significance of the need for such a specific finding is that disciplinary action so grounded is one of the bases for disqualification set forth in Section 15A(b)(4).

[57] Section 15A(h)(1). For an example of a case in which the Commission set aside the action of the National Association of Securities Dealers Inc., see *Investment Bankers of America Inc.*, SEC Securities Exchange Act Release No. 6886, Aug. 16, 1962, where the Commission remanded the matter back to the Association after reversing it on the major grounds for disciplinary action and sustaining it on lesser grounds.

[58] Section 15A(l)(1).

other person who, he had reason to believe, was violating with respect to such transaction any provision of the Act or rule thereunder or (B) has willfully violated any provision of the Securities Act of 1933 or any rule thereunder, or has effected any transaction for any other person who, he had reason to believe, was willfully violating with respect to such transaction any provision of that statute or rule thereunder.[59]

An officer or director of a registered national securities association may be removed by the Commission from office after appropriate notice and hearing if the Commission finds that he has willfully failed to enforce the rules of the association, or has willfully abused his authority.[60]

Sec. 24-9. Supervisory powers of commission—finding a person to be a cause of commission order. As seen, Section 15A(b) (4) sets forth disqualifications[61] as to membership in a registered securities association of a broker or dealer who, by his conduct while associated with a broker or dealer, was a cause of the suspension or expulsion of a member of a national securities exchange or registered securities association or of the barring or suspension of a person from being associated with all members of such an exchange or association, by reason of violation of a rule prohibiting conduct or omission inconsistent with just and equitable principles of trade, or who was the cause of a Commission disciplinary order.

In order for a person to be found to be a "cause" of a Com-

---

[59] Section 15A(l)(2)(A) and (B). It should be noted that the sanctions of Section 15A(l)(2)(A) may be imposed for mere violation of the Act or rule thereunder, as contrasted with the provision of Section 15A(l)(2)(B) that only willful violations of the Securities Act or rules thereunder may serve as a basis for the sanction. The Commission's authority to resort to the remedy of suspension or expulsion from a national securities association and of barring a person from being associated with a member was discussed earlier in the context of Commission proceedings against broker-dealers. See *supra*, Sec. 21-1. The Commission sometimes limits its sanction to suspension for a stated period from membership in an association as a lighter and more fitting remedy in the circumstances in the public interest, than, for example, the more drastic sanctions of revocation or expulsion. See e.g., *Brown Barton & Engel*, SEC Securities Exchange Act Release No. 6751, March 9, 1962, p. 5; *D. F. Bernheimer & Co., Inc.* SEC Securities Exchange Act Release No. 7000, Jan. 23, 1963, p. 7; *Bruns, Nordeman & Company*, SEC Securities Exchange Act Release No. 6540, April 26, 1961, p. 11; *Reynolds & Co.*, 39 SEC 902, 919-20 (1960); *Ira Haupt & Co.*, 23 SEC 589 (1946); *Kidder, Peabody & Co.*, 18 SEC 559 (1945); *E. H. Rollins & Sons Inc.*, 18 SEC 347 (1945); *Bond & Goodwin Inc.*, 15 SEC 584 (1944); *Franklin, Meyer & Barnett*, 37 SEC 47, 52 (1956).

[60] Section 15A(l)(3).

[61] See, *supra*, Sec. 24-3.

mission disciplinary order, it is not essential for him to have been an "immediate and inducing" cause, but merely to have contributed in more than a minor way to the violation upon which the Commission's order is based.[62] Thus an employer broker-dealer, failing properly to supervise his employees who commit the violation on which the Commission order is based, is a cause of such order.[63] Moreover, the fact that one person is primarily responsible for the violation does not mean that others who acted in concert or contributed to the result may not also be found to be causes for the disciplinary order.[64]

Additionally, a principal of a broker-dealer who has the basic responsibility for its conduct and the conduct of its employees may be found to be a cause for a disciplinary order by failing to carry out his responsibilities,[65] even though he may not have been in good health.[66]

In a leading court case on the subject, it was pointed out that the naming of a person as a "cause" has the effect of barring such person from the securities industry, and it was therefore concluded that the basic consideration is whether, in light of his actions, the public should be exposed to the hazard of his remaining in the securities field.[67]

Reference has already been made to the procedure for giving

---

[62] R. H. Johnson & Co. v. SEC, 148 F.2d 690 (2d Cir. 1952). And see, W. T. Anderson Company Inc., 39 SEC 630, 637 (1960). To establish that a salesman is a cause of a disciplinary order against a broker-dealer, more must be shown that this conduct was in some degree a factor in contributing to the violation which prompted the sanction. Berko v. SEC, 316 F.2d 137, 140-1 (2d Cir. 1963).

[63] R. H. Johnson & Co. v. SEC, 148 F.2d 690 (2d Cir. 1952).

[64] B. Fennekohl & Co., SEC Securities Exchange Act Release No. 6898, Sept. 18, 1962, p. 8.

[65] See Thompson & Sloan Inc., SEC Securities Exchange Act Release No. 6443, Jan. 3, 1961, p. 7.

[66] See Herbert Perry & Co., Inc., SEC Securities Exchange Act Release No. 6896, Sept. 13, 1962, p. 2. And see John Munroe, 38 SEC 308, 311 (1959); John T. Pollard & Co., Inc., 38 SEC 594, 598 (1958).

[67] Berko v. SEC, 316 F.2d 137 (2d Cir. 1963). This is known as the second Berko case, the first one remanded the matter to the Commission, 297 F.2d 116 (2d Cir. 1962). The second Berko opinion affirmed the Commission's order on reconsideration. For other recent cases shedding light on who will be held to be a "cause," see Aldrich Scott & Co., Inc., 40 SEC, 755, 778-9 (1961); Sutro Bros. & Co., SEC Securities Exchange Act Release Nos. 7052 and 7053, April 10, 1963; W. E. Leonard & Company, Inc., SEC Securities Exchange Act Release No. 7070, April 30, 1963; Fred L. Carvalho, SEC Securities Exchange Act Release No. 7129, Aug. 29, 1963. The test laid down in the second Berko opinion, supra, is substantially the same as the standards of "public interest" applicable to disciplinary orders of the Commission. See Sec. 19-2, supra, for a discussion of "public interest" in that context.

notice to an associated person who may be affected by Commission disciplinary proceeding against a broker-dealer and, in this connection, reference was made to Rules 15b-9 of the Act and 9(a) and (b) of the Rules of Practice.[68] The same rules, by their terms, are applicable to disciplinary proceedings in which such associated person may be named as a cause for the imposition of the disciplinary order resulting from such proceedings. Because of the Commission's view as to the binding effect of its disciplinary order on an associated person who has been given notice in accordance with these rules,[69] and because such rules specify the giving of such notice, a finding as to cause in regard to an associated person will be withheld if he did not receive the notice specified in the rule.[70]

Before leaving the subject of cause insofar as that is relevant to the disqualification of a person from membership or association with a member, it may be noted that by the terms of Section 15A(b)(4), the disqualification endures only so long as the order naming him a cause remains in effect. Thus, if the person be named as a cause of an order suspending a broker-dealer from membership on a registered securities association for a specified period, the person so named no longer suffers disqualification when the period has expired.

Sec. 24-10. Supervisory powers of commission—relief from disqualification. If a broker-dealer be disqualified from membership or continuance in membership by virtue of Section 15A (b)(3), or 15A(b)(4), or if, on the basis of the latter provision, a person should have an impediment which would mean expulsion from membership on the part of a broker-dealer who employed such person, there is a procedure provided for the broker-dealer

---

[68] *Supra*, Sec. 21-2. And see also *Security Investment Corporation*, 39 SEC 885, 891. Section 15b-9 of the Act; SEC Rules of Practice, Rules 9(a) and (b), 17 CFR 201.9(a) and (b).

[69] See *supra*, Sec. 21-2.

[70] See e.g., *Michael L. Spano*, SEC Securities Exchange Act Release No. 7003, Jan. 24, 1963, p. 1, at n. 1. *John G. Cravin Co., Inc.*, SEC Securities Exchange Act Release No. 7064, April 22, 1963, p. 2. However, if the person charged with being a cause was served with notice of the proceeding he has the burden of keeping himself informed of all developments and of taking steps to protect his rights. His failure to do so will not serve as a basis for not holding him to be a cause, if the evidence warrants a finding that he was a "cause" of the Commission's disciplinary order. *Harwyn Securities, Inc.*, SEC Securities Exchange Act Release No. 7153, Oct. 4, 1963, pp. 2-3. It has been seen, *supra*, Sec. 21-2, that, now, the Commission if it so desires can proceed directly against any person at all who has committed specified acts or is subject to specified disabilities. See Section 15(b)(7) of the Act.

member to apply for relief from the disqualification. He must first submit the matter to the association to determine whether it desires to admit or continue the broker-dealer in membership in the circumstances.[71] If the association decides that it desires such admission or continuance, it may file an application to the Commission for leave to do so.[72] Should the association decline to file such an application, the broker-dealer may do so himself.[73] Applications for relief will be denied if the Commission finds such a course to be in the public interest.[74] On occasions, they will be granted if found consistent with the public interest, generally upon the imposition of conditions.[75] On occasions also the Commission has granted relief where the application was made on behalf of a broker-dealer in cases where the disqualification attached to one of its principals.[76]

It may be noted that the proper procedure to follow for relief from disqualification is an application under Rule 15ab-1 rather than a petition to reopen the proceeding in which the disqualification occurred.[77]

---

[71] Rule 15ab-1.

[72] *Ibid.* Sections 15A(b)(3) and (4) have express provisions empowering the Commission to grant such relief.

[73] Rule 15ab-1. Paragraph (1) of Rule 15ab-1 provides that, to the extent they are consistent with that rule, the Rules of Practice apply to Rule 15ab-1 proceedings.

[74] For Commission orders denying the application or remanding the matter to the National Association of Securities Dealers Inc. See e.g. order re: *Bruce William Grocoff,* SEC Securities Exchange Act Release No. 6842, July 10, 1962, p. 2 (denied); *Edgar R. D'Abre,* SEC Securities Exchange Act Release No. 6817, June 8, 1962, p. 2 (remanded); *N. Sims Organ,* SEC Securities Exchange Act Release No. 6978, May 4, 1962; *Edgar R. D'Abre,* SEC Securities Exchange Act Release No. 7213, January 9, 1964 (following remand).

[75] See e.g. orders re: *Charles S. Peraino,* SEC Securities Exchange Act Release No. 6969, Dec. 13, 1962, p. 2; *Bryle Lerner,* SEC Securities Exchange Act Release No. 6805, May 15, 1962, p. 2; *William Whitehead,* SEC Securities Exchange Act Release No. 6766, March 27, 1962; *Robert Dermot French,* SEC Securities Exchange Act Release No. 6707, Jan. 11, 1962, p. 2. *Harry E. Jack,* SEC Securities Exchange Act Release No. 7059, April 16, 1963; *Alfred M. Sharp,* SEC Securities Exchange Act Release No. 7168, Nov. 8, 1963. For examples of where the Commission indicated in advance that it would in proper circumstances grant relief from disqualification, see *McClane & Co., Inc.,* SEC Securities Exchange Act Release No. 7163, Nov. 1, 1963, p. 3; *Siltronics Inc.,* SEC Securities Exchange Act Release No. 7158, Oct. 18, 1963, p. 3; *P. de Rensis & Co., Inc.,* SEC Securities Exchange Act Release No. 7114, Aug. 9, 1963; *Alexander Reid & Co., Inc.,* SEC Securities Exchange Act Release No. 7016, Feb. 7, 1963, p. 6; *George R. Ernstrom,* SEC Securities Exchange Act Release No. 7265, March 9, 1964. Cf. *Metropolitan Securities Inc.,* SEC Securities Exchange Act Release No. 7010, Jan. 31, 1963, pp. 3-4.

[76] See e.g., *Delago Securities Company Inc.,* SEC Securities Exchange Act Release No. 6450, Jan. 12, 1961, p. 2.

[77] See *Philip Newman Associates Inc.,* SEC Securities Exchange Act Release No. 6819, June 7, 1962.

CHAPTER 25

APPENDICES

Sec. 25-1. Appendix A—Selected recommendations from special study report (House Doc. No. 95, Pt. 5, 88th Cong. 1st Sess. (1963)).

Sec. 25-1 (a). Qualifications of persons in the securities industry.

(Chapter II, Part 5, pp. 45-48)

1. Under a regulatory scheme relying heavily on self-regulation, it is anomalous that some broker-dealers or investment advisers should remain outside of any official self-regulatory group so that their activities are subject only to direct regulation by the Commission. Membership in an appropriate self-regulatory group (exchange or national securities association or affiliate thereof) should therefore be a prerequisite to registration as a broker-dealer or investment adviser. If it should not prove feasible to establish a program of compulsory membership in a self-regulatory body for all broker-dealers and investment advisers subject to Commission jurisdiction, the added cost of governmental supervision should be passed on and directly borne by those in the industry who are not members of such a body, through fees or other assessments.

2. At present the only requirement for federal registration as a broker-dealer or investment adviser is that the firm and its principals have not previously misbehaved in specified ways, and there is a separate list of statutory disqualifications for NASD membership. These statutory disqualifications should be combined and made applicable to all broker-dealer and investment adviser firms and certain categories of individuals in the securities business, such as principals, supervisors and salesmen. There should be added to the combined list conviction within 10 years of crimes (a) involving theft, fraud, embezzlement, defalcation or criminal breach of fiduciary duty, or (b) arising out of the conduct of the business of a broker or dealer or investment adviser.

3. The Commission's present registration forms for broker-dealers and registered investment advisers fail to supply essential information for determining initial qualifications and for continuous regulatory needs. Every broker-dealer firm should be required to furnish initially, and keep current through annual or other periodic reports, information concerning: (a) major activities engaged in or to be engaged in; (b) exchange and NASD memberships; (c) number and location of branch offices; (d) clearing firms, correspondent firms and wire con-

258

nections; (e) size and composition of sales staff; (f) size and composition of any research department; (g) the individual in responsible charge of regulatory and self-regulatory matters within the firm, the supervisor of each major department or function (underwriting, retailing, research, trading, back office, etc.); the manager or supervisor of each branch office, and each individual authorized to handle discretionary accounts; and (h) the prior experience of any such individual, supervisor or manager. Every registered investment adviser should be required to supply and keep current information concerning (a) major activities to be engaged in; (b) research techniques used and/or other bases of recommendations; (c) size and composition of any research department; (d) the individual in responsible charge of any such research department, and/or in responsible charge of the firm's investment recommendations; and (e) the prior experience of any such individual.

4. The individual rather than the firm is the appropriate "unit" for many regulatory purposes, in the interest of fairness as well as efficiency. The present statutory registration scheme does not reach individuals at all, and the self-regulatory concept of "registered representatives" of particular firms does so only partially and indirectly. Without limiting the responsibility of firms for the personnel they employ or the right of firms to select their own employees, there should be established a system of licensing and registering individual salesmen, supervisors and other specified categories of personnel. Each such individual should be required to file a single basic registration form containing necessary data as to his present and prior employment, disciplinary matters, and eligibility under statutory disqualifications, together with a certificate as to his good character and, for applicants without adequate prior experience, as to his successful completion of any required examination. Copies of the basic registration form would be made available to affected regulatory and self-regulatory agencies. Subsequent changes in employment and disciplinary actions should be required to be reported and recorded in the individual file. Duly licensed persons would be, for regulatory purposes, eligible for employment by any firm.

5. Under such a system of licensing and registering individuals, disciplinary actions could, in appropriate cases, relate to individuals without necessarily involving current or future employers, as is now the case. The present system, under which the Commission may proceed only against a broker-dealer firm, often operates inefficiently or unfairly in that the Commission must move against an employee's firm or not at all. The Commission's powers in this respect should therefore be made more flexible even apart from the recommendation in paragraph 4, so that it will have the power to bring administrative proceedings directly against individuals involved in violations of the securities laws.

6. Apart from statutory disqualifications and requirements for

filing of basic data by firms and individuals, standards for entry into the securities business should encompass (a) competence, in the sense of knowledge and experience, (b) character and integrity, and (c) financial capacity and responsibility—the first two applying essentially to individuals and the third essentially to firms. In all three areas there have been significant accomplishments but there are serious gaps and deficiencies that need to be remedied promptly, as set forth in the following paragraphs.

7. The basic regulatory control in respect of competence is the examination. Present examinations and examination programs can and should be considerably improved, refined and coordinated. The standard examination should cover a core of basic subjects for salesmen, supervisors and principals, with appropriate supplemental questions for supervisors and principals, and with such further supplementation as any particular agency may desire for its own purposes. For certain recognized specialties, special supplementary questions should be provided; individuals whose activity (and license to act) is to be limited to any such specialty may be permitted to qualify through appropriately limited examinations. To achieve maximum results with minimum burdens, a National Board of Securities Examiners should be established by and for the various regulatory and self-regulatory agencies, to administer existing programs and foster improved programs. Through the same or a similar agency, the various existing training programs should be coordinated, extended and improved.

8. Quite apart from knowledge as tested through examination procedures, appropriate experience in the securities business should be a requirement for individuals in certain crucial roles. The individuals for whom there should be an experience requirement include at least one principal in each registered firm and, if other than such principal, the individual designated as being in charge of regulatory and self-regulatory matters, the supervisor of selling activities, the supervisor or manager of each branch office, and the supervisor of research activities. Appropriate periods and types of prior experience are left for future definition.

9. The matter of part-time salesmen has been the subject of considerable difference of opinion among members of the financial community and regulatory agencies. There appears to be no reason to exclude part-time salesmen as such, but they should be subject to exactly the same qualification requirements as full-time salesmen.

10. Of all the types of qualifications needed for the securities business, perhaps the most important, but also the most difficult to assure by formal regulation, is that of character and integrity. As rapidly as possible a system involving local "character and fitness" committees, as in the legal profession, should be established. More immediately, the responsibility for maintaining a proper level of character and integrity of all personnel must reside in the individual

firm, but with effective enforcement of this responsibility by the self-regulatory agencies. In addition, regulatory and ethical standards should receive greater emphasis in training and examination programs of the self-regulatory agencies. If the latter are to fulfill the role for which they are thought to be uniquely suited, they must also, of course, exert leadership in defining and elevating ethical standards for their members, above and beyond legal requirements.

11. A minimum net capital requirement is of high importance as one of the several different approaches to assuring a broker-dealer community of principals and firms reasonably qualified in terms of responsibility and commitment. The requirement need not and should not be a uniform one for all firms but should be appropriately scaled to reflect the type and size of business engaged in. Subject to exceptions and refinements to be worked out in the future (such as special provision for small proprietorships engaged only in sale of open-end investment company shares), and subject to an appropriate "grandfather" clause or adjustment period, every broker-dealer should be required to have at the commencement of business, and maintain at all times thereafter, net capital of at least $5,000, plus (say) $2,500 for each branch office and (say) $500 for each salesman employed at any time.

12. Since the underwriting of public offerings involves special obligations and responsibilities, any firm engaging or proposing to engage in underwriting securities offered to the public pursuant to the federal securities laws, whether on a "firm commitment" or "best efforts" or any other basis, should be required to have and maintain minimum net capital of $50,000 plus (say) 2 percent of the aggregate amount of underwriting commitments or undertakings in the most recent 12-month period (but not less than the amount required under paragraph 11).

Sec. 25-1 (b). Broker-dealers, investment advisers, and their customers—activities and responsibilities.

(Chapter III, Part 5, pp. 54-56)

1. The supervision by broker-dealers of the selling activities of their personnel, particularly in branch offices, should be generally strengthened by the adoption of appropriate procedures including, but not necessarily limited to: the designation of one home office senior executive responsible for internal supervision and regulatory and self-regulatory matters generally; increasing the branch manager's supervisory role while de-emphasizing his selling activities in branches having large numbers of salesmen; and in large firms with many branches, the tightening of home office control procedures, with more extensive use of electronic data processing equipment programmed to expose overtrading, undue concentration in speculative securities and other potential abuses.

2. The self-regulatory agencies should establish clearer standards and stronger surveillance and enforcement procedures to assure more effective supervision by their member firms. While the recent publication of the New York Stock Exchange's guide to supervision and management of registered representatives and customer accounts represents a significant step in this direction, the implementation of the standards there set forth will call for strengthening of surveillance. The NASD control procedures in respect of selling practices are also in need of substantial strengthening. More regular and frequent examinations of branch offices are called for, and examinations should include interviewing salesmen, and in appropriate cases customers, when accounts show heavy trading or concentration in speculative issues.

3. The Commission should adopt rules to facilitate and reinforce controls by firms, the self-regulatory bodies and the Commission over selling practices. Such rules should, for example, require: that every retail transaction be designated "solicited" or "unsolicited" in the permanent records of a broker-dealer; that all customer complaints be kept in a single file and available for inspection and examination by the Commission, the NASD, and the exchanges; and that customer account cards or similar records include such information as investment goals, occupation and type of service desired.

4. Greater emphasis should be given by the Commission and the self-regulatory bodies to the concept of "suitability" of particular securities for particular customers. The NASD, which has taken leadership in this respect by adopting a general suitability rule, should provide further definition of content and more effective surveillance and enforcement. The NYSE, which has less clearly recognized suitability as a standard of conduct, should make greater efforts to define its content and undertake necessary surveillance and enforcement. This area would seem to be a particularly appropriate one to be dealt with through Statements of Policy (similar to that now applicable to investment company selling literature), which can provide the necessary balance between generality and specificity of standards. Such Statements of Policy should cover such matters as: possible guidelines as to categories or amounts of securities deemed clearly unsuitable in specified circumstances; practices deemed incompatible with standards of suitability, such as indiscriminate recommending or selling of specific securities to other than known customers; and approved and disapproved practices in the handling of discretionary accounts.

5. The importance of disclosure for the protection of investors has long been recognized in securities regulation, and it is of particular value in connection with selling practices. The present mandatory, officially filed disclosures by issuers (reports and proxy statements), extended and improved as recommended in Chapter IX, should have wider and more prominent use in selling activities, and the obligations of broker-dealers in this regard should be appropriately defined by

the self-regulatory agencies and the Commission. These obligations might include such matters as: actually consulting available officially filed data prior to recommending or selling specific securities; furnishing copies to customers in appropriate cases; and advising customers whether officially filed information is available with respect to any security recommended for purchase.

6. The almost universal industry practice of compensating salesmen in proportion to the volume of business produced may be assumed to be inherent in the nature of the business, but certain of its particular aspects may tend to introduce undue pressures or biases into the selling process. This would appear to be another appropriate area for continuing attention of the self-regulatory agencies, with the view to evolving rules and standards, in line with the best existing practices, that might eliminate or reduce the more extreme forms of pressure or bias in selling. Among possible measures in this direction that should be considered by broker-dealer firms and the self-regulatory agencies would be: making monthly compensation less specifically dependent on each month's production; eliminating a step-up of commission rates for transactions in a given month on reaching a stated volume for the month; discouraging undue compensation differentials for sales of different categories of securities where advisory bias may result from the compensation differential; and requiring disclosure of extra compensation in respect of particular types of transactions.

7. The sanctions now available to the Commission in respect of selling practice and similar violations—revocation of a firm's registration with the Commission, or expulsion from or suspension (for up to 12 months) of membership in an exchange or national securities association—are sometimes unsuitable to the needs of particular cases, especially where the disciplinary action relates to only one or few salesmen or only one of many branch offices of a firm. The Commission should have more flexible powers to deal with the latter type of situation, so that it may invoke measures appropriate for dealing with particular kinds and degrees of misconduct rather than being limited to the choice between no sanction or an excessive or inappropriate one.

(Chapter III, Part 5, pp. 59-60)

1. Investment advice furnished by broker-dealers, though an integral part of their business of merchandising securities, is incidental to that business and, for the small investor particularly, their facilities for providing advice are quite varied in quantity and quality. This being the case, a minimum protection for such investors is that firms should not be permitted to represent that they perform research or advisory services which they are not reasonably equipped to perform. The New York Stock Exchange, instead of indiscriminately encouraging its members to advertise their research and advisory facilities,

should adopt standards governing the representations its members may make in this regard, and the NASD should provide similarly for its membership.

2. Specific practices with respect to investment advice, whether expressed in market letters, advertisements or otherwise, should receive more positive and effective attention from the self-regulatory agencies. Such agencies obviously cannot assume responsibility for the staffing of their member firms or the quality or validity of specific recommendations, but they should assume responsibility for eliminating irresponsible or deceptive practices by their member firms. This area also lends itself to establishment of standards through Statements of Policy, covering such matters as (a) required disclosures in printed material of sources of information, research techniques used and/or other bases of recommendation, rather than general disclaimers as to sources and reliability of data in market letters; (b) required disclosures in written advice of existing positions, intended dispositions, and market-making activities, rather than general "hedge" clauses as to possible present conflicting positions or transactions; (c) required indication of the name of the person responsible for the preparation of market letters, and dating of such material; (d) in printed investment advice which purports to analyze issuers, required references to most recently filed official disclosures by issuers, and representations that such filed information has been examined, with specific identification of issuers for which no officially filed information is available; (e) prohibition of specific practices in connection with written or oral recommendations, such as predicting specific future price levels of particular securities, claiming "inside" information by reason of a directorship, and trading against recommendations or other self-dealing; and (f) required disclaimers in connection with salesmen's written or oral recommendations not emanating from a firm's research department or otherwise sponsored by the firm.

3. The market letter surveillance program of the New York Stock Exchange should be strengthened and redirected toward achieving greater responsibility and restraint in the use and contents of such letters. More effective market letter surveillance should also be undertaken by the NASD and the other exchanges, or a coordinated program of self-regulatory agencies should be evolved.

4. Reckless dissemination of written investment advice by broker-dealers, whether or not for a separate fee, or by registered investment advisers, should be expressly prohibited by statute or by rules of the Commission and the self-regulatory agencies and should be made expressly subject to civil liability in favor of customers reasonably relying thereon to their detriment. Without limiting the general principle, written investment advice which purports to analyze issuers but fails to consider most recently filed official disclosures of issuers should be one of the factors to be considered in determining whether such advice is recklessly disseminated.

(Chapter III, Part 5, pp. 61-62)

1. The net capital rules of the Commission and the self-regulatory agencies should be amended to require broker-dealers to maintain a reserve of (say) 15 percent of the aggregate amount of free credit balances in the form of cash or short-term U. S. Government securities; or in the alternative, if a lesser reserve is maintained, to charge the difference to net capital. In addition, broker-dealers holding free credit balances should be required to give customers at least quarterly notice of the amounts of such balances. Such notice should include information to the effect that their free credit balances may be withdrawn at any time; that while held by the firm they are not segregated and may be lent to other customers or otherwise used in the business of the firm; that interest is not paid on such balances (or the circumstances in which interest is paid); and that financial statements of the broker-dealer firm are available for inspection.

2. The Commission should be empowered to adopt rules requiring that excess margin and fully-paid securities be segregated and marked in a manner which clearly identifies the interest of each individual customer.

3. The Commission should be empowered to adopt rules requiring that there be a "reasonable relationship" between the amount of each customer's securities that can be hypothecated or lent by the broker-dealer and the amount of indebtedness of such customer; and also requiring that broker-dealers obtain the specific, prior written consent of a customer before borrowing or lending his excess margin or fully-paid securities.

4. Consideration should be given to the feasibility of providing greater flexibility in the so-called "haircut" provisions of the net capital ratio rules and in their administration, in order to take account of different functions, market circumstances and needs. Additionally or alternatively, consideration should be given to exempting specified quantities (perhaps 500 shares) of securities in the inventory of a "primary market maker" as defined in Chapter VII.

5. Section 60(e) of the Bankruptcy Act should be amended to provide: (a) that customers' securities that have been appropriately segregated within four days after receipt so that their ownership can be ascertained, whether or not specifically identified (e.g., the bulk segregation system), and customers' free credit balances if similarly segregated, will be considered to be "identified specifically" within the meaning of Section 60(e)(4) notwithstanding that such segregation may have occurred less than four months prior to bankruptcy or during insolvency; (b) that the term "stockbroker" clearly include "dealers" as well as "brokers"; and (c) that the term "customers" include persons depositing cash for the purchase of securities. In addition, the Bankruptcy Act should be amended to empower the Commission to

petition that an insolvent broker-dealer be adjudicated a bankrupt, so as to assure equitable treatment of claimants under Section 60(e).

(Chapter III, Part 5, p. 63)

1. The NASD should reconsider the adoption of rules under the Uniform Practice Code permitting marking to the market on a greater range of contracts than is now permitted. The experience of the Pacific Coast Stock Exchange with respect to mandatory marking to the market appears to have been highly satisfactory and the self-regulatory organizations should consider the desirability of the adoption by them or their affiliated clearing houses of rules requiring marking to the market for all clearing house transactions.

2. A requirement for mandatory buy-ins might be of material assistance in reducing the volume of fails to deliver. It is recognized, however, that the adoption of such a system might raise certain problems such as the unavailability of securities which could be bought in at a fair price. The self-regulatory organizations and the Commission should give further study to the feasibility and utility of such a requirement for various types of markets or categories of securities.

3. The NASD should promptly reconsider the adoption of appropriate rules which would permit the NASD Board of Governors to establish hours of trading for all members or for specified classes.

4. The industry, with the cooperation of the Commission, should give continuing attention to possibilities for modernizing and improving existing securities handling, clearing and delivery systems, with the goal of evolving institutions and procedures which would permit the reduction of physical transfers of securities and centralization of functions now performed by broker-dealer back offices insofar as possible.

(Chapter III, Part 5, p. 66)

1. The many facets of the securities business, including the typical combinations of broker and dealer functions, underwriting functions, quasi-banking functions, and advisory relationships with issuers of securities and with customers, involve potential conflicts of interest and obligation of many kinds and degrees. This would appear to be the kind of area in which the self-regulatory agencies, with support from governmental agencies where violations of legal duties are involved, can be instrumental in defining and effectuating higher ethical standards. With all credit to the limited efforts they have made, the self-regulatory agencies have left many important subjects virtually untouched; for example, although the NYSE has recently advised its members concerning conduct in connection with the holding of directorships, the NASD, which has special responsibilities in respect of over-the-counter markets, apparently has never addressed itself to the conflicts involved in the role of the broker-dealer who is a corporate

director while engaging in inter-dealer and retail transactions in the corporation's securities. The self-regulatory agencies, no less than the Commission, should institute more positive, continuing programs for the study of important problems of conflict of interest in the securities business, with a view to speaking out on particular questions in the form of cautionary messages, policy statements, codes of ethics, or rules of fair practice, as circumstances may require.

Sec. 25-1 (c). Primary and secondary distribution to the public.

(Chapter IV, Part 5, pp. 71-73)

1. The Commission's administration of the registration provisions and related exemption provisions of the Securities Act has been one of its most outstanding achievements, and the statute itself has proved generally adequate and workable. Nevertheless, there are limited respects in which provisions of that statute and the administration thereof or of related provisions of the Exchange Act should be modified in order to adapt them more closely to experienced needs. The troublesome and sometimes dangerous phenomenon of "hot" issues is primarily associated with "first" issues, i.e., first public offerings of securities of a particular issuer. Accordingly, such "first" issues, whether fully registered or exempt under Regulation A, should receive particular attention, with a view to preventing certain practices that appear to have contributed unnecessarily to "hotness," while not interfering with normal and legitimate practices in connection with underwriting of "first" or any other issues or the flow of venture capital into new business.

2. Appropriate rules should be adopted by the NASD and/or the Commission, applicable to "first" issues of common stock generally, designed to eliminate or temper certain factors which, either independently or in interaction with each other, appear to have produced artificially high but ephemeral premiums in many instances. Among the types of rules that would appear appropriate for consideration and adoption would be rules (a) requiring that, with respect to allotments resulting from solicitations or indications of interest prior to the effective date, notices of allotment (in the form of confirmations or otherwise) be given to purchasers as promptly as reasonably possible, any delay of more than (say) 24 hours after the effective date to be deemed prime facie unreasonable; (b) requiring that, again with respect to allotments resulting from solicitations or indications of interest prior to the effective date, certificates of stock be delivered or made available for delivery to purchasers as promptly as reasonably possible, any delay of more than (say) two weeks after the effective date or more than (say) one week after the underwriting closing to be deemed prima facie unreasonable; (c) prohibiting all broker-dealers from initiating a trade market for a limited period of (say) 72 hours after the effective date, except for stabilizing activities in conformance

with Rule 10b-7 and such other exceptions as may be provided by rule or in specific circumstances; (d) clarifying or defining restrictions on soliciting, holding or transmitting, prior to the effective date, indications of interest or orders to purchase in the open market after the effective date; and (e) prohibiting all participants in the public offering, until the distribution is completed or for a period of (say) 40 days after the effective date, whichever is later, from soliciting or recommending purchases of the stock (including placing stock in discretionary accounts) at a price in excess of (say) 120% of the public offering price.

3. Acceleration by the Commission of the effective date of a registration statement or permitting clearance of a Regulation A filing, with respect to any "first" issue of common stock, should normally be conditioned on delivery of a prospectus or offering circular in substantially final form to each person to whom any participant in the distribution expects to make original allotments at least (say) 48 hours before any sales are made.

4. The 40-day period during which all dealers are required to deliver prospectuses should be extended to 90 days in the case of "first" issues of common stock, except as may be otherwise permitted by rule or in specific circumstances. The same provisions should apply to offering circulars under Regulation A exemptions. (It is recommended below that the 40-day requirement be eliminated in connection with offerings of securities of issuers subject to the continuous reporting requirements of Sections 13, 14 and 16 of the Exchange Act.)

5. The NASD should strengthen its enforcement of the prohibitions against "free-riding and withholding" by requiring, in the case of any "first" issue of common stock for which a price in excess of (say) 120% of the public offering price is reached within (say) 40 days after the effective date, a report of the managing underwriter showing all stock allotted to any participant in the distribution (other than stock resold at or below the public offering price) or its principals or members of their immediate families or to any broker-dealer other than a participant, and the disposition thereof, if any. In general, since those violating the "free-riding and withholding" prohibitions may be in a position to realize profits greatly surpassing the fines customarily imposed by the NASD, substantially severer penalties should be imposed in flagrant cases so as to provide an adequate deterrent.

6. The NASD has taken a forward step in providing for the review of underwriting arrangements in connection with offerings of unseasoned companies. To provide guidance to its membership, the NASD should periodically publish summaries of specific rulings relating to the amounts of compensation and types of compensation arrangements that have been considered unacceptable in given circumstances.

7. Underwriters receiving options, warrants, or "cheap stock" in connection with any public offering should be required to report to the Commission and the NASD: (a) upon exercise of options or warrants, the date and price; (b) upon transfer of options or warrants, the data, consideration, and identity of transferee; and (c) upon disposition of underlying securities without a post-effective amendment, the date, consideration, identity of distributee or class of distributees, and the exemption relied on. The general subject of transfer of such options, warrants, or "cheap stock" to registered representatives, traders or others not directly involved in the underwriting of an offering should receive greater attention of the NASD, with a view to adoption of rules or a Statement of Policy defining circumstances in which such transfer is deemed consistent or inconsistent with high standards of commercial honor and just and equitable principles of trade.

8. In light of widespread misunderstandings or uncertainties among broker-dealers, as discussed in this and other portions of the Report, the Commission should take appropriate steps to clarify the application of Rule 10b-6 (a) during a period when stock is being held "for investment" by a broker-dealer, (b) in connection with various forms of "shelf" registration, (c) in connection with a planned reduction of inventory or "workout," and (d) in connection with unregistered distributions generally.

(Chapter IV, Part 5, pp. 74-75)

1. Any broker-dealer managing an unregistered distribution should be required to file with the Commission a brief notification as to the total amount of securities involved in the distribution; whether the distribution represents inventory or investment stock of the broker-dealer and/or is on behalf of one or more other persons (with or without identification of such other persons); the offering price and underwriting arrangements and/or discounts or commissions involved; and whether stabilizing transactions may be effected. Consideration should be given, also, to the feasibility of requiring, with respect to all or specified categories of unregistered distributions, an interval of time, say 48 hours, between the filing of the notification and the commencement of the distribution (in which case only the method of determining price and spread rather than actual amounts should be set forth). For purposes of this recommendation and the following one, the term "unregistered distribution" should be defined to include the sale by any broker-dealer, as principal (including any planned reduction of inventory or "work-out") or as agent, of any block of securities of such size as to require an underwriting or selling group and/or receipt or payment of compensation exceeding normal compensation for routine (non-block) transactions in similar securities, unless the block is sold to fewer than 25 purchasers and/or at an aggregate price of (say) $300,000 or less.

2. Any broker-dealer participating in an unregistered distribution as principal or as agent should be required to advise each customer in his confirmation of the substance of the matters to be set forth in the notification, and at the time of solicitation as to appropriate portions thereof.

(Chapter IV, Part 5, pp. 76-77)

1. The Commission should propose to the Congress that Section 15A of the Exchange Act be amended to provide that all distributors of and dealers in real estate securities in interstate commerce shall be required to be members of a registered securities association having such rules relating to the business in real estate securities carried on by its member as shall appear to the Commission to be necessary or appropriate in the public interest or for the protection of investors. Also, all individuals engaged in selling or distributing real estate securities should be subject to the registration requirements recommended generally in Chapter II for persons engaged in selling or distributing securities.

2. The Commission should further study the problems of speculative offerings, promoters' benefits, insider transactions, distributions, and the information furnished to security holders, and the adequacy of its power to deal with such problems.

Sec. 25-1 (d). Exchange markets.

(Chapter VI, Part 5, pp. 87-91)

1. The specialist system now in operation on the NYSE and Amex is different in significant respects from the system which existed when present regulatory policies were established, and is different also from the image of the specialist system as frequently projected. In its present form, it appears to be an essential mechanism for maintaining continuous auction markets and, in broad terms, appears to be serving its purposes satisfactorily. There is a need, not for any broad and drastic change in the system, but for a number of important, specific improvements in specialist practices and in regulatory concepts and methods, as set forth in the following paragraphs. For the most part, these can and should be accomplished through changes in the rules and procedures of the respective exchanges, except that, since the Commission is not presently empowered to enforce rules of the Exchange (see chapter XII), it would be desirable to define certain basic dealer responsibilities of specialists (paragraphs 2 and 3 below) in rules of the Commission under section 11(b) of the Exchange Act. The limited volume of transactions on the regional exchanges and the dependence of these exchanges on the dual trading system may make it impracticable to place such responsibilities on regional exchange specialists and for the present they should be excepted from any such rules under

section 11(b). Further studies are needed in the structure of regional exchange specialist systems, and questions of responsibilities and privileges of these specialists should be held in abeyance pending such studies.[1]

2. Section 11(b) of the Exchange Act states a policy of restricting specialists' dealings "so far as practicable to those reasonably necessary to maintain a fair and orderly market." The so-called Saperstein Interpretation promulgated in 1937 among other things limits specialists' dealer transactions to those reasonably necessary to maintain price continuity and minimize temporary disparity between supply and demand. The NYSE's policy and practice of indiscriminately encouraging specialists to increase their participation as dealers is incompatible with the restrictive tenor of these provisions. Although the changed market context since 1937 has seemingly changed the level at which the standard of "reasonably necessary" in the foregoing provisions must be applied, it is still an appropriate and desirable standard which needs restatement, in place of the NYSE's present emphasis. The relevant portion of the Saperstein Interpretation should be embodied in a rule under Section 11(b).

3. While specialists should be restricted in their dealer participation to what is reasonably necessary to maintain a fair and orderly market, an affirmative obligation on their part to participate to the extent reasonably necessary to maintain a fair and orderly market should be more clearly recognized and enforced. The rules of the NYSE now merely state that such participation is "commonly desirable," and in practice the Exchange has not held individual specialists to high standards of performance, with the result that considerable unevenness in the quality of markets in individual securities has been tolerated. A rule should be adopted under section 11(b) to state the obligation positively.

4. The NYSE should increase its specialist capital requirements in recognition of current market needs and specialist obligations. Instead of the present requirement of capital sufficient to carry 400 shares of each stock in which a specialist is registered, the nature of the market in most securities would seem to require that specialists have the capital ability to carry at least 1,200 shares, and preferably a higher amount such as 2,000 shares, of each issue; the exact figure or figures may be left for future definition by the exchange and the Commission jointly.

5. The NYSE and Amex should adopt rules relating to specialists' participation in openings and their trading as dealers, as follows:

(a) With respect to openings, such rules should be designed to prohibit specialists from participating in openings in such manner as

---

[1] For this reason most of the following paragraphs are applicable only to the NYSE and/or Amex although specific items may also be applicable to one or more regional exchanges insofar as they use a specialist system in respect of primary listings.

to upset the public balance of supply and demand, i.e., from using their position as dealer, or a broker for all participating parties, to change prices. The policy of such rules would be that opening prices should move, from the previous close, in the direction dictated by public supply and demand and not against it.

(b) With respect to trading after the opening, such rules should limit the ability of specialists to "reach" across the market, i.e., buying at the offer or selling at the bid, whether such transactions are to establish or to liquidate a position. Provisions should be made for exemptions from such rules with approval of floor officials and for systematic review by the respective floor departments.

(c) With respect to the general obligation of specialists to participate to the extent reasonably necessary to maintain a fair and orderly market, such rules should give emphasis to the concept of continuity with reasonable depth, i.e., participating in reasonable volume at each price level, and should also make clear that the obligation to participate requires that all quotations be reasonable ones in view of market conditions and not merely nominal ones.

6. The NYSE and Amex should adopt rules requiring that each specialist unit maintain a single trading account. All securities in which a specialist is registered which are owned by such specialist or his unit should be maintained in such account and not segregated for tax or other purposes. No recommendation is made with respect to specialist inventory practices for tax purposes. Nevertheless, in view of the testimony of some specialists that they occasionally trade to adjust inventories kept on a LIFO basis, it should be made clear that trading so motivated is not permissible.

7. The NYSE and Amex should adopt rules governing the brokerage function of specialists and should clarify various related floor procedures, as follows:

(a) The respective exchanges should adopt rules affirmatively defining market and limited price orders and variations thereof, and defining specialists' (and floor brokers') responsibilities with respect to each type of order.

(b) The existing ban against specialists' accepting "not-held" orders should continue. If necessary, consideration should be given to increasing floor brokerage rates to compensate floor brokers adequately for their efforts in handling discretionary orders.

(c) Specialists on the NYSE and Amex should be prohibited from granting "stops" (either by allocating customers' orders or as principal) at any price at which a specialist holds an unexecuted customer's order capable of execution at such price.

(d) The present policy of the NYSE which permits executions resulting from stops to be omitted from the tape should be changed by a rule requiring that every transaction taking place on the floor be reported on the tape. The policy requiring the selling broker to report transactions should be strictly enforced.

(e) A specialist represents conflicting interests, his own and that of customers, whenever he purchases from or sells to his "book," i.e., from or to a customer whose brokerage order he holds. Policies should be formulated to prevent specialists from dealing with or for customers at unfair prices in relation to the general market conditions or the specialists' own transactions including but not limited to situations where a specialist sells to his customer at the limit price when he knows of a large offering or buys from his customer at the limit price when he knows of a large buy order. Whenever a specialist deals with the book a floor member representing the firm which forwarded the order should initial the specialist's memorandum of each such transaction. In its routine surveillance the exchange should systematically review transactions covered by such memoranda in light of subsequent transactions by the specialist.

(f) To keep within as narrow limits as possible the conflicts of interest inherent in a specialist's combination of functions, NYSE and Amex specialists and their firms should be prohibited from servicing the accounts of public customers, or receiving commissions on such accounts "introduced" by them at other firms.

8. No information is now publicly available with respect to specialist dealer activity in individual stocks. The NYSE and Amex should report to the Commission on a weekly basis each specialist's purchases and sales as principal in each issue traded. Such reports should be made public so as to give interested investors an indication of the degree of activity, exclusive of specialist participation, in particular issues. On the other hand, in its public statements on specialist activities the NYSE has tended to exaggerate the degree of stabilizing that specialists accomplish or could be expected to accomplish. The Exchange's "tick" test, whatever its other uses, is not by itself significant as an evaluation of "stabilizing" of the market by specialists and should not be so represented.

9. The NYSE and Amex should undertake studies, in conjunction with the Commission, as to methods or plans by which the capacity of specialists to acquire larger blocks of stock within the framework of the auction market could be otherwise strengthened. Among other possibilities, consideration should be given to (a) the establishment of an exchange-administered capital fund from which specialists could borrow under appropriate limits and safeguards; (b) the establishment of a capital fund, through contributions from the brokerage income of all specialists, that would be administered by specialists' representatives and/or the Exchange itself and would be available for taking positions beyond the financial capacity of an individual specialist; or (c) establishment of a system of limited self-insurance by specialists as a group. Reference is made to recommendation 4 above with respect to increasing the specialist capital requirement and the recommendation in part F of this chapter concerning the possibility of creating a category of "auxiliary specialists."

10. The NYSE and Amex should be required to report to the Commission any indication that a registered specialist unit is in violation of its specialist capital rule or has received a margin call. These exchanges should adopt rules providing in substance that any member firm which clears for or finances specialists may not terminate clearing arrangements or call for additional margin without adequate prior notice to the exchange. Where a specialist in financial difficulties cannot promptly secure additional capital sufficient to bring his account above the required margin maintenance, his stocks should be reassigned temporarily or permanently to units with capital adequate to handle them.

11. The NYSE has pioneered in the development of surveillance techniques regarding specialists' performance and has devoted considerable energy to this area. Nevertheless, its present techniques are not sufficiently refined to deal adequately with certain important aspects of the specialist's role and obligations. Among needed improvements on this Exchange as well as the Amex are the following, which should be developed promptly by the exchanges in conjunction with the Commission:

(a) For many routine surveillance purposes it would be invaluable, but it has not heretofore been practical, to have a means of preserving or reconstructing a specialist's book for a given period; modern automation techniques may well remove the practical difficulties and should be promptly explored.

(b) Surveillance of over-participation as well as under-participation should be strengthened; as a basic check, regular reporting to the respective exchange of income of specialists, segregated between brokerage income and dealer income, should be required.

(c) In general, surveillance should be directed toward assuring that each specialist is performing his obligation to maintain a fair and orderly market in each security, with appropriate procedures and sanctions for enforcement and with the ultimate purpose of allocating and reallocating securities where required to assure high standards of performance with respect to all securities.

(d) In addition to present tests to evaluate performance, tests for evaluating specialist purchases, sales, and positions in relation to price movements should be evolved, with the object of determining the market effects of specialist dealer activities.

(Chapter VI, Part 5, pp. 101-102)

1. The two series of data on short selling presently compiled by the New York and American Stock Exchanges are inadequate for regulation. The series are neither compatible nor are they useful in indicating the degree of short selling in individual issues, the effect of such selling on the price stability of a security, or whether the provisions of the Commission's rules are being observed. Accordingly, the exchanges should initiate systems of reporting that will provide

more frequent information on the volume of short sales in particular stocks classified as between the public and the principal classes of members. Monthly data on the short interest should show corresponding information in the selected individual stocks. In addition, consideration should be given the feasibility of indicating exempt short sales and furnishing information on the other types of short sales such as "against the box," arbitrage and hedging. The Commission also should consider the extent to which short sales data should be reported by other exchanges. The Commission should designate the information to be furnished to it on a regular basis, and should also determine the extent and type of short selling data to be made available to the public.

2. It is difficult to determine the extent to which short sales are being made on "minus" or "zero minus" ticks in the guise of exempted arbitrage transactions, but there is some indication that advantage is being taken of this exemption. The stock exchanges should examine current procedures for marking transactions as "short-exempts" and institute checks to insure that this marking is accurate, and thereafter the Commission should review and evaluate the procedures adopted.

3. Present rules appear inadequate to relieve the added pressure that short selling may create during a severe decline in the general market or a declining price trend in a particular security. Despite the rules, a relatively large volume of short selling occurred in particular stocks, including "market leaders" and "trading favorites," during the period of decline preceding the market break of May 28, 1962 and at critical junctures on that day, and many additional opportunities existed when short selling could have occurred. Accordingly, the present up-tick limitation should be supplemented by a rule or rules designed to cope more effectively with the potentially depressing effects of short selling during price declines. While the Special Study is not prepared to suggest the exact form of such rule or rules of general application, among the possibilities to be considered would be: the prohibition of short selling in a particular stock whenever its last sale price was below the prior day's low; or alternatively, whenever the last sale price was a predetermined dollar amount or percentage below a base price (e.g., the prior day's close or low or the same day's opening) as specified in the rule; or instead, given the circumstances of such a decline, a limitation of short sales in any particular stock to a predetermined proportion of the amount of stock available at the prevailing market. As a further precaution for times of general market distress, the Commission's rules should provide for temporary banning of short selling, in all stocks or in a particular stock, upon an appropriate finding by the Commission of need for such action.

Sec. 25-1 (e). Over-the-counter markets.

(Chapter VII, Part 5, pp. 126-130)

In view of the heterogeneity of over-the-counter securities and markets and the need for categorization of components, as emphasized in the above discussion, the following program is put forth with recognition that the measures recommended are not necessarily equally applicable to all securities, broker-dealers or markets, so that the appropriate scope and limitation of particular measures may require a more exact definition in the process of implementation. It is also recognized that, while the following recommendations are designed as a total integrated program, the form and timing of the implementation of certain of them might have the effect of lessening the need for others.

1. In the over-the-counter markets, there is a dichotomy between inter-dealer (wholesale) and public (retail) markets in many important respects, but there is a close and continuous relationship between wholesale and retail markets for any particular security. Inter-dealer and public quotation systems are vital to the operation of these markets and, whether handled by private enterprise or by a self-regulatory agency, they are vested with a public interest and should be brought under appropriate supervisory control of the Commission. At the same time, the operator of any such system would be vested with authority and responsibility to regulate the use of its system by broker-dealers through appropriate rules and procedures consistent with the rules of the NASD and the Commission.

2. Broker-dealers, although entirely free to change their inter-dealer quotations in the course of trading as at present, should be positively obligated to buy or sell 100 shares (or other indicated "size") of a quoted stock at their prevailing quotations, unless clearly designated as not firm, and should be required to keep a timed record of changes in quotations. All quotations entered in an inter-dealer quotation system should be firm, unless otherwise designated, when supplied. The NASD should establish appropriate programs for surveillance and enforcement of these obligations. The NASD and/or the Commission should have the power and responsibility to deny or temporarily suspend any broker-dealer's right to enter quotations in an inter-dealer quotation system with respect to a particular security or all securities, for willful abuse of a quotation system (e.g., by entering other than bona fide quotations) or willful violation of any special rules applicable to inter-dealer quotations.

3. Other rules applicable to inter-dealer quotation systems and/or to broker-dealers using such systems should require: (a) that quotations entered by one broker-dealer on behalf of another to be designated by appropriate symbols with clear differentiiation between correspondent arrangements and other arrangements involving this practice, and with clear indication where two or more quotations in different names represent a single quotation; (b) that "OTC-listed" securities (see Chapter IX)[1] be differentiated from all other securities by appropriate symbols, and that securities eligible for extension of credit (see Chapter X) be designated by separate symbols; and (c) that, consistent with the recommendation in paragraph 9, persons other

than broker-dealers be eligible to become subscribers to inter-dealer quotation systems, and that broker-dealers be required to make available to their regular public customers, upon request, any quotation system to which they may be subscribers. In addition, upon establishment of a system for identification of "primary market makers" as recommended in paragraph 4, consideration should be given to a further rule providing that primary market makers for a particular security should have the exclusive right (subject to possible defined exceptions) to enter two-way quotations in any inter-dealer quotation system; whereas any other broker-dealer, although free to enter one-way or OW or BW quotations, should be permitted to enter two-way quotations only as correspondent for an identified primary market maker.

4. Because of the large numbers and varieties of securities and participants involved in the over-the-counter markets, the quality and depth of the market for any particular security and the reasonable expectations of investors in such security are intimately related to the number and identity of dealers making an inter-dealer market. As a foundation for various immediate or longer-term improvements in the operation and regulation of over-the-counter markets, a system for official identification of the "primary market makers" in each security (tentatively defined for this purpose as "any broker-dealer who, with respect to a particular security, holds himself out, by entering two-way quotations in any inter-dealer quotation system or otherwise, as being willing to buy from and sell to other broker-dealers for his own account on a continuous basis") should be established by the Commission or the NASD as promptly as necessary mechanical arrangements can be worked out. Such a system would contemplate that each primary market maker in a particular security would file, prior to or promptly after becoming such, a data card showing the name of the security and the dealer's relation to the issue or issuers (as underwriter, director, optionee, etc.); that a primary market maker ceasing to act as such, either permanently or temporarily, would give notice to that effect; and that the Commission or the NASD would maintain, for public inspection or circulation, an official "primary market list" of those dealers who are primary market makers for each security at any given time.

5. The Commission and the NASD should make it part of their continuous agendas to seek further possibilities for strengthening the mechanisms of inter-dealer markets and the protection of investors in relation thereto, particularly in light of the possibilities of automation referred to below. Among other subjects for possible coverage in future rules, interpretations or Statements of Policy, to be applied either generally or in respect of specified categories of securities or of broker-dealers, would be: rights and obligations of primary market makers in maintaining competitive, fair and orderly markets; the grant of "cheap stock," warrants or options to primary market makers (see ch. IV.B); standards of supervision and methods of compensation of

traders; intra-firm responsibility for and supervision of the insertion of quotations in an inter-dealer quotation system; provisions for the handling of limit orders; and possible special requirements or exemptions for primary market makers in broker-dealer capital rules, including a possible exemption from "haircut" provisions in respect of limited amounts of inventory of securities traded by a primary market maker (see chapter III.D).

6. While a public investor must ultimately rely upon the competence and probity of his broker-dealer for a good execution, under present rules and standards in over-the-counter markets the price paid or realized by an investor on the purchase or sale of a security may depend, to an excessive degree, on the diligence of the broker-dealer and the capacity in which he acts and/or on the identity of the investor. The NASD and/or the Commission should adopt rules and standards requiring all broker-dealers executing retail transactions, whether or not they are primary market makers in the particular security and whether the transaction is on a principal or agency basis, (a) to make reasonable effort, in light of all circumstances including the kind and size of order, to ascertain the best inter-dealer quotations (and to show in their permanent records the number of markets checked), and (b) to provide an execution as favorable as may reasonably be obtained in light of the kind and amount of securities involved and other pertinent circumstances.

7. Under present rules and standards in over-the-counter markets the disclosure of facts on which the investor may judge the price and quality of an execution depends in part on whether the broker-dealer acts as agent or principal. So-called "riskless" transactions, i.e., those in which a broker-dealer who neither is a primary market maker nor has a bona fide inventory position elects to execute a customer's purchase order by buying from another broker-dealer and reselling to the customer (or the reverse in the case of a customer's sale order) on a "net" basis without disclosure of markup or commission, are inherently susceptible to abuse and (subject to possible defined exceptions) should not be permitted to take that form; that is, a broker-dealer who neither is a primary market maker nor has a bona fide inventory position should be required (subject to defined exceptions) to execute customers' orders on an agency basis.

8. The NASD's markup policy is in need of substantial clarification and strengthening in respect of other than "riskless" transactions. In particular, an integrated broker-dealer's obligation and standards of retail pricing in relation to its contemporaneous cost or its current inter-dealer quotations, especially in the case of securities for which there is no independent market, should be defined, by the Commission and/or the NASD, more clearly and positively than has been done in the interpretations or administration of the present markup policy.

9. As a further basic improvement in retail over-the-counter markets the present retail quotation system of the NASD should be

supplanted by a system designed to show generally (with appropriate exceptions to deal with exceptional categories of securities or situations, if any) the best prevailing inter-dealer bid and asked quotations that can be reasonably ascertained and the number of primary market makers for each security. Any other quotation system designed for public dissemination, including electronic systems, should be required to conform to the same provisions. By appropriate explanatory legends and by NASD-sponsored educational efforts the investing public can and should be advised that published quotations in such form are inter-dealer quotations rather than retail quotations and hence are subject to markups, markdowns or commissions in retail transactions.

10. The NASD should re-examine and strengthen, in a manner consistent with the above, its methods of handling "local" quotations, the functioning of its local quotations committees, and its procedures for coordinating and supervising the work of such committees.

11. The NASD should also give consideration to ways and means of improving its retail quotation system in other respects, including, but not necessarily limited to, supplying indications of dividends, ex-dividends' insolvency or reorganization proceedings, etc., in the manner of stock exchange quotations.

12. To the extent that space limitations prevent inclusion in any newspaper or similar quotation system of more than a fraction (presently about one-sixth) of all securities quoted in inter-dealer systems, the privilege of being included in the NASD's "national" or "regional" list should be limited to the "OTC-listed" category (see chapter IX), and within that category the selection should be based on appropriate rules of the NASD or other operator of the particular quotation system.

13. The NASD and/or the Commission should re-examine present requirements with a view to improving disclosures, at the time of soliciting a retail purchase or in confirmations, of essential information relevant to particular types of retail transactions. Among other possibilities that should receive early consideration in this connection would be rules of the following kinds: (a) A broker-dealer soliciting a customer's purchase of any security for which there is no independent market other than its own, or any security out of its own inventory, or any security in which there is a spread of, say, 20 percent or more in prevailing interdealer bids and offers, should be required to disclose such fact or facts at the time of solicitation. (b) The confirmation of a customer's purchase or sale involving 100 shares or less (or, in the case of securities priced at $5 per share or less, involving say, $1500 or less), if handled on a principal basis, should be required to show the best inter-dealer quotation on the opposite side of the customer's transaction (i.e., the inter-dealer bid in the case of a customer's sale or the inter-dealer offer in the case of a customer's purchase) reasonably ascertainable at time of execution. (c) The confirmation of a customer's purchase (but not sale), whether handled

on a principal or agency basis, should provide an indication of the prevailing spread between interdealer bids and offers by showing a representative bid quotation.

14. With an already strong communications network, there is on the horizon the likelihood of a computer system that would assemble all interdealer quotations and instantaneously determine best quotations for particular securities at any time. If such a system were established, the further possibility of using it in connection with executions and to compile actual price and volume data for over-the-counter transactions would exist. Any such automated system would clearly be affected with a public interest and should be under regulatory supervision. The NASD is the natural source of leadership and initiative in dealing with matters of automation in respect of over-the-counter markets. It should actively carry forward the very limited study of automation possibilities applicable to over-the-counter markets that the Special Study has been able to undertake and should report to the Commission from time to time as to the progress of the industry in this area. The Commission and the NASD should jointly consider possibilities for developing and coordinating automation programs in such manner as to fulfill their respective regulatory needs, as well as operational needs of the markets, with maximum effectiveness and minimum duplication and expense.

15. In the absence of a completely automated system for recording transaction data, consideration should be given by the Commission and the NASD to the feasibility of establishing a reporting system designed to obtain maximum price and volume data, without undue burden, for actual transactions in over-the-counter securities or for specified categories of transactions and/or securities.

16. Inter-dealer or retail over-the-counter transactions in exchange-listed securities present special problems because of their actual or potential interaction with auction markets. In implementing the recommendations in this chapter for over-the-counter markets generally, appropriate exceptions and/or special requirements should be provided for over-the-counter transactions in exchange-listed securities. Other recommendations on this subject appear in chapter VIII.D.

Sec. 25-1(f).   Trading markets—interrelationship.

(Chapter VIII, Part 5. pp. 142-144)

1. The rapid growth in recent years of an off-board market for the trading of listed common stocks has made this an increasingly important segment of the national securities markets. Although the stocks are listed on the exchanges, the market operates as a part of the over-the-counter markets. It thus has elements of each market but is distinguished in important respects from both (and for this reason has been designated in this part as the "third market"). As in the case of multiple markets generally, the third market requires

evaluation of the advantages of competition with reference to possible impairment of the depth of the primary market. Under existing circumstances, it appears that the over-the-counter market for listed stocks has been beneficial to investors and the public interest.

2. The Study found an acute lack of data concerning the third market. Correction of this deficiency is an indispensable prerequisite to understanding and evaluating this market. As a basis for the gathering of essential information concerning the off-board trading of listed securities, the broker-dealers who hold themselves out to other broker-dealers and others as being willing to buy and sell listed stocks for their own accounts should be identified. The system of identification should generally follow the pattern recommended for "primary market makers" in the conclusions and recommendations in chapter VII, but there is no need to await the establishment of mechanical arrangements for such identification; the relatively small number of market makers and securities involved in the third market should permit the institution of the necessary identification programs with a minimum of delay.

3. Pursuant to section 17(a) of the Exchange Act, the Commission should, by appropriate rule or regulation, secure information concerning the third market on a continous basis from at least two sources. The market makers (identified under paragraph 2) should be required to file reports on their trading in listed securities in such detail as to volume and price as the Commission may find reasonably necessary. Other broker-dealers engaged in off-board trading in listed securities, but not making markets, should be required to file periodic reports of transactions in listed securities of (say) 300 share or more, i.e., transactions effected as agent for both buyer and seller, not involving a listed market maker.

4. There appears to be no more basis for broker-dealers to engage in riskless principal transactions with public customers in listed stocks than in unlisted stocks, discussed in chapter VII. Broker-dealers trading in listed stocks for which they are not making markets officially identified under paragraph 2 or without a bona fide inventory should be required to effect the orders of public customers for listed stocks on an agency basis, in accordance with the recommendations in chapter VII.

5. Short selling by the customers of the market makers, though apparently limited in extent at the present time, contains the seeds of a problem if utilized to escape the regulations governing the exchange markets. All sales to market makers should be marked either "long" or "short" in conformance with such regulations as the Commission may issue, and the market makers should report such sales to them under paragraph 3 above.

6. The trading of market makers directly with individuals in the third market also appears to be negligible in amount. At the same time, however, expansion of this area of operation in the future

contains the potential of a situation requiring regulation to safeguard the interest of investors. The market makers should be required to file with the Commission data concerning such transactions necessary to permit adequate oversight and anticipation of regulatory needs.

Sec. 25-1(g).   Open-end investment companies (mutual funds).

(Chapter XI, Part 5, pp. 170)

1. The Study was not concerned with and has not attempted to evaluate the merits of mutual fund shares as an investment medium, and nothing contained in this Report should be construed as an endorsement or criticism of investment company shares generally or of those of any particular company, or as a basis for purchasing or redeming any such shares. However, certain factors peculiar to the mutual fund industry create pressures toward undesirable selling practices. Evidence suggests the existence of such practices to an unfortunate degree. Industry representatives and the NASD, in consultation with the Commission, should jointly undertake a program designed to eliminate such tactics and devices through the adoption of interpretations of the Rules of Fair Practice. The further development of secondary supervisory controls by industry members is desirable, and the NASD should increase its activities in the surveillance of selling practices outside of the area of advertising and sales literature. As recommended in chapter II, membership in the NASD or another registered securities association should be required of all mutual fund selling organizations, and any such association should be required to maintain standards equivalent to those adopted by the NASD in accordance with this recommendation. Reference is also made to the recommendations in chapter II concerning the qualification and registration of salesmen.

Sec. 25-1(h).   The regulatory pattern.

(Chapter XII, Part 5, pp. 183-184)

4. The enforcement and surveillance techniques of the [New York Stock] Exchange range from highly effective ones to quite inadequate ones. Through expansion of the present use of automation or otherwise, more significant and sensitive techniques of surveillance of members' conformity with rules and standards applicable to floor activities can and should be developed, along lines recommended in chapter VI. As to off-floor activities, the Exchange's programs for surveillance of market letters, selling activities, and members' supervision of branch offices should receive early and substantial attention, along lines recommended in chapter III.

5. The Exchange's handling of customers' complaints against member firms should be re-oriented. Complaints of serious import should occasion serious investigation of facts, to determine whether disciplinary action is warranted. In cases of this kind, the Exchange should act in a self-regulatory role and not in a protective role toward its members; it has recently made moves in this direction. The Exchange's arbitration machinery, generally efficient and fair though it appears to be, should not be used as a substitute for or in derogation of the Exchange's exercise of its disciplinary responsibilities.

6. For self-regulation to be effective the Exchange should impose punishments that fit the infractions involved, particularly those involving ethical standards in dealing with the public, where marked leniency has sometimes been shown. While formality in disciplinary matters should not be sought for its own sake, there should be enough of it to provide basic fairness and also to assure adequate accountability at all levels of the self-regulatory process. As a general principle, with such general or specific exceptions as the Commission may approve, disciplinary matters resulting in the imposition of a penalty by the Advisory Committee or the Board of Governors should be publicly reported; staff-imposed sanctions should be periodically reported to the Commission.

(Chapter XII, Part 5, pp. 193-196)

1. The NASD's job of self-regulation is a peculiarly difficult one, involving as it does a unique combination of these factors, among others: (a) Its membership is very large and not pre-selected—it is compelled to open its doors to all qualified persons, and the qualifications have not been particularly selective. (b) Its membership is nationwide and virtually all-embracing, so that differences in practices and concepts resulting from different kinds and sizes of firms and their different locations and varied activities must be encompassed and in some degree reconciled. (c) Its scope of responsibility is very broad—virtually as broad and varied as the securities business—but at the same time it has primary responsibility in the vast but relatively uncharted over-the-counter area. (d) Its emphasis has been on members regulating and disciplining themselves as distinguished from being regulated and disciplined by a hired staff, yet the enormity of the job to be done is difficult to reconcile with the limited demands that can be made on individuals volunteering time away from their main business. (e) Its purpose of promoting voluntary compliance with ethical standards beyond the reach of formal regulation has limited its resort to codification or other "legalistic" techniques that might ease its burden of day-to-day regulation.

2. Despite many accomplishments in its relatively brief history, the NASD has fallen short of its potential as a self-regulatory agency —not only in sometimes failing to reach adequate results in areas that

it has undertaken to deal with, but in failing to deal with some areas that would seem to have called for self-regulatory attention. If the Association is to fulfill its role as the principal self-regulatory agency for non-exchange members and is not to collapse under the weight of its job in relation to its organizational structure, the structure must be basically modified and strengthened. This would be true even assuming no increase in the breadth or depth of the Association's activities; the need may be even greater in light of the substantive conclusions and recommendations in various chapters of this report that would enlarge its role of self-regulation.

3. A prime and urgent need is to realign functions and responsibilities, as between member officials and paid staff and also as among member officials, so that the chairman and Board of Governors may perform their paramount role of leadership in policy determinations. The recommendations in the following two paragraphs, which stop considerably short of what the major exchanges have done in the direction of diminished reliance on member committees and increased reliance on full-time staffs, must be regarded as minimum organizational changes needed at this time.

4. Without limiting the concept of self-regulation by members themselves, but rather in furtherance of that concept, the NASD's paid staff should be increased in size, stature and responsibility. The office of executive director should be upgraded to that of president and he should be made a voting member of the board and some or all of its standing committees. With adequate assistance of vice presidents and department heads, he should have responsibility for continuous administration by the entire staff, both in national and district offices, subject to the overall direction and control of the Board of Governors. To further these objectives, consideration might be given to granting tenure for a limited period of years to a holder of the office, as in the case of some of the stock exchanges. The staff should have a larger role in all enforcement and disciplinary activities, both for the purpose of assuring systematic and consistent attention to surveillance and enforcement of established rules and policies and for the purpose of relieving volunteer members of routine burdens of enforcement and discipline until the stage of actual decision of individual cases. The staff should also be equipped, available, and utilized to conduct studies or otherwise assist elected officials and member committees in formulating policies and programs of self-regulation on a continuing basis.

5. Further to enable the chairman and members of the Board of Governors to concentrate on larger problems and programs, the National Business Conduct Committee under appropriate liaison with the Board of Governors should have final power of decision in disciplinary matters, except where the board in its discretion "takes jurisdiction" because of the novelty or importance of particular cases or questions. Apart from disciplinary matters, important topics and

programs requiring more concentrated attention than the board itself can give should be the province of permanent or ad hoc member committees under appropriate liaison with the board. An Executive Committee that can be expected to meet more frequently than the full Board of Governors should be given increased authority to act on its behalf in the intervals between board meetings. With regard to the foregoing and all other forms of member participation in the affairs of the Association, the enlarged and strengthened staff recommended above should be equipped and available to provide guidance, assistance and continuity.

6. The Association should give consideration to ways and means of obtaining a better distribution of seats on district committees and the Board of Governors by size and type of firm. Among the possibilities as to board representation which might be explored would be an amendment to the by-laws permitting election or appointment of a limited number of governors-at-large in instances where the present geographic emphasis results in lack of size or functional representation for a particular class of firms. At the district level, existing by-law provisions appear to be sufficiently flexible to achieve these objects to a greater degree than is now the case.

7. The NASD's modes of surveillance of members' conduct are quite limited even in relation to the present scope of its self-regulatory concern, and there is considerable diversity in methods and extent of surveillance as among districts. In any event surveillance machinery will need to be strengthened to cope with the wider scope of the Association's activities under the substantive recommendations made in other chapters. The basic limitation of staff (see paragraph 4) should be corrected as promptly as possible, with the national office staff generally directing and coordinating the surveillance activities of district staffs. Automated data-processing undoubtedly offers many possibilities for enlarged and more efficient surveillance activities of the entire organization (as well as for other important uses, see chapter VII.E) and for this additional reason should be the subject of prompt and continuing attention of the NASD.

8. Disciplinary procedures, protected by statutory prescriptions and provisions for Commission review, have been generally fair. However, a lack of clear definition and/or adequate publication to the membership of some of the Association's broad standards of conduct, coupled with the regional emphasis that has been characteristic of its self-regulatory approach, has resulted in some unevenness and possible inequity in disciplinary results. The principal problem, of considerable seriousness even though not exclusive to the NASD, has been with respect to efficiency and speed in handling disciplinary cases. Among possible procedural improvements, direct secretaries, under the general supervision of the national office staff, should have the responsibility of reviewing all inspection reports, and they as well as appropriate members of the national staff should have broader

authority to investigate apparent violations disclosed in such reports or in public complaints, including greater freedom to question members and customers directly. They should make recommendations to the district business conduct committees for formal complaint proceedings, and should, as at present, regularly report to the national office regarding all matters investigated. Consideration should be given to eventually delegating to the national office the authority to file formal complaints and to utilizing full-time hearing officers in some or all formal disciplinary proceedings where this would lighten the burden of hearings now imposed on district committees or other members; ultimate decision on the record should be made by the district committees, subject to review, as at present but with the modification suggested in paragraph 5 above. As a general principle, with such general or specific exceptions as the Commission may approve, disciplinary matters resulting in the imposition of penalties should be publicly reported; informally imposed sanctions such as letters of caution should be periodically reported to the Commission.

9. The NASD historically has operated on a relatively limited budget in relation to its responsibilities, although recently there have been substantial increases. In any event its future role may require further increases, even though, in accordance with other recommendations in the Report, the total financial burden of regulation and self-regulation hopefully may be reduced by raising business entry standards and through a better division of labor and coordination of effort among regulatory and self-regulatory agencies. Apart from possibly increased budgetary needs, the Association's present fee structure may be inequitable insofar as it takes into account the amount of underwriting business but not the amount of trading activity of its members, and also in having overall ceilings regardless of size of a member's business. The NASD should pursue studies looking to early revision of its fee structure in relation to the business of its members and its own budgetary requirements.

(Chapter XII, Part 5, pp. 201-204)

1. Regulation in the field of securities should continue to be based on the principle of giving maximum scope to self-regulation, wherever and to the extent that a regulatory need can be satisfactorily met through self-regulation. As a corollary, it is an essential role of government, i.e., the Commission, to assure that there is no gap between the total regulatory need and the quantity and quality of self-regulation provided by the recognized agencies. However broad or narrow this gap may be in particular areas or at particular times, governmental power and performance must be sufficient to assure that the self-regulatory agencies are performing in the manner and degree expected of them and that direct regulation is available and effective where a self-regulatory agency is unwilling or unable to fulfill a regulatory need. Governmental participation is necessary also to assure that action taken in the name of self-regulation fairly serves

a valid public purpose and is not for a purpose inimical to antitrust or other public policies; and conversely, that bona fide self-regulatory action is inhibited because of a risk of liability in the absence of Commission review (cf. *Silver* v. *New York Stock Exchange*). While the Commission must have ample powers to accomplish these purposes, as more particularly set forth in the following paragraphs, they should continue to be regarded essentially as residual powers, to be exercised as needed but in such manner as to allow maximum initiative and responsibility to the self-regulators. Regulation in the area of securities should, in short, be a cooperative effort, with the government fostering maximum self-regulatory responsibility, overseeing its exercise, and standing ready to regulate directly where and as circumstances may require.

2. In the present statutory scheme there are marked differences between the provisions defining the Commission's powers in respect of exchanges (particularly Sections 6, 11 and 19 of the Exchange Act) and those applicable in respect of the NASD and any other "national securities associations" (Section 15A). These differences may in part reflect differences in the origins and natures of the two types of agencies, and may in part reflect the time interval of several years in the enactment of the two sets of provisions. In any event reexamination of these differences and of related Commission responsibilities is now warranted in light of subsequent experience and developments, including the *Silver* decision. In this reexamination the principles set forth in paragraph 1, that there should be maximum reliance on self-regulation but with ample governmental power in reserve, should apply.

3. In respect of rules (in the broadest sense) of the self-regulatory agencies, it is one of the important continuing responsibilities of the Commission to examine them upon initial promulgation and to reexamine them from time to time in light of changing circumstances. To provide reasonable opportunity for examination of exchange rules prior to their initial effectiveness, the pattern now applicable to the NASD, calling for 30-day advance filing and Commission power to disapprove before effectiveness (Section 15A(j)), should be made generally applicable to rules of exchanges, with appropriate provision for longer or shorter intervals to be established in respect of particular types of rules or in special circumstances. As recommended in paragraph 7, the Commission should be equipped in personnel and program to make adequate pre-effective study of new rules and to maintain general oversight over the existing bodies of rules in changing circumstances.

4. The present statutory pattern applicable to exchanges, under which the Commission has comprehensive power to adopt its own rules as to major substantive matters (Sections 10 and 11) and to amend or supplement exchanges' rules as to other matters to assure fair dealing and protection of investors (Section 19(b)), has no direct counterpart in respect of over-the-counter markets. The Commission does have

very considerable substantive rule-making power under Section 15(c), but has no authority to amend or supplement NASD rules on substantive matters. The Special Study has been unable fully to explore the legal question of the potential scope of Section 15(c) in relation to the scope of possible regulatory needs and objectives. Further study of this question should be undertaken promptly and, if and to the extent such study indicates that the Section 15(c) powers are insufficiently broad in these respects, the regulatory gap should be closed through legislation giving the Commission the necessary direct rule-making power or, alternatively, the power to amend or supplement an association's rules.

5. In respect of disciplinary proceedings, minimum requirements of "due process" should be applicable to proceedings of exchanges that may result in denial of membership or employment or in imposition of fines, suspensions or expulsions of members or employees, or that may affect the right of specific nonmembers to do business with members. It may be possible to accomplish this without statutory amendment by voluntary exchange action or by the exercise of the Commission's power under Section 19(b) (as suggested by the Supreme Court in *Silver*, footnote 16 to majority opinion) or alternatively under Section 23. In the same manner, or by statutory amendment if necessary, another imperative need indicated by the *Silver* decision, but extending beyond the facts of that case, should be met promptly: to provide for Commission review of at least certain types of exchange disciplinary matters in the manner now applicable to associations (Section 15A(g)).

6. Consistent with giving maximum scope to self-regulation (paragraph 1) and avoiding duplication in the total regulatory effort so far as possible (see part J), the Commission should seek to reorient its own regulatory effort in respect of trading and markets, as rapidly as circumstances justify, in the direction of reducing its direct participation in areas that are, or can and should become, adequately covered by self-regulation, e.g., periodic examinations of books and records of broker-dealers, and giving greater emphasis to (i) continuous oversight of the self-regulatory performance of exchanges and national securities associations in all areas in which reliance is placed upon them, (ii) regulation of such exchanges and associations in areas where they themselves are operating in a quasi-public-utility capacity, e.g., in their own operation of market mechanisms, (iii) enforcement proceedings in areas that self-regulation cannot or does not effectively reach, including Securities Act cases, cases involving novel and important issues, cases involving persons other than or in addition to members of self-regulatory bodies, cases involving need for subpoenas and/or the need for immediate injunctive action, and cases of a serious or flagrant nature involving fraud or manipulation or in which criminal prosecution is indicated, and (iv) enunciation of rules and

standards of conduct arising out of its continuing awareness of market developments and its enforcement experience.

7. The Commission's Division of Trading and Exchanges, perhaps renamed "Division of Trading and Markets," should be enlarged and strengthened in keeping with the foregoing. It should be so organized and staffed that it will be in a position to maintain more effective liaison with all of the self-regulatory agencies, examine their rules and rule changes, keep informed as to their enforcement activities, and generally oversee and evaluate their performance on a continuous basis and advise the Commission with respect thereto. Its Branch of Economic Research should be expanded so that considerably greater emphasis can be given to compilation, analysis and, where appropriate, publication of data concerning important aspects and developments of the trading markets.

(Chapter XII, Part 5, pp. 205-206)

1. This report indicates various ways in which the quantity and quality of self-regulation and/or governmental regulation need strengthening. On the other hand, available mechanisms, budgets, and personnel of some agencies already seem overtaxed, and at the same time there appears to be considerable duplication of effort among the various agencies in certain respects, adding to the burdens on the agencies themselves and on broker-dealers subject to multiple regulation. In the interests of the public, the regulatory agencies and the securities industry, further and continuing attention should be given to possibilities for coordinating efforts and allocating responsibilities in a more efficient and productive pattern, without limitation on any self-regulatory agency's freedom to have specal measures or programs for its own membership. Among such possibilities would be further standardization of application and report forms for firms and individuals, to be used by all interested agencies with appropriate supplementation by each to serve its special needs; further development of centralized examining and investigating procedures, again with appropriate supplementation to meet special needs of each agency; coordination of efforts in defining standards of conduct in areas of common concern; clearer recognition of one agency or another as having primary enforcement responsibility in respect of particular categories of firms or subject matters; and stronger lines of communication among agencies to facilitate channeling of information relevant to the interests of each. In the Federal regulatory scheme, as recommended in paragraph 8 of part I, the Commission's role should involve greater emphasis on oversight of self-regulators and on regulatory matters that self-regulation cannot effectively reach, avoiding, so far as possible, direct duplication of effort with self-regulatory agencies. This will necessarily require the self-regulatory bodies to refer promptly to the Commission those disciplinary matters which they are unable to prosecute effectively.

Sec. 25-2.   Appendix B—List of SEC regional and branch offices.

Regional Offices

Region 1. New York, New Jersey.—225 Broadway, New York, N. Y., 10007

Region 2. Massachusetts, Connecticut, Rhode Island, Vermont, New Hampshire, Maine.—Federal Building, Post Office Square, Boston, Mass., 02109

Region 3. Tennessee, North Carolina, South Carolina, Georgia, Alabama, Mississippi, Florida, and that part of Louisiana lying east of the Atchafalaya River.—Suite 138, 1371 Peachtree Street, NE., Atlanta, Ga., 30309

Region 4. Illinois, Indiana, Iowa, Kansas City (Kansas), Kentucky, Michigan, Minnesota, Missouri, Ohio, Wisconsin.—Bankers Building, Room 630, 105 West Adams Street, Chicago, Ill., 60603

Region 5. Oklahoma, Arkansas, Texas, and that part of Louisiana lying west of the Atchafalaya River, and Kansas (except Kansas City).—United States Courthouse, Room 301, Tenth and Lamar Streets, Fort Worth, Texas, 76102

Region 6. Wyoming, Colorado, New Mexico, Nebraska, North Dakota, South Dakota, Utah.—Room 802, Midland Savings Building, 444 17th Street, Denver, Colo., 80202

Region 7. California, Nevada, Arizona, Hawaii.—Room 821, Market Street, San Francisco, Calif., 94103

Region 8. Washington, Oregon, Idaho, Montana, Alaska.—9th Floor, Hoge Bldg., 705 Second Ave., Seattle, Wash., 98104

Region 9. Pennsylvania, Maryland, Virginia, West Virginia, Delaware, District of Columbia.—Room 302, 310 Sixth Street NW., Washington, D. C., 20549

Branch Offices

Cleveland, Ohio, 44113.—Room 1628, Standard Building, 1370 Ontario Street.

Detroit, Michigan, 48226.—Room 1503, Washington Boulevard Building, 234 State Street.

Houston, Texas, 77002.—Room 2226 Federal Office and Courts Building, 515 Rusk Ave.

Los Angeles, Calif., 90028.—Room 309 Guaranty Building, 6331 Hollywood Blvd.

Miami, Fla., 33132.—Room 1504, 51 SW., First Ave.

St. Louis, Mo., 63103.—Room 4266A Federal Building, 1520 Market Street.

St. Paul, Minn., 55101.—Room 1027, Main Post Office and Customhouse, 180 East Kellogg Blvd.

Salt Lake City, Utah, 84000.—Room 1119, Newhouse Building, 10 Exchange Place.

Sec. 25-3. Appendix C—SEC list of publications.

Revised October 25, 1963

THE FOLLOWING PUBLICATIONS MUST BE ORDERED
DIRECTLY FROM AND REMITTANCE MADE PAYABLE TO:
Superintendent of Documents
Government Printing Office
Washington, D. C. 20402

SEC NEWS DIGEST. Daily summary of important SEC developments. $15 per annum. Copies will be sent Air Mail for an additional $16.80 or a total cost of $31.80 per annum.

OFFICIAL SUMMARY. $1.50 per year—15¢ a copy. (75¢ additional for foreign mailing.) A monthly summary of security transactions and holdings reported under the provisions of the Securities Exchange Act of 1934, the Public Utility Holding Company Act of 1935 and the Investment Company Act of 1940 by officers, directors, and certain other persons.

STATISTICAL BULLETIN. $1.50 per year—15¢ a copy. (75¢ additional for foreign mailing.) Issued monthly. Presents data on new securities offerings, registrations, trading on exchanges, stock price indexes, round-lot and odd-lot trading, special offerings, secondary distributions, and other financial series including those releases under Classifications 11 to 14 and 16 inclusive.

QUARTERLY FINANCIAL REPORTS—*Manufacturing*. $1.25 per year, Domestic; $1.75 per year, Foreign; $2.25 per year, Domestic air mail. Reports beginning with the third quarter of 1955 presenting quarterly balance sheet and income data for all United States manufacturing corporations. Joint study of SEC and FTC.

ACTS AND RULES AND REGULATIONS: *PRICE* *

Organization, Procedures and Rules of Practice........ 30¢
Rules of Practice.................................. 15¢
Securities Act of 1933............................ 20¢
   Rules and Regulations under the 1933 Act........... 45¢
Securities Exchange Act of 1934.................... 25¢
   Rules and Regulations under the 1934 Act........... 50¢
Public Utility Holding Company Act of 1935.......... 20¢
   Rules and Regulations under the 1935 Act........... 35¢
Trust Indenture Act of 1939 and Rules and Regulations. 25¢
Investment Company Act of 1940.................... 25¢
   Rules and Regulations under the Investment Company
    Act... 30¢
Investment Advisers Act of 1940.................... 15¢
Regulation S-X (form and content of financial statements
   under 1933, 1934, 1935 Acts and Investment Company Act of 1940).............................. 50¢

ACCOUNTING SERIES RELEASES:
Compilations of Releases to and including Nos. 1-77... $1.25
Compilations of Releases to and including Nos. 78-89..   .45

* Prices subject to change without notice.

SEC ANNUAL REPORT TO CONGRESS:
First to Twenty-first (out of print)
Twenty-second (June 30, 1956)...................... .70
Twenty-third (June 30, 1957)....................... .75
Twenty-fourth (June 30, 1958)..................... .75
Twenty-fifth (June 30, 1959)...................... 1.00
Twenty-sixth (June 30, 1960)...................... 1.00
Twenty-seventh (June 30, 1961).................... 1.00
Twenty-eighth (June 30, 1962)..................... .60

SEC DECISIONS AND REPORTS: (buckram bound)
Volumes 1-36, inclusive, quoted upon request
(Dates, inclusive—July 2, 1934 to January 31, 1956)
Volume 37 (February 1, 1956 to June 30, 1957)....... 4.00
Volume 38 (July 1, 1957 to March 31, 1959)........... 4.25
Volume 39 (April 1, 1959 to June 30, 1960)........... 4.25
Volume 40 (July 1, 1960 to May 31, 1962)............ 5.00

SEC JUDICIAL DECISIONS (buckram bound)
Volume 1 (1934-1939) (Supply Exhausted)
Volume 2 (1940-1942)............................. 4.50
Volume 3 (January 1, 1943-June 30, 1944)........... 4.25
Volume 4 (July 1, 1944-September 30, 1946)......... 4.50
Volume 5 (October 1, 1946-December 31, 1948)....... 5.00

SURVEY OF CORPORATE PENSION FUNDS (October,
1956) .... .30
Privately-Placed Securities (September, 1952)......... .30
Cost of Flotation of Corporate Securities (June, 1957).. .45

A STUDY OF MUTUAL FUNDS (1962), prepared for
SEC by The Wharton School (U. Pa.)—Hse. Doc.
#2274, 87th Cong., 595 pages..................... 1.50

REPORT OF SEC SPECIAL STUDY OF SECURITIES
MARKETS (1963) Hse. Doc. #95, 88th Cong., Parts 1
through 4, 2994 pages........................... 10.00

DIRECTORY OF COMPANIES FILING ANNUAL REPORTS
WITH THE SECURITIES AND EXCHANGE COMMISSION UN-
DER THE SECURITIES ACT OF 1934. $1.25 per copy. Published
annually. Lists companies alphabetically and classified by industry
groups according to the Standard Industrial Classification Manual of
the Bureau of the Budget.

Sec. 25-4. Appendix D—SEC classification of releases.
Mailing Lists are maintained in following classifications only:
1. NEWS DIGEST:
   A daily resume of orders, decisions, rules and rule proposals
   issued by the Commission under the several laws it administers,
   together with a summary of financing proposals contained in
   Securities Act registration statements and of other Commission
   announcements. Available ONLY by subscription from the
   Superintendent of Documents, U. S. Government Printing

Office, Washington 25, D. C. at $15 per annum. THE COMMISSION DOES NOT MAINTAIN A MAILING LIST FOR THE NEWS DIGEST.

2. RULE PROPOSALS:

A special classification for those who wish to receive *all proposals* (except those referred to in item 8 below) for adoption of new rules or forms or amendment of existing rules or forms (under any of the SEC laws) in order to have an opportunity to submit views and comments thereon. *Registrants* affected by any such proposal will receive copies thereof whether or not they are on this list. For new or amended rules or forms, *if and when adopted,* see other release classifications.

3. ALL RULES UNDER SECURITIES ACT OF 1933:

(including those with respect to oil and gas royalties, securities and dealers) and under the Trust Indenture Act of 1939: This classification is *only* for new or amended rules as finally adopted. See classification 2 for *proposed* new or amended rules or forms.

4. ALL RULES UNDER SECURITIES EXCHANGE ACT OF 1934:

This classification is *only* for new or amended rules, as finally adopted. See classification 2 for *proposed* new or amended rules or forms.

5. HOLDING COMPANY ACT OPINIONS AND RULES:

Special classification for those interested in Commission decisions and rules adopted under this Act (frequently, a *summary* of a decision is distributed in lieu of the full text thereof). See classification 2 for *proposed* new or amended rules or forms.

6. ALL RULES UNDER INVESTMENT COMPANY ACT 1940:

This classification is *only* for new or amended rules, as finally adopted. See classification 2 for *proposed* new or amended rules or forms.

7. ALL RULES UNDER INVESTMENT ADVISERS ACT OF 1940:

This classification is *only* for new or amended rules, as finally adopted. See Classification 2 for *proposed* new or amended rules or forms.

8. ACCOUNTING:

Paper-bound booklets containing Accounting Series Releases Nos. 1 to 77 inclusive (price $1.00) and Accounting Series Releases Nos. 78 to 89 inclusive (price 45 cents) may be purchased from the Superintendent of Documents, Government Printing Office, Washington 25, D. C. Proposed new or amended accounting rules will be distributed to persons whose names appear on the accounting list. When any such revision in the accounting rules or other accounting release is adopted, one copy thereof will generally be distributed to each person on this list. However, where the new rule or release is lengthy or may not be of wide, general interest, a brief summary of the role or release will be distributed to this list. In such event, one copy of the text of the rule or release may be obtained by request from our Publications Unit.

9. CORPORATE REORGANIZATIONS:
   Announcements relating to the Commission's activities under Chapter X of the Bankruptcy Act, as amended, and advisory reports (or *summaries* thereof) filed with Courts pursuant thereto.

10. SECURITIES TRADED ON EXCHANGES:
    Annual directory and quarterly supplements of securities traded on national securities exchanges.

11. INDIVIDUALS' SAVING:
    Releases issued quarterly presenting data on the volume and composition of individuals' saving.*

12. WEEKLY TRADING DATA ON NEW YORK EXCHANGES:
    SEC stock price indexes and daily round-lot and odd-lot transactions effected on the New York and American Stock Exchanges.*

13. PLANT AND EQUIPMENT EXPENDITURES:
    Releases issued quarterly presenting data on plant and equipment expenditures of United States business, both actual and anticipated. Joint study of SEC and Department of Commerce.*

14. NET WORKING CAPITAL:
    Releases issued quarterly presenting data on current assets and liabilities of all United States corporations.*

15. QUARTERLY FINANCIAL REPORTS:
    Releases issued quarterly summarizing balance sheet and income data for U. S. manufacturing corporations reflected in reports of joint SEC and FTC study. (Copies of reports available at GPO at cost of $1 per year.)

16. NEW SECURITIES OFFERINGS:
    Releases issued quarterly presenting data on all new securities offerings by corporations in the United States. More detailed data available in the Statistical Bulletin.*

17. CORPORATE PENSION FUNDS:
    Releases issued annually presenting estimates of corporate pension fund assets and their composition and data on receipts and expenditures.

18. LITIGATION RELEASES:
    Releases announcing actions to enjoin violations of SEC laws and rules and developments in such actions, as well as developments in criminal prosecutions for securities violations.

---

* Information is also included in the SEC monthly STATISTICAL BULLETIN.
ORDER DIRECTLY FROM AND REMITTANCE MADE PAYABLE TO:
Superintendent of Documents
Government Printing Office,
Washington 25, D.C.
$1.50 per year.—15¢ a copy—40¢ additional for foreign mailing.

Sec. 25-5. Appendix E—Form BD.

FORM BD

Revised
March 2, 1959

SECURITIES AND EXCHANGE COMMISSION
WASHINGTON 25, D. C.

FORM OF APPLICATION FOR REGISTRATION AS A BROKER AND DEALER OR TO AMEND SUCH AN APPLICATION UNDER THE SECURITIES EXCHANGE ACT OF 1934

- -

THIS IS AN APPLICATION FOR REGISTRATION. [ ]

CHECK
ONE
BOX

Instructions—All Items in the Form must be answered in full. If this is an application by a predecessor on behalf of a successor broker-dealer not yet formed or organized, see instruction 7 below.

THIS IS AN AMENDMENT TO AN APPLICATION. [ ]

APPLICANT OR REGISTRANT REPRESENTS THAT TO THE EXTENT THAT INFORMATION PREVIOUSLY FILED IS NOT CORRECTED, SUCH INFORMATION IS TRUE, CORRECT, AND COMPLETE.

Instructions—If Items 3 (b) or 3 (c) are amended, they must be answered in full. With respect to any other items, furnish only the corrected information.

FULL NAME OF APPLICANT OR REGISTRANT . . . .

NAME UNDER WHICH BUSINESS WILL BE CONDUCTED . . . .

ADDRESS OF PRINCIPAL PLACE OF BUSINESS. (Complete address of actual location) . . . .

IF NAME, OR NAME UNDER WHICH BUSINESS WILL BE CONDUCTED, IS HEREBY AMENDED, SHOW PREVIOUS NAME HERE . . . .

GENERAL INSTRUCTIONS

1. This Form must be executed and filed in duplicate with the Securities and Exchange Commission, Washington 25, D. C. An exact copy should be retained by the applicant or registrant.

2. If the space provided for any answer is insufficient, the complete answer shall be prepared on a separate sheet which shall be attached to the Form and identified as "Answer to Item _____." and reference thereto shall be made under the item on the Form.

3. Individuals' names shall be given in full.

4. A Form which is not prepared and executed in compliance with applicable requirements may be returned as not acceptable for filing. However, acceptance of this Form shall not constitute any finding that it has been filed as required or that the information submitted is true, correct, or complete.

5. Rule 15b-8 requires a statement of financial condition to be filed in duplicate with every application for registration. Consult Rules 15b-7 and 17a-7 to determine whether any non-resident of the United States named in the Form is required to file a consent and power of attorney, or a notice or undertaking with respect to books and records.

6. Rule 15b-2 (b) requires that if the information contained in the application, or in any supplement or amendment thereto, is or becomes inaccurate for any reason, an amendment must be filed promptly on Form BD correcting such information.

7. If the Form is filed as an application by a predecessor broker-dealer on behalf of a successor not yet formed or organized, the information furnished shall relate to the successor to be formed. The Form shall be executed by the predecessor. Section 15 (b) of the Securities Exchange Act of 1934 and Rule 15b-3 provide that registration shall terminate on the forty-fifth day after the effective date unless prior thereto the successor shall adopt the application as its own. This procedure cannot be used where the successor is a sole proprietor.

DEFINITIONS

Unless the context clearly indicates otherwise, all terms used in the Form have the same meaning as in the Securities Exchange Act of 1934 and in the General Rules and Regulations of the Commission thereunder.

1. IS APPLICANT OR REGISTRANT TAKING OVER SUBSTANTIALLY ALL OF THE ASSETS AND LIABILITIES <u>AND</u> CONTINUING THE BUSINESS OF A REGISTERED BROKER OR DEALER?

YES ☐ NO ☐

IF SO, NAME OF PREDECESSOR: --

ADDRESS OF PREDECESSOR: --

DATE OF SUCCESSION: --

2. TO BE FILLED OUT ONLY IF APPLICANT OR REGISTRANT IS A SOLE PROPRIETOR

FULL NAME --

RESIDENCE ADDRESS --

3. TO BE FILLED OUT ONLY IF APPLICANT OR REGISTRANT IS A CORPORATION

(a) STATE OR PLACE IN WHICH INCORPORATED--

DATE OF INCORPORATION --

(b) <u>COMPLETE</u> LIST OF OFFICERS AND DIRECTORS, AND PERSONS WITH SIMILAR STATUS OR FUNCTIONS:

Full Names	Designate Titles of Each Officer	Designate Directors by Stating "Director"

(c) IS ANY PERSON, DIRECTLY OR INDIRECTLY, THE BENEFICIAL OWNER OF 10 PERCENT OR MORE OF ANY CLASS OF ANY EQUITY SECURITY OF APPLICANT OR REGISTRANT?

YES ☐ NO ☐

IF SO, As to each such person state:

Full Name	Class of Security

4. TO BE FILLED OUT ONLY IF APPLICANT OR REGISTRANT IS A PARTNERSHIP

(a) LIST FULL NAMES OF GENERAL PARTNERS

RESIDENCE ADDRESS OF EACH GENERAL PARTNER WHO DOES NOT RESIDE IN THE UNITED STATES

(b) LIST FULL NAMES OF LIMITED OR SPECIAL PARTNERS

LIMITED OR SPECIAL PARTNERS (Continued)

2

5. TO BE FILLED OUT ONLY IF APPLICANT OR REGISTRANT IS <u>OTHER THAN</u> A SOLE PROPRIETOR, PARTNERSHIP OR CORPORATION.

TYPE OF ORGANIZATION OR ASSOCIATION: _____

FULL NAME OF EACH PERSON, INCLUDING A TRUSTEE, WHO DIRECTS, MANAGES OR PARTICIPATES IN DIRECTING OR MANAGING ITS AFFAIRS, AND THE RESIDENCE ADDRESS OF ANY SUCH PERSON WHO DOES NOT RESIDE IN THE UNITED STATES.

Full Name	Residence Address if Non-Resident

6. DOES ANY PERSON NOT NAMED IN ITEMS 2 TO 5, INCLUSIVE, DIRECTLY OR INDIRECTLY, CONTROL BUSINESS OF APPLICANT OR REGISTRANT? YES ☐ NO ☐

IF SO, Furnish Full Name	Business Address	Residence Address of Any Such Person Who Does Not Reside in the United States

7. LIST EACH PERSON NAMED IN ANSWERS TO ITEMS 2 TO 6, INCLUSIVE, AND WITH RESPECT TO EACH FURNISH THE FOLLOWING INFORMATION CONCERNING ANY CONNECTION WITH OR FINANCIAL INTEREST IN ANY BROKER OR DEALER (OTHER THAN REGISTRANT OR APPLICANT OR ANY PREDECESSOR) WITHIN THE PAST 10 YEARS. IF ANY SUCH PERSON HAS HAD NO SUCH CONNECTION, THE WORD "NONE" SHALL BE STATED WITH RESPECT TO SUCH PERSON:

Full Name	Name of Broker-Dealer	From Month	Year	To Month	Year	Exact Nature of Connection or Interest

8

8. STATE WHETHER THE APPLICANT OR REGISTRANT, ANY PARTNER, OFFICER, DIRECTOR OR BRANCH MANAGER OF APPLICANT OR REGISTRANT (OR ANY PERSON OCCUPYING A SIMILAR STATUS OR PERFORMING SIMILAR FUNCTIONS), ANY PERSON DIRECTLY OR INDIRECTLY CONTROLLING OR CONTROLLED BY APPLICANT OR REGISTRANT, INCLUDING ANY EMPLOYEE:

(a) HAS BEEN FOUND BY THE COMMISSION TO HAVE WILLFULLY MADE OR CAUSED TO BE MADE IN ANY APPLICATION FOR REGISTRATION OR REPORT REQUIRED TO BE FILED WITH THE COMMISSION UNDER THE SECURITIES EXCHANGE ACT OF 1934, OR IN ANY PROCEEDING BEFORE THE COMMISSION WITH RESPECT TO REGISTRATION, ANY STATEMENT WHICH WAS AT THE TIME AND IN THE LIGHT OF THE CIRCUMSTANCES UNDER WHICH IT WAS MADE FALSE AND MISLEADING WITH RESPECT TO ANY MATERIAL FACT, OR TO HAVE OMITTED TO STATE IN ANY SUCH APPLICATION OR REPORT ANY MATERIAL FACT WHICH WAS REQUIRED TO BE STATED THEREIN   YES   NO   ☐ ☐

IF SO, FURNISH THE FOLLOWING INFORMATION WITH RESPECT TO EACH SUCH PERSON

Full Name of Person	Position with Applicant or Registrant	Title of Action

(b) HAS BEEN CONVICTED, WITHIN 10 YEARS, OF ANY FELONY OR MISDEMEANOR (i) INVOLVING THE PURCHASE OR SALE OF ANY SECURITY; (ii) ARISING OUT OF THE CONDUCT OF THE BUSINESS OF A BROKER, DEALER, OR INVESTMENT ADVISER; (iii) INVOLVING EMBEZZLEMENT, FRAUDULENT CONVERSION, OR MISAPPROPRIATION OF FUNDS OR SECURITIES; OR (iv) INVOLVING VIOLATION OF SECTION 1341, 1342 OR 1343 OF TITLE 18 UNITED STATES CODE (MAIL FRAUD, FRAUD BY WIRE (INCLUDING TELEPHONE, TELEGRAPH, RADIO OR TELEVISION).)   YES   NO   ☐ ☐

IF SO, FURNISH THE FOLLOWING INFORMATION WITH RESPECT TO EACH SUCH PERSON:

Full Name of Person	Position with Applicant or Registrant	Name and Location of Court and Date of Conviction

(c) IS PERMANENTLY OR TEMPORARILY ENJOINED BY ORDER, JUDGMENT, OR DECREE OF ANY COURT FROM ACTING AS AN INVESTMENT ADVISER, UNDERWRITER, BROKER, OR DEALER, OR AS AN AFFILIATED PERSON OR EMPLOYEE OF ANY INVESTMENT COMPANY, BANK, OR INSURANCE COMPANY, OR FROM ENGAGING IN OR CONTINUING ANY CONDUCT OR PRACTICE IN CONNECTION WITH ANY SUCH ACTIVITY, OR IN CONNECTION WITH THE PURCHASE OR SALE OF ANY SECURITY.   YES   NO   ☐ ☐

IF SO, FURNISH THE FOLLOWING INFORMATION WITH RESPECT TO EACH SUCH PERSON:

Full Name of Person	Position with Applicant or Registrant	Title of Action Name and Location of Court, and Date of Judgment or Order

(d) HAS BEEN FOUND BY THE COMMISSION OR ANY COURT TO HAVE VIOLATED ANY PROVISION OF THE SECURITIES ACT OF 1933, OR OF THE SECURITIES EXCHANGE ACT OF 1934, OR OF THE INVESTMENT ADVISERS ACT OF 1940, OR OF THE INVESTMENT COMPANY ACT OF 1940, OR OF ANY RULE OR REGULATION UNDER ANY OF SUCH ACTS.   YES   NO   ☐ ☐

IF SO, FURNISH THE FOLLOWING INFORMATION WITH RESPECT TO EACH SUCH PERSON:

Full Name of Person	Position with Applicant or Registrant	Title of Action and, if by a Court, Name and Location, and Date of Judgment or Order

(e) HAS BEEN FOUND BY THE COMMISSION OR ANY COURT TO HAVE AIDED, ABETTED, COUNSELLED, COMMANDED, INDUCED OR PROCURED THE VIOLATION BY ANY OTHER PERSON OF THE SECURITIES ACT OF 1933, OR THE SECURITIES EXCHANGE ACT OF 1934, OR THE INVESTMENT ADVISERS ACT OF 1940, OR THE INVESTMENT COMPANY ACT OF 1940, OR OF ANY RULE OR REGULATION UNDER ANY OF SUCH ACTS, OR TO HAVE FAILED REASONABLY TO SUPERVISE ANOTHER PERSON WHO COMMITTED SUCH A VIOLATION.   YES   NO   ☐ ☐

IF SO, FURNISH THE FOLLOWING INFORMATION WITH RESPECT TO EACH SUCH PERSON:

Full Name of Person	Position with Applicant or Registrant	Title of Action and, if by a Court, Name and Location, and Date of Judgment or Order

(f) IS SUBJECT TO AN ORDER OF THE COMMISSION ENTERED PURSUANT TO PARAGRAPH (7) OF SECTION 15(b) OF THE SECURITIES EXCHANGE ACT OF 1934, AS AMENDED, BARRING OR SUSPENDING THE RIGHT OF SUCH PERSON TO BE ASSOCIATED WITH A BROKER OR DEALER, WHICH ORDER IS IN EFFECT WITH RESPECT TO SUCH PERSON.   YES   NO   ☐ ☐

IF SO, FURNISH THE FOLLOWING INFORMATION WITH RESPECT TO EACH SUCH PERSON.

Full Name of Person	Position with Applicant or Registrant	Title of Action

9. APPLICANT OR REGISTRANT CONSENTS THAT NOTICE OF ANY PROCEEDING BEFORE THE COMMISSION IN CONNECTION WITH THE APPLICATION OR WITH REGISTRATION THEREUNDER MAY BE GIVEN BY SENDING NOTICE BY REGISTERED MAIL OR CONFIRMED TELEGRAM TO THE PERSON NAMED BELOW, AT THE ADDRESS GIVEN:

NAME _____

ADDRESS _____

EXECUTION

THE APPLICANT OR REGISTRANT SUBMITTING THIS FORM AND THE PERSON BY WHOM IT IS EXECUTED HEREBY REPRESENT THAT IT CONTAINS A TRUE, CORRECT, AND COMPLETE STATEMENT OF ALL INFORMATION REQUIRED TO BE FURNISHED.

Dated the _____ day of _____, 19_____

Sole proprietor . . . .   _____
                                                            (Proprietor)

Partnership or other unincorporated organization {

_____
(Name of Partnership (or Organization))

By _____
(General Partner (or Managing Agent))

Corporation . . . . {

_____
(Name of Corporation)

By _____

_____, a principal officer.
(Title)

If this form is filed by a sole proprietor, it shall be signed by the proprietor; if filed by a partnership, it shall be signed in the name of the partnership by a general partner; if filed by an unincorporated organization or association which is not a partnership, it shall be signed in the name of such organization or association by the managing agent, i. e., a duly authorized person who directs or manages or who participates in the directing or managing of its affairs; if filed by a corporation, it shall be signed in the name of the corporation by a principal officer duly authorized.

GUIDE FOR BROKER-DEALER FORM BD

(Editor's Note: This Guide does not reflect the September 15, 1964 revisions in #8 of Form BD.)

READ THIS GUIDE before filling out forms

UNACCEPTABLE APPLICATIONS NUMBER 40%
because directions are not read carefully and followed.

TO AVOID HAVING YOUR APPLICATION RETURNED
study this guide, Form BD, and the rules. Pay particular attention to the following items where three-fourths of the errors occur:

★ Item 1, page 2, Form BD   ★ The financial statement (for completeness)
★ Item 3, page 2, Form BD   ★ The date of the financial statement
★ Item 7, page 3, Form BD   ★ The oath or affirmation accompanying the financial statement

---

This is simply a supplementary guide to help you avoid the most common errors. It does not take the place of reading the rules and the instructions in Form BD.

FORM BD
Revised
March 2, 1959

SECURITIES AND EXCHANGE COMMISSION
WASHINGTON 25, D. C.

FORM OF APPLICATION FOR REGISTRATION AS A BROKER AND DEALER OR TO AMEND
SUCH AN APPLICATION UNDER THE SECURITIES EXCHANGE ACT OF 1934

CHECK ONE BOX

THIS IS AN APPLICATION FOR REGISTRATION.

Instructions—All Items in the Form must be answered in full. If this is an application by a predecessor
on behalf of a successor broker-dealer not yet formed or organized, see instruction 7 below.

THIS IS AN AMENDMENT TO AN APPLICATION.

APPLICANT OR REGISTRANT REPRESENTS THAT TO THE EXTENT THAT INFORMATION PREVIOUSLY
FILED IS NOT CORRECTED, SUCH INFORMATION IS TRUE, CORRECT, AND COMPLETE.

Instructions—If Items 3 (b) or 3 (c) are amended, they must be answered in full. With respect to any
other items, furnish only the corrected information.

FULL NAME OF APPLICANT OR REGIS-TRANT . . . .

NAME UNDER WHICH BUSINESS WILL BE CONDUCTED . . . .

ADDRESS OF PRINCIPAL PLACE OF BUSI-NESS. (Complete address of actual location) . . .

IF NAME, OR NAME UNDER WHICH BUSI-NESS WILL BE CONDUCTED, IS HEREBY AMENDED, SHOW PREVIOUS NAME HERE . . . .

GENERAL INSTRUCTIONS

1. This Form must be executed and filed in duplicate with the Securities and Exchange Commission, Washington 25, D. C. An exact copy should be retained by the applicant or registrant.

2. If the space provided for any answer is insufficient, the complete answer shall be prepared on a separate sheet which shall be attached to the Form and identified as "Answer to Item ...." and reference thereto shall be made under the item on the Form.

3. Individuals' names shall be given in full.

4. A Form which is not prepared and executed in compliance with applicable requirements may be returned as not acceptable for filing. However, acceptance of this Form shall not constitute any finding that it has been filed as required or that the information submitted is true, correct, or complete.

5. Rule 15b-8 requires a statement of financial condition to be filed in duplicate with every application for registration. Consult Rules 15b-7 and 17a-7 to determine whether any non-resident of the United States named in the Form is required to file a consent and power of attorney, or a notice or undertaking with respect to books and records.

6. Rule 15b-2 (b) requires that if the information contained in the application, or in any supplement or amendment thereto, is or becomes inaccurate for any reason, an amendment must be filed promptly on Form BD correcting such information.

7. If the Form is filed as an application by a predecessor broker-dealer on behalf of a successor not yet formed or organized, the information furnished shall relate to the successor to be formed. The Form shall be executed by the predecessor. Section 15 (b) of the Securities Exchange Act of 1934 and Rule 15b-3 provide that registration shall terminate on the forty-fifth day after the effective date unless prior thereto the successor shall adopt the application as its own. This procedure cannot be used where the successor is a sole proprietor.

DEFINITIONS

Unless the context clearly indicates otherwise, all terms used in the Form have the same meaning as in the Securities Exchange Act of 1934 and in the General Rules and Regulations of the Commission thereunder.

1

APPLICATION

Check here if:
1. You are not currently registered, or
2. You are registered, but are changing type of organization, for instance, sole proprietor to partnership, or partnership to corporation, or
3. You are a successor to a presently registered broker-dealer.

AMENDMENT

Check here if:
You are currently registered, and neither 2 nor 3 above apply. See Rule 15b-2(b)

Name of sole proprietor, partnership, corporation, or association.

Trade name if different.

IN AN AMENDMENT, answer only if there is new information to report.

An additional address may be shown if marked "Mail Address."

IN AN AMENDMENT, answer only if there is new information to report.

USE ONLY IN AN AMENDMENT, and only to show change in name.

If the form of organization also changes, YOU MUST FILE AN APPLICATION, not an amendment.

This should be <u>answered</u> only IN AN APPLICATION.

Item 3(a) should be answered only IN AN APPLICATION.

For date - give day, month, year.

IF YOU ARE FILING AN APPLICATION, this Item must be answered with a <u>complete</u> list.

IF YOU ARE FILING AN AMENDMENT, this Item should be answered only if the information previously furnished under this Item is no longer accurate. If the Item needs amending then it must be answered with a <u>complete</u> list.

Relates to issued and outstanding or subscribed stock.

1. IS APPLICANT OR REGISTRANT TAKING OVER SUBSTANTIALLY ALL OF THE ASSETS AND LIABILITIES <u>AND</u> CONTINUING THE BUSINESS OF A REGISTERED BROKER OR DEALER?   YES ☐   NO ☐

IF SO, NAME OF PREDECESSOR: ....

ADDRESS OF PREDECESSOR: ....

DATE OF SUCCESSION: ....

2. TO BE FILLED OUT ONLY IF APPLICANT OR REGISTRANT IS A SOLE PROPRIETOR

FULL NAME ....

RESIDENCE ADDRESS ....

3. TO BE FILLED OUT ONLY IF APPLICANT OR REGISTRANT IS A CORPORATION

(a) STATE OR PLACE IN WHICH INCORPORATED..

DATE OF INCORPORATION ....

(b) COMPLETE LIST OF OFFICERS AND DIRECTORS, AND PERSONS WITH SIMILAR STATUS OR FUNCTIONS:

Full Names	Designate Titles of Each Officer	Designate Directors by Stating "Director"

(c) IS ANY PERSON, DIRECTLY OR INDIRECTLY, THE BENEFICIAL OWNER OF 10 PERCENT OR MORE OF ANY CLASS OF ANY EQUITY SECURITY OF APPLICANT OR REGISTRANT?   YES ☐   NO ☐

IF SO, As to each such person state:

Full Name	Class of Security

4. TO BE FILLED OUT ONLY IF APPLICANT OR REGISTRANT IS A PARTNERSHIP

(a) LIST FULL NAMES OF GENERAL PARTNERS   RESIDENCE ADDRESS OF EACH GENERAL PARTNER WHO DOES NOT RESIDE IN THE UNITED STATES

(b) LIST FULL NAMES OF LIMITED OR SPECIAL PARTNERS   LIMITED OR SPECIAL PARTNERS (Continued)

2

Do not answer this Item if
you have answered Item 2
as a sole proprietor, or Item
3 as a corporation, or Item
4 as a partnership.

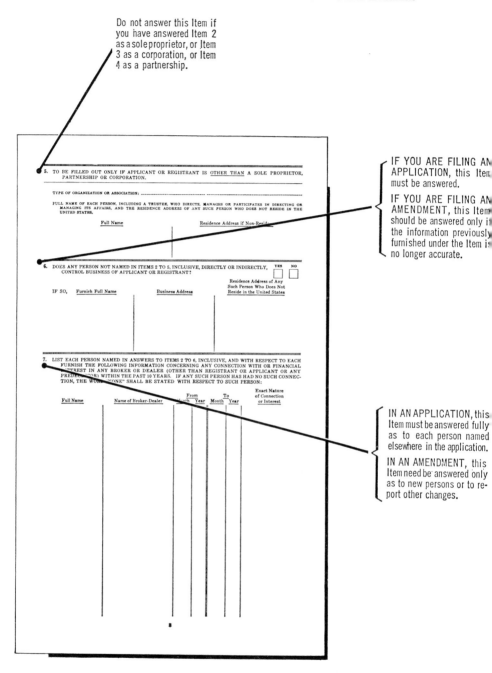

5. TO BE FILLED OUT ONLY IF APPLICANT OR REGISTRANT IS OTHER THAN A SOLE PROPRIETOR,
PARTNERSHIP OR CORPORATION.

TYPE OF ORGANIZATION OR ASSOCIATION: ....

FULL NAME OF EACH PERSON, INCLUDING A TRUSTEE, WHO DIRECTS, MANAGES OR PARTICIPATES IN DIRECTING OR
MANAGING ITS AFFAIRS, AND THE RESIDENCE ADDRESS OF ANY SUCH PERSON WHO DOES NOT RESIDE IN THE
UNITED STATES.

Full Name   Residence Address if Non-Resident

6. DOES ANY PERSON NOT NAMED IN ITEMS 2 TO 5, INCLUSIVE, DIRECTLY OR INDIRECTLY,   YES   NO
CONTROL BUSINESS OF APPLICANT OR REGISTRANT?

Residence Address of Any
Such Person Who Does Not
IF SO,   Furnish Full Name   Business Address   Reside in the United States

7. LIST EACH PERSON NAMED IN ANSWERS TO ITEMS 2 TO 6, INCLUSIVE, AND WITH RESPECT TO EACH
FURNISH THE FOLLOWING INFORMATION CONCERNING ANY CONNECTION WITH OR FINANCIAL
INTEREST IN ANY BROKER OR DEALER (OTHER THAN REGISTRANT OR APPLICANT OR ANY
PREDECESSOR) WITHIN THE PAST 10 YEARS. IF ANY SUCH PERSON HAS HAD NO SUCH CONNEC-
TION, THE WORD "NONE" SHALL BE STATED WITH RESPECT TO SUCH PERSON:

                                                                    Exact Nature
                                        From   To   of Connection
Full Name   Name of Broker-Dealer   Month Year Month Year   or Interest

IF YOU ARE FILING AN
APPLICATION, this Item
must be answered.

IF YOU ARE FILING AN
AMENDMENT, this Item
should be answered only if
the information previously
furnished under the Item is
no longer accurate.

IN AN APPLICATION, this
Item must be answered fully
as to each person named
elsewhere in the application.

IN AN AMENDMENT, this
Item need be answered only
as to new persons or to report other changes.

8. STATE WHETHER THE APPLICANT OR REGISTRANT, ANY PERSON NAMED IN ITEMS 2 TO 6, INCLUSIVE, ANY SALESMAN OR OTHER EMPLOYEE, OR ANY OTHER PERSON DIRECTLY OR INDIRECTLY CONTROLLING OR CONTROLLED BY REGISTRANT:

(a) HAS BEEN CONVICTED, WITHIN 10 YEARS, OF ANY FELONY OR MISDEMEANOR INVOLVING THE PURCHASE OR SALE OF ANY SECURITY OR ARISING OUT OF THE CONDUCT OF THE BUSINESS OF A BROKER OR DEALER. YES ☐ NO ☐
IF SO, FURNISH THE FOLLOWING INFORMATION:

Full Name of Person	Position with Applicant or Registrant	Name and Location of Court and Date of Conviction

(b) IS PERMANENTLY OR TEMPORARILY ENJOINED FROM ENGAGING IN OR CONTINUING ANY CONDUCT OR PRACTICE IN CONNECTION WITH THE PURCHASE OR SALE OF ANY SECURITY. YES ☐ NO ☐
IF SO, FURNISH THE FOLLOWING INFORMATION:

Full Name of Person	Position with Applicant or Registrant	Title of Action, Name and Location of Court, and Date of Judgment

(c) HAS BEEN FOUND BY THE COMMISSION TO HAVE VIOLATED ANY PROVISION OF THE SECURITIES ACT OF 1933 OR THE SECURITIES EXCHANGE ACT OF 1934, OR ANY RULE OR REGULATION UNDER EITHER OF SAID ACTS. YES ☐ NO ☐
IF SO, FURNISH THE FOLLOWING INFORMATION:

Full Name of Person	Position with Applicant or Registrant	Title of Action

9. APPLICANT OR REGISTRANT CONSENTS THAT NOTICE OF ANY PROCEEDING BEFORE THE COMMISSION IN CONNECTION WITH THE APPLICATION OR WITH REGISTRATION THEREUNDER MAY BE GIVEN BY SENDING NOTICE BY REGISTERED MAIL OR CONFIRMED TELEGRAM TO THE PERSON NAMED BELOW, AT THE ADDRESS GIVEN:

NAME ....

ADDRESS ....

EXECUTION

THE APPLICANT OR REGISTRANT SUBMITTING THIS FORM AND THE PERSON BY WHOM IT IS EXECUTED HEREBY REPRESENT THAT IT CONTAINS A TRUE, CORRECT, AND COMPLETE STATEMENT OF ALL INFORMATION REQUIRED TO BE FURNISHED.

Dated the .... day of ...., 19......

Sole proprietor . . . . (Proprietor)

Partnership or other unincorporated organization {
.... (Name of Partnership (or Organization))
By .... (General Partner (or Managing Agent))

Corporation . . . . {
.... (Name of Corporation)
By ....
............................, a principal officer. (Title)

If this form is filed by a sole proprietor, it shall be signed by the proprietor; if filed by a partnership, it shall be signed in the name of the partnership by a general partner; if filed by an unincorporated organization or association which is not a partnership, it shall be signed in the name of such organization or association by the managing agent, i. e., a duly authorized person who directs or manages or who participates in the directing or managing of its affairs; if filed by a corporation, it shall be signed in the name of the corporation by a principal officer duly authorized.

KEY TO APPLICABLE ITEMS FOR FORM BD

FORM OF OWNERSHIP	APPLICATION	AMENDMENT
Sole Proprietorship	Complete information on page 1 Items 1, 2, 6, 7, 8, and 9 on pages 2, 3, and 4 Execution on page 4 Financial statement on separate sheets	Complete information on page 1 as necessary to report changes. New information only under items 2, 6, 7, 8, and 9 on pages 2, 3, and 4 Execution on page 4
Corporation	Complete information on page 1 Items 1, 3, 6, 7, 8, and 9 on pages 2, 3, and 4 Execution on page 4 Financial statement on separate sheets	Complete information on page 1 as necessary to report changes. Items 3(b) and 3(c) on page 2 in full, if the change occurs in these items New information only under items 6, 7, 8, and 9 on pages 3 and 4 Execution on page 4
Partnership	Complete information on page 1 Items 1, 4, 6, 7, 8, and 9 on pages 2, 3, and 4 Execution on page 4 Financial statement on separate sheets	Complete information on page 1 as necessary to report changes. New information only under items 4, 6, 7, 8, and 9 on pages 2, 3, and 4 Execution on page 4
Other form of ownership	Complete information on page 1 Items 1, 5, 6, 7, 8, and 9 on pages 2, 3, and 4 Execution on page 4 Financial statement on separate sheets	Complete information on page 1 as necessary to report changes. New information only under items 5, 6, 7, 8, and 9 on pages 3 and 4 Execution on page 4

Sec. 25-7. Appendix G.

Attached is a Guide intended to assist applicants, registrants and their counsel in the preparation and completion of applications for registration as a broker-dealer and supplemental documents.

All answers in such documents must be accurate, complete and truthful.

Attention is directed particularly to the following requirements:

1. Financial reports filed must be strictly factual and accurately reflect the true and complete financial condition as of the time of preparation of such report. Hypothetical or pro forma reports are improper.

2. All prior broker-dealer affiliations for the past ten years must be reported (see Item 7 of Form BD). This includes all forms of employment of whatever character (e.g., salesman, cashier, bookkeeper, etc.) and all financial interests, direct or indirect, without exception.

3. Information must be supplied in Item 6 (Form BD) with respect to all persons exercising any direct or indirect control over the registrants' business unless they have been named in preceding items.

All information must be kept current, and amendments must be promptly filed to correct information no longer accurate or to reflect information required to be reported (see 17 CFR 240.15b-2(b):

including changes in address, in control or in officers, directors, partners or 10% stockholders called for under Items 3 and 4 (Form BD); and any criminal, civil or administrative actions called for under Item 8 (Form BD).

Extreme care must be exercised in completing these documents since all information reported on Form BD and documents supplemental thereto is relied upon by the Commission in performing its statutory duties and by the public in obtaining information concerning registered broker-dealers.

WARNING

Failure to include or file information required to be reported or the making of any false statements may result in the institution of administrative or civil proceedings. Moreover, intentional misstatements or omissions of material facts constitute federal criminal violations punishable by up to five years imprisonment and fines up to $10,000 for each offense. (See 18 U.S.C. 1001 and 15 U.S.C. 78 ff (a)).

A copy of this notice should be stapled to and returned with your application.

GUIDE FOR
PREPARATION OF
OATH OR AFFIRMATION AND
FINANCIAL STATEMENT.

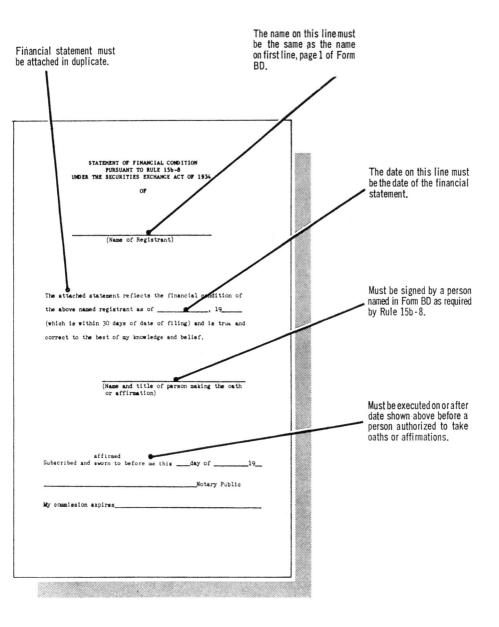

The name on this line must be the same as the name on first line, page 1 of Form BD.

Financial statement must be attached in duplicate.

STATEMENT OF FINANCIAL CONDITION
PURSUANT TO RULE 15b-8
UNDER THE SECURITIES EXCHANGE ACT OF 1934

OF

_____
(Name of Registrant)

The attached statement reflects the financial condition of
the above named registrant as of _____, 19_____
(which is within 30 days of date of filing) and is true and
correct to the best of my knowledge and belief.

_____
(Name and title of person making the oath
or affirmation)

affirmed
Subscribed and sworn to before me this ____day of _____19__

_____Notary Public

My commission expires_____

The date on this line must be the date of the financial statement.

Must be signed by a person named in Form BD as required by Rule 15b-8.

Must be executed on or after date shown above before a person authorized to take oaths or affirmations.

The statement of financial condition required by Rule 15b-8 must be that of the person or entity applying for registration and in sufficient detail to disclose the nature and amount of all assets and liabilities (of each category) and the resultant net worth. A pro forma statement as of a date in the future is not acceptable, although pro forma information may be included as a footnote or exhibit.

A sole proprietor must show all of his assets and liabilities and net worth, not just those assets dedicated to the broker-dealer business. If any assets are jointly owned, such should be indicated.

If any liabilities are secured, the nature and amount of collateral should be indicated.

A schedule of any securities in which the applicant has an interest must be included, showing the number of units of each security and market value as of the date of the statement.

A corporation should reflect its capitalization.

The statement required by Rule 15b-8 need not be prepared by an independent accountant.

Sec. 25-9. Appendix I—Form 7-M.

Revised December 9, 1958.

FORM 7-M THIS FORM SHALL BE FILED IN DUPLICATE ORIGINAL

SECURITIES AND EXCHANGE COMMISSION
Washington 5, D. C.

IRREVOCABLE APPOINTMENT OF AGENT FOR SERVICE OF PROCESS, PLEADINGS AND OTHER PAPERS BY INDIVIDUAL NON-RESIDENT BROKER OR DEALER

1. I, _____,

(Name)

of _____,

(Residence address in full)

doing business as_____,

(Name under which business is conducted)

at _____,

(Business address in full)

hereby designate and appoint, without power of revocation, the United States Securities and Exchange Commission as my agent upon whom may be served all process, pleadings, and other papers in any civil suit or action brought against me in any appropriate court in any place subject to the jurisdiction of the United States, with respect to any cause of action which (a) accrues during the period beginning when my registration as a broker or dealer becomes effective pursuant to Section 15 of the Securities Exchange Act of 1934 and the rules and regulations thereunder and ending either when such registration is cancelled or revoked, or when the Commission receives a notice to withdraw from such registration, whichever is earlier, (b) arises out of any activity, in any place subject to the jurisdiction of the United States, occurring in connection with the conduct of my business as a broker or dealer, and (c) is founded, directly or indirectly, upon the provisions of the Securities Act of 1933, the Securities Exchange Act of 1934, the Trust Indenture Act of 1939, the Investment Company Act of 1940, the Investment Advisers Act of 1940, or any rule or regulation under any of said Acts; and

2. I hereby consent, stipulate and agree, without power of revocation, (a) that any such civil suit or action may be commenced against me by the service of process upon the Commission and the forwarding by the Commission of a copy thereof by registered mail to me at the last address of record filed by me with the Commission, (b) that all service of process, pleadings, or other papers upon the Commission and the forwarding by the Commission of a copy thereof by registered mail to me at the last address of record filed by me with the Commission shall be taken and held in all courts to be as valid and binding

as if due personal service had been made upon me, and (c) that service upon the Commission may be effected by delivering copies of said process, pleadings or other papers to the Secretary of the Commission or to any other person designated by it for such purpose, and that the certificate of the Secretary of the Commission or of such other person reciting that said process, pleadings or other papers were received by the Commission and that a copy thereof was forwarded to me at the last address of record filed by me with the Commission shall constitute evidence of such service upon me.

IN WITNESS WHEREOF, I have executed this irrevocable power of attorney, consent, stipulation and agreement at_____
this_____day of_____A. D., 19__.

(Seal)

NOTE: The person executing this irrevocable power of attorney, consent, stipulation and agreement should appear before a person authorized to administer acknowledgments in the jurisdiction in which it is executed and acknowledge that he executed it as his free and voluntary act. The acknowledgment should be in the form prescribed by the law of the jurisdiction in which it is executed. *The form of acknowledgment suggested below should be used only if it is consistent with the requirements of the law of such jurisdiction.*

The failure of any acknowledgment to meet applicable requirements shall not affect the validity or effect of the foregoing irrevocable power of attorney, consent, stipulation and agreement.

Province (or State) of_____⎫ ss.
County of_____⎭

I, _____,

(Name)

_____, in and for

(Official position of person administering acknowledgment)

(said County in) the Province (or State) aforesaid, to hereby certify that

_____ personally appeared

(Name of person appointing agent for service, etc.)

before me this day and signed and sealed the above instrument as his free and voluntary act for the uses and purposes therein set forth.

Given under my hand and seal this _____day of
_____, A. D., 19__.

(Seal)   _____

(Signature of official)

_____

(Official position)

My commission (or office) expires:

_____

(Date)

Sec. 25-10. Appendix J—Form 8-M.

Revised December 9, 1958

FORM 8-M   THIS FORM SHALL BE FILED IN DUPLICATE ORIGINAL

SECURITIES AND EXCHANGE COMMISSION
Washington 25, D. C.

IRREVOCABLE APPOINTMENT OF AGENT FOR SERVICE OF PROCESS, PLEADINGS AND OTHER PAPERS BY CORPORATION* NON-RESIDENT BROKER OR DEALER

1. The _____ ,

(Name of corporation)

a corporation incorporated under the laws of_____

(Name of jurisdiction under whose laws

_____, and having its principal place of business at

corporation was organized)

_____ , hereby designates

(Address in full)

and appoints, without power of revocation, the United States Securities and Exchange Commission as the agent of said corporation upon whom may be served all process, pleadings, and other papers in any civil suit or action brought against it in any appropriate court in any place subject to the jurisdiction of the United States, with respect to any cause of action which (a) accrues during the period beginning when its registration as a broker or dealer becomes effective pursuant to Section 15 of the Securities Exchange Act of 1934 and the rules and regulations thereunder and ending either when such registration is cancelled or revoked, or when the Commission receives a notice to withdraw from such registration, whichever is earlier, (b) arises out of any activity, in any place subject to the jurisdiction of the United States, occurring in connection with the conduct of business of said corporation as a broker or dealer, and (c) is founded, directly or indirectly, upon the provisions of the Securities Act of 1933, the Securities Exchange Act of 1934, the Trust Indenture Act of 1939, the Investment Company Act of 1940, the Investment Advisers Act of 1940, or any rule or regulation under any of said Acts; and

2. Said corporation, _____ ,

(Name of corporation)

hereby consents, stipulates and agrees, without power of revocation, (a) that any such civil suit or action may be commenced against it by the service of process upon the Commission and the forwarding by the Commission of a copy thereof by registered mail to it at the last address of record filed by it with the Commission, (b) that all service of process, pleadings, or other papers upon the Commission and the forwarding of a copy thereof by registered mail to it at the last address of record filed by it with the Commission shall be taken and held in all courts to be as valid and binding as if due personal service had been made upon it, and (c) that service upon the Commission may be effected by delivering copies of said process, pleadings or other papers to the Secretary of the Commission or to any other person designated by the Commission for such purpose, and that the certificate of the Secretary of the Commission or of such other person reciting that said process, pleadings or other papers were received by the Commission and that a copy thereof was forwarded to said corporation at the last address of record filed by it with the Commission shall constitute evidence of such service upon it.

IN WITNESS WHEREOF, the President and Secretary of said corporation _____, by the
(Name of corporation)
authority and direction of the Board of Directors of said corporation, have executed this irrevocable power of attorney, consent, stipulation and agreement for and on behalf of said corporation at_____
_____, this_____day of_____A. D., 19__.

Attest_____   _____
                (Secretary)   (Corporate name)
(Corporate Seal)   By_____
                                              (President)

NOTE: The persons executing this irrevocable power of attorney, consent, stipulation and agreement should appear before a person authorized to administer acknowledgments in the jurisdiction in which it is executed and acknowledge that they executed it on behalf of said corporation as its free and voluntary act. The acknowledgment should be in the form prescribed by the law of the jurisdiction in which it is executed. *The form of acknowledgment suggested below should be used only if it is consistent with the requirements of the law of such jurisdiction.*

The failure of any acknowledgment to meet applicable requirements shall not affect the validity or effect of the foregoing irrevocable power of attorney, consent, stipulation and agreement.

Province (or State) of_____⎫ ss.
County of_____⎭

I, _____, a _____
                (Name)   (Official position of
_____, in and for (said County in)
person administering acknowledgment)
the Province (or State) aforesaid, do hereby certify that _____
                                                                                          Name of
_____, and _____ personally
(President)   (Name of Secretary)
appeared before me this day, stated that they are respectively the president and secretary of the _____,
                                                          (Name of corporation)
that they are the same persons named in the foregoing instrument as

the president and secretary of said corporation, that they have been duly authorized to execute said instrument for the corporation, and that they signed and sealed said instrument for and on behalf of said corporation as its free and voluntary act for the uses and purposes therein set forth.

Given under my hand and seal this _____ day of _____ A. D., 19__.

(Seal)

_____
(Name of Official)

_____
(Official position)

My commission (or office) expires:

_____
(Date)

* This form should be appropriately revised for use by a broker-dealer which is an unincorporated orgnization or association other than a partnership.

Revised December 9, 1958

CERTIFICATE OF RESOLUTION AUTHORIZING IRREVOCABLE APPOINTMENT BY CORPORATION OF AGENT FOR SERVICE OF PROCESS, PLEADINGS AND OTHER PAPERS

At a duly constituted meeting of the Board of Directors of _____, a corporation duly
(Name of corporation)
organized and existing under the laws of _____
(Name of jurisdiction under whose laws
_____, held at the office of said corporation at
corporation was organized)
_____, on the _____ day
(Address in full)
of _____, 19___, the following resolution was adopted:

Be it resolved that the president and secretary of this corporation _____, be and they
(Name of corporation)
hereby are authorized and directed to execute in legal form and to deliver to the United States Securities and Exchange Commission on behalf of this corporation in such form as may be prescribed by or acceptable to the United States Securities and Exchange Commission:

(1) A power of attorney designating and appointing, without power of revocation, the United States Securities and Exchange Commission as the agent of this corporation upon whom may be served all process, pleadings and other papers in any civil suit or action brought against this corporation in any appropriate court in any place subject to the jurisdiction of the United States, with respect to any cause of action which (a) accrues during the period beginning when its registration as a broker or dealer becomes effective pur-

suant to Section 15 of the Securities Exchange Act of 1934 and the rules and regulations thereunder and ending either when such registration is cancelled or revoked, or when the Commission receives a notice to withdraw from such registration, whichever is earlier, (b) arises out of any activity, in any place subject to the jurisdiction of the United States, occurring in connection with the conduct of business of this corporation as a broker or dealer, and (c) is founded, directly or indirectly, upon the provisions of the Securities Act of 1933, the Securities Exchange Act of 1934, the Trust Indenture Act of 1939, the Investment Company Act of 1940, the Investment Advisers Act of 1940, or any rule or regulation under any of said Acts; and

(2) A stipulation, consent and agreement, likewise without power of revocation, (a) that any such civil suit or action brought against this corporation may be commenced against this corporation by service of process upon the United States Securities and Exchange Commission and the forwarding by the Commission of a copy thereof by registered mail to this corporation at the last address of record filed by this corporation with said Commission, (b) that all service of process, pleadings or other papers upon the said Commission and the forwarding of a copy thereof by registered mail to this corporation at the last address of record filed by this corporation with the Commission shall be taken and held in all courts to be as valid and binding as if due personal service had been made upon this corporation and (c) that service upon the Commission may be effected by delivering copies of said process, pleadings or other papers to the Secretary of the Commission or to any other person designated by the Commission for such purpose, and that the certificate of the Secretary of the Commission or of such other person reciting that said process, pleadings or other papers were received by the Commission and that a copy thereof was forwarded to this corporation at the last address of record filed by this corporation with the Commission shall constitute evidence of such service upon it.

Province (or State) of _____⎫ ss.
County of _____⎭

　　I, _____,
　　　　　　　　　　(Name of Secretary)
being duly sworn, depose and say that I am Secretary of _____
　　　　　　　　　　　　　　　　　　　　　　　Name of
_____, and that the foregoing is a true and
　　corporation)
correct copy of a resolution adopted by the Board of Directors of said corporation on the _____ day of _____, A. D., 19__,

as the same appears on the records of said corporation now in my custody and control.

IN WITNESS WHEREOF, I have hereunto set my hand and affixed the seal of said corporation.

(Corporate Seal) _____

(Secretary)

Subscribed and sworn to before me this _____ day of _____, A. D., 19___.

(Seal) _____

(Name of Official)

_____

(Official position)

My commission (or office) expires:

_____

(Date)

NOTE: The Secretary of the corporation should appear before a person authorized to administer oaths in the jurisdiction in which it is executed and duly swear that he is the Secretary of such corporation and that the resolution is a true and correct copy of the resolution adopted by the Board of Directors of said corporation, The form of affidavit suggested above should be used only if it is consistent with the requirements of the law of the jurisdiction in which it is executed.

Sec. 25-11. Appendix K—Form 9-M.

Revised December 9, 1958

FORM 9-M   THIS FORM SHALL BE FILED IN DUPLICATE ORIGINAL

SECURITIES AND EXCHANGE COMMISSION
Washington 25, D. C.

IRREVOCABLE APPOINTMENT OF AGENT FOR SERVICE OF PROCESS, PLEADINGS AND OTHER PAPERS BY PARTNERSHIP NON-RESIDENT BROKER OR DEALER

1. The partners of _____, a part-

(Name of partnership)

nership having its principal place of business at _____

(Address in full)

_____, hereby designate and appoint, without power of revocation, the United States Securities and Exchange Commission as the agent of said partnership as now or hereafter constituted, upon whom may be served all process, pleadings, and other papers in any civil suit or action brought against it in any appropriate court in any place subject to the jurisdiction of the United States, with respect to any cause of action which (a) accrues during the period beginning when its registration as a broker or dealer becomes effective pursuant to Section 15 of the Securities Exchange Act of 1934 and the rules and regulations thereunder and ending either when such registration is cancelled or revoked, or when the Commission receives a notice to withdraw from such registration, whichever is earlier, (b) arises out of any activity, in any place subject to the jurisdiction of the United States, occurring in connection with the conduct of business of said partnership as a broker or dealer, and (c) is founded, directly or indirectly, upon the provisions of the Securities Act of 1933, the Securities Exchange Act of 1934, the Trust Indenture Act of 1939, the Investment Company Act of 1940, the Investment Advisers Act of 1940, or any rule or regulation under any of said Acts; and

2. The said partners of _____,
(Name of partnership)
hereby consent, stipulate and agree, without power of revocation, (a) that any such civil suit or action may be commenced against it by the service of process upon the Commission and the forwarding by the Commission of a copy thereof by registered mail to it at the last address of record filed by it with the Commission, (b) that all service of process, pleadings, or other papers upon the Commission and the forwarding of a copy thereof by registered mail to it at the last address of record filed by it with the Commission shall be taken and held in all courts to be as valid and binding as if due personal service had been made upon it, and (c) that service upon the Commission may be effected by delivering copies of said process, pleadings or other papers to the Secretary of the Commission or to any other person designated by the Commission for such purpose, and that the certificate of the Secretary of the Commission or of such other person reciting that said process, pleadings or other papers were received by the Commission and that a copy thereof was forwarded to said partnership at the last address of record filed by it with the Commission shall constitute evidence of such service upon it.

3. This irrevocable power of attorney, consent, stipulation and agreement shall continue in effect notwithstanding the subsequent withdrawal or admission of any partner if (a) such withdrawal or admission does not as a matter of law create a new partnership, or (b) if a successor partnership continues to operate on the basis of the registration of the old firm, whether or not in accordance with the conditions prescribed in the Securities Exchange Act of 1934 or the rules and regulations thereunder. In the event of dissolution of the partnership this irrevocable power of attorney, consent, stipulation and agreement shall nevertheless continue in effect for any action against the former partners or the partnership in dissolution.

IN WITNESS WHEREOF, _____
(Name of general partner authorized to execute this
_____, duly authorized by all of the partners of said partnership,
instrument)
has executed this irrevocable power of attorney, consent, stipulation

and agreement for and on behalf of said partnership at _____
this _____ day of _____, A. D., 19__.

_____
(Partnership)

By _____ (Seal)

(General Partner)

NOTE: The person executing this irrevocable power of attorney, consent, stipulation and agreement should appear before a person authorized to administer acknowledgments in the jurisdiction in which it is executed and acknowledge that he executed it on behalf of said partnership as its free and voluntary act. The acknowledgment should be in the form prescribed by the law of the jurisdiction in which it is executed. _The form of acknowledgment suggested below should be used only if it is consistent with the requirements of the law of such jurisdiction._

The failure of any acknowledgment to meet applicable requirements shall not affect the validity or effect of the foregoing irrevocable power of attorney, consent, stipulation and agreement.

Province (or State) of _____⎱ ss.
Country of _____⎰

I, _____,

(Name)

_____, in and for (said
(Official position of person administering acknowledgment)
County in) the Province (or State) aforesaid, do hereby certify that
_____ personally appeared
Name of general partner)
before me this day, stated that he is a general partner of _____
_____, that he is the same person named
(Name of partnership)
in the foregoing instrument as a general partner of said partnership, that he has been duly authorized by all of the partners to execute said instrument for the partnership, and that, he signed and sealed said instrument for and on behalf of said partnership as its free and voluntary act for the uses and purposes therein set forth.

Given under my hand and seal this _____ day of
_____ A. D., 19__.

(Seal)
_____
(Name of Official)

_____
(Official position)

My commission (or office) expires:

_____
(Date)

Sec. 25-12. Appendix L—Form 10-M.
Revised December 9, 1958

FORM 10-M   THIS FORM SHALL BE FILED IN DUPLICATE ORIGINAL

SECURITIES AND EXCHANGE COMMISSION
Washington 25, D. C.

IRREVOCABLE APPOINTMENT OF AGENT FOR SERVICE OF PROCESS, PLEADINGS AND OTHER PAPERS BY NON-RESIDENT GENERAL PARTNER* OF BROKER OR DEALER

1. I, _____, of
(Name)

_____, hereby
(Address in full)

designate and appoint, without power of revocation, the United States Securities and Exchange Commission as my agent upon whom may be served all process, pleadings and other papers in any civil suit or action brought against me individually or as a partner of any partnership engaged in business as a broker or dealer, in any appropriate court in any place subject to the jurisdictcion of the United States, with respect to any cause of action which (a) accrues during the period beginning when the registration as a broker or dealer of any partnership of which I am a general partner becomes effective pursuant to Section 15 of the Securities Exchange Act of 1934 and the rules and regulations thereunder and ending either when such registration is cancelled or revoked, or when the Commission receives a notice to withdraw from such registration, whichever is earlier, (b) arises out of any activity, in any place subject to the jurisdiction of the United States, occurring in connection withe the conduct of business of a broker or dealer, and (c) is founded, directly or indirectly, upon the provisions of the Securities Act of 1933, the Securities Exchange Act of 1934, the Trust Indenture Act of 1939, the Investment Company Act of 1940, the Investment Advisers Act of 1940, or any rule or regulation under any of said Acts; and

2. I hereby consent, stipulate and agree, without power of revocation, (a) that any such civil suit or action may be commenced against me individually or as a partner of any partnership engaged in business as a broker or dealer, by the service of process upon the Commission and the forwarding by the Commission of a copy thereof by registered mail to me at the last address of record filed by me with the Commission, (b) that all service of process, pleadings or other papers upon the Commission and the forwarding of a copy thereof by registered mail to me at the last address of record filed by me with the Commission shall be taken and held in all courts to be as valid and binding as if due personal service had been made upon me, and

(c) that service upon the Commission may be effected by delivering copies of said process, pleadings or other papers to the Secretary of the Commission or to any other person designated by it for such purpose, and that the certificate of the Secretary of the Commission or of such other person reciting that said process, pleadings or other papers were received by the Commission and that a copy thereof was forwarded to me at the last address of record filed by me with the Commission shall constitute evidence of such service upon me.

IN WITNESS WHEREOF, I have executed his irrevocable power of attorney, consent, stipulation and agreement at _____, this _____ day of _____, A. D., 19__.

(Seal)

NOTE: The person executing this irrevocable power of attorney, consent, stipulation and agreement should appear before a person authorized to administer acknowledgments in the jurisdiction in which it is executed and acknowledge that he executed it as his free and voluntary act. The acknowledgment should be in the form prescribed by the law of the jurisdiction in which it is executed. *The form of acknowledgment suggested below should be used only if it is consistent with the requirements of the law of such jurisdiction.*

The failure of any acknowledgment to meet applicable requirements shall not affect the validity or effect of the foregoing irrevocable power of attorney, consent, stipulation and agreement.

Province (or State) of _____ ⎱
County of _____ ⎰ ss.

I, _____,

(Name)

_____, in and for (said

(Official position of person administering acknowledgment)

County in) the Province (or State) aforesaid, do hereby certify that _____, personally appeared

(Name of person appointing agent for service, etc.)

before me this day and signed and sealed the above instrument as his free and voluntary act for the uses and purposes therein set forth.

Given under my hand and seal this _____ day of _____, A. D., 19__.

(Seal)   _____

(Signature of Official)

_____

(Official position)

My commission (or office) expires:

_____

(Date)

* This form should be appropriately revised for use by a "managing agent" of a broker or dealer. Paragraph (d) of the rule defines a "managing agent" to mean any person, including a trustee, who directs or manages or who participates in the directing or managing of the affairs of any unincorporated organization or association which is not a partnership.

Sec. 25-13. Appendix M—Form of Undertaking Required by Rule 17a-7(b) (1).

"The undersigned hereby undertakes to furnish at his own expense to the Securities and Exchange Commission at its principal office in Washington, D.C. or at any Regional Office of said Commission specified in a demand for copies of books and records made by or on behalf of said Commission, true, correct, complete and current copies of any or all, or any part, of the books and records which the undersigned is required to make, keep current or preserve pursuant to any provision of any rule or regulation of the Securities and Exchange Commission under the Securities Exchange Act of 1934. This undertaking shall be suspended during any period when the undersigned is making, keeping current, and preserving copies of all of said books and records at a place within the United States in compliance with Rule 17a-7 under the Securities Exchange Act of 1934. This undertaking shall be binding upon the undersigned and the heirs, successors and assigns of the undersigned, and the written irrevocable consents and powers of attorney of the undersigned, its general partners and managing agents filed with the Securities and Exchange Commission shall extend to and cover any action to enforce same."

Sec. 25-14. Appendix N—Guide to preparation of subordination agreements.

The following is a guide to preparing a "satisfactory subordination agreement" within the meaning of Rule 240.15c3-1. As an administrative matter the New York Regional Office uses this guide as a yardstick in determining whether such agreements comply with this rule and related rules.

I.

SUBSTANTIVE PROVISIONS

The agreement must be a written agreement between the broker or dealer and a lender, which agreement is binding and enforceable in accordance with its terms upon the lender, his creditors, heirs, executors, administrators, and assigns, and which agreement satisfies all of the following conditions:

    (a) It completely and effectively subordinates to all claims of all present and future creditors of the broker or dealer any right or claim of the lender to demand or receive any payment with respect to, or the return of, the money or securities loaned, or to exercise any right with respect thereto. In the event of bankruptcy, reorganization, assignment for the benefit of creditors, arrangement, liquidation or similar proceedings in regard to the broker or dealer, all claims of all such creditors are to be satisfied in full before any claim of the lender with respect to the money or securities loaned is satisfied in whole or in part;

(b) It is for a specific term of not less than one year and is not subject to unilateral cancellation, termination, modification or amendment;

(c) It provides that it shall not be terminated, rescinded or modified by mutual consent or otherwise, if the effect thereof would be to make the agreement inconsistent with the conditions of Rule 240.15c3-1, or to reduce the net capital of the broker dealer below the amount required by such Rule. It also provides that before any part of the money or securities loaned is repaid or returned to the lender prior to the expiration of the term of the agreement, this office is to be given 30 days' prior written notice to enable it to determine whether the same would be consistent with this provision;

(d) It provides that no default in the payment of interest or in the performance of any other covenant or condition by the broker or dealer shall have the effect of accelerating the maturity of the indebtedness;

(e) It provides that any notes or other written instruments evidencing the indebtedness shall bear on their face an appropriate legend stating that such notes or instruments are issued subject to the provisions of a subordination agreement which shall be adequately referred to an incorporated by reference, the terms of which shall take precedence over any inconsistent terms of any such note or instrument;

(f) It provides that the securities or other property loaned to the broker or dealer pursuant to its provisions may be used and dealt with by the broker or dealer as part of his capital and shall in all respects be subject to the risks of the business as then or thereafter in any way conducted. (The language should be clear and unequivocal so that the lender will fully understand that the securities and/or other property are at the risk of the business).

(g) Any provision for substitution of securities should include the following terms:
   (1) All new securities are to be as marketable as the old;
   (2) All securities substituted for cash are to have a ready market;
   (3) The new securities are to have a market value not less than that of the old;
   (4) No substitution may produce a result inconsistent with Rule 240.15c3-1.

II.

PROCEDURE

The agreement shall be signed by each party thereto and each signature shall be acknowledged before a Notary Public. If the

Notary Public be of a state other than the state in which the broker or dealer has its principal place of business, a county clerk's certificate or comparable evidence of the notary's authority and the genuineness of his signature shall be attached.

The executed agreement is to be submitted to this office for review for compliance with Rules 240.15c3-1 and 240.17a-3, together with the following:

(a) Two conformed copies of the agreement;

(b) Two copies of an opinion of counsel covering the following:

    (1) Compliance with paragraph I(a) above;

    (2) In the case of a corporate lender, the existence of corporate authority to enter into the agreement and due execution thereof by corporate officers;

    (3) The binding effect of the agreement upon the parties thereto;

    (4) The good title of the lender to the securities or monies which are the subject of the loan and whether there is any incumbrance thereon that would impair the effectiveness of the loan.

(c) Satisfactory evidence that the broker or dealer has reflected the fact of subordination of the subordinated obligation by appropriately identifying it on the broker's or dealer's books in a special account such as "Special Account, John Doe, Subordinated."

(d) Two conformed copies of any notes or other written instruments evidencing the indebtedness subordinated by the agreement, or a written representation that none exists.

Sec. 25-15. Appendix O—Customer's agreement (association of stock exchange firms).

ASEF—Form 101—Revised July, 1955

Gentlemen:

In consideration of your accepting one or more accounts of the undersigned (whether designated by name, number or otherwise) and your agreeing to act as brokers for the undersigned in the purchase or sale of securities or commodities, the undersigned agrees as follows:

1. All transactions under this agreement shall be subject to the constitution, rules, regulations, customs and usages of the exchange or market, and its clearing house, if any, where the transactions are executed by you or your agents, and, where applicable, to the provisions of the Securities Exchange Act of 1934, the Commodities Exchange Act, the present and future acts amendatory thereof and supplemental thereto, and the rules and regulations of the Federal Securities and Exchange Commission, the Board of Governors of the Federal Reserve System and of the Secretary of Agriculture in so far as they may be applicable.

2. Whenever any statute shall be enacted which shall affect in any manner or be inconsistent with any of the provisions hereof, or whenever any rule or regulation shall be prescribed or promulgated by the New York Stock Exchange, the Federal Securities and Exchange Commission, the Board of Governors of the Federal Reserve System and/or the Secretary of Agriculture which shall affect in any manner or be inconsistent with any of the provisions hereof, the provisions of this agreement so affected shall be deemed modified or superseded, as the case may be, by such statute, rule or regulation, and all other provisions of the agreement and the provisions as so modified or superseded, shall in all respects continue and be in full force and effect.

3. Except as herein otherwise expressly provided, no provision of this agreement shall in any respect be waived, altered, modified or amended unless such waiver, alteration, modification or amendment be committed to writing and signed by a member of your organization.

4. All monies, securities, commodities or other property which you may at any time be carrying for the undersigned or which may at any time be in your possession for any purpose, including safekeeping, shall be subject to a general lien for the discharge of all obligation of the undersigned to you, irrespective of whether or not you have made advances in connection with such securities, commodities or other property, and irrespective of the number of accounts the undersigned may have with you.

5. All securities and commodities or any other property, now or hereafter held by you, or carried by you for the undersigned (either individually or jointly with others), or deposited to secure the same, may from time to time and without notice to me, be carried in your general loans and may be pledged, re-pledged, hypothecated or re-hypothecated, separately or in common with other securities and commodities or any other property, for the sum due to you thereon or for a greater sum and without retaining in your possession and control for delivery a like amount of similar securities or commodities.

6. Debit balances of the accounts of the undersigned shall be charged with interest, in accordance with your usual custom, and with any increases in rates caused by money market conditions, and with such other charges as you may make to cover your facilities and extra services.

7. You are hereby authorized, in your discretion, should the undersigned die or should you for any reason whatsoever deem it necessary for your protection, to sell any or all of the securities and commodities or other property which may be in your possession, or which you may be carrying for the undersigned (either individually or jointly with others), or to buy in any securities commodities or other property of which the account or accounts of the undersigned may be short, or cancel any outstanding orders in order to close

out the account or accounts of the undersigned in whole or in part or in order to close out any commitment made in behalf of the undersigned. Such sale, purchase or cancellation may be made according to your judgment and may be made, at your discretion, on the exchange or other market where such business is then usually transacted, or at public auction or at private sale, without advertising the same and without notice to the undersigned or to the personal representatives of the undersigned, and without prior tender, demand or call of any kind upon the undersigned or upon the personal representatives of the undersigned, and you may purchase the whole or any part thereof free from any right of redemption, and the undersigned shall remain liable for any deficiency; it being understood that a prior tender, demand or call of any kind from you, or prior notice from you, of the time and place of such sale or purchase shall not be considered a waiver of your right to sell or buy any securities and/or commodities and/or other property held by you, or owed you by the undersigned, at any time as hereinbefore provided.

8. The undersigned will at all times maintain margins for said accounts, as required by you from time to time.

9. The undersigned undertakes, at any time upon your demand, to discharge obligations of the undersigned to you, or, in the event of a closing of any account of the undersigned in whole or in part, to pay you the deficiency, if any, and no oral agreement or instructions to the contrary shall be recognized or enforceable.

10. In case of the sale of any security, commodity, or other property by you at the direction of the undersigned and your inability to deliver the same to the purchaser by reason of failure of the undersigned to supply you therewith, then and in such event, the undersigned authorizes you to borrow any security, commodity, or other property necessary to make delivery thereof, and the undersigned hereby agreees to be responsible for any loss which you may sustain thereby and any premiums which you may be required to pay thereon, and for any loss which you may sustain by reason of your inability to borrow the security, commodity, or other property sold.

11. At any time and from time to time, in your discretion, you may without notice to the undersigned, apply and/or transfer any or all monies, securities, commodities and/or other property of the undersigned interchangeably between any accounts of the undersigned (other than from Regulated Commodity Accounts).

12. It is understood and agreed that the undersigned, when placing with you any sell order for short account, will designate it as such and hereby authorizes you to mark such order as being "short," and when placing with you any order for long account, will designate it as such and hereby authorizes you to mark such orders as being "long." Any sell order which the undersigned shall designate as being for long account as above provided, is for securities then owned by the undersigned and, if such securities are not then de-

liverable by you from any account of the undersigned, the placing of such order shall constitute a representation by the undersigned that it is impracticable for him then to deliver such securities to you but that he will deliver them as soon as it is possible for him to do so without undue inconvenience or expense.

13. In all transactions between you and the undersigned, the undersigned understands that you are acting as the brokers of the undersigned, except when you disclose to the undersigned in writing at or before the completion of a particular transaction that you are acting, with respect to such transaction, as dealers for your own account or as brokers for some other person.

14. Reports of the execution of orders and statements of the accounts of the undersigned shall be conclusive if not objected to in writing, the former within two days, and the latter within ten days, after forwarding by you to the undersigned by mail or otherwise.

15. Communications may be sent to the undersigned at the address of the undersigned given below, or at such other address as the undersigned may hereafter give you in writing, and all communications so sent, whether by mail, telegraph, messenger or otherwise, shall be deemed given to the undersigned personally, whether actually received or not.

16. Any controversy between you and the undersigned arising out of or relating to this contract or the breach thereof, shall be settled by arbitration, in accordance with the rules, then obtaining, of either the Arbitration Committee of the Chamber of Commerce of the State of New York, or the American Arbitration Association, or the Board of Arbitration of the New York Stock Exchange, as the undersigned may elect. It the undersigned does not make such election by registered mail addressed to you at your main office within five (5) days after receipt of notification from you requesting such election, then the undersigned authorizes you to make such election in behalf of the undersigned. Any arbitration hereunder shall be before at least three arbitrators and the award of the arbitrators, or of a majority of them, shall be final, and judgment upon the award rendered may be entered in any court, state or federal, having jurisdiction.

17. This agreement and its enforcement shall be governed by the laws of the State of New York and its provisions shall be continuous; shall cover individually and collectively all acounts which the undersigned may open or re-open with you, and shall endure to the benefit of your present organization, and any successor organization, irrespective of any change or changes at any time in the personnel thereof, for any cause whatsoever, and of the assigns of your present organization or any successor organization, and shall be binding upon the undersigned, and/or the estate, executors, administrators and assigns of the undersigned.

18. The undersigned, if an individual, represents that the under-

signed is of full age, that the undersigned is not an employee of any exchange, or of any corporation of which any exchange owns a majority of the capital stock, or of a member of any exchange, or of a member firm or member corporation registered on any exchange, or of a bank, trust company, insurance company or of any corporation, firm or individual engaged in the business of dealing, either as broker or as principal, in securities, bills of exchange, acceptances or other forms or commercial paper. The undersigned further represents that no one except the undersigned has an interest in the account or accounts of the undersigned with you.

Very truly yours,

Witness, _____   _____

Dated, _____   _____

     _____   _____

       (City)   (State)

CUSTOMER'S LOAN CONSENT

Until you receive written notice of revocation from the undersigned, you are hereby authorized to lend, to yourselves as brokers or to others, any securities held by you on margin for the account of, or under the control of, the undersigned.

Dated, _____   _____

       (City)   (State)

Witness, _____   _____

Sec. 25-16. Appendix P—Sample Escrow Agreement—best efforts, all-or-none underwriting.

To _____ Bank, Escrow Agent

The undersigned, _____ as Underwriter, and (a corporation), as Issuer, have entered into an underwriting agreement pursuant to which the Underwriter has agreed to use its best efforts to sell and distribute 100,000 shares of Common Stock of the Issuer at an aggregate price of $300,000.00. The nature of the underwriting commitment is that, unless all of the 100,000 shares have been sold and paid for within 60 days from the effective date of the public offering, the offering will be withdrawn and all of the money will be refunded to the respective purchasers.

The public offering is required to be commenced not later than the tenth full business day after the effective date of the Notification filed with the Securities and Exchange Commission pursuant to Regulation A of the Rules and Regulations promulgated under the Securities Act of 1933, as amended.

The gross proceeds from the sale of the offered shares, up to a total of $300,000, will be deposited by the Underwriter with you as Escrow Agent on the terms and conditions hereinafter set forth. At or before the time of making the initial deposit hereunder, you will be notified in writing by the Underwriter of the effective date of the public offering.

Purchasers of the stock will be instructed to remit the purchase price in the form of checks, drafts or other instruments for the payment of money, payable to your order as ESCROW AGENT. Such payments will be remitted directly to the Underwriter by the purchasers and each day's receipts will be delivered by the Underwriter to you before 3:00 P.M. on the following business day, together with duplicate copies of its confirmation slips showing the names and addresses of the persons subscribing for the offered shares. Any cash received by the Underwriter on account of the purchase price of such shares will likewise be delivered to you before 3:00 P.M. on the following business day.

The aforesaid checks, drafts, etc., are to be collected by you, but only if properly endorsed or otherwise in such forms as shall permit the immediate collection by you, and the proceeds thereof, together with all cash delivered to you hereunder, are to be held in escrow until the total amount of such cash and proceeds reaches the sum of $300,000.00.

In the event that you do not receive from the Underwriters, within 60 days from the effective date of the public offering as reported to you by the Underwriter, cash and checks, drafts, etc., aggregating $300,000.00. or in the event that such cash and checks, drafts, etc. in the aggregate sum of $300,000,00 are received but not collected within the aforesaid period and a normal collection period, even though such collection period may extend beyond such period, you shall issue and deliver by ordinary mail your checks to each person named in a confirmation slip delivered to you by the Underwriter to the address shown on such slip, for the amount set forth thereon, and you shall notify the issuer and the Underwriter of your distribution of the funds received and collected by you, as aforementioned; provided, however, that such distribution shall be made only in respect of funds in hand in cash with you at such time.

Written notice of the Effective Date of the Notification and Offering Circular, aforementioned, shall be given to you on the date thereof by _____, counsel for the Underwriter.

Upon your collection of the full $300,000.00, you shall pay therefrom to the Underwriter, $_____ less your compensation and the balance to the issuer and deliver to the issuer's then acting Transfer Agent, the instruction received by you with respect to the issuance and delivery of the said 100,000 shares and you will be under no further responsibility with respect to this Escrow Agreement.

It is understood and agreed, further, that you shall:

(a) be under no duty or responsibility to enforce any of the terms or conditions of the underwriting agreement between the Issuer and the Underwriter or to enforce payment of the purchase price for any shares of Common Stock of the Issuer subscribed to pursuant to the public offering and sale contemplated herein;

(b) be under no duty or responsibility to accept any confirmation slips hereunder from the Underwriter unless the same are accompanied by cash, checks, drafts or other instruments for the payment of money which are immediately negotiable and collectible, but you shall promptly notify the Underwriter of any discrepency between the amount set forth on any confirmation slip and the sum or sums delivered to you therewith, nor will you be required to keep records or any information on checks, drafts or other instruments received or collected by you except as to the amount of same;

(c) be under no duty or responsibility to enforce collection of any check, draft or other instrument for the payment of money delivered to you hereunder, but you shall promptly notify and return to the Underwriter any check, draft, etc., upon which payment is refused, together with the confirmation slip which was delivered to you with such check, draft, etc.;

(d) be protected in acting upon any notice, request, certificate, approval, consent, confirmation slip or other paper believed by you to be genuine and to be signed by the proper party or parties, it being understood that all notices, requests, certificates, approvals, consents, confirmation slips or other papers delivered to you on behalf of the Underwriter, shall be signed by _____.

(e) be deemed conclusively to have given and delivered any notice required to be given or delivered hereunder if the same is in writing, signed by anyone of your authorized officers and mailed by ordinary first class mail in a sealed postpaid wrapper, addressed to the Issuer at _____.
And to the Underwriter at _____.

(f) be entitled to consult with your counsel and shall not be liable for any action taken or omitted by you in accordance with the opinion and advice of such counsel whether such counsel be a member of your house counsel staff or independent counsel.

(g) be indemnified by the Underwriter and Issuer against any claim or charge made against you by reason of your acting or failure to act in connection with any of the transactions contemplated hereby, except as a result of your gross negligence or wilful neglect; and

(h) be entitled to reasonable compensation and be reimbursed for expenses (including collection expenses), including fees and expenses of your counsel, which compensation and reimbursement shall be paid by the Underwriter.

Yours very truly,

_____
Underwriter

The foregoing escrow arrangements are satisfactory in form and substance to us and you are authorized to proceed in accordance therewith.

_____
Issuer

The foregoing terms and conditions of the escrow agreement as set forth above are hereby accepted and agreed to this _____ day of _____.

_____
Escrow Agent

Sec. 25-17. Appendix Q—Form X-17A-1 (Stabilization Report).

Adopted February 13, 1942
Revised February 1, 1958

SECURITIES AND EXCHANGE COMMISSION
Washington 25, D. C.

FORM X-17A-1

Report Pursuant to Rule 240.17a-2

Title of security covered by this report _____

Filed by _____ As manager ☐ Not as manager ☐
(Check one)

Period covered by this report _____
(See paragraph III below)   (Use trade dates only)

INSTRUCTIONS

I. **WHO MUST FILE:** (a) Any issuer, vendor, underwriter, dealer or other person who makes, for his sole account or for the account of a syndicate or group, any stabilizing purchase to facilitate an offering of a security registered under the Securities Act of 1933, or offered pursuant to an exemption from registration under Regulation A or any offering where the aggregate offering price exceeds $300,000, should file "as manager." (b) Every other member of any such syndicate or group should file "not as manager."

II. **WHAT TRANSACTIONS MUST BE REPORTED:** All purchases, sales and transfers in the stabilized and offered securities for your own account or as a broker, and if the offering be a rights offering, in the rights.

III. **PERIOD TO BE COVERED:** Begins on the ninth business day prior to the first day on which the offering was made or on the business day prior to the day on which the manager made the first stabilizing purchase, whichever is earlier, and ends on the day stabilizing was terminated. If the _manager_ has a short position at termination he must continue to file until the short position is covered. (See paragraph IV, part (c), below.)

IV. **INSTRUCTIONS FOR A SOLE STABILIZER OR FOR A MANAGER:** (a) Any person who makes a stabilizing purchase for his sole account (e.g., sole underwriter, issuer, vendor, etc.) should file reports *only* "as manager." (b) Any person who makes transactions on behalf of a syndicate or group should report **"as manager"** only the transactions made on behalf of such syndicate or group. Transactions for his own account as an underwriter should be filed in a separate report "not as manager." (c) A person reporting "as manager" should file an initial report with the Commission not later than the third business day after the day on which his first stabilizing purchase was made. An additional report should be filed for each subsequent day on which he makes a transaction in either the stabilized or offered security (or rights of any) until such stabilizing is terminated. If he has a short position at termination he should continue to file until such short position is covered. All reports covering transactions subsequent to the initial stabilizing purchase should be filed the day after the transaction was made. (d) **Separate reports should be filed for each security offered or stabilized.** (e) The manager should promptly notify the members of his syndicate or group of the date and time when stabilizing is begun and again when it is terminated. This information, together with the stabilizing price, should also be sent to the Commission.

V. **INSTRUCTIONS "NOT AS MANAGER":** (a) A person reporting **"not as manager"** should file a single report with the Commission on Form X-17A-1 *after stabilizing has terminated,* and within five business days after such termination. (See "Period To Be Covered," paragraph III above.) (b) In item 1, immediately below these instructions, enter all of your agency transactions for the account of others during the "Period To Be Covered," and in item 3, on the other side of this form, enter all take-downs, purchases, sales, and transfers for your own account that were made during the "Period To Be Covered," and total columns C and H. (c) In item 2 indicate your net position at the opening of the first day of the "Period To Be Covered," usually the ninth business day prior to the offering date, and in item 4 indicate your net position at the end of the "Period To Be Covered," the termination of stabilization. (d) **A separate report should be filed for each security offered or stabilized.**

Item 1. PURCHASES AND SALES AS BROKER FOR ANOTHER

Set forth your brokerage transactions in the above security effected during the period or day covered by this report. Purchases or sales on the same day and at the same price may be grouped. USE TRADE DATES, NOT BLOTTER OR DELIVERY DATES. DO NOT ENTER BOTH SIDES OF A TRANSACTION UNLESS YOU ACTED AS BROKER FOR BOTH BUYER AND SELLER. If you had no transactions as broker during the period, write "none."

BOUGHT			SOLD		
DATE	AMOUNT	PRICE	DATE	AMOUNT	PRICE

Item 2. NET POSITION AT BEGINNING

A person reporting **"not as manager"** should set forth below his complete net position as principal at the beginning of the "Period To Be Covered." (See paragraph III above.) A person reporting **"as manager,"** in his initial report, should set forth his complete net position as manager at the beginning of the "Period To Be Covered," and in each subsequent report set forth his complete net position at the beginning of the day covered by each report. **Important**—If you had no position, check the box marked "Even."

_____ Long _____ Short Even [_____]
(Amount)   (Amount)

Item 3. PURCHASES, SALES, AND TRANSFERS AS MANAGER OR AS PRINCIPAL

A person reporting "as manager" should report here all his transactions as manager during the period or day covered by this report. Others should report *all* purchases, sales, and transfers as principal. Use column B or G to identify the transaction using the following words or their abbreviations. Unusual transactions may be explained in a footnote. NOTE.—The term "transfer" means any change in the control of a position in a security unaccompanied by a change in ownership.

ISSUER (ISS) .... A purchase directly from the issuer or vendor, other than through the exercise of rights, of the securities to be distributed.

MANAGER (MGR) ...... A purchase, sale, or transfer from or to the manager.

PARTICIPANT (PART) . A purchase, sale, or transfer from or to any participant in the distribution other than the issuer, vendor, or manager.

EXCHANGE (EXCH) .... The surrender, acquisition, or issuance of a security through exchange, conversion, or redemption.

EXERCISE (EXER) ...... The exercise of rights or the acquisition or issuance of securities through the exercise of rights.

RETAIL (RET) .... Retail sales of the security being distributed at the public offering price.

CANCELLATION (CXL) . The cancellation of a previous purchase, sale, or transfer.

CUSTOMER (CUST) ..... A purchase or sale, not on an exchange, from or to a customer not in the securities business, other than a transaction which may be identified by one of the above titles.

OTC .... A purchase or sale, not on an exchange, other than a transaction which may be identified by one of the above titles.

NYSE, etc. .... A purchase or sale on an exchange. The abbreviation should identify the exchange.

Transactions identified as ISSUER, MANAGER, PARTICIPANT, EXCHANGE, EXERCISE, RETAIL, or CANCELLATION on the same day and at the same price and concession or premium may be grouped under each such heading and totals entered in columns C and H. Times may be disregarded with respect to all transactions so identified. Consecutive purchases or sales on any one day at the same price (and concession or premium, if any) and identified as CUSTOMER, or OTC, or on a particular exchange, may also be grouped. Enter in column E the period of time during which any such group of purchases were effected and the time at which any single purchase so identified was effected. USE TRADE DATES, NOT BLOTTER OR DELIVERY DATES.

BOUGHT					SOLD			
A	B	C	D	E	F	G	H	I
DATE	TYPE OF TRANSACTION	AMOUNT	PRICE [1]	TIME	DATE	TYPE OF TRANSACTION	AMOUNT	PRICE [1]
	TOTAL					TOTAL		

[1] Indicate amount of any concession or premium by use of minus or plus signs (e.g., 100—1½ or 100+½).

Item 4. NET POSITION AT END

A person reporting **"not as manager"** should set forth below his complete net position as principal at the termination of stabilization. A person reporting **"as manager"** should set forth his complete net position as manager at the end of the period covered by his initial report, and in each subsequent report set forth his complete net position at the end of the day covered by each report. **Important—If you had no position, check the box marked "Even."**

_____ Long _____ Short Even [_____]
(Amount) (Amount)

All statements contained herein are true and complete to the best knowledge and belief of the undersigned.

Dated at _____, the _____ day of _____, 196__

By_____
(Signer must be a principal officer or member of the firm)

Sec. 25-18. Appendix R—SEC Release No. 6778 (Prompt Consummation Of Transactions).

For RELEASE Monday, April 16, 1962

SECURITIES AND EXCHANGE COMMISSION
Washington 25, D. C.

SECURITIES EXCHANGE ACT OF 1934
Release No. 6778

SECURITIES ACT OF 1933
Release No. 4476

The Securities and Exchange Commission has announced that during recent months it has received numerous complaints from customers that they have encountered considerable delay in receiving securities they purchased from broker-dealers. Inquiry indicates that in a number of these cases the dealers sold the customers securities which they did not own (short-sales), and did not, for a substantial period of time, effect the off-setting purchase transactions for purposes of delivery. This release is being published to caution broker-dealers that this practice generally involves violations of the anti-fraud provisions of the federal securities laws.

In substance, the anti-fraud provisions of the federal securities laws prohibit any act, practice or course of business which operates as a fraud or deceit, and any untrue statement or misleading omission of a material fact, in connection with the purchase or sale of a security.[1]

---

[1] Section 17(a) of the Securities Act of 1933, Section 10(b) of the Securities Exchange Act of 1934 and Rule 10b-5 thereunder, and Section 15(c)(1) of the Securities Exchange Act of 1934 and Rule 15c 1-2 thereunder.

The courts and the Commission have consistently held that a dealer impliedly represents that he will deal fairly with the public,[2] and that this implied representation of fair dealing includes an implied representation that the transaction will be consummated promptly unless there is a clear understanding to the contrary.[3] In *Lewis H. Ankeny*, 29 S.E.C. 514, at p. 516, the Commission stated:

> "Inherent in the relationship between a dealer and his customer is the vital representation that the customer will be dealt with fairly, and in accordance with the standards of the profession. *Duker & Duker*, 6 S.E.C. 386, 388 (1939). At a minimum, he represents that he will act in accordance with reasonable trade custom. Trade custom requires a dealer to consummate transactions with customers promptly, and in every transaction an implied representation to this effect is made, unless there is a clear understanding to the contrary. If a dealer intends not to consummate a transaction promptly, and fails to disclose this intention to his customer, he omits to state to that customer a material fact necessary to make the above representation not misleading, in violation of the anti-fraud provisions of the Securities Act and the Exchange Act."

The misrepresentation inherent in the above situation is aggravated when the dealer recommends the security and sells it to the customer in a short-sale, but delays effecting the covering transaction to acquire the security. Under these circumstances it is not unreasonable to assume that the dealer delayed the execution of his covering transaction because he believed that by postponing such transaction he would be able to acquire it at a cheaper price; and the failure to disclose this material fact compounds the violation.

Dealers who sell securities to customers should exercise diligence to deliver the securities promptly, and if they have any reason to believe they will be unable to deliver promptly, they should disclose to the customer all material facts with respect thereto before the transaction is entered into.

Sec. 25-19. Appendix S—Excerpts from SEC statement of policy.

(As amended November 5, 1957)

The Securities and Exchange Commission with the assistance of the National Association of Securities Dealers, Inc., in 1950 reviewed samples of advertising and supplemental sales literature used in the sale of investment company shares, much of which was not filed with

[2] *Charles Hughes & Co., Inc.* v. S.E.C., 139 F.2d 434 (CA-3, 1943); *Norris & Hirschberg, Inc.*, 21 S.E.C. 685 (1946), aff'd 177 F.2d 228; *Duker & Duker*, 6 S.E.C. 386 (1939).

[3] *Lewis H. Ankeny*, 29 S.E.C. 514 (1949); *Jessee S. Lockaby*, 29 S.E.C. 271 (1949); *W. F. Coley & Company Inc.*, 31 S.E.C. 722 (1950); *Carl J. Bliedung*, 38 S.E.C. 578 (1958); *Ned J. Bowman*, SEA Rel. 6257 (1960); and *Miller, Smith & Co., Inc.*, SEA Rel. 6663 (1961); cf. *Stephens* v. *United States*, 41 F.2d 440 (CA-9, 1930), cert. denied 282 U. S. 880 (1930).

this Commission. This review revealed the existence of many practices in connection with the use, form and content of certain advertising and sales literature which, in the opinion of the Commission, might violate statutory standards, including provisions of the Securities Act of 1933 and the Investment Company Act of 1940.

The Commission, therefore, has issued the following Statement of Policy so that issuers, underwriters and dealers may understand certain of the types of advertising and sales literature which the Commission considers may be violative of the statutory standards.

It should be emphasized that the following Statement of Policy, as amended, does not attempt to cover all possible abuses, and that literature which complies with this Statement may not be used if it is in fact misleading. Conversely, nothing in this Statement of Policy is intended to prevent the use of factual statements, fairly presented, concerning fundamental investment policies and objectives, investment restrictions or other characteristics of a particular investment company.

"Sales literature" as used hereafter shall be deemed to include any communication (whether in writing, by radio or by television) used by an issuer, underwriter, or dealer to induce the purchase of shares of an investment company. Reports of issuers to the extent they are transmitted to shareholders and do not contain an express offer are not deemed to be "sales literature" within the meaning of this definition but shall conform to this Statement of Policy. Communications between issuers, underwriters and dealers are included in this definition of "sales literature" only if such communications are passed on either orally or in writing or are shown to prospective investors or are designed to be employed in either written or oral form in the sale of securities.

For the purpose of interpreting this Statement of Policy, a piece of sales literature shall be deemed materially misleading by reason of an implication, as contemplated herein, if such sales literature (1) includes an untrue statement of a material fact or (2) omits to state a material fact necessary in order to make a statement made, in the light of the circumstances of its use, not misleading.

It will be considered materially misleading hereafter for sales literature___

Rates of Return

(a) To represent or imply a percentage return on an investment in the shares of an investment company unless based upon___

      (1) Dividends from net investment income paid during a fiscal year related to the average monthly offering price for such fiscal year, provided that if any year prior to the most recent fiscal year is selected for this purpose, the rate of

return for all subsequent fiscal years, similarly calculated, shall also be stated; or

Show Asset Value Change

(2) Dividends paid from net investment income during the twelve months ending not earlier than the close of the calendar month immediately preceding the date of publication related to an offering price current at said date of publication;

in either case the basis of the calculation shall be shown and adjustment made for capital gains distributions and any other factor necessary to make the presentation not misleading. "Net investment income" as used above shall include net accrued undivided earnings included in the price of capital shares issued and repurchased and shall be as required to be included in the issuer's prospectus. Every such statement of return shall be accompanied by a statement to the effect that such return is based upon dividends paid in the period covered and is not a representation of future results. Either in the same text, or by reference in the same text to an historical table elsewhere in the same piece of literature, there must be shown the per-share asset value at the beginning and end of the period, or the increase or decrease (stated in percentage) in asset value.

Capital vs. Income

(b) (1) To combine into any one amount distributions from net investment income and distributions from any other source.

(2) To represent or imply an assurance that an investor will receive a stable, continuous, dependable, or liberal return or that he will receive any specified rate or rates of return.

Explain Risks

(c) To represent or imply an assurance that an investor's capital will increase or that purchase of investment company shares involves a preservation of original capital and a protection against loss in value. To discuss accumulation of capital, preservation of capital, accumulation of an estate, protection against loss of purchasing power, diversification of investments, financial independence or profit possibilities without pointing out or explaining the market risks inherently involved in the investment.

Government Regulation

(d) To make any reference to registration or regulation of any investment company under Federal or state authority without explaining that this does not involve supervision of management or investment practices or policies.

Custodial Services

(e) To represent or imply that services of banking institutions as custodian of securities, transfer agent, or dividend disbursing agent, provide protection for investors against possible depreciation of assets or that such institutions maintain any supervisory function over management in such matters as purchase and sale of portfolio securities or payment of dividends or provide any trusteeship protection, or to fail to state the extent of the limited role of the custodian whenever the advantages of custodial services are discussed.

Redemption

(f) To state or discuss the redemption features of investment company shares without explaining in such statement that the value of the shares on redemption may be more or less than the investor's cost, depending upon the market value of the portfolio securities at the time of redemption.

Comparisons Generally

(g) (1) To represent or imply that shares of an investment company are similar to or as safe as government bonds, insurance annuities, savings accounts or life insurance, or have the fixed income, principal, or any other features of a debt security.

(2) To represent or imply that the management of an investment company is under the same type of investment restrictions or is operated under limitations similar to or has fiduciary obligations such as those imposed by governmental authorities on savings banks and insurance companies, except to the extent that it is so restricted or limited by its statement of policy on file with this Commission.

Comparisons With Market Index or Other Security

(h) To use any comparison of an investment company security with any other security or medium of investment or any security index or average without pointing out—
> (1) that the particular security or index or average and period were selected; and,
> (2) that the results disclosed should be considered in the light of the company's investment policy and objectives,

the characteristics and quality of the company's investments, and the period selected; and,

(3) the material differences or similarities between the subjects of the comparisons; and,

(4) what the comparison is designed to show; and

(5) anything else that may be necessary to make the comparison fair.

New Capital

(i) To represent or imply that investment companies in general are direct sources of new capital to industry or that a particular investment company is such a source unless the extent to which such investments are made is disclosed.

(j) (Item j is omitted)

Management Claims

(k) To make any extravagant claims regarding management ability or competency.

(l) To represent or imply that investment companies are operated as, or are similar to, "co-operatives."

(m) To represent or imply that investment company shares generally have been selected by fiduciaries.

Continuous Investment Programs

(n) (1) To use the phrase "dollar averaging" or "averaging the dollar" (although the phrases "dollar cost averaging" or "cost averaging" are not objectionable) in referring to any plan of continuous investment in the shares of an investment company at stated intervals regardless of the price level of the shares.

Cost Averaging and Contractual Plans

(2) To discuss or portray the principles of dollar cost averaging, or to discuss or portray any Periodic Payment Plan referred to in section 27(a) of the Investment Company Act of 1940, without making clear—

(i) that the investor will incur a loss under such plan if he discontinues the plan when the market value of his accumulated shares is less than his cost; and

(ii) that the investor is investing his funds primarily in securities subject to market fluctuations and that the method involves continuous investment in such shares at regular intervals regardless of price levels; and

(iii) that the investor must take into account his financial ability to continue such plan through periods of low price levels; and

(iv) that such plans do not protect against loss in value in declining markets.

(3) To discuss or portray any other type of continuous investment plan without making clear that such type of investment plan does not assure a profit and does not protect against depreciation in declining markets.

Sales Commissions

(o) To fail to include in any sales literature which does not state the amount or rate of the sales commission (except communications which deal only with routine business matters or which do not purport to discuss or describe any investment company or investment company security) a clear reference to the prospectus or prospectuses for information concerning the sales commission, and other information.

(p) To fail to include in any sales literature which is designed to encourage investors to switch from one investment company to another, or from one class of security of an investment company to another class, the substance of the following statement in a separate paragraph in type as large as that used generally in the body of the piece:

> **"Switching from the securities of one investment company to another, or from one class of security of an investment company to another, involves a sales charge on each such transaction, for details of which see the prospectus. The prospective purchaser should measure these costs against the claimed advantage of the switch."**

Industry Performance against Company Performance

(q) To represent or imply that the performance of any particular company may be measured by or compared with or related to the performance of a particular industry unless the extent and scope of the portfolio of the particular company is such that its performance will generally approximate that of the industry.

Reprints

(r) To employ material in whole or in part from published articles or documents descriptive of or relating to investment companies unless such material, or the literature including such material, complies with this Statement of Policy and in addition such material is not taken out of context in a manner which alters its intended meaning.

Sec. 25-20. Appendix T—SEC Securities Exchange Act Release No. 4445—Distribution by broker-dealers of unregistered securities.

For RELEASE Friday, February 2, 1962

SECURITIES AND EXCHANGE COMMISSION

Washington, D.C.

SECURITIES ACT OF 1933
Release No. 4445
SECURITIES EXCHANGE ACT OF 1934
Release No. 6721

Recent decision of the Courts and of the Securities and Exchange Commission have raised important questions concerning the standards of conduct expected of a registered broker-dealer in connection with the distribution to the public of substantial blocks of unregistered securities, particularly in situations where the securities are those of relatively obscure and unseasoned companies and where all of the circumstances surrounding the proposed distribution are not known to the broker-dealer.[1] Particularly significant are the following: What steps the broker-dealer should take to make sure that he is not participating in an illegal distribution in violation of Section 5 of the Securities Act of 1933? What investigation he should make concerning the issuer in order to avoid violations of the anti-fraud provisions of the federal securities laws in the course of the distribution, and particularly Section 17 of the Securities Act and Section 10(b) of the Securities Exchange Act and Rule 10b-5 thereunder?

In view of certain apparent misconceptions with regard to the responsibilities of a broker-dealer under these circumstances, it seems appropriate to set forth for the guidance of the industry and the Bar certain standards that the Commission believes applicable.

With regard to the registration requirements of the Securities Act of 1933, certain basic principles should be borne in mind. In the first place, Section 5 of the Securities Act of 1933 broadly prohibits the use of the mails or facilities of interstate commerce to sell a security unless a registration statement is in effect. A dealer or other person claiming the benefit of an exemption from this requirement has the

---

[1] *United States* v. *Francis Peter Crosby*, 294 F.2d 928 (C.A. 2, 1961); *SEC* v. *Culpepper*, 270 F.2d 241 (C.A. 2, 1959); *Gilligan, Will & Co.* v. *SEC*, 257 F.2d 461 (C.A. 2, 1959); *SEC* v. *Mono-Kearsarge*, et al, 167 F.Supp. 248 (D. Utah, 1958); *Barnett & Co.*, SEA Rel. 6310; *Best Securities*, SEA Rel. 6282.

burden of proving entitlement to it.[2] Where unregistered securities are offered to a dealer for distribution, exemption is commonly claimed under the first and third clauses of Section 4(1) of the Securities Act which, speaking generally, exempt transactions not involving any distribution by, or for an issuer or for a person controlling, controlled by, or under common control with the issuer. Consequently, in order for this exemption to be available, a dealer must not be participating directly or indirectly in any such distribution. He may become such a participant even if he has no direct contractual relationship or privity with an issuer or person in a control relationship if he, in fact, engaged in steps necessary to such a distribution.[3] Section 4(1) exempts trading transactions between individual investors with respect to securities already issued. It does not exempt distributions by issuers or control persons or acts of other individuals who engage in steps necessary to such distribution.[4] Consequently, a dealer who offers to sell, or is asked to sell a substantial amount of securities must take whatever steps are necessary to be sure that this is a transaction not involving an issuer, person in a control relationship with an issuer or an underwriter. For this purpose, it is not sufficient for him merely to accept "self-serving statements of his sellers and their counsel without reasonably exploring the possibility of contrary facts."[5]

The amount of inquiry called for necessarily varies with the circumstances of particular cases. A dealer who is offered a modest amount of a widely traded security by a responsible customer, whose lack of relationship to the issuer is well known to him, may ordinarily proceed with considerable confidence. On the other hand, when a dealer is offered a substantial block of a little-known security, either by persons who appear reluctant to disclose exactly where the securities came from, or where the surrounding circumstances raise a question as to whether or not the ostensible sellers may be merely intermediaries for controlling persons or statutory underwriters, then searching inquiry is called for.

The problem becomes particularly acute where substantial amounts of a previously little known security appear in the trading markets within a fairly short period of time and without the benefit of registration under the Securities Act of 1933. In such situations, it must be assumed that these securities emanate from the issuer or from persons controlling the issuer, unless some other source is known and the fact that the certificates may be registered in the names of various individuals could merely indicate that those responsible for the distribution are attempting to cover their tracks.

---

[2] *SEC* v. *Ralston Purina*, 346 U. S. 119 (1953); *Gilligan, Will & Co.* v. *SEC*, *supra*, note 1; *SEC* v. *Culpepper*, *supra*, note 1; and *Edwards* v. *United States*, 312 U. S. 473 (1941).

[3] *SEC* v. *Culpepper*, *supra*, note 1.

[4] *SEC* v. *Chinese Consolidated Benevolent Association*, 120 F.2d 738 (1941), cert. denied, 314 U. S. 618; *SEC* v. *Culpepper*, *supra*, note 1.

[5] *SEC* v. *Culpepper*, *supra*, note 1. See also *SEC* v. *Mono-Kearsarge Consolidated Mining Company*, *supra*, note 1.

In *United States* v. *Crosby*,[6] the court found persuasive the contention of defendant dealers that, in selling large blocks of unregistered stock of Texas-Adams Oil Co., Inc., in reliance on a legal opinion based upon incomplete facts, they were "doing business as usual" and, to their best knowledge, according to acceptable standards. The court perhaps found this argument persuasive in the context of that criminal conspiracy trial, since no evidence to the contrary was before it. The experience of the Commission, however, clearly demonstrates that the conduct of these dealers did not meet acceptable standards. Not only did the transactions in fact violate Section 5 of the Securities Act, as the court found, but the surrounding circumstances made such violations altogether likely. Shortly after the transfer of control of Texas-Adams to a small group of related persons, large blocks of unregistered stock commenced to appear in the market, accompanied by a drumfire of optimistic publicity from the management, obviously designed to keep the price of the stock up. In such situations, responsible dealers, aware that they have the burden of proving the availability of an exemption,[7]__and confronted with both an absolute liability to buyers under Section 12(1) of the Securities Act, and with the possibility of civil, administrative, or criminal proceedings—proceed with far more caution than was displayed in the Texas-Adams case, and the Commission expects, and will continue to expect, all dealers to do so. It was up to these dealers to make an appropriate investigation as to who their seller was[8] and not simply to rely upon the opinion of the seller's attorney that no control relationship existed.

There have been a number of cases in which dealers have unsuccessfully sought to justify a claim to exemption under Section 4(1) of the Securities Act simply by securing from the sellers, actual or ostensible, representations that such persons are neither officers, directors, nor large stockholders of the issuer, and submitting such representations to an attorney who then gives an opinion to the effect that, assuming the correctness of such representations, exemption under Section 4(1) is available. Obviously, an attorney's opinion based upon hypothetical facts is worthless if the facts are not as specified, or if unspecified but vital facts are not considered. Because of this, it is the practice of responsible counsel not to furnish an opinion concerning the availability of an exemption from registration under the Securities Act for a contemplated distribution unless such counsel have themselves carefully examined all of the relevant circumstances and satisfied themselves, to the extent possible, that the contemplated transaction is, in fact, not a part of an unlawful distribution. Indeed, if an attorney furnishes an opinion based solely upon hypothetical facts which he has made no effort to verify, and if he knows that his opinion

---

[6] *Supra,* note 1.

[7] *Ralston-Purina supra,* note 2. *Gilligan, Will, supra,* note 1; *SEC* v. *Culpepper, supra,* note 1.

[8] The seller turned out to be a nominee for the controlling group and the brother-in-law of one of them.

will be relied upon as the basis for a substantial distribution of un-registered securities, a serious question arises as to the propriety of his professional conduct.[9]

A broker-dealer undertaking the sale of a block of securities under the circumstances referred to herein has the further problem of avoid-ing conduct which will violate the anti-fraud provisions of the federal securities laws. In making such a distribution, he will probably find it necessary, or at least desirable, to recommend purchase of the se-curity by his customers. The Commission has, however, repeatedly held that it is a violation of the anti-fraud provisions for a broker-dealer to recommend a security unless there is an adequate and rea-sonable basis for the recommendations[10] and, further, that such recom-mendations should not be made without disclosure of facts known or reasonably ascertainable, bearing upon the justification for the recommendation.[11] As indicated, the making of recommendations for the purchase of a security implies that the dealer has a reasonable basis for such recommendations which, in turn, requires that, as a prerequisite, he shall have made a reasonable investigation. In addi-tion, if such a dealer lacks essential information about the issuer, such as knowledge of its financial condition, he must disclose this lack of knowledge and caution customers as to the risk involved in purchasing the securities without it.[12]

In view of the foregoing principles, it would appear that if a dealer undertakes the retail distribution of a block of securities with-out obtaining reliable information concerning the issuer, there is a substantial risk that he will violate the anti-fraud provisions of the securities laws, either by making recommendations without an ade-quate basis or by failing to disclose the absence of available informa-tion. Indeed, a serious question arises as to whether a dealer who undertakes an aggressive retail distribution to individuals of an ob-scure, unregistered security, with regard to which reliable information is not readily available, can meet his obligation to treat customers fairly and in accordance with the standards of the profession.[13] The mere fact that a security may allegedly be exempt from the registra-tion requirements of the Securities Act of 1933 does not relieve a dealer of these obligations. On the contrary, it may increase his re-sponsibilities, since neither he nor his customers receive the protection which registration under the Securities Act is designed to provide.

---

[9] In *United States* v. *Crosby, supra,* note 1, the court appears to have regarded the giving of such opinions as significant evidence supporting a jury finding that an attorney was guilty as a co-conspirator.

[10] *Leonard Burton,* SEA Rel. 5798; *Barnett & Co., supra,* note 1. *MacRobbins & Co.,* SEA Rel. 6462; *Midland Securities Inc.,* SEA Rel. 6524.

[11] *Leonard Burton, supra,* note 10; *Best Securities, supra,* note 1.

[12] *MacRobbins & Co., Inc., supra,* note 10.

[13] *Best Securities, supra,* note 1.

Sec. 25-21. Appendix U—SEC Securities Exchange Act Release No. 7290—Proposed rule Restricting floor trading.
For RELEASE Thursday, April 9, 1964

SECURITIES AND EXCHANGE COMMISSION
Washington, D. C.

SECURITIES EXCHANGE ACT OF 1934
Release No. 7290

The Securities and Exchange Commission announced that it has under consideration a proposal to adopt a rule under the Securities Exchange Act of 1934 ("Exchange Act") and particularly Sections 11(a) and 23(a) thereof to limit or restrict floor trading on national securities exchanges. In releasing the text of the proposed rule, the Commission invited views and comments of the securities industry and of any interested groups or persons. The rule makes provision for exemption of smaller national securities exchanges where the volume of floor trading is not substantial.

"Floor trading" is trading by members of national securities exchanges for their own account while personally present on the trading floor of an exchange. For reasons explained below the discussion will relate primarily to floor trading on the New York Stock Exchange.

The functions of members participating in execution of securities transactions on the floor of the New York Stock Exchange ("Exchange") are of three types: specialists, floor brokers, and odd-lot dealers and their associate brokers. The rules of the Exchange permit members of all three types to also engage in floor trading. In his capacity as a floor trader, the member's role is unique, for it is only in that capacity that he is not assigned, and does not assume, any responsibility in the handling of orders on the Exchange. Floor brokers and specialists must meet fiduciary standards of behavior in executing agency orders. Odd-lot dealers acting through their associate brokers on the floor consider themselves obligated to fill every odd-lot order placed with them. Specialists must, in certain situations, buy stock or sell stock. The actions of a member as a floor trader are dictated only by his personal desire to trade profitably, for his own account, on the floor of the Exchange.

At the present time, there are over 400 members of the Exchange who engage intermittently in floor trading. Of these, there are approximately 35 members of the New York Stock Exchange whose primary activity is floor trading. The number of members predominantly engaged in floor trading has remained fairly constant over the years but since 1950 the number of casual floor traders has shown a significant increase. The volume of floor trading, on the other hand, has declined since 1937 from 61 million shares to 44.7 million shares in 1961, or from 6.8 percent of total Exchange purchases and sales to

2.1 percent. At the same time, studies have consistently shown that floor trading is concentrated in the more active stocks. Thus, in certain stocks floor trading has amounted to over 35 percent of total reported volume on selected days; during shorter periods, floor traders have, on occasion, participated in virtually every transaction in particular stocks.

The proposed rule would restrict floor trading by a member of a national securities exchange for any account in which he has an interest or in which he is vested with more than the usual broker's discretion by prohibiting such trading unless it comes under specified exemptions or conditions. The proposed rule would exempt transactions of specialists and odd-lot dealers in the performance of their respective functions. Bona fide arbitrage transactions and stabilizing transactions effected in connection with the distribution of securities would be exempted. Certain other transactions effected with the approval of a floor official to assist in maintaining a fair and orderly market would also be exempted. Finally the proposed rule exempts transactions effected in conformity with a plan which is designed to eliminate floor trading activities not beneficial to the market, adopted by an exchange and approved by the Commission.

The Commission's proposal is directed solely to the question of floor trading and is not concerned with the issue of off-floor trading generally, except where off-floor trading is employed to evade the floor trading restrictions. Furthermore, the Report of the Special Study of Securities Markets made no recommendation in the area of segregation, i.e. that members be prohibited from both dealing in stocks, and acting as brokers, and the Commission is not considering any such proposals.

In view of the interest which has been expressed in this matter, it seems appropriate to provide some explanation of the background of the proposal.

LEGISLATIVE HISTORY

In Section 2 of the Exchange Act Congress found it "necessary to provide for regulation and control" of securities transactions and related practices and "to make such regulation and control reasonably complete and effective, in order to . . . insure the maintenance of fair and honest markets. . . ." Particular evils at which such regulation was to be directed as set forth in Section 2 were manipulation, excessive speculation and sudden and unreasonable fluctuations in the prices of securities. Goals sought to be obtained are "fair dealing," "a fair and orderly market" and such regulation as is "necessary or appropriate in the public interest or for the protection of investors."[1] To this end, manipulation and the use of manipulative and deceptive

---

[1] See Exchange Act, Section 6(d), Section 11, and Section 19(b); See also Report of the Special Study of Securities Markets, Pt. 2, pp. 13ff.

devices are defined and prohibited, and excessive trading by members and the activities of certain classes of members are subjected to regulation. It is in the context of these evils and these objectives that the Commission views its duties and responsibilities in respect to floor trading.

Trading by members of exchanges for their own account was a matter which particularly concerned Congress in its consideration of the legislation of 1934. As enacted, that statute included in Section 11(a) the following broad grant of authority to the Commission:

"Section 11. (a) The Commission shall prescribe such rules and regulations as it deems necessary or appropriate in the public interest or for the protection of investors, (1) to regulate or prevent floor trading by members of national securities exchanges, directly or indirectly for their own account or for discretionary accounts. . . ."

Earlier drafts of the legislation contemplated complete segregation of the function of broker and dealer and, as an incident thereto, major modifications in the specialist system and the complete prohibition of floor trading. Congressional attention in this area was primarily focused upon the first two of these propositions, and the legislative history with respect to the treatment of floor trading in the statute is scant. Testimony by proponents of the legislation noted the special advantages enjoyed by floor traders because of their presence on the floor, their tendency to trade with the trend, and the conflicts of interest involved in acting as both a floor trader and commission broker. In defense of floor trading it was argued that the practice contributed to the maintenance of continuous and liquid markets. Thus the theme was set for subsequent discussions of the problem.

The reason for the ultimate decision to vest responsibility in the Commission to regulate or to prohibit floor trading was stated by Congressman Lea on the floor as follows:

"When we came to the question of the broker and the dealer, a good deal of controversy was involved as to what control should be established; whether or not these positions should be separated; whether or not we would permit a man to act in the capacity of both broker and dealer; whether or not we should permit floor trading or permit specialists to be on the floor; and other problems.

"In attempting to deal with these questions I am candid to admit that the committee proposed to confer a large regulatory power on the regulatory Commission.

"There were two reasons for this: the first was that we recognized we are not experts and tried to act with a caution becoming our inexperience. Where in doubt as to what should be done, we thought it better to resolve the doubt in favor of maintaining the present business practices than to establish some fixed rule that might prove unfortunate. In the second place, where we gave the regulatory Commission the power, it would be a flexible power. If the Commission finds a mistake has been made, it can readily change its rules to more favorable ones and thus accomplish the purposes of Congress." (78th Cong. Rec. 7862 (1934))

The reasons for vesting in the Commission the responsibility to regulate or prohibit floor trading were thus essentially two-fold: lack of experience with these problems on the part of Congress, and the need for flexibility. In view of this legislative history, the Commission regards this provision of the Exchange Act as a mandate to attempt regulation of floor trading; but if such regulation does not accomplish the statutory purposes, the alternative, expressly provided by Congress, is prohibition.

OBJECTIONS TO, AND DEFENSE OF, FLOOR TRADING

Orders to buy and sell securities flow through commission houses to the floor of the Exchange from buyers and sellers in all parts of the world. The Exchange holds itself out as, and in the general is, an efficient and effective mechanism for the orderly execution of these orders. It maintains a specialist system designed to provide reasonable price continuity and to maintain a fair and orderly market in each issue traded. The floor trader, however, by his short-swing speculations frequently interferes with the orderly execution of public brokerage orders in a normal fashion through the facilities provided for that purpose by delaying consummation of a public transaction or causing it to be executed at a different price than it otherwise would, to the detriment of one or the other of the public customers involved. Floor traders, to the extent that they engage in destabilizing transactions make it more difficult for the specialist to perform his functions. The public has no way of knowing the impact of floor trader's activities on the functioning of the market generally or in particular securities.

The potential harmful effect of the floor trader upon prices and, in some instances, upon the volume of trading in a security stems from his central position in the market place, his freeedom from obligations such as those to which the specialist is committed, his mobility on the floor, and his agility in the actual trading process.

In pursuance of the Congressional mandate the Commission has since 1934 performed studies of floor trading on at least 15 occasions. The most comprehensive were those conducted in 1936, 1945, and, most recently, in 1962-63 by the Special Study of Securities Markets (Pt. 2, pp. 203-242).

Commission studies make it clear that floor trading possesses special characteristics which result from floor traders' presence on the floor. From this strategic position, trading activity may be observed minutes before it appears on the tape, and bids or offers may be made or withdrawn in a matter of seconds. In addition, presence on the floor carries with it the benefit of what has been termed the "feel of the market"—a heightened sense of market tenor and trend. This is attributable, among other things, to the exchange of observations among floor members, and familiarity with the trading techniques of specialists or floor brokers, with a resulting ability to foresee short-term market movements by informed observation of the activities of other persons on the floor.

This position has important consequences. Being first on the scene as a market movement commences, the floor trader can buy stock quicker and at a lower price, or sell it quicker and at a higher price. This, of course, is done at the expense of some members of the public.

It is thus apparent that the floor trader enjoys certain advantages over public investors as well as other professionals not on the floor. A question consequently arises as to the extent to which the floor trader's ability to exploit these advantages must be restricted in order to meet the statutory objective of "fair and honest markets" and its strictures against sudden and unreasonable fluctuations in securities prices.

There is inherent in floor trading an opportunity and an incentive to engage in a course of conduct which is inconsistent with the statutory purposes and scheme. For example, a floor trader, familiar with the fact that certain commission brokers handle a large number of orders and do not execute them all at once, can anticipate from their appearance in the market that further substantial buying is forthcoming; and, it is extremely doubtful whether trading on this information, which is unavailable to the investing public, is consistent with "fair dealing" or with the anti-fraud provisions of Rule 10b-5 under the Exchange Act.

Where floor traders rush to a security in which buying exists or is anticipated, and, by a succession of purchases at rising prices, interspersed with those of the public, arouse and capitalize upon public reaction to the activity shown on the tape, the consequences are hardly distinguishable from those of a manipulation, whether or not a violation of Section 9 of the Exchange Act is intended or can be established. Similar questions arise where he trades in anticipation of the rally which is apt to follow the "clean up" of a large sell order overhanging the market.

Evidence in the Commission's possession indicates that such conduct does occur and, indeed, a substantial number of members on the floor have complained of such activities. In the nature of things, it is impossible to determine how often these things happen. But, as noted, the opportunity and incentive for such conduct is inherent in floor trading; and, while the Exchange endeavors to prevent such abuses, its efforts to do so have not been successful. Indeed, under present concepts of floor trading, these efforts could hardly be expected to be successful except perhaps by an inordinate expenditure of time and money.

These problems are compounded where commission brokers handling public orders simultaneously engage in floor trading. A conflict of interest at once arises between the commission broker's duty of fidelity to his customer and his opportunity to personally profit from his customer's investment decisions—perhaps at the customer's expense. Floor trading may also distract brokers, as well as specialists, from the performance of their responsibilities. This conflict has been recognized in an exchange rule which prohibits a member from trading for his own account in a security if he has an unexecuted customer's market order in that security, and by member firms which have restricted or prohibited floor trading by their floor members. The exchange rule and the voluntary action of some firms do not insure that the floor broker's duty of fidelity to his customer is not compromised by his own floor trading activity.

Floor trading has been defended on the grounds that added market liquidity and continuity have been a beneficial byproduct of the presence of professionals on the floor. The exchanges have suggested that this advantage to the market as a whole more than outweighs the possible injury to public investors. Commission studies, however, demonstrate, first, that added liquidity standing alone cannot justify floor trading that is otherwise harmful and, secondly, that floor trading actually tends to have a destabilizing influence on prices. Studies have shown that floor traders are generally buyers in rising markets and sellers in declining markets, with respect to both the market as a whole and to individual stocks. Their trading, as a result, has been found to be inimical to the orderly functioning of the market, tending to accentuate price movements. These studies also have consistently found that floor trading is heavily concentrated in the active stocks, where additional liquidity is least needed. In addition, the maintenance of orderly markets and continuity is the responsibility of the Exchange, which it has implemented by placing affirmative obligations on the specialist.

It was recognized in the Report of the Special Study and again in the report of a consultant retained by the Exchange to study floor trading, that on occasion certain floor traders provide a useful service in the auction market. This service is mainly in the area of providing capital on the floor of the Exchange to aid in the orderly assimilation and liquidation of large blocks of securities without disruption of the auction market. Also, on other occasions, certain floor traders are willing to commit capital to aid in situations where there is temporary imbalance between supply and demand for a stock. These functions are mainly assumed by a small group of well-capitalized traders who are in a position to commit substantial capital for a period of time. However, the Exchange has neither placed any obligation on floor traders to assume these functions which are only voluntarily performed from time to time nor has it restricted floor trading to those members who are most likely to perform these useful functions.

THE REGULATION OF FLOOR TRADING

The history of regulation of floor trading on the New York Stock Exchange under the Exchange Act is described in some detail in the Report of the Special Study of Securities Markets (Pt. 2, pp. 226-237). The following is a summary of certain salient aspects of that history.

Over the years since the enactment of the Exchange Act, the Commission has relied upon rules adopted by the Exchange to regulate and control floor trading rather than adopting its own rules. In 1935, the Commission suggested that the exchanges adopt certain rules to regulate floor trading. The reasons given for this choice were the desire to encourage flexibility in the administration of the rules and to facilitate adaptation of the regulation to varying conditions on the several exchanges.[1]

When, in 1936, the Commission evaluated the functioning of floor trading, it concluded that, notwithstanding the existence of exchange rules, the undesirable characteristics of floor trading persisted. It was determined, however, not to abolish floor trading but to strengthen its regulation by additional rules. One of these proposals would have required a complete segregation of floor trading from the floor brokerage function. This proposal was not carried into effect.[2]

The next major evaluation of floor trading occurred in 1945. Following a comprehensive study, the Division of Trading and Exhanges filed with the Commission a report made public on January 16, 1945. This report found that the evils of floor trading persisted; that floor traders enjoyed a "formidable" advantage over the general public; that floor trading distracted brokers from their duties to the public; and that floor traders traded with the trend and were a destablizing influence. This report also concluded that the existing exchange rules were ineffective to meet the problem and that the only adequate solution was complete prohibition of floor trading.[3]

The Commission tentatively determined to abolish floor trading in August 1945, but after considering the matter and holding conferences with the Exchange, it determined not to abolish floor trading in light of repeated assurances that the exchanges would develop effective self-regulation of this activity. The Commission said:

[1] Report on the Feasibility and Advisability of the Complete Segregation of the Functions of Dealer and Broker, p. 60, 1936.

[2] The other proposal, adopted in 1937, called the "daylight margin" rule, required each member to have on deposit each night an amount equal to the margin required to carry the maximum position assumed during the day.

[3] The report concluded that ". . . [a] review of the exchanges' enforcement of these rules over the past 10 years demonstrates that neither these nor any similar rules administered by the exchanges serve to restrain floor trading in the slightest measurable degree."

"We have reviewed the information available to us from the sources just described, including the discussions subsequent to the conference of May 16, and are satisfied that floor trading as now conducted gives an undue advantage to floor traders over the public; that frequently it accelerates market movements and accentuates fluctuations in particular securities or groups of securities; and that more often than not it detracts from the stability of the market. We are convinced that it is essential to make effective as soon as practicable regulation that will minimize or eliminate those influences of floor trading which impair the stability of the market.

"The New York Stock Exchange has urged us, in lieu of abolishing floor trading at this time, to afford it the opportunity to apply certain regulations which it believes will minimize the undesirable features of floor trading, yet preserve certain asserted benefits. The New York Curb Exchange has expressed its desire to put similar rules into effect. . . .We propose to give [the exchanges] that opportunity . . . If at any time it becomes evident to us that the Exchanges' rules either in the form now proposed, or as they may be modified, are inadequate for the effective regulation of floor trading, we shall reconsider the recommendations of our staff, or any appropriate modification of those recommendations, and take such action as, in our opinion, will provide an adequate solution of the problems created by floor trading."

Shortly after this statement the Exchange adopted rules designed to meet the problem. Two of these rules, Rule 108 dealing with parity or precedence and Rule 109 prohibiting "stopping" of stock for floor traders, have continued in effect substantially unchanged. The more important rule, now Rule 110, has undergone a steady process of amendment and erosion which is described in the Report of the Special Study (Pt. 2, pp. 233-237).[1]

Although various Commission staff studies between 1945 and 1961 reported critically upon floor trading practices, the next major evaluation was the Report of the Special Study. Certain of the findings of that Report are summarized above under the heading "Objections to, and Defenses of, Floor Trading." The Study concluded that the existing regulation of floor trading by the exchanges "has not only been generally ineffective but in a most important respect it has been misdirected"; and that "despite the great variety and complex-

---

[1] The relaxation of the floor trading rules coincided with important changes in 1949-50 in the constitution and policies of the Exchange as a result of proposals made by a group of floor members known as the Committee of 17. In general, the committee recommended that the board be increased in size and that the active floor members be given greater representation. The committee also recommended that the Exchange make greater efforts in the areas of public relations and advertising. Finally, it proposed that the Exchange repeal certain floor trading rules which it claimed were inhibiting a free market.

ity of exchange rules experimented with to date . . . floor traders still retain their significant private trading advantages in a public market, continue to concentrate their activities in the more active stocks, and continue to accentuate price movements." The Study recommended that floor trading be prohibited by Commission rule and that the feasibility of utilizing present floor traders as "auxiliary specialists" be explored.[1]

In a letter to the Congress, dated July 23, 1963, the Commission commented on the Special Study's recommendation as follows:

"In light of the very serious and basic problems presented by the continuation of floor trading, as brought out by the Report of the Special Study and as evidenced by prior studies, and of the lengthy and apparently unsuccessful efforts to resolve them, the Commission agrees that a rule proposal abolishing floor trading on the New York and American Stock Exchange should be developed, unless those exchanges demonstrate that its continuance would be consistent with the public interest."

From the earliest days of the Commission's administration of the Act to date, the Commission has relied for the regulation of floor trading upon rules adopted by the exchanges. Numerous approaches have been attempted, and rules have been adopted, amended, and repealed.

One salient fact emerges from this history. Notwithstanding its reliance upon exchange rules, there has been no time in the past thirty years when the Commission, which has the statutory responsibility, has been in a position to make a finding that exchange regulation had satisfactorily resolved the problems of floor trading. Not only has the Commission's staff, as a result of numerous studies, consistently concluded that regulation by the Exchange was inadequate, but on the three occasions in 1936, 1945 and 1962 when the Commission formally addressed itself to the matter, it expressed a similar conclusion.

CURRENT DEVELOPMENTS

After the release of the Report of the Special Study, with the Commission's comment on floor trading, quoted above, the Exchange stated that it wished to take advantage of the opportunity afforded to it by the Commission. In October, 1963, the Exchange retained Cresap, McCormick & Paget, a management consultant firm, to make a study of floor trading. Also a Special Committee of Governors of the Exchange was appointed to consider the matter. In formulating a response to the Commission, the Special Committee and the Exchange had available to them not only the Report of the Special Study and the Cresap recommendations, but also the factual and analytical materials developed in the course of that firm's study. The

---

[1] Report of the Special Study, Pt. 2, pp. 241-242.

Exchange thus had ample basis upon which to formulate a regulatory program which would isolate and preserve the beneficial aspects of floor trading while effectively eliminating its demonstrated abuses.

After the Exchange received the Cresap report on February 14, 1964, copies were made available to the Commission. On March 4 the Exchange presented to the Commission its own proposals. It was the view of the Commission that neither the recommendations of the Cresap report nor the less restrictive proposals submitted by the Exchange represented any new departure or meaningful change in existing practices. The Exchange was informed that its proposals did not recognize the existence of the problems presented by floor trading and constituted only a series of rules little different from those which had been tried at one time or another during the long history of ineffectual regulation.

In the course of formulating its own position the Commission has studied, among other things, the various materials collected by the Cresap firm. These materials included completed questionnaires with the Cresap firm had sent to all members of the Exchange to elicit their firm's policies or practices and their own experiences, observations and comments on floor trading. A study of the answers of these members, as well as statistical data relied on in the report, were useful to the Commission in the formulation of its own program.

In the course of several meetings with the Exchange held between March 9 and March 30, 1964, the Commission staff presented such a program to the Exchange. The alternative approach suggested by the Commission's staff was directed at preserving the benefits of floor trading while controlling and limiting its harmful effects. This approach was based on several concepts. First, floor trading would in effect be restricted to professionals having substantial capital and capable of supplementing the activities of specialists in acquiring or disposing of blocks, thus eliminating the casual, amateur floor trader whose capital was insufficient to enable him to take or maintain any substantial positions. The shortswing trading with the trend done by this type of floor trader\has been one of the principal problems of floor trading and makes no contribution to the market. Secondly, the function of floor trading would have to be sufficiently separated from that of acting as a commission broker so that the floor broker's duty of fidelity to his cuustomer's interest would not be compromised by his floor trading activities. Thirdly, in order to minimize the ability of the floor trader to compete with the investing public, floor traders would not be entitled to priority over public orders. In the fourth place, destabilizing transactions by floor traders would be restricted by methods similar to those proposed by the Exchange but with more rigorous standards. Finally, in view of the regulatory history which has seen cycles of regulation followed by erosion of exchange rules, it was deemed essential that any plan be subject to control by the Commission. This would be done through a rule of the Commission under

Section 11 of the Exchange Act generally prohibiting floor trading with an exception for trading conducted pursuant to a plan filed by the Exchange and approved by the Commission, which would leave day to day administration and enforcement of the plan to the Exchange. The Exchange initially refused to accept these principles, contending that they would be tantamount to abolition of floor trading.[1] However, on March 30, Exchange representatives agreed to accept these proposals and on April 2 the Exchange's Board of Governors approved the basic elements of a plan to implement them which would be filed with the Commission under the rule being proposed today.

As described above, the new pattern of regulation falls into two parts. The first is a Commission rule which generally prohibits floor trading on national securities exchanges, except for transactions "effected in conformity with a plan designed to eliminate floor trading activities which are not beneficial to the market." The New York Stock Exchange has agreed to file under the proposed rule a plan which conforms to the proposals set forth by the Commission in the course of discussions held with the Exchange. The essential elements to be contained in the plan are the following:

1. A member activity known as the "registered trader" would be established by the Exchange.

2. Each member registered as a trader would be required to meet an initial minimum capital requirement of $250,000 over and above the capital required for the member's other activities.[2] In order to engage in floor trading, members would also be required to show a familiarity with the requirements applicable to registered traders through an appropriate examination.

3. Registered traders would be prohibited from executing brokerage orders and floor trading in the same security during a single trading session.

4. A series of new rules would compel registered traders to conduct their business in a way calculated to contribute to the orderliness of markets and to prohibit them from engaging in transactions which have disruptive effects:

    a. Destabilizing acquisitions of a security above the previous day's closing price in such security would be prohibited;

    b. At least 75 percent of all registered trader acquisitions and 75 percent of all liquidations (except for liquidations at a loss) would have to meet a "stabilization" test (i.e., purchases below the last different price and sales above the last different price

---

[1] Letter to Exchange members from G. Keith Funston, President of the NYSE, dated March 14, 1964, on the subject: Discussion with SEC on Floor Trading.

On March 19, 1964, the Exchange Board of Governors decided to make certain amendments to the floor trading rules of the Exchange. It was the view of the Commission, that these amendments failed to meet the floor trading problem.

[2] If losses in a registered trader's account exceed about $75,000, additional capital would have to be deposited.

would be considered stabilizing.) This performance test would
be computed on a monthly basis.

c. Present Exchange rules which now prohibit members from
trading on the floor in such a way as to "dominate" markets
in the acquisition of a position would be extended to cover
liquidations of positions.

5. Registered traders in the acquisition of positions would have
to yield the floor to orders originated off the floor by giving up priority based on time and parity with or precedence based on size over,
such orders, and would also yield precedence based on size when liquidating positions.[1]

6. The Exchange will, within the limits of system capabilities,
proceed with the automation of the surveillance of registered traders'
transactions as a first step in the automation of the surveillance of
all floor activities.

It is the Commission's present judgment that this new program
of regulation should preserve the constructive market purposes of
floor trading while eliminating its harmful effects. The part-time occa-
sional floor trader, who was responsible for many of the problems in
this area, should disappear. According to the Exchange, during the
last six months some 420 members engaged in trading on the floor.
Under the new program, the Exchange estimates that about 20 to
30 members would register and thereby be eligible to engage in floor
trading. Registered traders would not be in a position to use the
knowledge fo their customers' orders in their trading activities and
their ability to compete with the public generally would be substantially curtailed. A high capital requirement would limit floor trading
to those members who can supplement the activities of specialists in
acquiring and disposing of blocks. Finally, the Exchange's commitment to automate surveillance would insure that the performance
standards in the plan are enforced. It is anticipated that the net effect
of such a plan would be to create a small group of professional dealers whose activities should be of maximum assistance to the public
in the execution of orders on the Exchange. The Commission will in
the course of its program of exchange inspections determine whether
the new program has the desired effects.

The American Stock Exchange has also been studying the ques-

---

[1] Where two or more parties have placed bids (or offers) in a security at
the same price, technical rules of the Exchange determine who is entitled to the
transaction. These are known as "priority," "precedence," and "parity." "Priority"
holds that the bid or offer which is first in time is entitled to the first execution.
If all orders were placed simultaneously, or if the party entitled to priority has
effected his transaction, the principle of "precedence" becomes determinative,
holding that bids (or offers) are to be executed in order of size. All bids for
amounts as large or larger than the amount of stock offered are considered of equal
size, or on a "parity." These bidders then "match" (flip a coin) to determine who
is entitled to the execution. If none of the bids is as large as the amount offered
(or no offer as large as the bid) they are executed in order of size, with parties
having bids (or offers) of equal size "matching" to determine the order of execution.

tion of floor trading and has submitted a statement to the Commission. That exchange has requested that the problem of floor trading on its floor be considered separately upon the ground that it believes that the requirements and problems of its market are different from those of other markets. The Commission has determined to grant this request. However, it is of the view that if the American Stock Exchange wishes to continue floor trading, any plan which it devises to meet its own requirements and problems must at the same time eliminate the detrimental aspects of floor trading described above.

Floor trading on regional exchanges in stocks also traded on the major New York exchanges does not appear to influence price movements or involve special advantages. The Commission has not made a study of floor trading in securities traded only on such regional exchanges which account for only a small part of the total volume on most of these exchanges. Under these circumstances, an exemption for floor trading on such exchanges would appear to be warranted at this time.

The text of the proposed rule is as follows:

Rule 11a-1—Regulation of Floor Trading.

(a) No member of a national securities exchange, while on the floor of such exchange, shall initiate, directly or indirectly, any transtion, the choice of security to be bought or sold, the total amount of any security to be bought or sold, or whether any such transaction action in any security admitted to trading on such exchange, for any account in which such member has an interest, or for any account with respect to which such member has discretion as to the time of execu- shall be one of purchase or sale.

(b) The provisions of paragraph (a) of this rule shall not apply to:

(1) any transaction by a specialist in a security in which he is so registered on such exchange;

(2) any transaction by an odd-lot dealer in a security in which he is so registered on such exchange;

(3) any stabilizing transaction effected in compliance with Rule 10b-7 to facilitate a distribution of such security in which such member is participating;

(4) any bona fide arbitrage transaction;

(5) any transaction made with the prior approval of a floor official of such exchange to permit such member to contribute to the maintenance of a fair and orderly market in such security; and

(6) any transaction effected in conformity with a plan designed to eliminate floor trading activities which are not beneficial to the market and which plan has been adopted by an exchange and declared effective by the Commission. For the purpose of this rule, a plan filed with the Commission by a

national securities exchange shall not become effective unless the Commission, having due regard for the maintenance of fair and orderly markets, for the public interest, and for the protection of investors, declares the plan to be effective.

(c) For the purpose of this rule the term "on the floor of such exchange" shall include the trading floor; the rooms, lobbies, and other premises immediately adjacent thereto; other rooms, lobbies and premises made available primarily for use by members generally; and the telephone and other facilities in any such place.

(d) Any national securities exchange may apply for an exemption from the provisions of this rule under Section 11(c) of the Act because of the limited volume of transactions on such exchange.

All interested persons are invited to submit their views and comments, on the Commission's proposed rule and the proposed plan of the New York Stock Exchange, to the Securities and Exchange Commission, Washington, D. C. 20549, on or before May 8, 1964. Except where it is requested that such communications not be disclosed, they will be considered available for public inspection.

By the Commission.

Orval L. DuBois
Secretary

INDEX

Numbers refer to sections.

Numbers refer to sections.

Numbers refer to sections.

Numbers refer to sections.

Numbers refer to sections.